The Founders of America

Maps by Tom Willcockson

W · W · NORTON & COMPANY · NEW YORK · LONDON

The Founders of America

☀ HOW INDIANS DISCOVERED THE LAND,

PIONEERED IN IT, AND CREATED GREAT

CLASSICAL CIVILIZATIONS; HOW THEY

WERE PLUNGED INTO A DARK AGE BY

INVASION AND CONQUEST; AND HOW

THEY ARE REVIVING ☀

Francis Jennings

The text of this book is composed in 10½/ 13 Janson,
with the display type set in Typositor Janson Italic.
Manufacturing by The Haddon Craftsmen, Inc.
Book design by Jack Meserole.
Cartography by Tom Willcockson.

Library of Congress Cataloging-in-Publication Data
Jennings, Francis, 1918–
        The founders of America : how Indians discovered the land,
    pioneered in it, and created great classical civilizations, how they
    were plunged into a Dark Age by invasion and conquest, and
how they are reviving / Francis Jennings.
            p.   cm.
        Includes bibliographical references (p.   ) and index.
        1. Indians of North America—History.   I. Title.
    E77. J53   1993
970. 004´97—dc20   92- 14487

ISBN 0-393-31232-1

W. W. Norton & Company, Inc. , 500 Fifth Avenue, New York, N. Y. 10110
W. W. Norton & Company Ltd. , 10 Coptic Street, London WC1A 1PU

    3 4 5 6 7 8 9 0

CONTENTS

LIST OF MAPS

We have lived upon this land from days beyond history's records, far past any living memory, deep into the time of legend. The story of my people and the story of this place are one single story. No man can think of us without thinking of this place. We are always joined together.

—A Taos Pueblo man quoted by Alfonso Ortiz

INTRODUCTION

Do the Americas have a common history? To the extent that all the Americas, from their earliest settlement to the present day, have had in occupation the peoples called Indians, the answer is *yes*. Indians are the link that binds "Latin America" to "Anglo-America." All the Americas are Indian America. Every European invader and colonizer was met by Indians, whether he came from Spain, Portugal, France, England, Sweden, or the Netherlands in the earlier days of Europe's "discovery," or whether he came from Italy or Russia or Germany in the nineteenth century. Whether he was Catholic, Protestant, Jew, Muslim, Buddhist, or Atheist, he came to the land of Indians; and no matter whether he sat down on ocean shores, river valleys, mountains, plains, or deserts, he found Indians there first.

The common history of the Americas should be the history of American Indians. Is it not strange, then, that this common history is always broken up to be portrayed in a reflection of the part-history of some other people? It is as if one peered through a kaleidoscope full of prisms and mirrors of European making in order to see the whole Indian persons standing in front of the tube.

As pioneers, Indians swarmed over the continents and islands from the Arctic to Tierra del Fuego, creating communities, establishing networks of trails and trade, and adapting the land everywhere to human purposes. Imperial city states rose in Mexico and Peru, and the "Suns" of Mexico extended colonies and cultural influence into North America in ways comparable to the Roman Empire's relations with northern Europe. This was the "classical" era of Indian North America.

European invasion destroyed those classical urban dynamos and brought on a Dark Age for the native peoples which was cursed by their conquerors as *savagery* and *heathenism*. A maxim among historians says that the conquerors write the history. True to this adage, European conquerors praised themselves as bringing *civilization* and *salvation* to the Americas. Masked by these uninformative hollow abstractions, there were real persons, events, and relationships, empirical realities often widely discrepant from statements made about them.

This book differs from most others, apart from format and organization, in three major ways:

15

1. The book avoids the romantic fallacy by which some students correct for savagery mythology by idealizing the victims of conquest. American Indians have never been savages of either ignoble or noble varieties because savagery is the product of imagination forcing facts into preconceived molds. The hardest part of historical writing is to penetrate prescribed roles to the real persons of real events. Indians included the entire range of human types.

2. It asserts that the persons known as Indians came as pioneers into the Americas and coped with the wilderness they found in this hemisphere, transforming it into diverse human habitats. They created a multitude of human cultures and societies, varying from simple, kin-structured bands into immense and complex cities. Europeans who came later did not conquer wilderness; they conquered Indians. They did not discover America; they invaded it.

3. The book rejects absolutely the concept of *race* and all its implications. The organizing themes herein are *culture* as the product of human ingenuity and tradition, and *caste* as the product of conquest. Whereas the race concept assumes biologically inherent, unchangeable qualities of superior-inferior differentiation between the conquerors and those over whom they dominate, culture and caste assume that social differentiation was created by social behavior and is consequently modifiable by social behavior.

These three themes are intertwined and interdependent. On such assumptions, not only the history before writing gains new life. What happened after Europeans invaded and brought writing with them has been interpreted anew as encounters between societies with varied cultures rather than the march of civilization and progress against savagery and wilderness. Such encounters of real people bear no resemblance to the death struggles imagined to have occurred between abstractions. Real people do business as well as do battle—and they did. The ways in which Indians and Europeans mixed together have been presented herein with as much care as the ways in which they kept apart. The *frontiers* of the book's subject matter are regions of interaction rather than lines of division. The book contains no maunderings about abstract absolutes locked in mythical opposition. Some examples are noticed of how each society changed in response to the other until both merged in the new large society which was neither wholly Indian nor wholly European, but distinctively American.

The book has an unusual organization. It does not fit into what the literary people call an established canon of study. The canon literature is what we find in textbooks. It focuses on the dominant people of a nation state, Americans or Mexicans or Canadians, as separate, distinct folk with separate, distinct histories. This is unacceptable and inaccurate for Amerindians who are spread all over those national boundaries.

The book is an essay rather than a compendium. It omits South America and much else that I found too much to handle. My main attention has been given to the North America of the present-day United States and (to a less extent) Canada, but the book gets there by way of the complex urban culture and society of pre-conquest Mexico (omitting the Mayas). I do not believe that the cultures of North America can be properly understood without some knowledge of the far-reaching influence and colonization from Mexico. My thesis is that Toltec Mexicans invaded and colonized the Mississippi Valley and the American Southeast centuries before Europeans came in sight. Under the name of *Mississippians*, the Toltecs were overthrown by "barbarian" tribes from the Northwest so that the Mississippians were invisible to newcoming Europeans. They have had to be literally unearthed by archaeologists.

Important as it was, this Toltec frontier was but one, and a relatively recent one, of the multitude of frontiers among the multitudes of varied Indian peoples whose relations with each other ranged from close cooperation to perpetual hostility. Over the centuries, the entire continent was covered by these frontiers.

After invasion and conquest by the great power of Spain, the history of Mexican peoples took a different direction from that of peoples farther north. For the latter, a variety of situations arose when nationals from Europe invaded from every point of the compass, *not* just from east to west, and always involving the Europeans' competition with each other. Frequently, through patron-client relationships, Indians became surrogates for European purposes. Finally, after the emergence of the new empire of the United States, the book focuses on the Indian peoples submerged under that political entity.

Obviously such range precludes comprehensive treatment of events, and many readers may be upset by omission of favorite subjects. I plead stringencies of space and scope. The book focuses on processes and examples in an effort at synthesis or what the scientists like to call a *paradigm*. Evidence frequently demanded novel interpretations, but they are not presented as definitive; rather they are exploratory. Successors will correct errors and make improvements. More power to them.

Another hazard exists for the historian who reaches out to disciplines other than his own; and I have consulted archaeology, anthropology, linguistics, demography, and tribal traditions, having mastered none of them.

Though everyone praises interdisciplinary research, actual practitioners quickly find that one must pick and choose particular schools or authorities in every one of those disciplines; there is no such thing as consensus. Naturally the scholars whose opinions are not chosen will lump the interdisciplinarian with their enemies in their own professions. Then, also, each scholarly discipline has its distinct systems of conception and modes of procedure, and the professors of each are apt to be impatient of interlopers. Happily, some genial souls understand the need for talking to each other across the fences, and even for listening to each other. We can but try.

But is it *objective* history or just fantasy? The question is legitimate, though somewhat loaded, and the answer is that the book is not fantasy. Much imagination necessarily has gone into its creation, especially in the account of large-scale events that occurred outside the ken of literate observers. One has to make sense somehow of the sort of evidence available where written documents do not exist. Sometimes the problem is worsened by plenty of writings. "Language is what we use to deceive each other," wrote Voltaire, and the aphorism is never truer than when we have something to hide. The whole of American Indian history is a battleground on which scholars struggle mightily over interpretations that often are directly contradictory. There is no way to soar above the battles, and I am certain that there is no way for one writer always to be on the winning side. *C'est la vie.*

I have taken standard precautions. Works of solid scholarly substance have been consulted at every step. Some risks have been taken, however, to force issues that should not be avoided any longer. I expose my biases as candidly as I know how. (The writer who claims to be above bias is trying to keep his axe-grinding out of sight.) It seems to me that objectivity imposes a double requirement—faithfulness of the writer to his source material and also, equally important, candor of the writer to his reader. Error is natural and within limits forgivable; lying, never.

Like many another academic historian, I have spent most of my career working in a narrow specialty. The method sharpens one's wits and enhances appreciation of the revelations to be found in obscure bits of evidence, but it tends to tunnel vision. Sometimes it seems also to fetter the inquirer with a greater desire for security than a willingness to investigate risky curiosities. The writer is always looking over his shoulder for pursuing critics. It is a curse of our time. So much learning is available in our massive culture that serious scholars fear to experiment and explore lest they arouse the ire of erudite wiseacres with turfs to defend.

My first response to the idea of a new synthesis of American Indian history was fear of ridicule at the mistakes inevitable upon going so far out of my snug specialty, but curiosity changed my mind. (And I no longer need to worry about tenure or promotion.) The time seemed overdue for a broadened perspective, so I accepted the challenge. Let me stress again that what follows is not the utterance of an oracle, but rather a report of large vistas, many of which are new to me, offered in the hope and expectation of expansion, precision, and correction by other hands. I have tried to take the reader along on that voyage, to share difficulties and excitements, and, if all goes reasonably well, to gain the sense of exultant satisfaction that comes from an enriched mind.

ACKNOWLEDGMENTS

For this subject, I needed much help and advice, so my debts are many. To the Rockefeller Foundation for priceless undistracted time for meditation on the subject while a guest at Villa Serbelloni at Bellagio, Lake Como. To the Henry E. Huntington Library for a fellowship during which much of the preColumbian material was researched and drafted. Most of all, to the Newberry Library for hospitality, collegiality, and resources beyond compare.

A special debt is owed to colleagues and "alumni" of the Newberry's D'Arcy McNickle Center for the History of the American Indian. William R. Swagerty, now at the University of Idaho, volunteered great quantities of archaeological studies and much good (though sometimes evaded) advice about prudence in their use. "Alumnus" Henry F. Dobyns introduced me to demography. Cornell University's John V. Murra taught the commerce of the Andes. Colleagues Marge Curtis, Fred Hoxie, Harvey Markowitz, Jay Miller, Richard Sattler, and Helen Hornbeck Tanner have contributed probably more than they are aware of. Tom Wilcoxson, of the Newberry's Hermon Dunlap Smith History of Cartography Center, professionalized my crude drafts of maps. Omniscient John Aubrey found specific answers to my frequently vague questions. The efficient guardians of Special Collections seemed amused rather than annoyed by my forays into their domain. "Dean" Richard H. Brown has, more or less patiently, paid bills, with fervent encouragement to finish the thing.

My editor, James L. Mairs, browbeat me into the labor of collecting many illustrations, a task that taught me how pictures have become a special problem. Many institutions now charge large fees for the right to publish pictures from their possessions. Costs for quantities quickly become prohibitive. Either a book's price must increase to cover the cost or the author's royalty must decrease. Neither implication is appetizing. I am all the more grateful, therefore, to the Newberry Library for waiving publication fees for something over half of this book's pictures, and thereby making their inclusion possible. My publisher has picked up most of the costs for the rest, but the following agencies deserve mention for cooperation and reasonableness (they are also noticed individually under the pictures each provided):

American Museum of Natural History; American Philosophical Society; Arizona State Museum, University of Arizona; Ashmolean Museum; British Columbia Archives and Records Service; Cahokia Mounds State Historic Site; Canadian Museum of Civilization; Haffenreffer Museum of Anthropology of Brown University; Library of Congress; Millicent Library, Fairhaven, Mass.; Montana Historical Society; Museum of New Mexico; New York State Museum; Rhode Island Historical Society; Secretaria de Turismo de Mexico; Smithsonian Institution's National Museum of American Art, Museum of American History, and National Museum of the American Indian.

Contributions of various sorts have been made by the following individuals who must not be held responsible for my errors:

James Axtell; A. Pierce Bounds; Olive Patricia Dickason; Jane Edwards; Art Einhorn; William N. Fenton; Bernard Fontana; Robert Steven Grumet; Barbara Hail; Erik Hemmingsen; Ted Hunter; William Iseminger; Gerald Milanich; Lt. Col. Clayton R. Newell; Alfonso Ortiz; Daniel K. Richter; Dean R. Snow; Helen Hornbeck Tanner; Jacob E. Thomas.

As every work of history is, in a sense, cumulative from the author's entire previous career, the acknowledgments of my earlier writings should be understood as included here by reference. No historian is an island entire of himself—certainly not this one.

PART ONE

Classical Indian America

CHAPTER 1

Conquest of the Wilderness

Who were the first Americans, and how did they get here? Tribal traditions speak of ancestors springing up "out of this very ground," but there are too many such traditions at too many places; and there is too much solid evidence that tribes have moved about. We must appeal to physical science for help with what is usually called prehistory. Sometimes, when I think of the enormous labors that have been put into assembling and sifting knowledge from odd bits of human detritus, and the immeasurable ingenuity and skill used in the process, I marvel at the miracle of revelation that has resulted, despite its gaps and flaws. It should not be given a demeaning name. It is assumed herein that what the scientists disclose is not *pre*history, but simply history by other means. Call it history of preliterate peoples.

Physical anthropologists have examined skulls, bones, and teeth of the earliest humans in the continent and have concluded that they were fully developed specimens of *homo sapiens*. There is no evidence anywhere in the Americas, as on other continents, of prehuman hominids. Therefore the residents of these continents must have come from somewhere else.

Whence and how? The physical types of these pioneering Americans show that they were not descended from Europeans or Africans, but have much affinity with tribal peoples of northeastern Siberia. Granted, ocean currents might have drifted a few strays into the Americas from other places. A correspondent of Washington Irving reported that a Japanese junk had been wrecked near Queen Charlotte's Island off the Pacific coast in the winter of 1833 (!) and that he had seen two survivors before the Hudson's Bay Company sent them to England—all this after the junk had drifted out of control across the Pacific. And there are tantalizing correspondences between ancient ceramic designs in Japan and Ecuador. But Irving's correspondent noted a grim fact that cannot be ignored: the two survivors he had seen in 1834 escaped not only the fury of the Pacific Ocean, but also the wrath of American natives who killed the rest of the junk's crew. It is open to much doubt that a boatload or two in ancient times could have survived long enough to make a significant impact on predecessors who had migrated in numbers, whether by land or by fleets following the coasts from the north. An accidental contact or two is not the same thing as peopling two continents.

It seems appropriate to give some evidence for this judgment. Until quite recently, students of the region centered on the Bering Strait had to rely upon sources limited by the cold climate and the cold war between the United States and the Soviet Union. The physical climate prevented all but a minimum of archaeological digs. The politics kept scholars separate until the two nations thawed a little, at which time the Smithsonian Institution of the United States and the Institute of Ethnography of the Soviet Union joined hands to produce in 1988 an exhibit and a large book of interpretation called *Crossroads of Continents: Cultures of Siberia and Alaska*. Besides these splendid additions to knowledge, the Smithsonian is gradually publishing a twenty-volume *Handbook of North American Indians* with chapters by specialists on "prehistory" devoted exclusively to the Alaskan side of the Bering Sea. Together, these great projects reveal a wealth of information previously inaccessible even to experts. *Crossroads*, especially, attends to the physical and cultural links between tribal peoples in Siberia and Alaska, and provides much sensible information about the "land bridge" that once united them.

This "bridge" existed because the glaciers locked up so much water that the oceans were much lower 20,000 years ago than they are today. At 1,000 miles wide, north to south, and stretching from Siberia to Alaska, it was really more than a bridge. It has been called a subcontinent, and it lasted as long as the glaciers. Scientists today believe it was a habitat for "hundreds of native-born generations" from which many persons later migrated into Alaska and beyond.

This subcontinent (called Beringia) seems to have been pretty soggy. Though it contained higher elevations, one didn't walk casually dry-shod everywhere on it because it was full of marshes and bayous; but it was a fine habitat for people who understood boats and how to harvest the waters. One scholar finds it "hard to imagine" any human living there "who was not a skilled boatman." We must imagine the situation because enough glaciers did melt so that the physical evidence is now 300 feet down in the mud under Bering Strait and Sea. We do not really know whether Neolithic Siberian peoples used boats similar to those still used in Siberia and Alaska today, but neither can we say they did not; and we know that the waters between the continents today teem with fish and aquatic mammals, not to speak of vast flocks of birds that breed in that north country during the summers. It is almost impossible to think that intelligent humans would not take advantage of such opportunities. It is assumed herein that they did.

It seems self-evident that people accustomed to living at the edge of the sea would have followed along the shore *as it then existed*, pushing ever farther southward if only out of curiosity. But that shore exists no more, sunk as it is under 300 feet of ocean. There are reasonable grounds to think that some migrants came on foot. Though it is often presumed that glaciers blocked passage into North America, the glaciers were spotty even at maximum extent; they came and went as Earth cooled and warmed. They did not melt down all at once. Rather, they pulled back, so to speak, glacially. Even so early as 18,000 years ago, an ice-free corridor existed between glacier complexes so that it would have been possible for humans to travel down the east side of the Canadian Rockies into territory of the present-day (non-Alaskan) United States. Saying it was possible is not saying that it happened. At present there is no indisputable evidence that it did happen.

Accepting Siberia as the source region, we must remember the thousand-mile north to south breadth of the "land bridge" to Alaska. It has implications of time as well as space. It requires us to abandon the normal assumption that the earliest migrants must have crossed over *what is now* the shortest distance between the continents at about the latitude where Nome, Alaska, now stands. On that assumption, a Soviet archaeologist denies that migration could have occurred earlier than 20,000 years ago because northeastern Siberia remained unpopulated until then. Given that assumption, it is hard to argue with the conclusion that people could not migrate from a place where no people existed.

But when it is realized that migration could have occurred a thousand miles south of Nome, and very much more attractively for people who lived well at the water's edge, possibilities change. From Kamchatka a route for "boat people" is marked out still today by the Aleutian Islands. When the water was 300 feet lower, those islands would have been almost like the Florida keys. Fishermen with a taste for aquatic birds and mammals could have coasted along that route long before their hunting brethren spread up into northeastern Siberia and across to Nome's region.

Such migration would not necessarily have been unique. The lowered sea level affected other parts of the world also, for instance by making a broad connection for Celts to cross from the continent of Europe to what are now the British Isles. Geologists tell us that the Thames River formerly flowed into the Rhine.

Lydia T. Black has written that "the Lower Amur [River] basin and the Maritime Provinces of the Soviet Far East, the Primorie, were, in all probability, one of the major staging areas from which groups of Asiatic Mongoloids spread to the American continents in remote antiquity *and* from which groups of Asiatic Mongoloids spread to the Asian northeast in much more recent periods." (Emphasis added)

Her observation neatly eliminates the objection that far-northern Siberia lacked population until 20,000 years ago, because she assumes that the more southerly Amur basin was the source region for *both* Siberia and Alaska. The American migrants could easily (and sensibly) have ignored and bypassed the north country by crossing to the Kamchatka peninsula along Hokkaido and the Kurile Islands. Following Kamchatka's coast northward they could have skirted the deep waters to get to the Aleutian Islands. In the conditions of seas 300 feet lower than at present, the island chains would have exposed much larger bodies of land much closer together.

There is other evidence. Cultural similarities between peoples of Kamchatka and the Aleutians include both material and mythological traits. Similarities between Aleut and Kamchatka sod houses have no apparent cause except "direct contacts between these peoples," according to a Soviet scientist, and Kamchatka legends about the Raven as hero and trickster correspond closely to those of the Alaskan Tlingits.

In such a perspective, some credence must be given to archaeologists who insist on human occupation of the Americas at very early dates. (Nobody can speak certainly on the subject.) Perhaps the most extreme date guessed for early occupation is L. S. Cressman's for 70,000 years ago. Dean R. Snow estimates as long as 27,000 years ago. Linda Newton ranges from 25,000 to 40,000 years ago; she sends migrants to South America about 20,000 B.C., and has them arrive at the tip of Tierra del Fuego by 9,000 B.C.

The great problem with tracing "boat people" is that the evidence of their passing would lie along shores that have been drowned by seas rising as the glaciers melted. What may be evidence appears on Santa Rosa Island off the southern California coast, which was separated from the mainland by a very short distance during the glacial period when the seas were low. What is taken to be hearth charcoal has been dated there as far back as about 28,000 years B.C. by one scholar, but he is challenged by another who allows dates only "in excess of 10,000 years."

Belief in very early dates is not confined to scholars of the United States. A French-Brazilian party has radiocarbon-dated charcoal samples from hearths in Brazilian rockshelters, ranging from 32,000 to 17,000 years ago; and it found artifacts nearby dating from 15,000 to 12,000

Water Routes in the Glacial Age

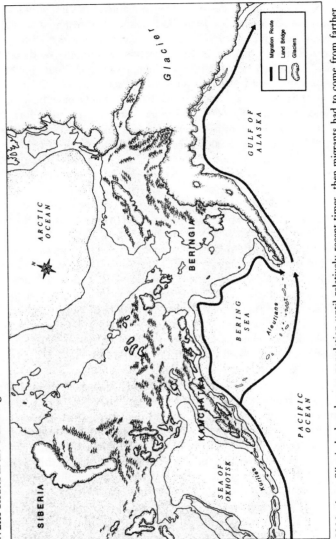

If Northern Siberia had no human population until relatively recent times, then migrants had to come from farther south, either through the subcontinent of Beringia or by skirting its shores as shown here.

years ago. A series of articles by recognized authorities in *Natural History* magazine between November 1986 and January 1988 suggested early dates.

There is good reason to believe that some immigrants walked instead of, or in addition to, paddling. Radio-carbon technology has dated Meadowcroft Rockshelter near Pittsburgh, Pennsylvania, at about 14,000 years ago, and it would not be easy to get from Alaska to western Pennsylvania by canoe. The immigrants who walked would likely have been hunters accustomed to following herds of big game to wherever the forage was best, and we now know of rifts in the glaciers that would have made that possible. However, by 12,000 years ago Beringia was already under melt water. Some migrants could have walked across before that time, but from then on travelers must either have walked across winter ice or have come by boat.

Having said all that, suppose that migrants did make their way to the Americas as early as 40,000 years ago—what would be the implications for history of that great feat? Not much, actually.

Those migrants could not have been very numerous because their way of life then fitted the mythical descriptions that Europeans foisted onto Indians of far more advanced cultures. As the editors of the *Atlas of Ancient America* remark, "The Paleo-Indian way of life, so similar in many respects to that of the Upper Paleolithic people of Eurasia, could have supported only a few people over very wide areas." Requiring sixty-five square kilometers (twenty-five square miles) to support each person, they could not have made much of an impact on the land.

For that very reason they spread out far and thinly. The most astonishing fact about human occupation of the Americas is the speed with which it occurred. If thousands of years seem like plenty of time to spread over the continents, one must remember that the peoples concerned had no wheeled vehicles and no riding animals; they got about on their own legs and by canoe, and whole families marched together into what was then in reality uncharted wilderness, finding their food as they went and coping with wondrous hazards. (Old European maps sometimes filled in unknown spaces with the phrase, "Here be Tygers." For America's earliest pioneers, the tigers were often real—and saber-toothed, no less.)

Considerable physical evidence has been dug from North American sites dated at 15,000 to 17,000 years ago, and these years coincide with the melting-withdrawal of the most recent glacier system. Regardless of revisions that may be made in future, the withdrawal of the glaciers seems like a practical starting point for this history.

Migration happened more than once; perhaps it was fairly continuous over a long period of time though large-scale immigration seems to have stopped when the seas rose to drown Beringia. The immigrants brought along a great variety of languages and cultures, and developed them further in their new homes. Though the general genetic stock of American Indians is Asian, and specifically from Siberia, they have evolved their own branch from that stock during the long ages of their separation from Asia. The modern peoples of Siberia and America are remote cousins. Some have preserved conscious ties of kinship. An Alaskan native researching at the Newberry Library told of the tradition among her far-northern people of walking out on the ice to meet "cousins" on the Soviet side.

The immigrants' variety almost defies description. Thousands of Indian societies evolved from the original Asian stocks, each with its own language and culture, and, at any given time, its own territory. They moved about in many directions, and their cultures changed through time, not always progressively. An anthropologist has remarked that Indian life-way differences exceeded those of Europe in 1492.

In the most general way, we may speak of an epoch during which Indians harvested their subsistence without doing anything deliberately to produce it. As omnivores today, we must remind ourselves that the earliest immigrants came through northern regions where edible plants were scarce and of short seasonal duration. The earliest interior Indians lived primarily by hunting and fishing as Eskimos have continued to do. Whenever those first migrants did come over, they developed an efficient weapon unknown in the Old Country—the "fluted" projectile point made by chipping the sides of spear and dart points—and they became mighty hunters. As they moved inland, they became specialists in big game (never neglecting smaller prey). They fanned out to follow mastodons, woolly mammoths, huge bison, and deer, all the way to the Atlantic Coast in one direction and to the Gulf of Mexico in another. Others moved by land or water southward along the Pacific shores. By about 12,000 years ago, they had spread to all the unglaciated corners of both American continents.

These "Paleo-Indians" were far from homogeneous. They adapted locally and diversely to the extraordinary variety of climatic and topographical conditions in the Americas. Eskimos of the "Thule" culture, from whom all present-day Eskimos are descended, were so precisely adapted to Arctic conditions that these people of the cold never attempted to migrate south to warmth; they spread eastward instead, from Alaska to Greenland across the top of Canada. They sought territories and waters where the conditions they understood could be coped with by the skills they had mastered.

We are so accustomed to the phrase "hunting and gathering" that it is necessary to stress *fishing* as a major feature of hunting cultures. Eskimos have drawn sustenance from the teeming life in and on the waters regardless of biological classifications: fish, shellfish, aquatic mammals, birds, and the mammals that roam over the ice—all are food for the Eskimo.

For other peoples also. On the Northwest Coast of North America, fishing is overwhelmingly dominant in native cultures, and we may be certain that it was prominent among the immigrants who paddled down the Pacific shores to South America—those shores now under the risen ocean.

In the sub-arctic regions of northern Canada, some hunting Indians followed caribou bands in the animals' cyclical migrations; others traveled less and trapped more as was true also in the eastern woodlands. On the great prairies, bison became the staple of subsistence, trapped in pits and stampeded over cliffs by hunters on foot. (There were no horses before Spanish invasion.)

Water was, then as now, an absolute requisite for human existence, and the immigrants kept within reach of it, the more the better, but some of them learned to cope with the arid conditions they found in Mexico's Sonora Desert and the Southwest region of the United States. They invented "catchments" to hold the water of rare rains, and they learned how to dig shallow wells. They identified succulent plants and cacti that stored water for the long dry periods, and drained them. And these people whose ancestors had come from the far north became botanical experts without peer in order to harvest nutrition and medicines from wild plants in the semi-desert. Nor did they lack for protein; even in the desert there is animal life available for hunters whose tastes are not delicate.

Several large-scale migratory dispersions are recognizable today from a variety of evidence. We have already noticed the migration of Eskimos from Alaska to Labrador and Greenland. After finding devices to survive within the narrow limits imposed by their severe climate, these extremely conservative people maintained a workable culture with little change over thousands of years; and they kept aloof from remote neighbors to the south. We know their track because they left traces in "readable" shape along the way.

Other peoples moved down the Pacific Coast, either as it was in glacial times or later as it has become in the geological present. As glacier-era shores are now under water, we must infer movement along them from archaeological remains in South America and on the California island of Santa Rosa. There may also have been movement inland, as noted above, southward along the east slope of the Sierra Nevada range, through

Probable Variety of Migration Routes 10,000 years or More Ago

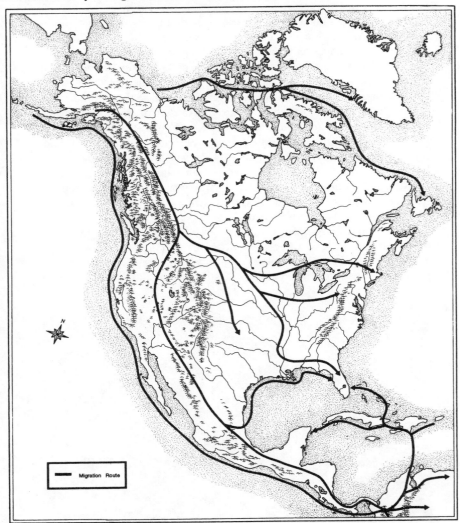

The routes on this map are suggested by archaeological findings to date. To identify details or precise times of movement is impossible in the current state of knowledge. This map suggests the variety and extensiveness of migrations.

the Great Basin of the United States, and thence through Mexico and Central America.

Thus we see a giant angle of vectors diverging eastward and southward from Alaska. For the moment, let us observe the peoples fanning out within that angle only to notice that they were different from those who traveled along the Pacific shores—quite distinct in languages and substantially so in material culture. More of that further on.

In contrast to the Eskimos' conservatism, some of the peoples along the Pacific were the most radical innovators of the Americas. In Mexico, Central America, and South America from Ecuador to Bolivia, they developed the continents' most advanced societies. In strong contradiction to European myths arising after 1492, *most* pre-Columbian peoples lived in these advanced societies, which will require separate chapters. As Russell Thornton has remarked, "Urban areas of one form or another have been a facet of the life of various native peoples of the Western Hemisphere for thousands of years."

Migration from Asia seems to have happened again and again through the centuries. At least three great tides of migration are suggested by archaeology, and smaller numbers could easily have crossed without leaving clear evidence of their passing. It is likely that all of these migrants

Not everyone made the trip from Siberia. Wouldn't this sight have surprised Cortés's conquistadors?

came either from Beringia or later across the Bering Strait by boat. What this implies is that peoples alien to each other came sooner or later into contact with each other. Frontier regions evolved thousands of years before the notion of *The* Frontier with Europeans was conceivable. Reactions varied. Sometimes the peoples warred for slaves and women, who represented the most portable form of wealth among peoples who had not learned to domesticate animals (always excepting the llama and omnipresent dog). Sometimes the peoples exchanged valued goods; evidence exists of trade in very ancient times, often over long distances hinting at intermediate "brokers."

The most extensive and most historically influential frontier zone in North America came into existence after the invention of planting led to the development of urban societies within present-day Mexico, often mentioned as "civilized" in comparison with the "savage" or "barbarian" peoples still living by hunting, fishing, and gathering. Such vague, emotionally connotative terms describe only the attitude of a writer. They are used herein only to represent viewpoints held by peoples under discussion.

Coping with cold. Eskimos and Aleuts made their livings in environments that seem too harsh for human habitation. They showed almost incredible ingenuity to overcome the natural odds against them. They preserved body heat during winter by wearing layers of fur that look ridiculous but function warmly. For shelter, in lands without trees, they made houses of sod; and in winter they converted oppressive snow and ice into building materials. The same snow and ice made roads for dogsled transportation.

Food might be invisible on land in the winter, but these experts knew where it lurked in the sea. They invented ways of fishing through holes in the ice, and of hunting sea mammals in much the same way.

When the ice thawed, they hunted whales in kayaks and canoes, and without mother ships for refuge. Their vessels were marvels of lightness, flexibility, and maneuverability that have never been surpassed by the most advanced modern technology.

Except where noted, this small portfolio of pictures were drawn from observations made before 1824. The traditional way of doing things clearly predominates.

Main source: Journal of A Second Voyage for the Discovery of a North-West Passage from the Atlantic to the Pacific; performed in the years 1821–22–23, in his majesty's ships, *Fury* and *Hecla*, under the orders of Captain William Edward Parry, R.N., F.R.S. *(London: John Murray, 1824).* COURTESY OF THE NEWBERRY LIBRARY.

Where there was no wood to build fires for warmth, layers of fur preserved body heat.

Seal hunting in western Greenland as portrayed by missionary Hans Egede, 1736. COURTESY OF THE NEWBERRY LIBRARY.

Whale hunting in western Greenland as pictured by Hans Egede, 1736. COURTESY OF THE NEWBERRY LIBRARY.

The windbreak was a necessity during long, patient waiting for a seal to surface. COURTESY OF THE NEWBERRY LIBRARY.

Walruses are big, strong animals even when harpooned. A hunter must prepare to brace himself. COURTESY OF THE NEWBERRY LIBRARY.

Fish traps below ice. The clothing is modern. The technique is traditional. COURTESY OF THE SMITHSONIAN INSTITUTION MUSEUM FOR NATURAL HISTORY.

CANOE OF THE SAVAGE ISLANDS
Hudson's Strait

AN ESKIMAUX OF IGLOOLIK
In a bird-skin jacket carrying his canoe down to the water

WHALE HUNT OF THE KODIAK ISLAND NATIVES

CHAPTER 2

The Dynamo

About 10,000 years ago, the domestication of wheat and barley was invented in Southwest Asia (called by Europeans "the Near East"). Almost contemporaneously, about 9,000 years ago, some Indians in the valley of Tehuacán in south-central Mexico began to plant the seed of teosinte, the grass-like ancestor of maize *(Zea mays)*, soon to be called "corn." Independently, at about the same time, other Indians of northeastern Mesoamerica cultivated pumpkins and gourds. (The term *Mesoamerica* has been coined to identify the advanced societies of central and southern Mexico and Yucatán. It distinguishes them from the northern regions of present-day Mexico.)

Having germinated the seed of an idea, these Mesoamericans went on to experiment with other sorts of seeds: beans, chili peppers, avocados, bottle gourds, squash, and notably cotton. With cotton, which was to play a special role in subsequent history, they expanded horticulture from subsistence to other functions.

On several counts these tremendous inventions are worth more than casual mention. Standard mythology has held that hunting was the mode of all Indian life. Indians' subsistence, wrote Chief Justice John Marshall in 1823, "was drawn chiefly from the forest." Now, however, a scholar notes that the Indians of North and South America originated cultivation of crops that today "aggregate more than half" of the world's agricultural wealth.

Specifically: potatoes, corn or maize, long-staple cotton, tobacco, rubber, tomatoes, chocolate, peanuts, pineapples, avocadoes, tapioca, quinine, maple syrup, chicle, vanilla, cashew nuts, red peppers, cocaine. In the United States, corn has become the nation's principal crop, "exceeding in production and value all its other cereal crops combined." Yet the Indians who began this mammoth agricultural enterprise are supposed to have been savage hunters.

This transformation by the magic of words is another reminder that history is written by conquerors who rationalize their behavior by the cant of conquest. Lawyers express that cant by inventing fictions that fit their purposes rather than observable facts, and the man on the bench solemnly declares, as Chief Justice Marshall did, that white is black.

There were, indeed, aboriginal Indians who lived by the hunt, as once there were also aboriginal Europeans who did likewise. Chief Justice Marshall seized upon the tail of this elephant and said the elephant was mighty like a snake. But by the time of first contact between Europeans and Indians, *most* Indians lived by planting. Europe had developed more powerful ways of making war (to be noticed further on). The Americas, in the words of Edwin F. Walker, "had developed an agriculture far above that of any European country." But we run ahead of our story.

How did it happen that the invention of planting occurred to hunters in Southwest Asia and independently in two regions of Mesoamerica at times so close to each other after all the long millennia of the hunting-fishing-gathering ways of life? Is this a mystery of human psychology or is it to be explained by some wandering Johnny Appleseed who somehow carried the notion from place to place? Diffusion of culture does not occur without human carriers, and in this case the experts' consensus opts for independent invention without trying to explain why it happened.

Early horticulture apparently was a hit-and-run affair, supplementing hunting and fishing rather than substituting for them. Ralph Linton has remarked persuasively that food *gathering* in most parts of the world has been more important than hunting, despite the fact that "hoeing is a much less entertaining occupation than hunting." Food *raising* began "where the population was already dependent upon wild vegetable foods and where they had become accustomed to the laborious processes involved in gathering roots and seeds." Planting can be regarded as a specialized way of gathering, probably introduced by the women who did the gathering in hunting societies that had sexual division of labor.

Some scholars are puzzled about the transition from hunting-fishing-gathering to crop cultivation. They have calculated that much less labor provides a subsistence sufficiency from hunting than is required for planting. They have overlooked what might be called the iron law of population size: in proportion as human numbers increase, the adequacy of wild food resources diminishes. Land enough for ten people is not enough for twenty. Though the constant moving about of hunters militates against a high rate of successful births, their populations do gradually increase to strain the resources of their habitat. They overhunt and overfish, and gather for themselves the wild plants needed to nourish game.

Thus the comparison of labor time required to hunt as less than time required to plant is fallacious because of its unstated false assumption that sufficient game is always available. Humans began to plant—i.e., to *produce* food—because they had to. (In the Old World they also domesticated animals whose increase could be controlled more reliably than game populations, but this major advance in material culture never occurred in the pre-Columbian Americas.) The alternatives of contraception or reciprocal homicide have certainly been tried often in history, but at some point the extra labor of planting has seemed preferable.

Planting did not result in immediate transformation of life styles. Hunting bands might stop in one place long enough to sow seeds, returning in a regular cycle to harvest the crop; but as populations grew, nearby bands of hunters increasingly competed and clashed over hunting territories. An alternative to continual desperate war for access to means of subsistence was to settle in one place and cultivate for maximum crop yield. Villages appear in the archaeological record of Mesoamerica's Tehuacán Valley at about 5,000 years ago.

Two areas became prominent in the early history of Mesoamerica: the lowland region around the modern city of Veracruz, and the highland "Basin of Mexico," a sort of topographical bowl formed by hills around what used to be Lake Texcoco. (The metropolis of Mexico City sprawls over it now.) Though Tehuacán, where maize culture originated, was in the high country about 160 miles southeast of Mexico City, its growth was outpaced by that of a people called Olmecs in the lowlands of Veracruz province on the gulf coast. These Olmecs added commerce to their strategy for growth, and they prospered.

From about 3400 to 2900 years ago, by one scholar's reckoning, the Olmecs traded in obsidian and jade from key trade route intersections. These were highly valued commodities. Throughout pre-Columbian times, Mesoamericans attributed spiritual qualities to jade and held it more precious than gold. Obsidian was valued for another reason. Though it could be, and was, crafted into highly decorative objects, this glass formed by volcanic explosions was made into tools and weapons with razor-sharp edges; it was the nearest approach in America to Damascus steel.*

Olmecs put up big buildings, and lugged the stone for them from

---

*One must distinguish archaeologists' comments about general phenomena from what they say about their narrow specialties. For example: Linda Newton holds off village life *at Tehuacán* until about 5,000 years ago, and holds down "dramatic increase" in population *there* until about 2,500 years ago, but one must read closely to see the narrowness of her reference; while J. C. Langley, in the same volume, has his Olmecs dominant already by 3,400 years ago and performing prodigies of construction. Sometimes I wonder if archaeologists read each other's work.

quarries distant nearly fifty miles away—without wheels or work animals. This would have been impossible without large gangs of human laborers under strict control. It appears that religious sanctions, as in ancient Egypt, were instrumental in maintaining the power and privilege of a ruling class, and this strong religious dominance continued throughout Mesoamerican history. To venture somewhat beyond the positive evidence, we can infer that the idea of democracy was inconceivable to both masters and men. This must be a tentative finding because of the state of the sources. Whether as artifacts or glyphs, these sources were prepared by order of the masters, and such records serve the interests of the masters. If there were egalitarian rebels, we shall probably never know of them.

Olmecs were a tropical lowland people. Progress among the highlanders of the Basin of Mexico may have been slowed by the aridity of their climate, which they eventually learned to offset by irrigation and terracing. The highlanders' influence rose as Olmec influence declined (possibly because of new competition in the trading network). The rise of the highlanders coincides also with their expansion into marginal lands, made feasible by the new techniques of irrigation and terracing. Whether technological progress was sufficient reason for social advance is not clear. That it brought on a sharp increase in population seems beyond doubt, and where all work was done by human labor the greater number of laborers determined the greater power.

As Olmec influence waned, a period ensued in which local and regional cultures assumed more prominence for the archaeologist. By about 2,000 years ago, approximately the beginning of our calendar's Christian era, the city of Teotihuacán rose to prominence. This was a true city, far larger than most in Europe at that time. (London had not yet been settled. Paris held fewer than 10,000 persons until after A.D. 300. About 50,000 strong, Teotihuacán expanded until by about A.D. 650 it held at least 125,000 persons. A sacred city built over a sacred spring, its strong political controls were essentially theocratic. The city was built near a volcano that had created rich deposits of obsidian, and its craftsmen became expert in working that material. A large network of long-distance trade added to the city's prestige as a venerated holy site.

The period of Teotihuacán's glory saw growth throughout Mesoamerica. The city of Monte Albán, in the southern highland valley of Oaxaca, expanded to about 30,000 persons; and the famous, if rather mysterious, Mayas of Yucatán also prospered, though none of the dispersed cities of the Mayas ever achieved the size and power of Teotihuacán. Yet the Mayas made two especially notable intellectual triumphs.

They contrived a system of hieroglyphic carving in stone, and they made a calendar—again, carved in stone—of marvelous intricacy and accuracy based on meticulous astronomical observations. Its precision is greater than that of modern Europe's Gregorian calendar.

For about 2,000 years, during a period while the Roman Empire grew and was disrupted, Mesoamerica advanced in numbers and cultural achievements. These were not altogether the same as what was happening in the Old World. Among other things, Mesoamericans never invented nor developed an alphabetical system of writing, and that lack had grave consequences. Nor did the Mesoamericans ever domesticate large work animals, so most labor had to be performed by human muscle. Even our joke about reinventing the wheel is not funny in this respect, for the Mesoamericans never did invent functioning wheels nor wheeled vehicles of any kind except on children's toys. Yet their cities grew and threw up immense structures for worship and government. To modern minds this acceptance of human labor as the only source of usable energy is incomprehensible. Yet the very rational forebears of our own culture, the Greeks of the ancient golden age, had steam-engine toys for children and never thought through the possibilities for harnessing them to work. What inference is to be drawn, I wonder?

Mesoamerica's lack of domesticated animals is worth a moment's reflection for it means that the people there, like most American Indians, still harvested meat from what nature provided instead of producing it as they produced plant food. To be sure, they kept turkeys and dogs and ate both, and they probably also ate some of the birds that they kept in cages for salable plumage. One other exception must be the slaves sacrificed to their gods who hungered only for human hearts; the rest of the victim was eaten by the god's devotees.

But Mesoamerica had no mutton, pork, beef, or horseflesh, nor milk, butter, nor any kind of cheese; and in a land so densely populated, few wild animals were available to the hunter. Except for fish, it seems clear that most Mesoamericans must have been involuntary vegetarians.

Something unknown and terrible happened in the eighth century A.D. About A.D. 750, Teotihuacán was suddenly abandoned, and by A.D. 900 Monte Albán and the Mayan cities were also abandoned. At about this time, "barbarian" Chichimecs invaded from the north. We must turn to Louisiana for clues.

Archaeology establishes that about A.D. 800, strong Mesoamerican influence appears in the Mississippi Valley, including most suggestively the culture of a superior variety of maize and the building of truncated pyramids or "platform mounds" on the Mexican style. A Natchez Indian tradition attributes this powerful influence to actual colonization from Mesoamerica. The tradition was recorded and published in 1758 by a Louisiana Frenchman called Antoine Simon Le Page du Pratz who got it from "the keeper" of the Natchez temple. Le Page was curious as to why the Natchez seemed to be so different from surrounding Indians: "I was inclined to believe that they were not originally of the country which they then inhabited."

Here is the priest's response. "Before we came into this land we lived yonder under the sun (pointing with his finger nearly south-west, by which I understood that he meant Mexico); we lived in a fine country where the earth is always pleasant; there our Suns had their abode, and our nation maintained itself for a long time against the ancients of the country, who conquered some of our villages in the plains but never could force us from the mountains. Our nation extended itself along the great water [the Gulf of Mexico] where this large river loses itself; but as our enemies were become very numerous, and very wicked, our Suns sent some of their subjects who lived near this river, to examine whether we could retire into the country through which it flowed. The country on the east side of the river being found extremely pleasant, the Great Sun, upon the return of those who had examined it, ordered all his subjects who lived in the plains, and who still defended themselves against the antients of the country, to remove into this land, here to build a temple, and to preserve the eternal fire." This does not imply that the Mississippi Valley lacked population before the Toltecs colonized. As in Mexico, they had to deal with "the ancients of the country."

There are reasons for believing this tradition, and further discussion of Teotihuacán's colony in the Mississippi Valley will appear a little further on. It is enough here to note that the influence of that great city shows in a different direction as far south as Guatemala where a miniature replica was built, apparently also by colonists.

Teotihuacán was destroyed and its center burnt by unknown invaders before the Aztecs arrived. The city's ruling elite fled, but their departure did not signify the end of the toiling peasantry on the land, nor did it mean that Teotihuacán's cultural advances were irretrievably lost. The emigrants carried old values and skills to their new colonies, and in Mexico's central highland heartland the new city of Tula arose, magnificently recreating the wonders of its predecessor.

This was the capital of the Toltecs who flourished between A.D. 900 and 1110. According to legend, these Toltecs "came over the waters from the north," though a modern scholar, Michael D. Coe, is not disposed to accept all the legends about Tula. Coe calls the Toltecs a combination of "disparate tribal elements"; to wit, the Tolteca-Chichimeca from the interior of the plains, and the Nonoalca who were "sculptors and artisans from the old civilized regions of Puebla and the Gulf Coast." Legend ascribed wondrous inventions to the Toltecs that Coe, working from other source materials, derived from Teotihuacán. Here is another of the multitude of pitfalls in the way of the historian. Coe explains it as due to the ambiguity of the name Tula. It meant "something like 'the city,' " he writes, and was "indiscriminately applied to great centers like Teotihuacán and Cholula." Thus, for many scholars, "the Tula of the Toltecs must have been the admittedly magnificent Teotihuacán."

(Among the later followers of Hernán de Soto, "the Gentleman of Elvas" noticed that a town called Tula was encountered and ravaged by de Soto somewhere near the north coast of the Gulf of Mexico.)

As to language, it is agreed that the Toltecs of Tula spoke Nahuatl, which became, like Latin in Europe, the language of civilized societies everywhere in Mesoamerica. It is still a living language in Mexico.

Whether from Teotihuacán or Tula, the wonders of the ancients still struck awe into Aztec successors relating them after Spanish conquest. (It is strikingly reminiscent of medieval European attitudes toward ancient Rome.) "Their works were all good, all perfect, all wonderful, all marvelous." They were skilled and learned. They understood herbs and invented the art of medicine. "They understood the stars . . . they gave them names and understood their influence." And they left behind marvels of monumental architecture comparable to the most impressive to be found anywhere else in the world.

The great city states of Mesoamerica were theocracies held together by their gods, rituals, and priests, and governed literally in the fear of their lords. Human sacrifice was widespread, and when one notable ruler at Tula (indisputably Tula now) attempted to stop it, he met rebellion and was forced into exile. This was Topiltzin, who became identified in myth with the Feathered Serpent god Quetzalcoatl. In the legends, "he admonished them . . . 'you shall sacrifice before him only serpents, only butterflies.' "

Thereupon the traditionalists invoked their ancient fierce god Tezcatlipoca and drove Topiltzin / Quetzalcoatl away with all his Toltec followers. The refugees took to the sea, landing at Yucatán, where they conquered a kingdom and set up its capital at Chichen Itzá. It seems plain to me that others settled, either then or earlier, in the Mississippi Valley.

The bellicose warriors remaining at Tula expanded their rule over a wide region of central Mexico until they, in turn, succumbed to another wave of conquerors from the northern Chichimec tribalists. In the latter part of the twelfth century, Tula's Toltecs left their city to the mercies of the "barbarians," who burnt it; and migrated southward beyond their reach. Some of these Toltecs took over the old city of Cholula and kept it until Spanish conquest three and a half centuries later.

In due course, a new colony of Chichimec immigrants moved into the Basin of Mexico central highlands and fought their way to power. These were the Aztecs or Mexica who will have their own chapter below.

Throughout the "classic" and "post-classic" eras of Mesoamerican history, population continued to increase despite calamities of war and nature. Conquerors came and went, but peasants worked the land in ways hallowed by custom and tradition—and many still do, even in the midst of new industrial agriculture. But the cities grew by discharging other functions. Great temples and plazas witness the cities as centers of mass ritual, and products of handicrafts give evidence of more mundane commercial activity.

The cities were hubs of extensive and complex networks of trade for which goods manufactured by their skilled workmen (*Toltecs* means "artificers") were exchanged for raw materials from distant places. It seems highly likely today that those successive waves of Chichimec invaders had been inspired to migrate southward by sight of rich crafts and vague reports of the wealth of the cities. Traffic between the cities and the far-off northern lands was two-way.

Thus the influence of the Mesoamerican dynamo expanded far beyond the utmost limits controllable by its cities. Much evidence suggests migration and diffusion by commerce into South America as well as northward, but that is beyond the scope of this book. In North America, the traders from Mesoamerica met and mingled with other peoples, and colonists fought, taught, and treated with them in a gigantic, irregular frontier region that spanned the continent. As the history of Europe requires attention to interaction between ancient Rome and the peoples beyond its boundaries, so the history of North America demands notice of Mesoamerican relations with the tribalists to the north.

CHAPTER 3

Chaco Canyon

Mesoamerica, which has been called "Nuclear America," extended its influence into North America in at least two identifiable ways. Traders brought it to Arizona and New Mexico along chains of intermediary towns that led through the Sonora Desert to the splendor of Chaco Canyon,and colonists spread it in the U.S. Southwest, up the Mississippi Valley to the Great Lakes, and around or through the Appalachian Mountains to the Atlantic Coast. The trails are clear; the legend reported by Le Page du Pratz is mere confirmation. Oddly, in this instance, the data of the digs are more specific than human memory.

We are reminded that Mesoamerica "was the source, directly or indirectly, for many of the changes that began in the Southwest about 2000 B.C.," and further, that the region "can best be understood in terms of its marginal relationship to Mesoamerica."

A distinction must be made between diffusion of culture that just happens—what one archaeologist calls unregulated diffusion—and, on the other hand, the regulated type that comes about through deliberate instruction by visitors who stay for lengthy visits. Still more distinction must be made when a colony settles in, whether by invasion or invitation. Necessarily it brings its own culture in toto, which the indigenous people must adapt to as a pattern, whether by accepting it in place of their traditional system, by rejecting it completely, or by accepting it selectively with modifications to fit their physical circumstances or mental predispositions. For example, the pattern of planting associated with sedentary villages may be accepted; but if it comes from a land with plentiful water to an arid country, both planting and architecture will have to be adapted to the new physical situation.

For the Southwest, Mesoamerica was the source of some developments in culture that occurred haphazardly, such as early planting of maize and squash. This unregulated phenomenon hardly establishes a frontier between self-consciously different peoples. In those early days, three to five thousand years ago, there was not much real difference between hunters who supplemented diet by gathering wild plants and hunters who added to their gatherings something extra they had planted themselves. Differences became more marked when the planters settled in villages, populations grew, labor became diversified, and new, specialized crafts were created. Then the villagers produced things that the casually planting hunters could not make for themselves, trade became systematic, and the traders carried new ideas as well as material goods.

It must be stressed that indigenous peoples occupied the Southwest, though sparsely, before Mesoamericans made contact. These hunters have not been studied much, but they were there and they had developed variations on the Paleo-Indian theme. It is agreed that "the Archaic cultures of the West were distributed over a vast area from Oregon to the central Mexican Plateau, and from the flanks of the Sierra Nevada to the western slopes of the Rockies." The direction from which these peoples came is still uncertain though their ancestors must ultimately have moved south from Alaska. Some of them, perhaps most, seem to have moved through Idaho to the Great Plains and thence into the Great Basin at a time when its climate was wetter than it is now. Others may have come north from western Mexico, turning inland as they reached the Southwest. When they came, they settled and stayed, preserving, with utmost conservatism, a way of life that endured 10,000 years. (In default of a better term, *Southwest* is used herein for the southwestern region of what has become the United States.)

The southern peoples of this vast region diverged from the northerners after adopting cultural changes introduced from Mesoamerica. Communication continued throughout, but horticulture in the Southwest gradually required or initiated novelty in habitat, religion, and social organization as well as technology. What evolved in the sub-region of the Southwest became so different from the conservative hunting and gathering culture to the north that a cultural frontier in the fullest sense formed between them.

There was also a broad frontier between the Southwest peoples and those of Mexico. Proto-Pueblo cultures developed from their own traditions as modified by what they accepted from the south. The results were very different from mere replicas. These mixtures were not clones.

One must attend carefully to the meaning—or, rather, the various meanings—of that word *frontier*. It has a mythological significance of a line between the imagined entities of "civilization" and "savagery." In this sense, *frontier* is a justification of almost theological quality for conquest by the "civilized" people who are invariably the *us* of the writer. This meaning has no place in a serious history.

Colonization from Mexico

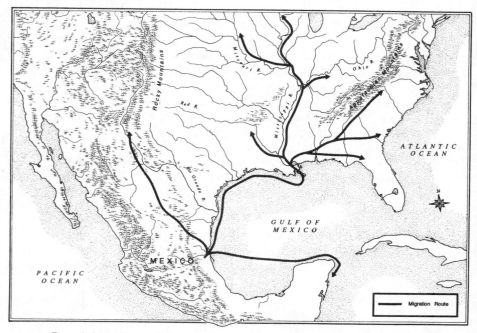

Recorded Natchez tradition, supplemented by the evidence of truncated pyramids and diffusion of maize, establishes these vectors. Old Guard scholars refuse to accept the fundamental idea (and the evidence) that Mexico's civilization had power to expand.

As between real peoples instead of the imaginary kind, frontiers can be cultural, military, political, or ethnic. They do not necessarily coincide, and only the political frontier is a line—sometimes not even that one. Frontiers are zones of contact and interchange between peoples and polities which may be marked by either accommodation or conflict, often by both; and they usually are the scene of syncretism and synethnicity. In less technical terms, the concerned peoples adapt their own cultures by amalgamating features from each other's lifeways (syncretism), and some persons from each people mate with those from the other (synethnicity), thus creating a new gene pool out of the combination of the older ones.

In the case of the Southwest gradually becoming distinct from the Great Basin people, we are talking about a *cultural* frontier. As Henry F. Dobyns succinctly writes, "The Southwestern frontier lay where horticulture ended." Communication was not cut off. Trade continued and perhaps increased, but the planting peoples of the Southwest and hunters of the Great Basin lived in different sorts of habitation, made their livings in different ways, and recognized themselves as significantly different from each other. Sometimes they contested for the same territories. The planters won, and the hunters went off to less desirable lands. (Something similar occurred in the nineteenth century when American farmers competed with herders for water and land.)

Experts do not agree upon the exact date of horticulture's beginnings in the Southwest. They interpret the scant evidence over a broad range from 5,500 years ago to 3,500 years ago, and a span of 2,000 years is not negligible. Though innovation occurred slowly, with accretions and substitutions being made individually and experimentally, three cultures in the Southwest had formed by A.D. 500 into patterns that distinguished that region from all the rest of North America. Because they did not have writing, we know them only by their material remains as the Hohokam, Anasazi, and Mogollon.

The first to become distinct in the digs were the Mogollon. They sprawled across today's boundary between Arizona and New Mexico, and they seem to have evolved from a Great Basin group who had acquired the idea of horticulture by means not known now, perhaps from traders. They were probably the ancestors of present-day Zuñis.

The Hohokam, it is generally agreed, were conquering invaders from the south, probably from somewhere in the Sonora Desert as they showed great versatility in adapting to desert conditions. They settled in Arizona in the triangle formed by the Salt River and Santa Cruz River (with Phoenix and Tucson at two of the triangle's corners). Their Mexican origins show especially in elaborate canal systems for irrigation, hundreds of miles of them, some branches of which extended individually as much as ten miles. They built platform mounds in an echo of Mesoamerican pyramids, and they played the ball game that was as obsessive in Mesoamerica as football in Texas today. It appears that the modern Pima–Papago Indians are descended from the Hohokam.

The Anasazi have been traced back to the "Four Corners" area where Utah, Colorado, Arizona, and New Mexico come together. Ancestors of today's Pueblo tribes (excepting the Zuñis), they are best known for their multistory adobe "apartment houses" whose concentrated inhabitants could not have been sustained without carefully tended farms.

A caution: although the Pueblos were village peoples, in contrast to the nomads farther north, they were not static. Some of them moved about in trade, and many were obliged to change habitation in response to natural calamities (such as prolonged drought) and war. Thus, for example, the Zuñis now live in only one town, where they congregated after seven others collapsed. Refugees from stricken communities sometimes amalgamated with their hosts after generations of coexistence. History here, as everywhere, is a story of flux.

With the exception of wars and the Hohokam colonization the greatest agency of change was trade.

Two kinds of trade appear in the evidence after A.D. 500: local or regional systems involving perishable goods, and long-distance systems that moved highly valued luxury items such as gaudy macaws, copper bells, precious stones, and ornamental marine shells. It appears that the long-distance traders traveled from one center of regional trade to another, moving in easy stages and probably doing some business at each until some of them reached the ultimate outposts. Two key communities along one route were Casas Grandes (northwestern Chihuahua) and Chaco Canyon on the Four Corners plateau of the Southwest. Little work has been done on the much larger Casas Grandes, but enough to show that trade had the usual effect there of stimulating crafts by a growing class of specialized artisans.

Chaco Canyon, which has been studied more intensively, was an Anasazi town, ancestral to present-day Pueblo peoples, at the far northern rim of horticulture. Chaco Canyon was influenced only by diffusion from Mesoamerica, which modified a distinctive, regionally developed culture. Thus there evolved what may be conceived as geographic strata or layers of culture. A strong pattern of populous urban society based on horticulture was centered at the Basin of Mexico and was imitated within a wide radius extending northward as far as to the Sonora Desert. Bits of the pattern, rather than the whole complex, were carried hundreds of miles farther to Chaco Canyon, and communities in the intervening region adopted what they liked and adapted it to cultures that came originally from quite other sources. North of Chaco Canyon was alien territory where Mesoamerican culture made little or no impression upon hunters and gatherers.

We are so accustomed to thinking of polar opposites that an effort must be made to visualize intermediaries—the "peoples in between"—with distinct lives of their own; but when that concept has been grasped, we can see an immense frontier *zone*—not a *line*—between the urbanites and the hunters. Its bounds were not as neat as lawyers and diplomats would prescribe, its edges on both sides were ragged and vague; but it cannot be classed without violence to fact as either urban or hunting. The Great Basin was much lusher then, before sheep, cattle, and increased aridity reduced its carrying capacity for edible plants. The Anasazi / Pueblos were planters and cultivators, and they built "apartment house" towns in the midst of their fields, but they had not forgotten how to hunt nor how to harvest the wild plants in their vicinity.

We have names for some of the towns whose fascinating ruins so impress tourists nowadays: Aztec, Salmon, Canyon de Chelly, Mesa Verde, Chaco Canyon. These are the visible remains of substantial communities in the northwest quadrant of New Mexico, with a few in southwestern Colorado. Remnants of many more may be waiting in the earth.

The culture of these Anasazi peoples seems to have come to maturity at about A.D. 1000, after which population increased notably until the late thirteenth century when something disastrous seems to have happened all over North America. Commerce was as essential as horticulture to the growth of this society. All roads led to Chaco Canyon, and the Chacoans built their own roads radiating out from their canyon center. These stimulate wonder by being so much like Inca roads thousands of miles away in Peru. Though designed for foot traffic only, the major roads were nearly thirty feet wide, and even the secondary roads extended more than twelve feet from side to side. They can still be mapped, by surveys and aerial photography, and they lie in straight lines between objectives, turning only at sharp angles where necessary and mounting over hills and bluffs by stairs carved into the living stone.

More than 400 miles of Chaco roads have been mapped, and the fact that only 100 miles of them lie in Chaco Canyon itself implies a widespread cultural system centered in the canyon and linking communities throughout 60,000 square miles.

What was the purpose of these roads? No signs have been discovered of the sort of military tyranny that would have required massed armies. Lacking beasts of burden, the Chaco people could not have formed great caravans on the Asiatic model. Certainly no string of porters would need roads thirty feet wide. Just as certainly, no community would have taken the pains and given the labor to build such engineering, sprawled over 400 miles, unless it was intended to fulfill a clearly conceived function.

We do know that these roads connected Chaco Canyon to outlying settlements patterned generally (but not identically) after the villages within the canyon, and, further, that signaling stations with line of sight visibility were located along them. Not so mysterious, this part of the arrangement fairly plainly suggests planned defensive measures.

Planning shows also in the towns. They did not follow the Mesoamerican grid pattern and compass orientation, but they were laid out regularly, often in a half-moon or "D" formation, and they were carefully designed to incorporate circular chambers—kivas—for ritual gatherings for worship and probably for politics also. In accordance with the most modern architectural precepts, the villages within Chaco Canyon were located on the north side and opened toward the south for passive solar heat. The largest canyon village, Pueblo Bonito, had more than 800 rooms layered on four floors, each receding from the front of the next below so that each had a sort of penthouse terrace. This, too, anticipated modern design. (The "Habitat" building designed in this fashion caused great excitement at the 1967 World's Fair in Montreal.) Pueblo Bonito was the largest apartment building in North America until New York City surpassed it in the nineteenth century, and Pueblo Bonito was only the largest of 125 villages in the "Chaco phenomenon."

Archaeologists dispute the probable size of the population in Chaco Canyon. The accepted figure, based on a count of rooms, used to be about 6,000 people. Some students now think that inflated. Observing that many rooms in Pueblo Bonito appear to have been disused for residence, the skeptics have settled on a figure of about 1,000 inhabitants. I am skeptical of these skeptics. I think they have overlooked the immensity of the Chaco people's constructions. Such things do not happen without much machinery or masses of laborers, and there were no machines or draft animals at Chaco. Apart from stonework, according to Kendrick Frazier, "as many as 100,000" giant ponderosa pines were lugged from many miles away for the pueblo buildings. Those storage rooms could have been dwellings during peak population, converted after a decline.

Big populations require much food, and the farmers of the Southwest were handicapped by the region's aridity. They coped successfully with that problem by controlling every drop of water that fell during brief rainy season storms. Even today, the Pueblo Hopis can be seen carrying pots of water to individual plants. Hard labor makes up for what nature withholds.

Kendrick Frazier comments, "Almost all Indian cultures of the Southwest developed some form of water control. The Hohokam of southern Arizona were indisputedly advanced in their water-control efforts. The Mogollon people of eastern Arizona and southwestern New Mexico were skilled in irrigation too. The Hisatsinom (Anasazi) in the Kayenta area of northeastern Arizona used a variety of water-control devices, most notably from A.D. 1150 to 1300. The people of Mesa Verde developed water systems as early as A.D. 900 and continued their use until abandonment about 1300. They had contour terraces, check dams, ditches, and reservoirs." All textbooks on "western civilization" stress Mesopotamia's use of irrigation as a sure indicator of the rise of civilization. The same logic dictates that Spanish invasion of the Southwest in the sixteenth century crippled the civilization being developed there. This fact must be accounted for in recent efforts by some historians to revive an imagined "transit of civilization" from Europe to the Americas. Sooner or later the semantic magician must face reality.

CHAPTER 4

Cahokia

When Cahokia Mounds was designated a United Nations World Heritage Site, it was formally recognized as an irreplaceable property of international significance. Cahokia Mounds belongs to an elite group of cultural and natural landmarks of special importance in the history of mankind.

—CAHOKIA MOUNDS MUSEUM SOCIETY

By means unknown, the knowledge of maize cultivation had diffused to eastern North America by about A.D. 200, but after A.D. 400 little evidence of maize appears in the archaeological record beyond the Southwest, until about A.D. 900. The hiatus remains mysterious. My speculation is that when maize reappeared it came by design rather than happenstance, because it was a new, improved variety freshly imported from Mexico. Colonies went out from turmoil in Mesoamerica—the same tumult that resulted finally in Teotihuacán's abandonment, and indications suggest that the colonies came from that city. The colonists established apparent commercial superiority over indigenous tribes in the Mississippi Valley on a scale that looks on the map very like an empire. They brought from Mesoamerica the habit of building truncated pyramids and of putting temples and administrative structures on the topmost platforms. The ruins of these pyramids appear now all along the Mississippi Valley and throughout the southeast United States south of Virginia. Moravian missionary John Heckewelder told of seeing such ruins in the eighteenth century near Detroit (apparently now beneath Wallaceburg, Ontario).

Once again, we must distinguish purposeful diffusion from the influence spread by the unregulated kind. Our signposts, so to speak, are those pyramids. Mesoamericans and Mississippians were not the only peoples to pile up earth in monuments, but their truncated pyramids can be easily distinguished in form and function from the varied *mounds* of the other peoples. Long before the Mississippians appeared in the Mississippi Valley, an unidentified community at Poverty Point, Louisiana,

Pyramids and "mounds." From the very beginning of Cortés's conquest of Mexico, the conquistadors recognized the great pyramids of Tenochtitlán/Tlatelolco as centers of religious and political power that were also military bastions. However, when similar structures were discovered in the United States, they were shrugged off by many scholars as mere "mounds" despite the resemblance. More recent study discerned functional as well as physical differences between the truncated pyramids, such as Cahokia, and the interment mounds of varied shapes, such as Marietta, Ohio, (shown above) and the great snake at Locust Grove, Ohio, (below)

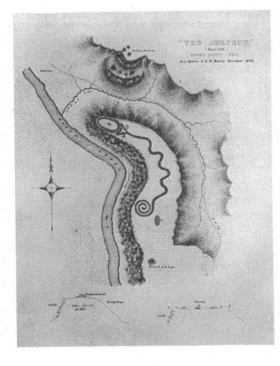

A spectacular "mound." This monument in the shape of a serpent swallowing an egg is protected in a state park at Locust Grove, Ohio. Its symbolic significance is still debated.

built six concentric rows of ridge mounds in half an octagon around a central plaza 600 yards in diameter. Dated at about 3,000 years ago, the ridges were not very high, standing at something like ten feet tall and seventy-five feet wide, separated from each other by nearly twice their widths. William N. Morgan estimates the population of this community at about 2,000 persons and suggests they traded over a network extending "to Florida, the Appalachians, and the Great Lakes."

Poverty Point was exceptional for its time, but a new cultural influence emerged about 2,500 years ago, apparently centered in southern Ohio. In archaeological jargon the patterns of this culture in its earliest manifestations are denoted "Adena," merging gradually into "Hopewell." Its still surviving mounds were built in every shape *except* pyramidal. They display circles, octagons, clover leaves, and animal effigies— even a large human effigy. Southern Wisconsin holds about 5,000 low effigy mounds usually functioning as graves. In south-central Ohio, near Locust Grove, a huge effigy of a serpent stretches more than 200 yards from extended jaws to coiled tail. Although this serpent stands now only about four feet high, the erosion measured during the past century suggests a much greater original height.

Once again, there is much evidence in these mounds of widespread trade. William N. Morgan notes "ample evidence of trade specialization" including "artifacts of stone, obsidian, flint, fresh water pearls, bone, antler, bear teeth, mica, marine conch shells, textiles, and copper sometimes overlaid with iron, silver, or gold." They indicate trade "westward into Kansas, southward into Mississippi and Louisiana, southeasterly across Alabama and Georgia into Florida, and northeasterly into New York." In a review of art objects, David S. Brose mentions copper rings and bracelets and, most significantly, cloth wrappings. Cloth could only have come at that time, directly or indirectly, from the Southwest or Mesoamerica.

The artifacts were mostly grave goods deposited with corpses. They and the mounds evidence communities of some wealth, attached to particular territories sufficiently large to motivate mound construction. Among other functions, the mounds would serve as marks of possession. These people lived primarily by hunting, fishing, and gathering, but they also planted squash, pumpkin, sunflower, goosefoot, and marsh elder. They did not plant maize.

If Mesoamerica's influence had reached so far as the Ohio Valley during the Adena–Hopewell era, it did so in most attenuated wisps. These mounds differed in form and function from Mesoamerica's pyramids, and maize was not anywhere in sight.

Cahokia. A painting by William R. Iseminger of the Cahokian community, circa A.D. 1100–1150. Compare the temple at Tenochtitlán. Notice at left the artist's portrayal of the circular "woodhenge" by which Cahokian priests regulated their calendar. COURTESY OF THE CAHOKIA MOUNDS STATE HISTORIC SITE.

Below. The site as it appears today with the interpretive center to welcome visitors in the foreground. "Monk's Mound" in the background is so called because Trappist monks built a monastery on it in the nineteenth century. COURTESY OF THE CAHOKIA MOUNDS STATE HISTORIC SITE.

Art objects from the great mound at Marietta, Ohio. Source: E. G. Squier. COURTESY OF THE NEWBERRY LIBRARY.

Ceramic pots from mounds in Ohio. Source: E. G. Squier. COURTESY OF THE NEW-
BERRY LIBRARY.

Clearly there were sources of cultural energy and invention in eastern North America as well as in the west, independent of colonization from Mesoamerica, and even of its strong influence. One expert suggests that horticulture may have originated independently in the East. When colonization came up the Mississippi Valley in the ninth or tenth century A.D., the newcomers had to come somehow to terms with indigenous peoples. The product of their accommodation is now known as Mississippian culture, which embraced much variety manifested in its art objects.

Although Mesoamerican intrusion seems established, the mode of this great operation is puzzling. It is unlikely that conquest, in its ordinary, military sense, took place. The newcomers' weapons were not better than those of the vastly more numerous native peoples among whom Mesoamericans settled. If anything, the bows and arrows of the natives had more power than the *atlatls*, or throwing spears, to which the warrior elites of Mesoamerica clung.

Yet Mesoamerican maize and truncated pyramids were soon to be found all along the Mississippi Valley and throughout the Southeast, and one of those now-eroded pyramids rose to a height exceeding all the structures save two in originating Mesoamerica. This was Cahokia (across the river, in Illinois, from St. Louis, Missouri), whose remains still impress and excite scholars as well as casual tourists. Cahokia was the center of an "empire" of *commerce*, and that fact is the clue to how a comparative handful of Mesoamericans could acquire domination over multitudes of strangers so much more numerous than themselves. They *knew* more. I hazard a hypothesis: newly introduced maize produced a surplus of food that was exchangeable wealth, and it would seem that groups of the Mesoamericans established themselves as trading elites among hunting peoples, teaching the wonders of horticulture to the hunters and acquiring prestige in the process. Whereupon they put up pyramids and placed themselves on top to make their superiority unquestionable.

How to account for the disappearance from North America of Nahuatl, "the language of civilization" in Mesoamerica? The newcomers may have held to their own language for communication among themselves, as the Natchez nobility maintained speech distinct from that of their "stinkard" inferiors. This would not be a great rarity in history: the courtiers of tsarist Russia spoke French to distinguish themselves from the rabble, and so did the Normans who conquered England. But the weight of numbers eventually overpowers such distinctions: Russians today speak Russian, and what Englishmen speak has been disputed only by Bernard Shaw's Professor Henry Higgins. The Mesoamericans who dominated the Mississippi Valley learned to talk in the varied languages of their underlings because they had to, and eventually they forgot the speech of their ancestors. Deprived of help from writing, I must speculate.

Whatever the real procedure may have been, it created domination by Mesoamericans over the mixed peoples now called Mississippian. They were numerous and varied, and adapted to diverse environments and indigenous traditions, but all their sites show evidence of trade. Some distinction must be made between the peoples who adopted both maize and truncated mounds, on the one hand, and those who took up maize cultivation without platform mounds. It seems to be the difference between regulated diffusion (though perhaps only of a commercial nature) and unregulated diffusion beyond. Maize and platform mounds are singled out here for simplicity's sake; many other cultural traits were also involved.

Assuming the distinction, Mississippian regulation, as evidenced by the platform mounds, extended at utmost from Aztalan in southeastern Wisconsin to Greenhouse in southern Louisiana. Though the Mississippi River was clearly Main Street for Mississippian trade, outlying colonies settled at intervals from Tennessee to South Carolina and south to Florida. Some few mounds are to be found westward in Arkansas and Oklahoma where the cultures of Caddoan Indians show evidence of Mississippian or Mexican influence; but the bulk of Mississippian society, mixed though it was, lay between the great river and the Atlantic. In this respect, archaeological evidence confirms the Natchez tradition that Mesoamerican colonists had made for the "east side" of the river.

Vast though these regions were, maize cultivation leaped far beyond them. Maize spread over the Northeast above the Ohio River and over to the Atlantic and as far north as climate permitted. The Hurons of southern Ontario became maize farmers in a very substantial way, and maize was cultivated across the southern shores of the Great Lakes and up the Missouri River where Mandans and Hidatsas established trading centers between planters and hunters.

On a much larger stage, a similar pattern repeats that of the Southwest. From Mesoamerica, colonies formed a core around which direct commercial relations formed, and beyond them a penumbra of maize growers. Beyond maize, Mesoamerican influence did not become appreciable. As in the Southwest, the final frontier lay where horticulture ended. Also, as in the Southwest, the hunting peoples on the other side of that frontier had made their way across the continent from an origin somewhere in or near Alaska. On the west-east axis the greatest number were speakers of the Algonquian family of languages, some of whom, like the Shawnees and Delawares, adopted maize culture, though others, like the Crees and Algonquins, adhered to the hunting life. Again, it must be understood that even the planters hunted and fished part-time.

Within the Mississippian core, a metropolis arose. This was Cahokia, the largest city north of Mexico. Four miles east of the Mississippi River, and across it from modern St. Louis, Cahokia was impressive by any standards for its era. A palisade surrounded a large plaza and nineteen platform mounds, of which the largest was "Monks Mound," rising originally in four tiers from the plaza floor. (It was so named because a monastery was built on it in the nineteenth century, that has since been removed.) After more than 500 years of erosion, it still stands more than ninety feet high. Though apparently occupied as early as A.D. 600, it appears to me to have been taken over by Mesoamerican colonists sometime between A.D. 700 and 900, when turmoil at Teotihuacán caused the Great Sun there to send forth those of his people whom he could not protect. (He himself, with the rest of his people, stayed behind in Mexico until Spain's invasion, after which he joined the colony at Natchez.) Cahokia's population rose to 10,000, 40,000, or 75,000 persons, depending on which estimator is accepted. Administrators of its modern historical park accept a peak population of 20,000. That the place was a true city can hardly be questioned, as suburban villages outside its palisade surrounded more than 100 tributary mounds.

Cahokia's sophistication is suggested by the discovery of a "woodhenge," a solar observatory consisting of forty-eight posts set in a large circle aligned with the points of the compass, and so arranged that a forty-ninth post outside the circle permitted an observer within to view the sunrise at the equinoxes and solstices in A.D. 1000. The Cahokians were as well acquainted with astronomy as the Celtic builders of Stonehenge in England, but allowance must be made for the great difference in their eras.

That Cahokia was the center of a wide-ranging commerce is generally agreed by archaeologists. This commerce sometimes involved foodstuffs. Examples from written history in other places show stable trading relationships between planters and hunters, each possessing what the other wanted; and there certainly were times when local shortfalls impelled trade for food with regions of plenty. Besides exchanging such basic staples, the Mississippians manufactured what David W. Penney calls "primitive valuables."

We must pause for a moment to conceive what gave value in commerce without money. Sidestepping the condescension of that word *primitive*, we can gain greater clarity by thinking of values cherished in tribal societies where status ranked higher than possessions. In such societies, men gained esteem by giving wealth away rather than by hoarding;

by ostentatious sacrifice, by showing more concern for public welfare than for selfish accumulation. With this exception: personal adornment of self and family was acceptable and striven for. In terms of economic analysis, goods were acquired for consumption, display, and redistribution rather than for the creation of capital. This system of values, obviously alternative to those that had evolved in the Old World, is the content of that word *primitive* which, equally obviously, tends to make it seem less worthy than the values held by Europeans. Again, however, an exception must be noted in the case of Europeans and Asiatics who renounced the world and its wealth in order to seek solace or serve humankind in religious communities. *Primitive* is not ordinarily used to designate such organizations or persons.

David Penney specifies profound meaning for his unfortunate phrase. The valuables of Mississippian commerce were objects that "created and maintained crucial obligations among individuals, families, clans, and communities."

Ancestor worship was widespread among the Mississippians, so tribute had to be paid to the deceased by burying valuable ornaments and implements with them, and even the implements were usually decorative. Surviving art works demonstrate the existence of master craftsmen in large numbers, for each such object required long hours of painstaking labor. For such grave goods, copper was a favorite material in the north, worked by cold hammering into many forms and comparable in this respect to gold in Europe: "valuable and beautiful, but not for mundane use." A technical term for this sort of object is *sumptuary implement*, and such goods were traded throughout the Mississippian system as church ornaments were made and sold in Europe.

Marine shells from the South Atlantic and Gulf shores were traded over great distances and worked into elaborate ornaments. Pipes and figurines carved from stone were exchanged in the southern Mississippi Valley and eastward, and pottery moved in all directions. Traders rejoiced in the mortuary function of so much of their wares because demand never ended.

Perhaps equally important was gift giving between individuals and between groups. Presents represented friendship, and reciprocity was mandatory. The man who could distribute presents so lavishly that returns could not possibly match his generosity acquired thereby great respect and the political influence that went with it. Skill in the processes of exchange led to the wealth that could be translated into power. Prestige was the tribal equivalent to capital.

Copper had to be mined, marine shells had to be harvested by patient collection, and clay and carvable stone had to be gathered from where they appeared in the earth. Such were the raw materials to be exchanged for the products of Mississippian crafts. At the outer fringes of the system, maize was exchanged for the furs and pelts of the hunting peoples, which had considerable value in societies without domestic cattle as a source of leather. Such peripheral subsystems are suggested by an example that Frenchmen found operating when they entered the St. Lawrence Valley. Though its dates of discovery were much later than the Mississippian era, its processes seem to have been around for a long time.

Much of what is presented in this chapter is not known certainly by anybody. Archaeologists dispute whether the Mississippians in fact were colonists from Mexico, and they dither a lot on the issue while failing to offer a credible alternative. I find the Natchez migration legend convincing as explanation of archaeological findings consistent with it. I notice that those who most emphatically reject this interpretation simply ignore the existence of the Natchez legend. That won't wash.

The documented detailed similarities between Natchez and Mexican cultures require explanation more persuasive than vague assumptions of independent origination. By contrast we have the specific, unambiguous, recorded statements of the Natchez chief priest and Great Sun ruler. They require respect.

NOTE

"WOODHENGE"
(*Courtesy of Cahokia Mounds Museum Society and Collinsville, Ill., Optimist Club*)

Fascinating information about the people who once built the great prehistoric city of Cahokia was revealed during the early 1960s. At this time, professional archaeologists were trying desperately to save archaeological information which was to be destroyed by the construction of a highway, which has since been relocated.

In 1961, one of the most outstanding accomplishments of the prehistoric Cahokians was discovered quite by accident. After a summer of intense excavation, Dr. Warren Wittry was studying excavation maps when he observed large oval-shaped pits which seemed to be arranged in a circle. He determined these pits once held wooden posts of red cedar that lined up with the rising sun at certain times of the year, serving as a calendar which he called Woodhenge. After further excavation, Dr. Wittry and other archaeologists discovered four more Woodhenges. These calendars had been built in the same place over a period of 200 years (A.D. 900–1100).

The first circle (date unknown) consists of twenty-four posts. The second circle had thirty-six posts, and the third circle (1000 A.D.) had forty-eight posts. The fourth (date unknown), which was not completely excavated, probably consisted of sixty posts. The fifth circle had only the thirteen posts in the sunrise arc. Had this been a complete circle, it would have had seventy-two posts; building only the sunrise arc suggests that red cedar trees were becoming scarce.

The functions of only three posts in the circle have been determined. These three posts mark the first day of each season. On the first day of spring and fall (equinoxes), the sun rises at the same location. A spectacular sunrise may be seen on those two days. The post marking this sunrise aligns with Monks Mound, where the leader resided. Viewed from Woodhenge, it looks as though Monks Mound is giving birth to the sun.

The other two posts mark the winter and summer solstice sunrises. During winter, the sun moves south, giving the impression that it might not return. Evidence of a fire pit was found in one of the circles near the winter solstice post; Dr. Wittry suggested that a fire had been built to warm the sun to encourage it to move back north. The winter solstice probably marked the beginning of a new year.

What the other posts were used for is unknown. Other posts located in the sunrise arc may have marked special festival dates related to the agricultural cycle.

The remaining posts around the circle may have been used to enclose the sacred area of Woodhenge. Speculations have been made that these posts were used to predict eclipses or mark the position of the moon or bright stars. There is no proof of this, however.

The third circle, which dates to 1000 A.D., was reconstructed in 1985. This circle, 410 feet in diameter, consists of forty-eight red cedar posts evenly spaced 26.8 feet apart. The posts were fifteen to twenty inches in diameter and stood about twenty feet high. Red ochre (an earthy iron oxide powder) found in the post pits suggests the posts were painted.

The post pits averaged seven feet long and 2.22 feet wide. The bottom sloped from the surface at one end to four feet deep at the other, forming a ramp to slide the posts down to facilitate their raising.

CHAPTER 5

Huronia

There are good reasons for thinking that the identifiable Indians of the bulk of the North American continent came from a later and much different cultural stock than the Indians of Mesoamerica. That the tribalists continued a rural hunting, fishing, and gathering way of life in contrast to the urban culture of Mesoamerica is plain even to cursory inquiry, but this might be explained simply by an assumption that the Mesoamericans had developed earlier on an evolutionary path that the others would follow, sooner or later. Such an explanation could gain credibility by the history of Mesoamerica's Mississippian colonists mingling with the "barbarian" predecessors in the great valley and teaching them maize cultivation.

The explanation fails, however, in other respects. True enough, the mingling Mississippians put up flat-topped pyramids with temples on top, but they did not follow mechanically along the Mexican path. They plainly rejected the practice of ripping out human hearts at their temples. Indeed, this is another reason for thinking them to be followers of Quetzalcoatl who had enjoined his Toltec followers to sacrifice "only serpents and butterflies." (The human-blood party overthrew him at Tula.)

Regardless of the Mississippian dominant people, the others among whom they chose to settle were clearly from another ethnic and cultural stock, seemingly proto-Siouan. The choice and use of weapons provides a clue to distinctions. Few will dispute that the bow and arrow represents an advance in efficiency over the spear-throwing atlatl, but Aztec warriors from the more advanced society spurned the bow as a "barbarian" weapon which was used in the Aztec armies only by Chichimec auxiliaries. Was it that the Aztecs wanted to get close to their enemy so as to capture him for sacrifice later to the gods? Or that the atlatl was a weapon proper for the nobility while the bow was to be disdained as low? (It was lower class in Europe where the nobles encased themselves in armor and fought man-to-man on horseback.) Whatever the reason, it did not prevail north of the Gulf of Mexico where bowmen achieved great proficiency and included chiefs.

Perhaps the most telling sign of the difference between the northerners and the Mexicans was the upbringing and treatment of children. The
parents of Tenochtitlán, by their own descriptions, were horrifyingly
cruel to their children. They did not spank or flog; instead they drew
blood—always blood!—by scratching the child with wicked thorns anywhere on the body, but particularly on the tongue. When the children of
aspiring or dutiful parents approached adolescence, they were delivered
to the temple boarding schools under supervision of priests who were
even stricter than the parents. Here the children lived under discipline as
strict as a Trappist monk's. The purpose may be compared to that of
nineteenth-century England's "public" schools—Eton, Harrow, and so
on—where youths were disciplined and bonded to be agents of imperial
rule. Aztec upper-class children were prepared, rather more rigorously
than the English, to assume dominant roles in government and religion,
ready to serve the cruel gods and rulers without compunction or senti-
ments of humanity for the victims thereof.

Such behavior would have utterly shocked the tribalists to the north
if they had known of it. Children among the hunters, and among planters
who also hunted, were invariably seen by European observers to have
great freedom. They were rarely beaten, a fact disapproved sternly by
Englishmen who did not believe in sparing the rod. When an Indian
father or mother wished to correct a child, they spoke gently to it. If this
failed of effect, mother poured a bowl of cold water over the incorrigible.
Life was so carefree for the Indian young that it served as a powerful
attraction to oppressed youth from English colonies who, when captured
in war, often refused repatriation, especially the indentured servants whose
personal experience with toil and punishment contrasted sharply with the
gentleness and freedom they found as adopted members of Indian families.

There is much irony in this matter of child rearing. The "civilized"
peoples—Aztecs and Europeans—prepared their children for the cruel
side of adult life by making life miserable in childhood. Only among the
"primitive" or "savage" peoples, which had fierce cruelty enough for outsiders, were children able to grow peacefully.

At least two waves of Indian migration from the Northwest preceded
European invasion of North America from the East and South. Athapascans surged southward through the American West in relatively recent
times, locating themselves as Apaches and *Apaches de Nabajó* in the Southwest. From linguistic evidence, it appears quite clearly that this migration occurred thousands of years later than the migrations of Uto-Aztecan

speakers who emerged as a distinct linguistic group somewhere around the border between Arizona and Mexican Sonora. Between 3,000 and 5,000 years ago, some of these Uto-Aztecans went south into Mexico to create the great cities in which Nahuatl was spoken. Others stayed behind to become Chichimec "barbarians." In contrast, the Apacheans broke away from Athapascans of the Northwest and entered the United States Southwest probably around A.D. 1400, after trekking along the eastern or western flanks of the Rocky Mountains. For this Southwestern region, there is no doubt that tribal immigration occurred more than once.

Archaeologists are also beginning to believe in separate waves of migration in other directions though they are tentative and vague about specifications. It is fairly well agreed that peoples of the linguistic "family" called Algonquian have occupied the northern regions of the continent for thousands of years. Now, however, it appears that other Algonquians came along later and spread across the continent from Northwest to East in a grand *völkerwanderung* so recent as to still be a subject of legend when missionary John Heckewelder picked up the tradition toward the end of the eighteenth century. To Heckewelder, the Algonquians were all "Delawares." Although he understood the distinctions of tribal identities, he believed that the Lenni Lenape of the Delaware Valley held some sort of revered status as the "grandfathers" of the other tribes. Notably, and exceptionally, they did not find it necessary to fortify their villages.

The special status of the Delawares is confirmed by a tradition among the Iroquoian Cayugas of Grand River Reserve in Canada. Respected Chief Jacob E. Thomas has preserved an account that the Delawares had been adopted by the Five Nations of the Iroquois league. (The Cayugas were one of those nations in the league.) The Delawares were established by this adoption as peacemakers to cement alliance between Iroquois nations and the Algonquian speakers among whom the Delawares were preeminent.

This Cayuga legend fits well into Heckewelder's recorded Delaware legend, which, by the way, was not a fantastic origin *myth*. Indeed, Heckewelder's tradition is unique only in its circumstantiality. Among the Algonquian Ojibwas, tradition carries their migrating people all the way east to the Atlantic Coast, then back again to spread across and around the Great Lakes. Together with the Potawatomis and Ottawas, they became known as the peoples of the Three Fires. We accept without argument the repeated waves of migration from the Northwest to the Southwest, culminating in the treks of the Athapaskan speakers in the fifteenth century A.D., thousands of years after the earliest arrivals; and we do not doubt the movement of Shoshone–Comanche peoples from the Northwest Southward into the Great Plains. For Algonquian speakers to migrate from the Northwest to the Northeast to join previously established groups seems equally credible.

Whatever one may think of the value of tribal traditions in detail, it is certain that the peoples of North America were not a homogeneous static blob of "savages," and equally certain that their migrations have been inadequately studied.

Heckewelder's Delaware tradition is enormously suggestive. It tells of a long journey that took the Delawares across the Mississippi River "where they fell in with" Iroquoian speakers whom they called the Mengwe. These Iroquoians "had likewise emigrated from a distant country," maddeningly unspecified as to direction, "and had struck upon this river somewhat higher up. Their object was the same with that of the Delawares; they were proceeding on to the eastward, until they should find a country that pleased them."

To Heckewelder's Delaware informants, the Mississippi was the *Allegéwi Sipu*, the river of the Allegéwi who were "a very powerful nation, who had many large towns built on the great rivers flowing through their land" and who also inhabited "the country east of the Mississippi." It is a very definition of the Mississippians, given long before archaeologists discovered them and confirming perfectly the Natchez tradition at the mouth of the great river.

Heckewelder's informants told further that the emigrants sought and obtained permission to cross the Mississippi, but that their vanguard on the east banks were treacherously attacked. Delawares and Iroquoians joined forces and carried on protracted war "in which many warriors fell on both sides." The allies triumphed eventually, and the Allegéwi "abandoned the country to the conquerors and fled down the Mississippi river, from whence they never returned." Seemingly this occurred about A.D. 1300, when the Mississippians are known to have retreated downriver.

The "Mengwe" chose lands "in the vicinity of the great lakes, and on their tributary streams," and the "Lenape" chose lands further south. Heckewelder's "Mengwe" means speakers of Iroquoian languages, and "Lenape" means Algonquians including the historic Delawares whom Heckewelder placed on the Delaware River "at the centre of their possessions." The legend follows them to the Susquehanna River and down to Chesapeake Bay as well as to the Hudson and Delaware rivers. Others of these Algonquians, perhaps as many as half, "retreated into the interior" west of the Mississippi. Some of them apparently chose to stay within the Mississippi Valley. As archaeology has established the presence in the Northeast of both Algonquians and Iroquoians long before the era of the legend, to accept its validity requires us to cast aside assumptions that each of these great folks migrated as an integral whole. As to that, the contrary assumption is really more plausible. Indian societies were marked by repeated fission.

I have followed the Rev. John Heckewelder's recorded tradition because he has proved to be responsible and reliable in other matters and because he consulted closely in retirement with the scholars of the American Philosophical Society. Anthropologist James Mooney has recorded the same tradition of the Allegéwi being forced south, interpreting it to mean that the Allegéwi were the modern Cherokees and the "Mississippi River" was the Ohio and Allegheny tributaries of the great river. Sometimes one must be as circumspect in dealing with anthropologists as with tribal traditions. I diverge from Mooney on several counts. He has been far from reliable in certain other matters (e.g., aboriginal Indian population), and he paid no attention to the Mississippians as such, so his version of the legend has a poor fit on archaeologically determined data.

(Since writing the preceding account, my attention has been called to the *Iroquoian* tradition recorded by the Seneca scholar Arthur C. Parker, which originates Iroquoians near the mouth of the Mississippi River on its western side. Parker's account broke off the Cherokees and took them eastward into the Appalachian mountains. Much later he sent other Iroquoians northward in the Mississippi Valley and then east, splitting into Hurons, "Five Nations," and Laurentian groups. See my map, p. 73.)

Archaeologists do not usually consult tribal traditions, preferring instead to rely on tangible material evidence, so my sketch here is at odds with the usual inference of a single Algonquian occupation in the Northeast thousands of years ago. Archaeology also does not have all the answers. Linguist Wallace Chafe has determined that the language of those Mengwe people (Iroquoians) was an offshoot of proto-Sioux-Caddoan-Iroquoian, probably diverging thousands of years ago. Since the historic Caddoans lived in the region of Arkansas and Texas, the linguistic divergence bespeaks a physical migration. One must ask "When?" and "By what route?"

Another careful linguist recently analyzed the vocabularies of known Iroquoian peoples to determine the age sequence of their languages: i.e., in what chronological order they diverged from the proto-Iroquoian speech that was parent to them all. Marianne Mithun concluded that the Cherokee language had seniority, followed by Nottoway, Tuscarora, and Meherrin, none of which is closely related to the Five Nations Iroquois of historical fame. These were all mountain dwellers in the interior of Kentucky, Tennessee, Alabama, Georgia, North and South Carolina,

Hypothesized Delaware and Iroquoian Migration Routes

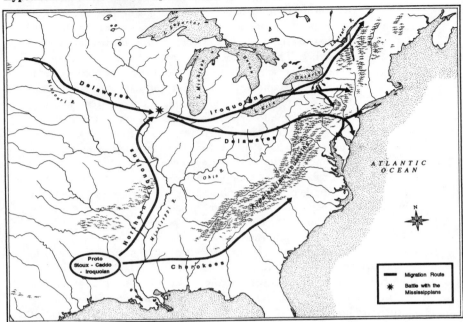

Sources for this map include oral traditions of Delawares and Iroquoians supplemented by evidence from linguistics and archaeology.

and Virginia—peoples of the Southeast. Next in line of departure from proto-Iroquoian were the Hurons and Wyandots (northerners), after which the Five Nations Iroquois split off. The sequence should include the Iroquoians of the St. Lawrence Valley, but none of their languages have survived though they spread over 125 sites established by archaeology.

Bearing these divisions in mind, let us return to Heckewelder's legend. It recounts that after the Mississippians fled downriver in defeat, the victorious allies continued advancing into the Northeast where they separated into many communities that had coagulated into tribes by the time that Europeans learned of them. Then, as the legend specified, *these* Iroquoians came to possess much land bordering on Lakes Huron and Ontario while the Delaware–Algonquians sprawled over the region between the Appalachian Mountains and the Atlantic.

This is not to say that they found howling wilderness in their new localities. Archaeologists have solid evidence of predecessors in the

Northeast from at least 10,000 years before the present. Indeed, some assert that the culture of the Iroquoian Onondagas evolved *in situ:* i.e., right where the Onondagas were discovered in times of written history. But, whoever they were, the preceders came from somewhere else at some time or another. They did not come into existence by spontaneous combustion. The *in situ* case rests largely on the evidence of pottery sherds that show sequence of technology and design, but language is at least as much part of culture as pottery is—and so are traditions. After about A.D. 1300 the Onondagas came to depend more heavily on maize than ever before, and the signs seem clear that they acquired this trait by way of the Mississippians. Somehow the evolution of Onondaga's material culture must be reconciled with the other evidence.

A possible explanation is conquest and assimilation. If we suppose that Iroquoian speakers came to Onondaga after helping to defeat the Mississippians, they could have brought maize dependency and their language to dominate over the local "Owasco" people (who may have been different Iroquoians) while merging some of the local traits with their own. On this assumption, it is not difficult to fit migration of persons to *in situ* development of culture because the dates show how this could have occurred. Archaeologists agree that the Mississippians withdrew downstream at about A.D. 1300, and "the first phase of the Iroquois [Onondaga] cultural tradition [as distinguished from preceding 'Owasco'] began at about A.D. 1300 or a few decades later."

In consideration of the great age of the Cherokee language compared to the other Iroquoian tongues, the proto-Cherokees probably broke off from the others at an early date and migrated by themselves. I offer a hypothesis based on the close fit of the oral traditions to linguistic and archaeological evidence: that the Iroquoian homeland, as far back as we can guess, was somewhere in Texas or Arkansas, that the Cherokees separated in a body to cross *from west to east* through the lower Mississippi Valley to the Smoky Mountains and there sent out Tuscaroras, Meherrins, and Nottoways.

Other Iroquoians, according to archaeologist Dean Snow, migrated *from south to north* "at about 2,000 and perhaps as much as 4,000 years ago," and by their intervention cut off eastern Algonquian speech communities from others in the west. In my hypothesis, when the Delaware–Algonquians started their final migration from the Northwest, their legend has them meeting up with *these* Iroquoians. I cannot even try to account for the time elapsing between 2,000 or 4,000 years ago and A.D. 1300.

The legend recorded by Heckewelder carries the Iroquoians along

Lake Erie's north shore, dropping off Hurons in Ontario and splitting the rest on arriving at Lake Ontario, some choosing the north shore of that lake and going down the St. Lawrence River to Hochelaga and Stadacona, others settling along the Finger Lakes region of New York; and, finally, it posits that from this last body offshoots went south to become Susquehannocks.

This is very obviously a large and complex structure—perhaps no more than a house of cards—to build upon an oral tradition and a few vague clues from archaeology and linguistics. But what better explanation can be reconciled to those clues? Critics have a responsibility to account for them. Much difficulty for interpretation is created by confusion among specialists studying the vectors of maize diffusion from Mexico. New technology has raised serious questions about a number of important findings derived from older methods, and some questions are now up in the air—a very murky air. In the present state of the evidence, my hypothesis cannot be offered as proved, but it does seem to fit what we do know, and I think it makes more sense than an assumption that the Onondagas popped up from nowhere to create a culture out of nothing.

The Delaware–Algonquian legend went on to tell of Iroquoians and Algonquians, that "for a long time, some say many hundred years, the two nations resided peaceably," but eventually came to blows. At this point, an Iroquois legend, as told to Cadwallader Colden early in the eighteenth century, picks up the story. The two legends, as might be expected, each blame the other side, but they agree as to the outbreak and continuation of hostilities. This was the situation when the French entered the St. Lawrence Valley in the sixteenth and seventeenth centuries.

For clarity, it must be emphasized that "Algonquian" and "Iroquoian" are umbrella terms coined by linguists, rather like "Romance" or "Teutonic," to cover the speakers of related languages who must be presumed to have had common ancestors—the proto-Iroquoians or proto-Algonquians. As descendants grew in numbers, they separated, and developed dialects that eventually became distinct languages identifying distinct peoples. As for the Iroquoians, their own traditional history states that before the formation of the Iroquois League, they had lived "apart from each other as separate nations and having nothing in common." The same localism was true of the Algonquians who surrounded most of the Iroquoians. When war began, therefore, there was no grand massing of all the Iroquoians against all the Algonquians. Although generally hostile feelings prevailed, actual fighting was a matter for individual tribes pitted against each other for specifically tribal objectives, something like the nations and religions involved in the Thirty Years War of Europe's seventeenth century.

In this complex of relationships, the most remote northern Iroquoians, the Hurons of lower Ontario, went their own way, maintaining peaceful trading relationships with Algonquian-speaking hunting peoples, and even warring aggressively against other Iroquoian peoples. They require special attention.

The Hurons of written history lived in a confederation of four tribes in southern Ontario between Lake Simcoe and the Georgian Bay of Lake Huron. It appears that their confederation was the product of successful trade by the earliest tribe on the scene, the Attignawantan, whose presence dated from mid-fifteenth century. These were joined a century later by the Arendarhonon, and still later by the Attigneenongnahac, and at about 1610 by the Tahontaenrat.

The confederation's location was strategic in several particulars: it offered much opportunity for canoe-borne transportation, and it was the northernmost region where maize could be grown reliably. These assets led to the growth of a planting society having excellent, peaceful relationships with surrounding Algonquian hunting peoples, especially those to the north where the climate precluded planting. Notably, the hunters who lived on the Canadian Shield, around Lake Nipissing, became friendly with the Hurons. "There is little reason to doubt," writes Bruce G. Trigger, "that these relations centered around a reciprocal exchange of corn, nets, and tobacco for skins, dried fish, and meat." It appears also, from later observation, that the Nipissings would shelter in Huronia when winters became too bitterly cold. It was a "symbiotic relationship." Something similar occurred in the Southwest when Plains Indians wintered among the Pueblos.

This was in strong contrast to the hostilities common between the Hurons and other Iroquoian peoples. The rule between these competitive rather than complementary Iroquoians was a desire to dominate that led toward consolidation and alliance of some tribes, and the building of defensive stockades around all the Iroquoian villages. It probably explains also why pre-Columbian Huron trade was almost entirely regional. Not many goods of an exotic nature found their way through the territories of hostile tribes.

All changed when Frenchmen appeared in the St. Lawrence River. Jacques Cartier's voyage to the river in 1534 was the first to be recorded though he may have had predecessors who were not eager for publicity. In 1535, Cartier came again, this time pushing up the river as far as

Montreal Island and spending the winter with Iroquoian hosts. He brought European trade goods, and he was followed by yet more Frenchmen.

We must not run too far ahead of events elsewhere. It is enough for present purposes to observe that frontier relationships of the Huron tribes before European arrival had produced increase in village size, perpetual hostilities toward other Iroquoians except those that joined in confederation or commerce, especially the highly successful symbiotic trade between the planting Hurons and the hunting Algonquians of the north. Frenchmen, when they appeared, represented a new frontier, new in particulars and in kind, but it evolved from the old.

In the East as in the Southwest, intertribal war was endemic when Europeans arrived. The Iroquois were engaged in constant hostilities with surrounding Algonquians, according to legends on both sides, a situation which may have stimulated the organization of the Five Nations confederacy or League of the Haudenosaunee (Iroquois) in one location and the Huron confederacy in another. The dates of formation of these confederacies are not certain though current thinking among some anthropologists sets the Iroquois League origin at about the fourteenth century. League chiefs have set it at about 1390 A.D.

In the Southwest, newcomer Apaches and Navajos surrounded Pueblo villages and adopted some cultural novelties learned from the Pueblos: horticulture at first, then weaving and the herding derived ultimately from Spaniards. "We civilized them," says a Pueblo friend, tongue in cheek—but that process took some time. After Spanish colonization the Athapaskan colonists became the horsemen and raiders whose image is familiar from Hollywood movies.

This is a mere sampling of the total situation, chosen to give life to generalities. By the end of the sixteenth century, Europeans of all colonizing nations found situations ripe for the divide-and-conquer strategies at which they were expert. The tribes were disunified and often mutually hostile. Whatever stabilization had been effected by the commercial network of the Mississippians was without a unifying political framework.

CHAPTER 6

The Dalles

On the northwestern side of Mississippia, maize was carried to the middle Missouri Valley by Mandans and Hidatsas, speakers of Siouan languages who had migrated, according to their legends, from somewhere toward the east, apparently near the Great Lakes. In their settled villages in North Dakota, they established trading centers, functioning similarly to the pattern at Huronia, where hunting peoples brought meat and hides to exchange for products of farm and craft.

Their near neighbors living lower on the Missouri (in South Dakota) were the Arikaras, a Caddoan-speaking people who had migrated northward, probably from Texas or Oklahoma. Also cultivators of maize and other farm produce, the Arikaras also traded with outlying hunters. Eventually, after their population dwindled from disease and war, they joined the Mandan / Hidatsas.

The vectors of maize cultivation come together here in the Dakotas after going off in different directions from Mesoamerica: the Mandan path leading through Mississippia while the Arikara path in all likelihood had taken its way from the Southwest. This juncture surely represented the farthermost limit of Mesoamerican influence in the Northwest, but it was by no means the endpoint of trade. Beyond maize, trade continued among the hunting peoples in their own fashion and involved goods they valued for their own reasons.

The Missouri villages were busy places. The evidence of recorded times has them being visited by members of the Crow, Assiniboin, Plains Cree, Cheyenne, Arapaho, Kiowa, Kiowa–Apache, and Plains Comanche tribes. Indians who never came near the Missouri villages acquired goods from them through tribal middlemen. The vast open spaces of the Northwest contained a network of commerce.

Among the hunting tribes an ancient institution moved goods about. This was the "rendezvous" that took place when small bands of hunting peoples at peace with each other converged during the summer at a prearranged meeting place. It was a time to bind the people together with ritual worship, arranged weddings, exchanges of presents, and group merrymaking. Unlike Mesoamerican and Mississippian markets, the rendezvous functioned more like a fair, providing a reliable outlet for the middlemen who had picked up a stock of goods from the Missouri year-round trade centers. Thus Crow middlemen shuttled between the Missouri Valley and the Shoshone rendezvous in southwestern Wyoming where they met other traders from the far Northwest as well as the congregated Shoshone bands.

Still another variant on trading methods appeared at The Dalles, on the Columbia River where it bounds the states of Washington and Oregon about sixty miles east of the modern city of Portland. Far beyond any possible direct influence from Mesoamerica, and beyond any but the most nebulous sort of indirect influence, a permanent trading center grew up at The Dalles unparalleled in North America for "variety of trade goods, the intensity and volume of trade, and the plethora of cultures that manufactured and processed these goods." Here the founding staple was not maize, which is conspicuous by its absence from that great variety of trade goods. Instead of abundance from the earth, the Indians at The Dalles lived and did business by harvesting a regular "crop" from the waters. Before Bonneville Dam changed everything in the twentieth century, the Columbia River narrowed at The Dalles and fell eighty feet in twelve miles. Incoming salmon, rushing upstream to spawn in the waters of their origin, crowded and struggled up the narrow rapids, guaranteeing a large annual catch for Wasco–Wishram and Wayam Indians living along the shores.

Salmon had the effect here that maize had elsewhere. It persuaded the local people to stay put in sedentary villages. It gave them a surplus beyond their own needs for subsistence, which they processed by drying and smoking and then exchanged with traders from the Yakima, Kittitas, Klikitat, Umatilla, and Nez Percé tribes. Traders who came for fish brought their own goods in exchange, and since they came from different directions with different kinds of goods, The Dalles became a sort of general store: "dealers in almost everything." Chinookans from the lower Columbia River could catch salmon enough for themselves, but they came for other goods. Middlemen on their own account, they brought marine products from the Northwest Coast—shells and shellfish, oils, whale and seal bone—to exchange for obsidian and stone tools from the Great Basin, skins and feathers from the Great Plains, baskets and minerals from the Plateau, and wild food plants from California where farming was not practiced because nourishing plants were so plentiful in the wild.

William R. Swagerty, who provides this information, remarks that "items traded at The Dalles have been found in archaeological sites from Alaska to California and over 1,000 miles east in the Missouri River trade centers." Here, as everywhere across the continent before European invasion, the native peoples cooperated through commerce when at peace. The frontiers of trade, in all their variations, were means of linkage instead of barriers of separation.

What can explain all these frontiers?—the vast regions of contact and interaction between Mesoamerican producing culture and its derivative societies, opposed to assorted peoples of extracting cultures?—the melange of smaller frontiers beyond the periphery of the great one?

Besides the contrasts in material cultures, another set demands to be accounted for: the multitude of languages. It cannot surprise that many tongues should come into being where there was no writing to stabilize any. Time and distance give birth to dialects, and they in turn evolve into new vernaculars. This has happened everywhere in the world.

Yet it is to linguistics, I think, that we must look for the clue, only dimly suggested by material culture, to the number and variety of aboriginal American Indian frontiers and peoples. Many as were their languages, large groups of them form "families" so related within each family that they may safely be assumed to have had a common ancestor—the proto-Uto-Aztecan, proto-Algonquian, proto-Iroquoian, proto-Siouan, proto-Athapaskan, and so on. These "proto" languages, totally unrelated to each other, must have been spoken in times of great antiquity by peoples who had evolved in separate territories with separate histories. At some point, impelled by motives only to be guessed at, each of them migrated.

To modern minds such conduct is inexplicable, almost incredible, but many better-known peoples serve as examples of such *völkerwanderungen* elsewhere on the globe. The Hellenes came out of Europe's interior to seize the Greek mainland and isles. Turks came out of Mongolia to conquer Persia. Huns surged from one direction into Europe, Goths and Norsemen from others.

The language families of American Indians imply such migrations of multitudes. Whether they came in search of big game, or whether increase of population impelled them to seek more room and resources away from their formative territories, must be matter for speculation. But the fact of migration, interpreted by the distinctness of languages, implies that these peoples migrated at different times—as many times as there were peoples—and the cultural frontiers of aboriginal America support that inference.

A portentous date carries the logic a significant step further. Archaeologists have observed that about A.D. 1300, great tumults occurred all over North America. As examples, the Mesoamerican city of Tula was overthrown and destroyed, Chaco Canyon was abandoned, and Mississippians left their outpost at Aztalan (in Wisconsin) to flee south to Cahokia. Sometimes the archaeologist guesses that the phenomena in a given locality occurred because of climatic change, perhaps because of increased aridity, but hints of other reasons emerge. Legends and ruined buildings tell of warfare at Tula. Much intertribal violence is evident among the Uto-Aztecan-speakers—the Chichimeca "barbarians"—of the Southwest, leading eventually to Aztec migration into the Basin of Mexico. The Delaware-Algonquian legend remembers bitter, protracted war against the Mississippians and is explicit that this is what forced the losers downstream. In itself this legend is a refutation of the aridity causation theory, and well it might be when one considers how well the Mesoamericans and their colonials understood irrigation.

I suggest that around about A.D. 1300, and continuing somewhat later, new waves of migrating peoples surged out of Alaska and / or the Canadian Northwest. Each one, as it advanced, impelled retreat by its predecessor who pushed against its own predecessor, and so on throughout the continent. Whatever caused these mass migrations continued to operate into the fifteenth century when the Navajo–Apache swarm broke off from their Athapaskan-speaking kin in Canada and surged southward to establish their own niches in the Southwest. This sort of thing *in Asia* is accepted as standard in our textbooks, to explain, for example, the waves of migration breaking upon Persia. Why do we not see it in America?

In a world where so many linkages and reasons for cooperation existed as the widespread networks of commerce demonstrate, there must have been strong causes for hostilities. Conquerors normally hunger for territory—land to be possessed and ruled—and rational tribal peoples had similar appetites. Written history shows them willing to battle desperately against encroachment by outsiders. Under pressure, they became encroachers themselves, and their separatism and ethnocentrism created frontiers of struggle instead of cooperation. Warfare begat destruction, loss of population, and the abandonment of great commercial centers. Tribal invasions began the destabilization of aboriginal societies that later was carried on so terribly by European invasions.

Inferred from archaeology and linguistics, this observation runs counter to most, if not all, recent histories, including my own. These were derived from written documents and ethnological research which lacked the chronological depth necessary to grasp the impact of the migrations of the peoples. There has been a tendency much evident among both historians and ethnologists, and descended from a long ancestry of European "image" literature, to conceive American Indians as different from other people. In its beginnings among European "discoverers," this attitude grew from an identification of Indians with physical nature so complete that they became significantly different from what the observers called civilized persons. Museums of their cultures are part of "natural history" institutions. Indians being so *natural*, their communities became in conception like herds of animals, bereft of real government and simply wandering over the land or alternatively bound to particular habitats. Indians defending themselves against encroachment in modern times have unwittingly lent credence to this preconception by professing that a particular tribe or community had become as one with a site at which their ancestors had lived from time immemorial.

In its entirety, all this is the myth of the savage Indian, a creature other than normally human as understood by Europeans. When the natural man is placed among the beauties of nature seen as benign, his savagery is noble. When he is likened to nature seen as cruel, he becomes a beast of prey and his savagery is horrible. In fact, Indians are not, and have not been, any more natural, nor any more savage, than human persons of the most advanced societies. What they are is *human*, with all the nobility and baseness, all the strength and frailty, all the virtues and vices latent in the human animal. What distinguishes them from Europeans has been their history, and the time is past due to get on with it.

CHAPTER 7

How Many Indians—and Why

Scholarly wisdom long held that Indians were so inferior in mind and works that they could not possibly have created or sustained large populations. An early formulation of the notion reached print when a French Jesuit missionary remarked in A.D. 1612 that the nomadic Indians of his acquaintance "roam through rather than occupy" vast stretches of territory. By simply assuming that *all* Indians were nomads, theorists of what is called international law were able to argue that *no* Indians really occupied the land, and logic then dictated that there could not have been many Indians. Spuriously inductive—had not Jesuit Biard observed those nomads?—this justification for conquest was recited again by the nineteenth-century American politician Lewis Cass who wrote that the land was "traversed but not occupied" by Indians, when Cass could see Indian farmlands and settled villages with his own eyes. And historians carried the myth into the twentieth century as Frederick Jackson Turner excluded Indians from the "settled area" and defined their territories as "free land," after which his disciple Walter Prescott Webb expanded the definition to "land which can be had for the taking."

Webb explained in a note that he was "ignoring the scattered Indian population. . . . In the present area of the United States the Indian population was probably not more than 500,000, one Indian to about six square miles." Thus the myth of the "incompetent savage" became a justification for conquest of Indians because supposedly they did not exist in numbers enough to matter.

After missionary Biard's remark in the seventeenth century, the myth became an upside-down pyramid of rationalization by theorists and logicians. Emerich de Vattel, a theorist of international law, argued that "while the conquest of the civilized Empires of Peru and Mexico was a notorious usurpation . . . colonies upon the continent of North America might, if done within just limits, have been entirely lawful. The peoples of those vast tracts of land rather roamed over them than inhabited them."

Regardless of theories spun across the Atlantic, actual observers often saw Indians who were not nomads, and reported phenomena quite different from Biard's. Indeed, Biard was a late comer to the world so new to Europeans. Fifteenth- and sixteenth-century Spanish conquerors in the Caribbean islands and on the continents had observed, awestruck, the teeming multitudes of chiefdoms and cities (of which, more below), and no one could accuse them of delusive sympathy for the peoples they were destroying. By the seventeenth century, epidemic diseases transmitted from Europe had raced far ahead of European colonizers to devastate Indians throughout the Americas; but "discoverers" along the Atlantic coast could still report large communities of horticultural Indians from Florida to Massachusetts.

Like Biard, they put estimates in writing, but their numbers vastly exceeded his as their observed cultures differed from his. Later proponents of savage incompetence had to explain away such reported phenomena. They used two techniques, of which one was simply to ignore inconvenient data or to dispose of them with a contradictory assumption. Thus the great populations of Mexico and Peru were shunted aside on the assumption that those peoples were not the same as the savages to the north. Vattel's cited comment is an example. The second technique involved disparagement of the estimating "discoverers" on grounds that they inflated numbers to increase the importance of their finds—or simply because of hyperactive imaginations. On these arbitrary bases, early estimates were halved by succeeding generations, and halved again in years following until a number was reached early in the twentieth century acceptable to the savagery mythmakers.

There was still a nagging problem of how to dispose of the effects of horticulture. Theory dictated that savages lived by the hunt; it was what made them roam. But Indians who had been seen to live by planting should theoretically have increased their populations. Among other considerations, agriculture was at the heart of civilization and its progress. Two quite diverse gentlemen invented diverse rationalizations. Albert Gallatin solved the problem by observing that the Indians who tilled the soil were women. Wrote Gallatin, "In order that the cultivation of the soil may promote that increase of mankind, which is limited only by the quantity of land fit for cultivation, it is necessary that the annual agricultural labor should produce a quantity of food, at least equal to the annual consumption of the whole existing population. The labor of women alone is not sufficient to produce that result."

Gallatin was an eminent statesman and respected scholar of linguistics. In the twentieth century, eminent ethnologist Alfred Kroeber took a somewhat different tack to get to much the same destination. Kroeber resorted once more to the Indian as a being essentially different from civilized Europeans. He laid down dicta: the Indian "was not a farmer in our sense of the word." Indians grew food only for their own households. Therefore, "the population remaining stationary, excess planting was not practiced," and then the ultimate dogma *ex cathedra*, "nor would it have led to anything in the way of economic or social benefit nor of increase of numbers."

It is hard to comprehend how such omniscient gall could have provoked anything but horse laughs; but, sad to say, it was long accepted by many scholars as the final authority on its subject. It should be a stern lesson as to the value of unexamined authority.

As his contribution to scientific method, Kroeber measured off areas on the map with a device called a planimeter, and arbitrarily assigned a density of population to each cultural area. For the horticultural areas of the eastern United States he assigned between five and thirty persons per thirty-eight square miles, a ratio of fewer than one person at maximum per square mile. But this was merely flummery to give an appearance of personal work to what was in reality only an opinion. As Kroeber confessed, it seemed best to him to "accept . . . in toto, rather than to patch" the estimates earlier calculated by the reputable ethnologist James Mooney. (In 1976, a physical anthropologist determined that "no one has determined the exact sources of the estimates of the methodology employed" by Mooney. After examining Mooney's notes, Douglas H. Ubelaker endorsed a finding that Mooney's numbers "represent neither the aboriginal number immediately prior to European contact nor the maximum aboriginal number prior to . . . population decline.")

Kroeber finally came up with a figure of 900,000 aboriginal Indians north of the Rio Grande and a grand total of 8,400,000 in the entire western hemisphere. His total was scrupulously fair to North and South America, assigning an even 4,200,000 to each. In all this, Kroeber flaunted his high status among ethnologists in response to challenges from other scholars. The beginning of sanity in the field had been expressed by H. J. Spinden in a 1929 Smithsonian Report. Spinden looked at archaeological findings and took direct issue with Mooney and the earliest statements made by Kroeber. Spinden concluded that "a halcyon epoch of far-flung trade" had existed at about A.D. 1200, indicating "say 50,000,000 to 75,000,000 souls" in the whole hemisphere. None too specific in these calculations, he nevertheless aimed in the opposite direction from Mooney and Kroeber, and for opposing reasons. Whereas they propounded

Indians as incompetents, Spinden observed evidence of Indian surpluses being created and exchanged.

The most damning indictment of Kroeber's methods and results came from fellow Californians Carl Ortwin Sauer (geographer), Sherburne F. Cook (physiologist), and Woodrow Borah (historian). These scholars worked primarily with Spanish written records from Latin America, a method that annoyed Kroeber who set up the wisdom of Mooney and himself as "a safer authority than Cortés or Las Casas, or registers of baptisms and deaths by priests knowing only some missions in one province." From Olympus, he decreed, "I am likely to reject most of them outright."

Less inclined to oracular bilge, his challengers continued their systematic drudgery in the sources, and the tide of scholarly opinion has now turned. Let us turn, too, from this sorry story so as to review the new situation.

Carl O. Sauer found references to a partial census of the island of Hispaniola (Haiti and the Dominican Republic) in A.D. 1496, ordered by Bartholomew Columbus (the admiral's brother) for purposes of taxation. Conducted by the cacique chiefs, whose interest was to minimize the figures and so reduce their tax burden, the census produced a total of 1,100,000 natives in the half of the island then under Spanish control. Early in the sixteenth century, Bartolomé de Las Casas, who was on the spot, thought that Hispaniola's total aboriginal population must have been three million persons. Geographer Sauer surveyed the island's favorable environment and the natives' methods of exploiting it, and agreed with Las Casas.

Woodrow Borah and Sherburne F. Cook caused a stir with their carefully researched studies of pre-Cortés Mexico and the devastation wrought by Spanish conquest. Summarizing in the *Proceedings of the American Philosophical Society*, they found that there was in Central Mexico when Cortés landed on the coast of Veracruz "a very dense population" having an average density "of one hundred twenty-five persons per square mile." The averages added up to a total for Central Mexico—the land of urban Indians—of 25.2 millions in A.D. 1518.

Sauer, Borah, and Cook conducted their part of the discussion in polite, professional prose, but anthropologist Henry F. Dobyns used blunt, angry language to challenge the dogma of the incompetent savage. Departing from the method of itemized researches used by other scholars, he concentrated on the known effects of epidemic disease. He worked backward from populations observed and reported in historic times, using an established ratio of loss caused by disease among peoples lacking immunities,

Some Aboriginal Indian Trade as of A.D. 1250

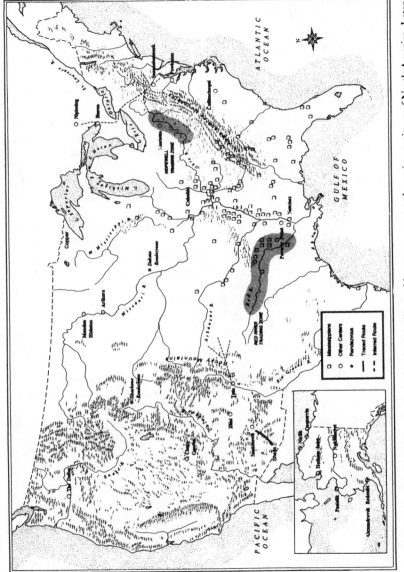

The ancestors of modern Indians conducted trade, by tribes and by persons, across the entire continent of North America. Later, when Europeans introduced the world market to America, they built upon pre-existing systems.

and calculated what maximum Indian populations must have been. By this means, Dobyns increased all previous estimates of North American Indian population to a range of between 90 and 112 millions, of which 10 to 12 millions lived north of the Rio Grande.

The revisionist publications of the 1960s churned up furious new debate. Demographer William M. Denevan edited in 1976 a collection of essays ranging widely; Dobyns returned to the fray with a new book in 1983; and in 1987 sociologist Russell Thornton broadened the discussion to include the whole sequence of decline and revival from 1492 to the present. There is still no consensus about aboriginal numbers, and special problems of interpretation emerge from scholarly differences over which era in aboriginal America to use as a base figure: the time of presumed maximum as of about A.D. 1200, or the time as of 1492 after some evident decline had occurred. The ambiguous figures range from one million to 18 million persons north of Mesoamerica.

This brief survey mentions only a sampling of the better known participants in the debate, chiefly to demonstrate how unsettled the issue has been and yet remains. The reader will have noticed the wide range of scholarly disciplines represented. I pretend to no authority whatever, but I venture some opinions after wrestling with the literature. First, there seems to be a general tendency toward acceptance of higher figures than Mooney and Kroeber proposed, but lower than those of Dobyns or Borah. (So far as Mesoamerica is concerned, however, the *Cambridge Encyclopedia of Latin America* accepts without qualification the Borah and Cook estimate of 25.2 million pre-Columbians in Central Mexico.)

My inclination, after observing the great North American trading networks of pre-Columbian times, is toward absolute rejection of Mooney–Kroeber, and especially of Kroeber's monumentally egotistic braying. There is little doubt in my mind that those old Indians did have the intelligence to exploit natural resources as well as humans could elsewhere in the world. However, their North American cultures (above Mexico) lacked certain skills that could have expanded populations to Old World dimensions. Of these lacks, the most conspicuous were herds and flocks of domesticated animals—an enormous source of meat, hides, and dairy products, especially after game animals became scarce. This lack undeniably must have restricted possibilities for growth. The lack of iron and steel metallurgy also limited the range of technology in terms of utensils and weapons; and the absence of wheeled vehicles, as well as beasts of burden, meant that Indians had to labor much harder than Europeans or Asiatics to achieve the same amount of product. Nothing could be falser than the myth of the Lazy Savage. *Everything* done by Indians was done by their own muscles.

It seems also that the intertribal clashes that upset Indian America throughout the successive waves of invasion from the Northwest could only have produced heavy casualties. What happened when Europeans added their own invasion accelerated and raised to a higher power a process that had begun as early as A.D. 1200. The continent's maximum population probably was reached at about that date.

Knowing that new local studies are raising figures everywhere, though they have not yet been collected, I will hazard a guess. My guess tilts toward the ten-million figure of Woodrow Borah and the early work of Henry F. Dobyns. This is for Indians north of the Rio Grande at about A.D. 1200.

A large component of that figure will have to come from the masses in the Northwest who have received very little attention except notice of their pouring out of the region. One must consider also a bias inherent in all archaeological work: i.e., it can go nowhere but up. Today's figures are minimum; tomorrow's new digs add new figures.

CHAPTER 8

The "Documents" of Pre-writing History

In any history the question is pertinent—sometimes, in another sense, impertinent: How do you know? It brings to mind the 1930s radio comic Jack Perle. Posing as "Baron Munchausen," he told the most preposterous whoppers, and when his straight man protested, he would chuckle and retort, "Vuss you dere? Sharlie?" Obviously, we vuss not dere in the era before writing. How then can we have even a remote idea of what happened, when, and where?

The practitioner of prehistory must be versatile. At bottom (so to speak) he is an archaeologist, but he must be acquainted with many sciences and arts. Though some ancient ruins appear still on the surface of the earth, most have been buried, for which reason the archaeologist must dig. In doing so, the professional distinguishes himself from the amateur curio collector by digging with a system called *stratigraphy*. The formidable name need not frighten. It stands for a simple yet profoundly important process based on the assumption that upper layers, or strata, were laid on top of lower layers, and therefore are of more recent origin. Logically, then, things found in the lowest layer preceded chronologically all those higher up. (In excavating ancient Troy, Heinrich Schliemann kept going down until he found nine Troys, one underneath the other.)

The archaeologist reconstructs cultural successions or sequences by study of manmade things (called artifacts) in higher or lower layers of soil; and if he knows a little about the geology of his excavation site, he may be able to put an approximate date on each layer, plus or minus an appropriate tolerance. What follows is a sampling of techniques.

Stratigraphy is most useful for sequence. For greater precision, the archaeologist has other strategies. Another formidable name—*dendroclimatology*—identifies the study of past climates by making cross sections of trees, counting their growth rings, and interpreting the spaces between them. Wide spaces may be ambiguous, but narrow spaces mean lack of rainfall, and the numbers are definite years. This method has been much used in the United States Southwest where cycles of aridity have dominated all human activity.

An extremely important technique is *radiocarbon-dating*. Developed only since 1947, it exploits the process by which cosmic rays stimulate the creation of carbon-14, which is absorbed by plants through photosynthesis and taken into animals at the top of the food chain. Carbon-14 decays at a regular rate when it stops being renewed at the death of its producer. Thus all organic matter can be analyzed for the age of its carbon-14 constituent, and fragments of wood and bone become an archaeologist's calendars.

Another technique from physics is *archaeomagnetic* dating, which relies on how Earth's magnetic field constantly shifts in intensity and direction. Such changes affect iron particles in clay, but they stabilize when heated past 200 degrees Celsius. Thus the clay at the bottom of a hearth will sometimes carry an approximate date.

Certain minerals are traceable to their originating mines by X-ray fluorescence which reveals the identifying "signature" of the lode. For instance, the precise origins of different types of turquoise and obsidian can be calculated with confidence. Catlinite can be mapped because it came from only one source in Minnesota. When artifacts of these materials are found at great distances from their sources, or when seashells are found far inland (especially when they show signs of crafting), we can be sure they were conveyed by human hands, and most likely in trade. Indeed, we can plot the distances, though we cannot say whether one long journey or several shorter ones were involved.

From biology come techniques called *palynology*—the study of fossil pollen—studies of *macrobotanical* remains (seeds and plant parts), and *faunal* studies—all of which are indicators of types of climate necessary or unfavorable to such life forms. Apart from the famous puzzle concerning why the dinosaurs disappeared, perhaps the most intriguing today is the extinction of the great mammals—mastodons and woolly mammoths, for example—in North America sometime around 11,000 or 12,000 years ago. Since remains of these animals have been found with human weapons stuck in them, the archaeologist knows that homo sapiens had arrived in North America before the demise of the large animals. Some scholars believe that humans hunted the great beasts to extinction, but others think that there must have been environmental traumas as well, perhaps arising from increasing aridity of climate.

Human remains, artifacts, and habitations are at the center of archaeological concerns. Specialists in physical anthropology can infer much about prevalent diseases from the evidence of human bones. We know, for example, that rheumatoid arthritis is a very ancient ailment. We can tell the average size of local populations where enough bones have been recovered; and we reason with some confidence that the lives of hunters and gatherers were generally short, not much exceeding twenty years. (It is unsettling to think that the natural way of life was not usually the healthiest.)

Teeth, as well as bones, survive through the centuries, and some specialists can suggest migration patterns from the evidence of dental types. Such suggestions gain strength when confirmed by patterns of blood types in populations alive today. No "pure" Indian blood is type O. Indians are not Rh negative—provided they are not descended from intermarriage with non-Indians.

Apart from the physical bodies of humans, their cultural products provide strong clues to how they lived and where they went. Habitations are highly informative. Only humans make fires, so the materials found around a charcoal hearth tell what tools were being used and what food was being eaten at a time set by carbon-14 dating of the charcoal. (But this is sometimes dubious.) Post-holes for house construction leave telltale marks in the soil long after the posts have rotted away; an expert measures distances between them to find house size, counts the number of houses in a settlement, estimates average family size, and gets a fair notion of population size as well as life styles.

There are techniques of analysis and comparison of *style* in artifacts. Arrowheads that are merely curiosities to most persons may tell the experienced archaeologist much if he knows where they came from, at what layer of soil, and what they were found in association with. Chipped in a certain way, an arrowhead or spearhead bespeaks a type of culture with a particular technology. Different technologies mark different cultures or different peoples. During the long epoch when humans lived primarily by hunting and gathering, such differences might indicate cultural sequences among the same people. But the casual collector who picks up an arrowhead without identifying site, depth, and associations destroys its value as a "document."

It is obvious that style in the crafting of tools and weapons tells something about what was needed for their making and more about how they were used. Style is useful also in the analysis of those other hard, inorganic artifacts: ceramics and works of art. With these the archaeologist acts partly as technician noting the processes of craft, and partly as art critic comparing designs, colors, textures, and so on. Such documents are enormously informative about religion and lifeways. (Anyone looking at the art of Northwest Coast Indians knows immediately how distinctive an art style can be. No matter where found, such an object locates its origin unambiguously.)

Archaeologists are apt to concentrate on material culture—i.e., tangible objects—but there are other products of culture that require the assistance of other specialists. Of these, beyond question, language is most important. We do not know of a time when humans lacked speech, and we can only speculate about how it originated, but what a multitude of languages our species has invented! Ever since the Brothers Grimm, linguists have developed methods to trace ancient connections between living languages; and, appropriately enough, the Grimms were also folklorists who preserved traditional tales. Even when these seem entirely fanciful, they reveal much about the outlook and ideology of the folk who have kept them alive.

There is a special kind of traditional story which provides detailed information available from no other sources. These are the narratives recorded by curious Europeans at times of early contact with preliterate peoples. They are difficult to deal with: typically vague and confused about chronology, often mythologically exasperating, and apt to be slanted by both the speaker and his recorder; yet such oral traditions of record may contain nuggets of information when compared carefully with other sources.

It should be clear from all this that the archaeologist has to be a renaissance scholar to extract data from "documents" that predate pen and ink. With such techniques he has reconstructed the prehistory of humankind in the Americas, which is to say history by other means. This work is still comparatively in its infancy, and unavoidable great gaps exist in the record. The materials of study are partly responsible as they have not been susceptible to collection according to any overall strategy, but rather have come to light in a hit-or-miss fashion when individual workers or organizations became interested in a particular situation. As often as not this interest arose by chance. (There is a famous story of how Schliemann used Homer's *Iliad* as a guide to find the ruins of Troy.)

There are other problems. A serious fallacy is propagated when, as sometimes happens, an archaeologist equates evolution of material culture with the history of a people. Ancient wisdom advises that man lives not by bread alone. People get involved in more matters than making ceramic or stone implements; and language and religion, especially, evolve independently of artisan skills.

Archaeology's difficulties are increased, it seems to me, by the odd combination of particularism in practice and universalism in theory that characterizes some of its hard-working devotees. A friend has remarked that an archaeologist may explain the history of the world after finding a broken pipe stem. Obviously joking, this was wild exaggeration for effect, but the remark rings true enough to sting. It does seem as though the diggers focus so tightly on their own sites and regions that they pay little attention to what is happening among others of their own kind. Naturally, such narrowness precludes systematic synthesis even as it encourages flights of fancy that sometimes propagate "universal" laws of history.

The interpretation of artifacts is at least as important as their accumulation. Anthropologists and archaeologists sometimes take sides in a bitter battle over diffusion of a culture versus its local evolution. Certain basic data must be kept in mind. Nowhere in the Americas did the people originate there, and they brought with them the culture of the place from which they came. Thus, no matter how their culture evolved from that base, the base originated in some such place as Siberia, Beringia, or Alaska.

We can argue sensibly, if we wish, that the culture changed enormously in its new location, but it changed *from* something. Thus, American culture today includes a dominant language that originated in England from components that go farther back and away. We use mathematical symbols that originated in India and were modified by Arabs. Our writing is based on an alphabet that went through its last big change in Rome, and our printing started in faraway Korea. Few persons will doubt that we have made changes in these basics and have combined them with many others to make a culture distinctively American, but we cannot say our culture originated here without violence to plain facts. It is the product of much diffusion in its components.

This example should clarify the problem. Instead of making broad, unqualified assertions about a culture diffusing or originating *in situ*, we must distinguish. I have in mind particularly an argument over the origin of the Iroquoian Onondagas in the course of which one archaeologist has blocked profitable inquiry by his dogma that the culture began right there in upstate New York. His evidence consists of surviving material objects which he displays in forbidding array.

He has overlooked those other material objects, the people themselves, who most certainly did not spring out of that very ground. Very confidently we may assume that they spoke some variant of the proto-Iroquoian language wherever they came from; and let it never be forgotten that language is an essential part of all human culture. Besides these assumptions, we have the positive evidence of sudden increase in maize cultivation which appeared at Onondaga about A.D. 1300 and became basic to the people's subsistence. We know that maize cultivation was invented in Mexico. As to its appearance in Onondaga, the only permissible question is how it got there.

The dimensions of the problem emerge from this example. Where did the people come from and when? How much did their language change in its new location? What else did they bring with them? What features of their culture did they innovate where they settled down? What features were introduced by travelers or colonizers?

Such questions can be answered by empirical research. To ask whether the whole culture diffused or evolved *in situ* is to set up a false issue over which its exponents can wrangle happily forever.

Ethnology has contributed insights to what pre-Columbian cultures might have been like by a method called "upstreaming." This consists of close examination of a tribe's culture as it exists today and as it was reported in the earliest written descriptions that have survived, and a hypothesis constructed by extrapolation into the past. The method is tricky because it depends heavily on identification of the perdurable elements in a culture, those that survive time and extraneous pressures, so it depends also, very heavily, on the interpreter's expertise. It also requires comparison with such findings of other disciplines as are available, and analysis of legendary and mythical lore, and oral tradition of events.

Linguistics provides clues. Among preliterate peoples, the components of speech change in detail as separate communities develop dialects that eventually become vernaculars, but certain elements of language endure intact. The brothers Grimm have taught linguists how to watch for standard ways that vowels and consonants drift to different sound within the same language. Beyond these, the basic modes of grammar and syntax often remain stable through many surface changes. And, as shown in chapter 5, above, checklists of vocabularies can be revealing about ethnic change.

Perhaps one should make allowances for the writers of preceding centuries who tried to make sense of American Indian history. Most of them dismissed everything before Columbus's epochal voyage with a sentence or two about how the Indians' ancestors had crossed from Siberia to Alaska and wandered over the hemisphere. Actually, not much else could be said in the absence of the information provided lately by archaeology, anthropology, demography, and linguistics. Purposeful imagination took the place of evidence. Conquerors and their justifiers transformed Indians into mythological monsters for the purpose of excusing conduct that would be inexcusable if the Indians had been seen as human. Other students and writers were misled by sincere belief in doctrinal precepts of religion and law which had been formulated in other lands and about other peoples. Our difficulty today is not so much with these men of good will as with their creeds. We think in semantic terms inherited from those creeds, and both religion and law are slow to permit revision. The new sciences conflict directly with the old myths beloved by descendants of conquerors. One must choose. One must assume that when theory or myth collides with demonstrable fact, myth must be upheld against fact or myth must be abandoned and replaced by understandings based on verifiable evidence.

It should be obvious that no one scholar, no matter how versatile, can become an adept in all the sciences and skills mentioned above. Fortunately for the historian, despite the impediments of jargon, Standard English enables us to communicate our findings between disciplines, and multidiscipline conferences have become common. There is even a national organization called the American Society for Ethnohistory which meets annually and publishes a journal to aid interdisciplinary cooperation. Textbooks, unhappily, are still deplorable, but even they are gradually being dragged into the light of new knowledge. The process is slow, but hopeful.

All of these approaches are fraught with obvious difficulties and susceptible to hazards peculiar to themselves, so that a historian is apt to breathe a sigh of great relief when finally he comes to an era of written source materials—but only for a moment. Writing may have more ways of misleading understanding than any of the unwritten sources. Writings made for public consumption provide gratifyingly explicit data, but all of them are made to serve the writers' purposes, which may vary widely from objective truth.

Thus the hieroglyphs of ancient Egypt exalted certain pharaohs whom the priestly glyph carvers approved; sacred texts of Christian scripture were altered by monkish scribes to conform to the most recent theological dogmas; and the national archives of modern times have an exasperating way of omitting attention to the desires and struggles of subjected peoples. George Orwell, in *1984*, showed tyrants rewriting history and the language of history in ways horrifying to think about; but Orwell was a long-delayed latecomer. More than 500 years earlier, at about A.D. 1430, the Aztec ruler Itzcoatl thought that the common people should be spared the knowledge contained in ancient books "for they contained many falsehoods," so he ordered them all burned and replaced by a new image that would exalt his conquering elite. After Spaniards conquered the Aztecs, the Spanish Inquisition ordered similar destruction for a similar purpose.

The modern historian has the task, therefore, of penetrating these propagandas designed to hide reality.

The reader must bear such difficulties in mind as we proceed to the grand and tragic climax of Mesoamerican history. As many new problems of interpretation appear as there are new sources. In these sources the people who appear as heroes at the summit of classic Mesoamerica are those for whom we have the most information, but when we consider the effects of the book-burners' propaganda and look again at the revelations of archaeology, these Aztec heroes appear in a different light, and their downfall becomes more readily understandable.

PART TWO

Oncoming Crisis

CHAPTER 9

Hispaniola

Many is the time I have wished that God would again inspire me and that I had Cicero's gift of eloquence to extol the indescribable service to God and to the whole world which Christopher Columbus rendered at the cost of such pain and dangers, such skill and expertise, when he so courageously discovered the New World.

* * *

And of all those distinguished and incomparable goods . . . that most worthy man Christopher Columbus was the cause, second to God but first in the eyes of men, being the discoverer and only worthy first admiral of the vast territory already known as the New World.

* * *

The admiral and his Christians, as well as all those who followed after him in this land, worked on the assumption that the way to achieve their desires was first and foremost to instill fear in these people, to the extent of making the name Christian synonymous with terror.

* * *

It was a general rule among Spaniards to be cruel; not just cruel, but extraordinarily cruel so that harsh and bitter treatment would prevent Indians from daring to think of themselves as human beings or having a minute to think at all.

—BARTOLOMÉ DE LAS CASAS, *History of the Indies*

The Antilles are a chain of islands delineating the Caribbean Sea as a nautical entity separate from the Atlantic Ocean to the east and the Gulf of Mexico on the northwest. The Lesser Antilles—including Trinidad, Grenada, Martinique, and Guadeloupe—sweep northward from the mouths of the Orinoco River in Venezuela toward St. Croix and the Virgin Islands. The Greater Antilles—Puerto Rico, Hispaniola, Jamaica, Cuba—extend from east to west past the Keys of Florida to about 100 miles from Yucatán.

By the fifteenth century A.D., these islands had become populated by migrants from South America, and perhaps earlier by a Mesoamerican colony. A small remnant of hunters, fishers, and gatherers called Ciboneys had been pushed to the westward tip of Cuba. Certain archaeological ruins in southwestern Hispaniola hint at earlier occupation by a people with culture similar to Mesoamerica's or Mississippia's. The major ethnic groups of the islands were speakers of Arawak and Carib languages, of whom we know most about the Island Arawaks, so-called to distinguish them from the multitudes in South America where Arawak is the most widely dispersed family of aboriginal languages.

Names are as troublesome to the historian here as anywhere else. The Island Arawaks are sometimes called Tainos by anthropologists. The island called *Hispaniola* in modern atlases was *Española* to Spaniards. *Caribbean Sea* honors those skilled canoemen, the Caribs, whose bellicosity and appetites gained them less favor when their name was dubiously corrupted into *cannibals*.

Hispaniola holds special interest because it became the first great conquest of invading Spaniards and a base for greater triumphs. Early in A.D. 1492, it held a population of about three million Island Arawaks organized into five chiefdoms of highly stratified societies at peace with each other. The people lived well in a mild climate with horticulture that produced crops three times a year. The chief staple was manioc, which had originated in the Orinoco or Amazon Valley, supplemented by yams or sweet potatoes, which seem to have originated in the Andes. Besides these, the Island Arawaks grew the combination of maize, beans, and squashes familiar as the product of Mesoamerica. Another clue to contact with Mesoamerica, directly or indirectly, is the ball game which was seen played and described by Spaniards as *bata;* its courts have been found all over the islands, and it was central to the politico-religious cultures of Mesoamerica. It is evident that the islanders had been in touch with the mainland from time to time.

That regular commerce with the mainlands was maintained is open to question. The islanders simply did not need exotic materials and had little to exchange that could not be had with less trouble by mainlanders from their own resources.

Until 12 October 1492, the islanders lived without want in a stable society. To understand the trauma that began on that fateful date, we must look to the other side of the Atlantic Ocean for the evolution of a culture of conquest and the invention of means to implement conquest.

Basic to all social development in Spain during Europe's Middle Ages was the invasion and occupation of most of the Iberian peninsula by Muslim Moors in the eighth century. For 700 years the Catholic Christians of Spain, who were united by little except language and religion, fought to gain independence from Moorish domination, and in the process their own religion became as devoted as the Muslim to Holy War. Crusades against Muslims in Spain expanded to invasions of North Africa and served as the inspiration for *the* Crusades in eastern Mediterranean lands.

Perpetual combat gave opportunity to military commanders in Castile, Leon, and Aragon to become proficient in battle and military diplomacy; and to recruit and train rugged troops with a long tradition of expertise in handling weapons. Spanish armies became the most formidable in Europe, especially after the invention of firearms reduced the power of knights in heavy armor.

As Castile expanded in the thirteenth century by conquering Muslim Andalusia, its crown acquired port cities, including Seville, which had long thrived on trade with North Africa. Castile's kings encouraged growth of a new maritime community with the goal of launching campaigns in North Africa, but trade and exploration rose naturally out of the process.

As of A.D. 1490, Spain began to colonize the Canary Islands and their indigenous people, the Guanches. In a foreshadowing of events to come, the resisting Guanches were defeated and subjected. To the conquerors' dismay, for they wanted those Guanches as a labor force, the indigenous people fell victims to diseases against which they had never acquired natural immunities, and, according to current belief, they died out entirely. It is hard to be sure about possible assimilated descendants of mixed parents.

While the colonization of the Canaries was going on, an experienced Genoese sea captain persuaded Ferdinand and Isabella, king of Aragon and queen of Castile, to charter an expedition in search of yet more islands, which he believed could be found by sailing westward into the Atlantic to reach "the Indies." Some authorities think that his goal was Japan.

What happened then, as we all know, was earthshaking, but even yet our knowledge is troublingly confused. Like many great events, Columbus's first voyage became almost absurd in the myths and puzzles surrounding it. Queen Isabella did not pawn her jewels to finance Christopher Columbus. (Romanticists are lethal to history.) Rather, his needed funds seem to have been provided by the director of the Spanish CIA of his day, the Santa Hermandad secret agency for "covert operations." Or Genoese bankers in Spain may have put up the money.

That Columbus was a skilled navigator is affirmed on all sides, but the precise details of his voyage are a little murky on several counts. We have no copy of his diary of this momentous first voyage to "the Indies."

Extracts made from it by Bartolomé de Las Casas are the fullest and firmest documentary source surviving.

We do know that Columbus sailed first to the Canaries, then set out due west into mystery. He tried to deceive the crews of his three vessels by keeping two logs of distance traveled: one for his personal information, the other to minimize distances and thus to allay the crews' fears about getting too far from home. Much guesswork was involved, and the irony is that his "phony" log was nearer correct than the secret one.

For many years, scholars have felt sure that Columbus first made landfall at Watling Island (his "San Salvador") in the Bahamas. Now a teapot tempest has blown up to divert him to Samana Cay, eighty miles south by east of Watling. No effort will be made here to judge details that seem insignificant in the larger perspective. The point simply is that he had arrived, and he knew it.

Or thought he did. For he dubbed the islands among which he now cruised "the Indies," and made their people into "Indians," and that is why our language now has to contend with *Indians* from India, and *Amerindians* from the Americas; and with the *East Indies* and the *West Indies*. So far as North Americans are concerned, of course, the West Indies are to the south, and the East Indies are far to the west and south; and East Indians live neither in India nor the Americas. Semantics involves history at least as much as logic.

In the long run, what counts about Columbus's voyage is that his crews and he did arrive intact in the West Indies, that they returned with their reports, and that they thus inaugurated a new epoch of world history.

They also initiated processes genocidal in effect upon the native peoples.

Columbus's great dream was to gain riches and power; discovery was just a means to that great end. When he looked upon the natives who welcomed him at the large island of Hispaniola he thought first of gold and the enslavement which was a commercial path to gold. He kidnapped some of the natives to take to Spain as living testimony to his discovery. And as slaves. In 1494, to look briefly ahead, he seized 1,500 slaves and sent 500 of them to the market in Seville.

Back in Spain he insisted upon confirmation of the noble titles and empowerment for which he had contracted before starting out; but his acquisitiveness met with royal disfavor because Spain's royalty did not relish the prospect of so much wealth and power in the hands of a subject who could become overmighty. Though Columbus made three more voyages and discovered much more land, and though his titles passed to his son, the crown's agents chopped the family down to size. Columbus returned to Spain in chains after his fourth voyage. He is honored more today than he was then.

Columbus's first voyage was magnificent, and its acclaim is richly deserved. What he did on arrival, however, was shameful, and it is usually passed over swiftly. When Columbus and his weary crews landed at Hispaniola, they welcomed the gifts presented by Arawak-speaking Tainos who at first mistook them for visitors from the sky. This illusion did not last long. Taino women quickly discovered the human mortality of these visitors, and Taino men learned that their presents were regarded as tribute. Not enough tribute. More was demanded, and more yet, and still more. The Columbus whose glory shines and whose praises ring throughout European and Euramerican societies for his unquestionably great feats of intelligence and seamanship—this Columbus showed a different sort of character to his welcoming hosts. To them he was a rapacious pirate and despot. For the Indian peoples of the Americas, 12 October 1492 is a day of black mourning.

Columbus immediately ended the idyllic existence of the peoples of the West Indies. He declared the Spanish crown's sovereignty over land and persons, and set in motion the processes of conquest. Unwitting natives, to whom gold was merely ornamental, directed and guided Spaniards to places where it could be found, and were promptly and brutally turned into miners. The cacique chiefs were made responsible for providing food and shelter for more and more incoming Spaniards, and were turned to hostilities against each other for slave raids. Taxes were levied. In 1498, Columbus's brother took a census to count heads in the half of Hispaniola then under Spanish control so that no native older than fourteen years could escape tribute. Rape by Spaniards of Indian women became normal, expected behavior, as did brutality toward all natives.

When promising sources of income disappointed Columbus because their treasure vanished into other purses before coming to his, he determined on the slave trade to enrich himself. Already, by 1495, 1600 Indians were seized by his order, far too many for the capacity of his ships. Five hundred and fifty were loaded on board, as many more given to the colonists left behind, and 400 turned loose, mostly nursing mothers. Mortality on the voyage to Spain was high: 200 of the slaves died and were thrown into the sea; the rest were landed at Cadiz. As noted by the reporter, "half of them sick . . . they suffer from the cold, and they do

An American visitor to the island of Dominica brought back pictures of Caribs who somehow survived the terrible epidemics and persecutions of their people. These pictures were made twenty years ago. Today the traditional culture is being eroded by more subtle pressures: automobiles, highways, electronics, and Coca Cola. Those *pictures can be spared here.*

A Carib who survived. Hilary Frederick shows his diploma from Lowville Academy, New York (1977), before returning to Dominica to become a chief of his people.

Carib Chief Hilary Frederick and his wife on the island of Dominica.

Present-day Caribs on Dominica. As in many regions where Africans formerly were held in slavery, some of the slaves escaped and mixed with the Indians.

not have a long life." Five years later, only twenty had survived. The casualties did not swerve Columbus from his goal: by 1498 he calculated on taking 4,000 slaves annually.

Bad as all this was, disease was worse. Biologically unprepared to resist diseases common among Europeans, the natives died so fast that even the Spaniards were astonished, accustomed though they were to plague and pestilence at home. In only a few years, their aim to live on Indian labor became an idle thought as the intended laborers died away. It was unthinkable for the proud conquistadors to work for their own subsistence, so they imported African slaves whose "Old World" immunities to epidemic were as strong as the Europeans'.

Effectively, all but completely, the devastation depopulated the West Indies of their indigenous peoples. My first draft of this book stated that the natives had been exterminated, but I have been surprised by an account and film of a surviving Carib community on Dominica who had synethnic relatives on St. Vincent and in Belize. The sheer staying power of such peoples deserves awestruck respect.

Nevertheless, these survivors now constitute only an infinitesimal fraction of the teeming renewed populations of the West Indies, made up of Europeans, Africans, Euramericans, and *East* Indians. If there are other descendants of the pre-Columbian natives, they have lost aboriginal identification by assimilating to other ethnic stocks.

Spaniards spread quickly through the islands. As the Canary Islands had served as a base from which to launch expeditions to the Antilles, so now these islands became bases for new and greater feats of conquest. Spaniards suspected the potential for such, but needed to gather information, manpower, and capital, and to get permissions from a nervous crown. Mesoamerica's great urban societies had a respite between the conquest started by Columbus in 1492 and the conquest begun by Hernan Cortés in 1519. Before turning to Cortés, let us look at some of the sources for information about the people he attacked.

CHAPTER 10

Truth and Sahagún

Having ventured out to the peripheries of Mesoamerican colonization, and beyond, we must return to the originating land and peoples to observe the grand traumatic climax of their independent history. We know much about how this came about. Relatively speaking, we have a plethora of sources, new in both quantity and kind, for the Aztecs who faced against invading Spaniards. As hinted in the preceding chapter, this situation creates new problems of selection and interpretation for a historian. The reader deserves a few words of preparation in order to pass fair judgment on what follows.

In the fifteenth century A.D., the Aztecs had books of a sort, but Itzcoatl's destructiveness makes earlier possession of books a rarity. Sixteen authentic pre-Columbian codices have survived; all are now in Europe. These *codex* books were not scrolls like ancient Europe's, but rather screenfolded sheets of paper made from bark, their folds opening into pages. A number of them have survived with inestimably valuable information, but they were *picture* books without written captions because the so-called writing of the Aztecs was painted in pictorial symbols, not drawn in representations of the sounds of speech: i.e., it was glyphic rather than alphabetical or syllabic.

Some of these books were made by Aztec "scribes" by order of missionary priests after Spain's conquest, as the missionaries wanted to know what sort of people they had to deal with. The captions that now appear on surviving codices were written by the missionaries, and the modern student must read these statements with the knowledge that the priests' informants—usually Aztec converts to Catholicism—may in some instances have deliberately misinformed from motives of their own. Besides this, the evidence is strong in the inscriptions themselves that the missionaries pumped a lot of their own religion and culture into their statements describing Aztecs and Mesoamerican predecessors. Nigel Davies writes that "the chroniclers' accounts of these happenings are visibly coloured by their familiarity with the Old Testament." Happily, however, much labor has been given by dedicated scholars to penetrating the defenses set up in the several ways of missionaries and their informants, and a large literature now exists of modern studies of Aztec culture based on analysis of the codices. This does not substitute for the work of archaeologists, anthropologists, linguists, and so on that we have noticed above. Rather modern scholars combine and systematize information drawn from all sorts of sources, written and other.

A second type of written record was made by Spanish conquistadors who spilled much ink onto paper in frantic maneuvers to justify their violence against each other as well as the Indians. In the process, they included much description of native persons and societies. Again the problem of self-serving slant arises to raise questions about the validity of description. Any lawyer will confirm that eyewitness testimony requires cross-examination to get at real facts, but it is nevertheless an extremely valuable kind of evidence, and the conquistadors' accounts have been examined very closely indeed. It follows that, for enlightenment about the conquered people, the editor's notes on Hernan Cortés's *Letters from Mexico* are often more helpful than the letters themselves, but notes and text must be read together.

This caution applies as well to the history written by the Dominican missionary Fray Diego Durán who, though born about 1537 in Seville, had grown up in Texcoco. As Ignacio Bernal remarks, "Durán, though a Spaniard by blood," was culturally "a mestizo or hybrid. His childhood gave him a fluent knowledge not only of Nahuatl but also of the indigenous culture . . . Though he writes in Spanish, he seems to be thinking in Nahuatl." Durán's linguistic fluency and human sympathy let him salvage much information from living links to the Aztecs' past whose lore would otherwise have died with them. However, this sort of information is not always confirmable, and sometimes is contradicted from other sources. Yet, when read critically, it is invaluable for detail and synthesis. Durán's manuscript lay buried in the National Library of Madrid until 1854 when a copy was made. Publication began in 1867. After many vicissitudes, the remainder of the manuscript appeared in print in 1880. Only after three centuries out of sight did Durán's work become generally accessible to scholars. In contrast, three of Cortés's letters were in print by 1525 and the "chronicles" of Cortés's fellow conquistador Bernal Díaz del Castillo was published in 1632. Until very recently, historically speaking, the Aztecs appeared only as their enemies and conquerors portrayed them.

By far the most reliable single source for Aztec culture was the manuscript that barely escaped destruction. Its own fascinating history encap-

Sahagún's History. These pages from the *General History of the Things of New Spain* illustrate the method of Fray Bernardino de Sahagún as he searched for reliable information about Aztec culture preceding Spanish conquest. His method had the invaluable side effect of creating a sort of "Rosetta Stone" for subsequent generations to interpret Aztec symbolism. Sahagún's converts explained, in their own Nahuatl language, the meaning of the Aztec glyphs, and Sahagún interpreted the Nahuatl explanation into Spanish. COURTESY OF THE NEWBERRY LIBRARY.

Madre

la propriedad de la madre es tener hijos y dar les leche, la madre virtuosa, es vigilante...

Madre mala

la mala madre es boba, necia...

hijos ohijas legítimos

Ay entre esta gente hijos legítimos y hijos bastardos...

¶ Nantli tenan yntenã pilhua chichiua, yn qualli yyollo cõchiani, tzicuictic, mopopoxo, ni yiel, yatocuani, yyollo ymâca, micauiani, tlacauapatia, tecemmati, teceemmati, tlaxocoyoma, tecamochiua, tlamiquauia, tlatlaixcaua, momotzoloa, motlatlaca.

¶ yn tenan tlauelilloc, yn amo qualli, tlacanexquimilli, xolopitli, tonalchqui, maxixlopauax, tlancpopoloani, tlaixpachilhuiani, tetlanaualchiuiliani, tetlanaualpelhuiani tlaxccauani, tlatlatziuhcauani tlatlauelcauani, haquentema, haquetcmati, haquemotecuiltauia, hatetamochiua, hatleipã tlachia, teatoyauia, tetepexiuia, teixpopoyotilia tochin macatl yyuui quitei, titia quitetoltia, patlauac Vtli quitenamictia.

¶ Tepiltzin teconeuh, yn tepiltzin tlacopilli, calitic cuneutl, chaneca conetl, tecuyotica tepiltzin, ychtlacaconetl, caxpãpilli...

Panquetzaliztli, ynqac tlacatla mouiuilopuch tli, ynipan tonalpoal cauaya...

Ynilhuil quicaya ypan innmetztli noviembre ic matlactli omei.

Atemoztli, ympan atemoztli ynovia tepetipac, nextlaoaloya, icmitoaya nãcuica, temoya, iniztlalol, Auh inmocuil tonoam inindachia, motlepacti aya, yealnepanta inixtlacoya tepicto yoã xoxocuiltchaya...

Ynilhuil quicaya ypan inmetztli decietbre, ye xilhuitl

sulates the hazards attendant on written records and their use. The history begins with the very earnest effort of Franciscan missionary friars to convert the Aztecs to their version of Christianity. In pursuit of that goal, they opened the Royal College of Santa Cruz in 1536, fifteen years after the armed conquest (and an even century before the founding of Harvard College). Fr. Bernardino de Sahagún labored at Santa Cruz, but he became suspicious that his apparent success in converting the natives was superficial and delusive. He scented continuation of idolatry under the appearance of Catholic orthodoxy, and he set out to discover the facts of pre-conquest society so that masked idolatry could be exposed and overcome.

His method was direct and so effective that he is often called the founder of anthropology in America. Since converted native students at Santa Cruz had been taught writing, he gave them questionnaires and requested answers written in their own Nahuatl language so as to be sure the informants were not hampered by lack of fluency in Spanish or Latin.

Interpreting and editing the responses, he produced a systematic *General History of the Things of New Spain* which was altogether too informative to suit the managers of the Spanish Inquisition. Although Sahagún had worked with approbation of royal officials, drastic changes occurred after the death of his chief protector, Juan de Ovando, president of the Council of the Indies, who had also befriended and admired the "protector of the Indians," Bartolomé de Las Casas. The circumstances remind us how much our knowledge depends on seemingly unrelated phenomena. In this instance, the Spanish crown's policies reversed because of pressures from the Catholic Counter-Reformation which included establishment of the Index of forbidden books (1559). In 1577, a royal decree ordered delivery to crown authorities of all writings—original manuscripts and all copies—on pre-Columbian societies and cultures. It advised further that officials in New Spain should ban any future writing "in any language . . . concerning the superstitions and way of life these Indians had."

Sahagún understood what this meant. He protested so vehemently that he was excommunicated, obviously on political grounds as his orthodoxy was beyond challenge even by Inquisition standards.

This tale gains relevance to our history because one copy of his manuscript escaped the book-burners. On the pretense of delivering it to the crown, Sahagún's friend, the commissary Fr. Rodrigo de Sequera, carried this complete copy of the *General History* to Spain. Whether it ever got there is open to question. What is certain is that it ended up in the Medicea-Laurenziana Library in Florence, Italy, where dedicated humanist librarians felt no compulsion to inform the Inquisitors of their acquisition.

Sahagún had translated the Nahuatl text into Spanish, so the manuscript was recognized a couple of times during the next three centuries, but without creating much interest. A French translation was published in 1880. In 1979 the Mexican Archivo General de la Nación issued a facsimile edition. Meanwhile, a history professor at the University of New Mexico brought a microfilm copy of the original to the United States where it was translated into English between 1945 and 1982. Another odd twist is that one of the sponsoring institutions for the translation was the University of Utah where interest was stimulated by Mormon doctrines about Indians. After all its wanderings and adventures, Sahagún's invaluable work is now available in Nahuatl, Spanish, French, and English, and its pictures are in the Mexican facsimile edition.

We turn now to the people who were the subject of all these writings—the Aztecs and their "empire."

CHAPTER 11

The Rise of Tenochtitlán

The Aztecs were Johnnies-come-lately in Mesoamerica, inheriting rather than creating the great culture of Teotihuacán and Tula. According to legend, the Aztecs had migrated into the Basin of Mexico from "Aztlan," hence their name, but nobody has been able to do more than make an informed guess about the whereabouts of Aztlan, which one expert thinks may be "as much a concept as a place." (The Mississippian name of Aztalan, in Wisconsin, excites wonder.)

Further, it seems likely that the people concerned were an aggregation of tribes rather than a single homogeneous unit. The historian Nigel Davies speculates that some of them may have lived under Mesoamerican influence for an undetermined time before being joined by more distant barbarians from the Northwest—which would be near or in the "Southwest" of present day United States.

However that may be, when the Aztecs and others united, they assumed the new name *Mexica*, not to be confused with the more inclusive modern Mexicans. The Mexica were those who grew to power after building twin cities on an island in the lake of the Basin of Mexico.

It is sometimes thought that the legendary "seven caves" of Aztec origins refers to a cavern under Teotihuacán which held mythical significance because of the sacred spring that bubbled up in it.

The "old people" told a different story to Sahagún. According to them the Mexica "came over the waters from the north," and the seven caves of their origin were "seven ships or galleys in which the first settlers of this land came." Sahagún was quite positive: "It is certain that they came in some vessels." As usual with tradition, ambiguity abounds. Were the old people referring specifically to the Mexica, or did "first settlers" mean peoples long preceding the Mexica, of whom there had been many? In any case the provocative reference to vessels has been passed over by modern students. It should be taken into account, one way or another.

The Toltec city of Tula was destroyed and its inhabitants scattered at about A.D. 1110. Shortly afterward, at about A.D. 1132, Chichimec

The Aztec Origin Legend. This cover of the Codex Mendoza (in color) told in symbolic code how the Aztecs found their new homeland at Tenochtitlán after migrating from the North. An eagle perched on a cactus was their sign that this was the place. (The Arabic numerals of sequence were added later, possibly by André Thevet, cosmographer to the king of France, who once owned the codex.) COURTESY OF THE NEWBERRY LIBRARY, CHICAGO, ILL.

northerners established themselves in Texcoco on the *east* shore of Lake Texcoco in the Basin of Mexico.

Nigel Davies has consulted other traditions to bring the Mexica to abandoned Tula in the year 1168, after which they entered the Basin of Mexico by a circuitous route winding around the *west* side of Lake Texcoco. It appears that Sahagún's migrants were different from Davies's. This supposition is strengthened by the semi-autonomous role played later by Texcoco in relation to the Mexica of Tenochtitlán.

The confusion can be clarified by simply remembering the disclosure that all the records of Tenochtitlán preceding 1430 had been destroyed and replaced by a new ideology according to ruler Itzcoatl's orders. This crucial fact is not mentioned by Nigel Davies who drew most of his data from annals based on Itzcoatl's approved ideology. Not surprisingly, the picture that emerges shows Itzcoatl's people as gloriously heroic and destined to rule the universe. As so portrayed, their god Huitzilopochtli is always prophetically right and always urging his true followers on the correct path.

This does not jell. If nothing else raised questions, we might wonder why the people of Texcoco, who had the same ethnicity and the same god, were not as glorious as the Mexica of Itzcoatl's city of Tenochtitlán.

To get behind the chosen-people propaganda requires attention to actual events. It seems plain that when the Aztecs from "Aztlan" had migrated to the Basin of Mexico they split up, some heading around Lake Texcoco's eastern shore, others around the west. At Texcoco, the newcomers joined previous residents to build a rich and powerful city. On the lake's western shores, however, the Mexica, despite their orthodoxy, long remained poor and harried. They brawled with their neighbors unsuccessfully so that they were shunted from one place to another until they ended up on a forlorn blob of mud in the lake. At this point their priests, ever ready with divine revelation, divulged the sacred secret that this soggy real estate, wanted by no one else, had been reserved by Huitzilopochtli for his chosen people. The really heroic feat of the Mexica was the creation of a city in such unpromising surroundings.

Like Dutchmen creating Holland, the Mexica dredged the bottom of the shallow lake to make a solid base for their new city of Tenochtitlán, and they fabricated farmland by more dredging of the rich bottom soil. They piled it up in rectangular islets called *chinampa*, held them in place with basketwork walls, and tripled production by growing three crops a year on them.

Meantime they hired out as auxiliary warriors to their big neighbors to the west, the Tecpanecs of Azcapotzalco, in course of which they necessarily acquired the Tecpanecs' enemies as their own. We cannot here follow all the intrigues and shifts of alliance that were conducted by the Basin of Mexico cities early in the fifteenth century. Nothing conceived by Niccolò Machiavelli outshone them in deceit and treachery as each city's nobles struggled for supremacy while their common people performed almost incredible prodigies of labor by direction of the priests of innumerable gods. There was no eight-hour day in Tenochtitlán.

Crisis came at the juncture when Azcapotzalco had achieved commanding dominance and its long-lived ruler died. A faction within this imperial city had watched distrustfully as Tenochtitlán's Mexica improved their position and gained subordinate power. In the struggle over Azcapotzalco's succession, this hostile faction came out on top by assassinating its chief opponent. The new ruler, a man named Maxtla, immediately prepared for war. He seems to have been a creature of habit, for the first of his preparations was to contrive the assassination of Tenochtitlán's ruler, Chimalpopoca, and his son. There is no lack of authorities, but they do not correlate well with each other; it seems almost as if anyone can become an expert by picking and choosing among the disputants. To me, the following rationale makes sense.

When the ruler of Tenochtitlán was killed, the city was supposed to capitulate and subject itself to Maxtla, and a peace party in Tenochtitlán advocated this submission. At this crucial moment, however, the war party took charge. The city's elders chose Itzcoatl as ruling *tlatoani*—he of the "chosen-people" ideology—and supported him with two strong ministers, Tlacaelel and Moctezuma I. These three reached out for allies among the other cities that had suffered under Azcapotzalco's domination, and gained cohorts from Texcoco, Tlaxcala, and Huexotzingo. Or so the official line has it. One may doubt whether much-disliked Tenochtitlán actually led in this diplomatic offensive, or whether it could have been successful if it had. A new actor appeared on the stage of high politics, the gifted ruler of Texcoco, who headed the actual embassies that persuaded other cities to join the coalition.

This was Nezahualcóyotl, kinsman to the ruling family in Tenochtitlán and claimant to the throne of Texcoco. He, too, had suffered from Azcapotzalco's tyranny. As a boy he had watched his father being killed by the tyrants' agents. He had gone into hiding and learned political survival skills that included conspiracy behind a mask of submission. His moment of opportunity came when the Mexica decided to resist Azcapotzalco. He gathered allies, recruited a Texcocan army, and took the field against the oppressors. The allies won.

In the wake of victory, Nezahualcóyotl gained great eminence by a

A lthough coastal Olmecs began the building of cities in Mexico, urban society and culture effloresced under the Toltecs, whose influence spread widely into North America as well as Central America. One mark of Toltec influence and/or colonization was the truncated pyramid topped by a temple. Such pyramids flaunted power in Toltec culture as cathedral-and-castle did in mediaeval Europe. Standing impressively high, overwhelming all other constructions, the Toltec pyramid was a bastion of military strength as well as religious ideology, and it gained sacred power from the bodies and attendant spirits of great ancestors buried within itself.

Wherever Toltecs went, they built their special pyramids. These are architecturally distinguishable even today from the mounds of other North American peoples which functioned primarily as structures of interment.

The Aztecs based their own culture on features borrowed from the Toltecs, including the enormous dominant pyramids in Tenochtitlán-Tlatelolco.

Teotihuacan was the home city of the Toltecs, originators of the culture adopted by the Aztecs. Some notion of the dimensions of Toltec monumental architecture can be gained from these partially uncovered ruins. Their immensity can be gauged by comparison with the human figures that appear so tiny in the photographs. COURTESY OF THE SECRETARIA DE TURISMA DE MEXICO.

Teotihuacán.

Chichen Itzá. A temple
built under Toltec influence
in the Maya country of
Yucatán. COURTESY OF THE
SECRETARIA DE TURISMA DE
MEXICO.

Tenochtitlán. The great temple reconstructed by Ignacio Marquina from Spanish
descriptions from surviving monuments. COURTESY DEPARTMENT OF LIBRARY SERVICES,
AMERICAN MUSEUM OF NATURAL HISTORY, NEW YORK (NEG. NO. 326597).

supremely clever device. He led his troops out to a sham battle against Tenochtitlán, declared defeat, rushed them home, and submitted Texcoco to Tenochtitlán. The submission was exceptionally mild. Tenochtitlán confirmed his authority in Texcoco where it had still been under challenge, and gave him voice and vote in the council of his supposed overlords. Having doubled its power, Tenochtitlán went on to a career of conquest that reconstituted and enlarged the former "empire" of Azcapotzalco.

The crucial war against Azcapotzalco occurred in or about the year 1428. As we have seen, Tenochtitlán's ruler Itzcoatl wiped out the records and created a new "history" in 1430. One reason for his doing so was to explain and justify the traumatic changes in Mexica society imposed upon it by the newly victorious militarists.

These very great changes in political and social organization were officially attributed to fulfillment of a contract between Itzcoatl and the common people. In this account the fearful commoners had protested before going to war against Azcapotzalco, whereupon Itzcoatl and his warriors offered a bargain. "If we do not achieve what we intend, we will place ourselves in your hands, so that our flesh becomes your nourishment. In this way you will have your vengeance." The commoners supposedly reciprocated, "If you are victorious, we will serve you and work your lands for you. We will pay tribute to you, we will build your houses and be your servants. We will give you our daughters and sisters and nieces. And when you go to war we will carry your baggage and food and your weapons upon our shoulders. . . . In short, we will sell and subject our persons and goods to your service forever."

Whether such a bargain had, in fact, been struck can be seriously doubted, but after victory the warriors acted as if it were a real compact authorizing a new constitution for the city and its possessions. The warriors seized and distributed among themselves most of the lands formerly held by Azcapotzalco, after first allotting "the largest and best fields . . . to the royal government." Some fields were assigned for support of the temples. But the common men "were not given land or anything else" even if they had fought in the war "except for some who had shown a certain amount of valor."

The consequence of this great concentration of landed property was a proportional concentration of political power among the warrior class. Because Mesoamericans had no durable currency they could not hoard monetary wealth. The only sources and embodiments of wealth were land and persons. By one decisive stroke, the militarists of Tenochtitlán acquired enormous new estates and land together with the serfs required to work them. No wonder that Itzcoatl burned the books that pictured previous history. "It is not necessary for all the common people to know of the writings," he explained. "Government will be defamed." The "writings," of course, were codex books of conventional pictorial symbols.

CHAPTER 12

The Aztec Empire

I must say at the outset, however, that it is impossible to state a general rule as concerns any part of Indian government and customs, for there are great differences in almost every province. Indeed, two or three different languages are spoken in many towns, and there is almost no contact or acquaintance between the groups speaking these different languages. I have heard this is general in the Indies, and from what I have seen in my travels, I can affirm it to be true. Consequently, if what I say here appears to contradict some other information, the cause must be the diversity that exists in all things in each province and not any lack of diligence on my part in seeking the truth. Nor should we wonder that some divergencies appear in the Indian accounts. To begin with, in the majority of cases the versions of the interpreters are faulty. In the second place, the Indians lacked an alphabet and writing and preserved all their past history in the form of pictures, most of which have been lost or damaged. Add to this that the memory of men is frail, and that most of the aged Indians who were knowledgeable about these matters are dead. These are the reasons why there are different accounts about everything. Yet another reason is the small value that men attach to the study of Indian antiquity, which they regard as something from which little or no profit can be derived.

—ALONSO DE ZORITA (ca. 1570)

After the critical conquest of Azcapotzalco, many persons from outlying regions flocked into triumphant Tenochtitlán so that the city became much more heterogeneous than before. No longer populated mostly by Mexica, it drew to itself culturally related people who claimed distant descent from Aztlan by way of different routes and genealogies. The Mexica naturally reserved privilege for themselves, but the new polity became multiethnic "Aztecs," within the city as well as among its tributaries.

This diversity was accentuated by the existence of Tenochtitlán's sister city Tlatelolco which had been founded on a nearby island about A.D.

1358 by related Mexica. With much labor the people of the two cities made their islands into one, but the cities maintained separate governments until A.D. 1473 when a quarrel between their rulers ended in Tenochtitlán's triumph over Tlatelolco. (Until this point, I have deliberately omitted Tlatelolco from this narrative in order to avoid confusion among all the names so strange to English-speaking readers.)

Previous to their conflict, the twin cities had worked together in external affairs and had dealt cooperatively with their physical environment. They had supplemental specialties: Tlatelolco was primarily mercantile, Tenochtitlán was primarily militarist. After conquest, these specialties continued. Tlatelolco's market became the largest in Mesoamerica and one of the largest in the world; but Tenochtitlán seized ultimate power resting finally on armed force.

Both cities almost exploded in growth after defeating Azcapotzalco in 1428 when they became "Aztec," and they quickly acquired all the problems of urban density. Like many ancient Old World cities, they had previously built an aqueduct to bring fresh drinking water from springs beyond their lake. (The lake must have been badly polluted. I have not read an account of waste disposal.)

Food sufficient for the multitude could not be produced from the chinampa gardens alone. Indeed, at the cities' maximum size of 250,000 inhabitants, chinampa supplied only 5 percent of requirements, productive though they were. The rest had to come from peoples surrounding Lake Texcoco, partly in tribute, partly in exchange for the output of the cities' craft workers. To handle such a huge volume of daily freight, an intricate and extensive transportation system was required, about which more details are provided further on.

Housing the people in such manner as to keep them from getting in each other's way demanded a city plan, and one was put into effect. At a time when Europeans still blundered onto and around each other along old cow trails turned into streets, the twin cities built on the rectangular grid that was to become the generally adopted pattern of modern metropoles. Within the grid, great squares were set aside for magnificent temples, palaces, and markets.

To bridge the transition between tribalism and statism, governments divided the cities into territorial sections called *calpulli*. Modern scholars sometimes call them "wards," sometimes see them as separate tribal groups occupying sequestered districts. These are but different aspects of the same thing: i.e., the gradual assimilation of independent tribes into a hierarchical, bureaucratic city state. Technological lacks, especially the absence of writing, prevented this transitional form from becoming a fully developed nation state, so that tributary towns retained their own institutions; but the capital cities were compact enough for face-to-face management in which tribal leaders came to function as dependent government officials.

Each calpul had its own temple for its special god, but all of them owed tribute to the great gods of the twin cities, especially the war god Huitzilopochtli; and all were required to provide tribute in goods and persons for the cities' wars and rulers.

The religious system overshadowed all other institutions. In the approved ideology adopted after Itzcoatl destroyed older records, the god Huitzilopochtli was the patron divinity who had chosen the Mexica-Aztecs to conquer and rule over the whole world. This divine patronage was contingent on unquestioning service and sacrifice by the chosen people. Human blood was supreme among all kinds of sacrifice. Indeed the priests of Huitzilopochtli believed and taught that blood was so essential that the world would come to an end if the sacrifices were interrupted. (In a manner of speaking, they were right: *their* world ended when Spanish Christians stopped the blood sacrifices.)

Unfortunately for the Aztecs, the very beliefs that inspired their warriors and terrorized their commoners involved practices that created deep divisions within the empire and made it vulnerable to attack. More about that further on.

At the top, the empire was ruled by an elected *tlatoani* (speaker) and a hierarchy of councils supervised by a great council of four powerful ministers. "Election" is perhaps too strong a word for the process by which the tlatoani was *chosen* from eligible candidates in the extensive royal family, but succession was not automatic from father to any particular son among his many spawn. The tlatoani ruled for life (though there were ways of curtailing that term). Besides his executive functions, he became a high priest—a necessary precaution where politics was so intertwined with religion.

The tlatoani's decrees were administered locally by calpulli headmen. Judges appointed from the top controlled misbehavior by swift justice and drastic sentences. In the special case of the great market of Tlatelolco, administration and judging were in the hands of merchant guilds, but the guilds were controlled by royal appointment of their chiefs. The word *guild* does not here connote the sort of autonomy held by the Lord Mayor of London and the livery companies who elevated him to office. The Aztec merchant guilds were tightly integrated in the state machinery.

The social structure was highly stratified. The royal family, sprung from the loins of one stud monarch, stood at its head. The ruler in question, named Acamapichtli, had married about twenty wives to insure loyalty of the clans who provided them, and his offspring, and their equally fecund offspring, quickly constituted a new nobility with special privilege. Nevertheless, merit was the principle governing appointment and tenure in office. Though only a noble could hold high position, he had to be a competent noble. This may have been a matter of expedience more than principle. The clique of warriors who seized power under Itzcoatl were descended like him, from the wrong ancestors for claims to hereditary right. Itzcoatl was only so-so royal; though he had been sired by the ruler Acamapichtli, his mother was a slave girl. When he triumphed against Azcapotzalco he consolidated power by lavishly granting conquered lands to his loyal followers: "brothers, cousins, and nephews." As frequently has happened elsewhere in the world, he conquered his own people by means of conquests abroad.

Rewards for outstanding performance included grand titles, estates, and rights to wear special ornaments, flamboyant headdresses, and gaudy clothing. A man's worth was instantly recognizable by his appearance. Privilege in Tenochtitlán was ostentatious, and unauthorized commoners who assumed the finery were summarily put to death.

Judges and priests might be drawn from the ranks of free commoners, but all officials, whether political or religious, had first been trained in schools under rigid priestly supervision. The Aztecs could look benignly on varied local customs, but they had no tolerance for heresy or heterodoxy.

For most of the free working classes, the only privilege was exemption from being sacrificed, but to preserve that exemption they must keep out of debt and not be convicted of serious crime. Working people worked *hard* and long. Their only freedom from strenuous toil came during the great religious festivals when they enjoyed the feasting and gruesome spectacles. Freemen were called *macehuales*. Below them in rank were the semi-free serfs attached to noble estates. At the bottom were slaves— persons captured in battle, or sold into slavery for debt, or condemned for crime—who were in constant jeopardy of becoming sacrifices at the next festival.

There was nothing democratic or libertarian about Aztec culture except for the possibility of upward social mobility for intelligent persons whose orthodoxy and obedience could not be questioned. Perhaps it should be added that justice seems to have been meted out without discrimination, but I must doubt the authorities who propound such a condition. It would be little short of miraculous in any country and any social system.

No creative novelties could come into existence where independence of thought was so systematically suppressed, but the Aztecs excelled in construction and organization. To facilitate transportation and allow quick marches by armies, they built three causeways between their island and the opposite lake shores. When salinity threatened to end production of the chinampa, Nezahualcóyotl suggested a dike to cut off the evaporating eastern waters from those purified by springs flowing in from the west. It was built, and by labor impressed from the conquered city of Xochimilco. To facilitate traffic by cargo-bearing canoes, the Aztecs dredged canals through the shallow, reed-clogged waters. Every day, a great tide of persons walked and paddled into the twin cities and out again.

Some bore tribute for the conquerors' warehouses. Others brought goods to the great market and carried off their exchanges. Without all this constant pumping up, the cities would have had to collapse like a deflated balloon.

To forestall utter chaos, so much activity required regulations of two kinds. The rulers prescribed amounts and kinds of tribute to be paid in from the provinces, and supervised the transportation system. Merchant guilds kept the market in order. They allocated space for every kind of product, and patrolled constantly to ensure fair dealing. Judges sat daily in Tlatelolco's market to deal summarily with disputes and crime.

Most exchange was conducted by barter, although rough standards of value were expressed in terms of cacao beans or quills filled with gold dust. Such "money" never transformed into the universal commodity of minted coins. Its unitary irregularity and lack of durability made it functionally inferior to the monies of Europe and Asia; and the Aztecs' lack of phonetic writing prevented the growth of an elaborate credit system although simple, man-to-man credit was extended and debtors sometimes had to sell themselves to pay.

Goods were moved between the cities and their hinterland by human muscle. Much was paddled by canoe to the lake shore where it was shifted to the backs of porters called *tlameme*. (Some of them, of course, trotted across the causeways.) A tlameme carried a basket held by a tumpline across his forehead so as to free his arms (somewhat like a modern knapsack except for the tumpline). Burdens varied according to circumstance and the tlameme's ability. Ross Hassig has calculated an average load of about fifty pounds to be carried about twenty miles each day. This portering was a hereditary vocation, and each tlameme belonged to an association in his home town where they were regulated by the local rulers. The same authorities kept pedestrian roads in order from town to town (in the absence of wheeled vehicles), and the burden bearers usually worked in relays from town to town although it seems that some might carry long distances. Hostelries were kept for them in each town. The Aztecs also maintained relays of runners along their roads to guarantee quick delivery of important news to the rulers and orders to the provincials. System and regulation prevailed everywhere.

Management of the subject cities was also systematic. The Aztecs did not attempt to integrate them into the administrative structure of Tenochtitlán–Tlatelolco. Instead they created what has been called a hegemonic empire. They required acknowledgment of suzerainty by a local ruling class, with payment of tribute. The *Codex Mendoza* itemizes articles of tribute delivered at varied intervals: e.g., honey, planks, wood, and copal every eighty days; mantles and copper plates every six months; war dresses, shields, grain, gold, and turquoise each year. Perhaps the lords of Tenochtitlán had some rule of thumb for apportioning tribute quotas, but they might change the amount at any time for any city according to their needs, circumstances, or whims.

Persons as well as goods were demanded in tribute. The appetite of Aztec gods for human blood was insatiable. Ordinary sources of victims—war captives, debtors turned slaves, and persons delivered in tribute—were insufficient to slake that terrible thirst, so the Aztecs devised a special source called "flowery wars." These were battles with towns kept deliberately independent for the sake of perpetuating combat so that Aztec warriors could seize prisoners and gain credit for offering them as sacrifices. Merchants also could gain divine credit by buying slaves in the special market at Azcapotzalco which they then ritually sacrificed; indeed, no merchant could rise high in his guild until he had performed this ritual.

Plenty of opportunities were provided for gaining such credit. Each of the numerous gods had a separate temple and a special feast day, and the war god Huitzilopochtli required frequent "feeding." The Spaniards who compiled *Codex Mendoza* for the information of Emperor Charles V reported without qualification that 20,000 victims were sacrificed in four days when Huitzilopochtli's tremendous new temple was dedicated in A.D. 1486. This seems a mite exaggerated even after allowing for the involvement of priests in fourteen temples. It calculates to about one victim every four minutes, twenty-four hours per day in all fourteen temples for all four days. Imagine the candidates waiting in line for their turns!

Even if hyperbolic, the spectacle was gory enough. Skipping details, we visualize the victim being led up the steps to the top of that towering temple where he / she was sprawled backward across the altar block, all four limbs held firmly down by assistants. The officiating priest plunged an ornate obsidian dagger into the victim's breast and wrenched out the heart as the god's offering. Blood flowed in rivers, and the corpse was kicked down that long, steep stair to the bottom where it was picked up by its dedicator to take home for dinner. But not all of it; a thigh was reserved for the tlatoani's kitchen.

This made a great and cautionary spectacle for the mob, like the fun Europeans had at witch burnings and executions by drawing-and-quartering. It appealed rather less to the cities providing the victims, not because of moral objections, for they also practiced human sacrifice, but because they resented having to send their own people for sacrifice on foreign temples. Incidentally, they were also losing a lot of manpower in a land where all wealth depended on human labor.

Thus, when Hernan Cortés and his men arrived in 1519, the situation was ready made for them to gain allies by exploiting accumulated resentment.

CHAPTER 13

Cultures in Conflict

So it came about that in the spring of the year A.D. 1519, the Spanish empire and the Aztec empire came, so to speak, within hailing distance of each other. Both were aggressively expansionist. At first glance, the Aztecs held overpowering advantage. Though they ruled over much less territory than the Spanish crown's, their peoples outnumbered Spain's by four to one, and were concentrated. They were more than twenty to one greater in numbers than Spain's outpost bases in the West Indies.

In terms of ideological motivation the two sides were evenly matched. If we stretch a word beyond its Eurocentric origins, both empires were on crusade. The Aztecs *had* to save the world from annihilation by getting prisoners' blood to feed the gods. The Spaniards *had* to save the world's souls to feed their Christ who had long since ceased in their conceptions to be the pacifist of the New Testament. In practice, though processes were conceived differently, the objectives of both sides required the shedding of much human blood. Both sides wanted more land. Both wanted more laborers to exploit. In addition, the Spaniards hungered for gold with an appetite inexplicable to the Aztecs because the uses of gold had not been institutionalized in Mesoamerica.

Spain held visible advantage in technology and social organization. To itemize:

- Ocean-going ships capable of controlling the seas so that troops and equipment might be delivered where desired without fear of retaliation.
- Spanish ability to reach out to Mexico while denying Aztec reach to Spanish bases meant that Spain could exploit divisions among Aztec subjects while the Aztecs could not get at peoples resentful of Spanish rule.
- Superior weaponry, including firearms, crossbows, hardened steel swords and lances; and defensively, mail armor.
- Horses and other domesticated animals. Spanish cavalry, which had been trained in a long tradition of combat with Moors in Spain, was

129

a formidable weapon in itself. Swine, sheep, and cattle were portable sources of high-energy food.
• Phonetic writing with which to "speak" across great distances and
thus to coordinate strategy and tactics.
• Gold and silver functioning as money and capital, and a complex
credit structure, which combined made possible the private Spanish
conquistador's accumulation of equipment, supplies, and mercenary
troops on a scale impossible for the Aztecs except by state power.
• A social and political structure that enabled the Spanish crown to
preoccupy itself with power struggles in Europe while permitting
private conquest under charter at no expense or trouble to the crown.

In the clash between the two empires, these advantages alone might
not have overcome the tremendous advantage of Aztec numbers, but the
conquistadors had an even more potent invisible weapon that guaranteed
long-run success however events might go in the short run. Epidemic
disease fought and killed in behalf of the Europeans. Smallpox was the
first new disease to smite the Indians whose hemispheric isolation had
spared their ancestors from Old World plagues, and had consequently
prevented natural selection of resistant survivors and their descendants.
The Aztecs and all the other inhabitants of the Americas were what epi-
demiologists call "virgin soil" for the inadvertent planting of smallpox,
influenza, measles, plague, chickenpox, diphtheria, scarlet fever, and a
host of other pestilences. Even the "common" cold was new and could be
deadly. An African slave among the forces of Cortés's competitor Pánfilo
de Narvaez brought smallpox from Cuba in 1520, after which it transmitted itself to both continents. On the way it reduced the population of
Central America catastrophically. When Cortés's men went into battle,
their Aztec foes (and Cortés's Indian allies too) were already suffering
from the effects of this malign disease.

In the light of all this, the marvel is not that Spanish conquest was so
swift, but that it took so long. Resistance was fierce. Spanish troops were
not supercilious about the Aztec warriors' fighting abilities. But hindsight
permits knowledge that the Aztecs never had a chance.

Ambivalence and division appeared on both sides. When conflict flared
up, some cities of the Mesoamericans joined invading Spaniards against
the Aztec overlords. On the Spanish side, ambivalence took different
forms in government and church, though these were hardly more than
varied aspects of the same hierarchy because clerics occupied many of the
highest posts in government. For that very reason, however, when some

priests began to feel qualms about treatment of natives in the conquered West Indies, government responded at once.

The crown was even doubtful about whether the Indies were worth keeping. Columbus was at violent odds with sundry conquistadors bent on enriching themselves rather than either him or the king. The conquistadors fought among themselves for greatest shares of Indian slaves and the gold that had been discovered in Hispaniola's hills. Officials of the crown wondered why so little of that gold came to the royal treasury, and in 1500 they sent a new governor to investigate.

He carried with him a royal decree guaranteeing the Indians personal liberty as vassals of the crown and as evidence of intent twenty Indians were returned to their homeland—the survivors of 300 who had been brought in slavery to Spain.

One of the returnees had been the slave of Bartolomé de Las Casas who was to become "the protector of the Indians." But in 1500 Las Casas inclined more toward the attitudes of the conquistador-colonists than to royal notions about humanity to Indians. The nephew of three of Columbus's companions on the latter's Second Voyage, and the son of another, Bartolomé followed them to Hispaniola in 1502 and acquired estates and Indian slaves in direct disobedience to the royal will. He even participated in the conquest of Cuba ordered by another priest-official, Governor Nicolás de Ovando, and did not react immediately when another Dominican refused him the sacraments in 1614 because he owned and exploited slaves. This in spite of the fact that Las Casas himself had been ordained to the priesthood before leaving Spain.

A ferment was working among the clerics. If some of them were as brutal as any soldier—Ovando, for example, ordered a massacre in Cuba—others discovered that religion should be a matter of conscience as well as politics. None was so treasonous as to suggest Indian independence, but several took advantage of the royal edict proclaiming Indians to be free men, in order to preach humanitarian treatment for the king's vassals. In 1511, Fray Antonio de Montesinos shocked the Spanish community on Hispaniola with a sermon raising the questions, "Are these Indians not men? Do they not have rational souls?"

In 1515, Las Casas underwent a conversion. Perhaps the denial of the sacraments a year earlier had affected him after all. He studied Ecclesiastes 4:1: "So I returned, and considered all the oppressions that are done under the sun: and behold the tears of such as were oppressed, and they had no comforter; and on the side of their oppressors, there was power; but they had no comforter."

Las Casas became convinced that Spaniards' souls were endangered by colonists' brutality toward the Indians who had never been given the light of true religion, and he dedicated his life to righting this great wrong. He sold his estates and his Indians—it does not appear that he freed the Indians—and he traveled to Spain and Rome to enlist the aid of the great and powerful. After many frustrations, he gained permission from Emperor Charles V to found a separate mission colony in Tierra Firme (Venezuela), and he returned to the Indies in high elation.

But events had not stood still during his absence. In 1517, an expedition from Cuba reached Yucatán where they sighted "a large town standing two leagues back from the coast . . . We had never seen so large a town in Cuba or Hispaniola." The Spaniards landed, were ambushed, and suffered heavy casualties, but they were able to seize much treasure of gold and jewels. What they brought back to Cuba aroused keen interest. More expeditions followed in 1518 and 1519. Thus it happened that while Las Casas argued at the emperor's court in behalf of the Indians, Hernan Cortés launched the greatest conquest yet.

PART THREE

The Dark Ages

CHAPTER 14

Trauma

We stopped to rest in one of the low passages [of the catacombs] with bones and dust surrounding us on every side . . . but when I thought how Christian men have dealt with one another; how, perverting our most merciful religion, they have hunted down and tortured, burnt and beheaded, strangled, slaughtered, and oppressed each other; I pictured to myself an agony surpassing any that this Dust had suffered with the breath of life yet lingering in it . . .
—CHARLES DICKENS, *Pictures from Italy*

Hernan Cortés destroyed Aztec military power in the two years between 1519 and 1521, thereby opening the continental mainland to Spanish conquest. What Cortés did, however, must be seen in perspective as the removal of an obstruction to more traumatic change. The peoples of Central Mexico had long been accustomed to military conquest; they labored on, paid their tribute to new masters, and the more things changed, the more they continued as before. Cortés opened the gate to a different sort of conquest, one that transformed the world of the American Indians besides sending repercussions back to Europe's Old World.

Military conquest was accomplished by familiar European techniques of massacre, devastation, terrorism, and resultant demoralization of native peoples. It was quintessentially the product of free private enterprise by mercenary killers whose functional identity lurks behind the glorious mask of *conquistador*. The crown contributed chartered permission, and the church contributed a blessing. Entrepreneurs assembled risk capital from private persons, and engaged other private persons to risk themselves for pay and the lure of plunder. All the persons concerned were intent on maximizing return to themselves individually, and behaved accordingly. Their armies, while in the field, were a law unto themselves, under no sort of external control except the enemy's resistance. Even the Spanish crown feared their power, and moved cautiously and tentatively to bring them under control.

It is a grim but necessary task to follow part way along the path of their horrors.

Cortés began his enterprise by betraying his master, Diego Velázquez, governor of Cuba, who had sent out explorers in preparation for his own career of intended conquest in Yucatán. In 1518, Velázquez commissioned Cortés to look for a fleet whose return to Cuba was overdue. Although his commission permitted Cortés to explore and trade, it omitted authority to colonize because Velázquez himself was soliciting a license from the Spanish crown to colonize. Cortés understood his restraints and the reason for them. He knew that he had to act fast and treacherously if he was to grasp the prize that Velázquez reached for. He knew also, as J. H. Elliott observes, that "nothing could more quickly obliterate the stigma of treachery and rebellion than a brilliant military success and the acquisition of fabulous riches."

When he disregarded Velázquez's instructions and landed at San Juan de Ulúa, Mexico, 22 April 1519, he quickly learned from natives of the greatness and riches of Tenochtitlán farther inland; and he resolved at once to take the place. By legal prestidigitation he freed himself formally from Velázquez by persuading his men to establish a municipality, Villa Rica de Vera Cruz, directly under the crown of Spain. The freemen of the town—who were Cortés's own men—then appointed Cortés captain and decided by their assumed royal authority to proceed to Tenochtitlán. They were only 508 men, but Spain's conquests in the West Indies had made them cockily confident, no matter what the odds in manpower.

Another lesson, taught by the 700 years of the reconquest of Spain from the Moors, reinforced by the West Indian campaigns, taught the military value of terrorism. People in mortal fear of the monsters suddenly appearing among them were unlikely to put up effective resistance. "This was their common custom," wrote Las Casas, "that they no sooner had set footing in any place, but they committed immediately some notorious violence upon the people, that the rest might stand in the greater fear of them." Cortés followed this policy all along his route to the interior.

The quoted remark by Las Casas was stimulated by a particular episode on Cortés's route, the massacre he directed at Cholula. Here is what happened, as described by himself in a justification of his action to the crown. He stated that the Aztec ruler Moctezuma had massed an army near the city in order to fall upon him. (Cortés's editor discounts this.) Then, "I decided to forestall an attack, and I sent for some of the chiefs of the city, saying that I wished to speak with them. I put them in a room and meanwhile warned our men to be prepared, when a harquebus was fired, to fall on the many Indians who were outside our quarters *and on those who were inside*. And so it was done, that after I had put the chiefs in the room, *I left them bound up* and rode away and had the harquebus fired, and we fought so hard that in two hours more than three thousand men were killed." [Italics added.] Here is another example of the powers of semantics. Cortés's men *fought so hard* against Cholulans who were *bound up*. More than the chiefs were in that room as other sources plainly say.

Cortés's meetings with Moctezuma, and the latter's hospitable reception of the Spaniards in Tenochtitlán, made a profound impression on the hardened soldiery. Tough old Bernal Díaz told that when Moctezuma was killed by his own people for betraying them, "Cortés wept for him, and all of our captains and soldiers . . . and it is not surprising, considering how good he was."

But the Aztecs rose against Moctezuma precisely because he had accepted soldiers who perpetrated in Tenochtitlán the same sort of massacre that Cortés had ordered in Cholula. Cortés had returned to the coast to deal with one of his recurring political problems among the Spaniards. He left eighty soldiers in Tenochtitlán under command of Pedro de Alvarado, a man regarded as especially cruel even by the Spaniards. Alvarado surrounded and assaulted a religious festival dance by unarmed Aztecs in a temple courtyard, after which the formerly peaceful city rose in rage.

Cortés returned with reinforcements, but had to beat a strategic retreat out of the city. Losses were heavy because Aztec warriors are not to be underestimated. "I do not know how to describe their tenacity in fighting," wrote Bernal Díaz who faced them in the fray; ". . . some three or four soldiers who were there with us and who had served in Italy swore to God many times that they had never seen such furious fighting . . . nor had they seen men like those Indians, with such spirit in closing their ranks as they advanced."

To be brief, Cortés could not conquer the Aztecs with his own resources unaided. When Alvarado pushed the policy of terrorism too far, the outraged people forgot their fear and rediscovered their power. In the fighting that followed, Spanish casualties were so great—Díaz put them at 860 men and 60 horses—that, even with the reinforcements Cortés had brought from the coast, he was left with only 440 men and 20 horses. All the survivors were wounded, including Cortés himself, and they had no firearms or ammunition left. (Díaz says the number left was even smaller, at 420 soldiers and 17 horses.) The remnant took refuge in the city of Tlaxcala which had maintained itself bitterly independent from the Aztecs, where they awaited more reinforcements.

Romance stresses how Cortés had burned his ships to make retreat impossible, but ships arrived from the Indies every month for the next nine months, adding substantially to the core of Spanish soldiers and the big battalions recruited by Cortés from natives. At the bottom of Spanish fortunes, Tlaxcala alone provided 4,000 warriors. Another ally came unbidden to create havoc. Díaz remarked casually that defending Aztecs "had been weakened by smallpox, which had caused great suffering and was spreading over the land." Even Cuitláhuac, the new ruler who had been elevated to take Moctezuma's place, died of smallpox after a reign of only eighty days.

Many writers have attributed Cortés's ultimate success to an Aztec superstition that Cortés was the god Quetzalcoatl returning to regain his kingdom, and a myth has gained currency that Quetzalcoatl was a bearded white man, but this does not stand up under examination. Davies calls it "a purely post-Conquest invention" and, according to Sahagún's informants, Quetzalcoatl was a mountainous *black* man.

Though the Spaniards were efficient and energetic at their murderous trade, it is inconceivable that they could have prevailed alone over the masses opposed to them. Their losses in the retreat from Tenochtitlán— two-thirds of their force—show that they were not supermen, and the Aztecs were not pushovers. We must agree with three modern authorities. Benjamin Keen commented, "The handful of Spaniards owed their victory . . . neither to Aztec superstition nor to their superior arms but to the aid of masses of Indians eager to throw off the Aztec yoke." J. H. Elliott identified "geological faults" within the Aztec empire, and concluded that the conquest "was as much a revolt by a subjugated population against its overlords as an externally imposed solution." And Miguel León-Portilla observed the political skill by which Cortés convinced Tenochtitlán's enemies that "the Spaniards were siding with them. In this belief they succeeded in defeating the Mexicas, not knowing for a while that their foreign allies were the only ones to profit from such a victory."

The oft repeated details of the conquest are irrelevant to present purposes. What is to the point is that the Spaniards continued to use the policy of divide-and-conquer by which native allies helped to suppress resistance wherever it showed. Cortés then faced the massive problem of what to do with his conquest after its accomplishment (to be discussed in the following chapter).

Central Mexico became a new base from which conquistadors ranged north and south, into the "American Southwest" and into Central and South America. Meantime, from the older bases in the West Indies, other would-be conquerors stormed into Florida, the "American Southeast,"

Cholula. At Cholula, invading Spaniards decapitated a Toltec pyramid and built a Roman Catholic church on its base. As with the Greeks of classic times, the Indians of classic Mexico knew how to gain spiritual power for their temples by building them on dramatic sites, and the Spaniards understood the necessity to transfer that sacred power to their own religion.

The purpose in building a Catholic church on top of the ruins of a pagan temple was to show how much more powerful and triumphant the God of Christians was than the gods of the pagans. In one respect this strategy backfired. As Bernardino de Sahagún discovered, the Indians worshipping in such a church often directed their veneration secretly to the gods of its sacred site.

and the coastal region of the Gulf of Mexico, leaving death and desolation in their wakes. No one else was as successful and fortunate as Cortés who won wealth and honor by crown favor even as he was quietly stripped of power by rulers who wanted no possible competitors for their authority.

In Peru the Pizarro brothers used Cortés's strategies of terrorism and division to overthrow the huge, fantastically wealthy empire of the Incas; but the conquistadors there could not control themselves. They greedily killed each other with almost as much zeal as they assailed the Incas, and the last survivor of the Pizarros went to prison for his pains. The last Inca outlived him. The greatest beneficiaries of the conquest were Spaniards who never lifted a sword except in ceremony, men who came later armed with royal powers and grants. But we must turn our eyes away from South America.

In the southern tier of what were to become states in North America, a sort of unplanned Spanish pincers movement invaded from east and west. Francisco Vasquez de Coronado took a host of ne'er-do-wells from Mexico to New Mexico and as far east as Kansas before accepting failure, but not before wreaking carnage among the Pueblo Indians. Among others, he encountered in 1540 the people of "Acuco," the "sky city" of Ácoma, one of the oldest continually occupied locations in North America. People had lived there at least from A.D. 1200, long before Europe dreamed of a New World, and the Hákukwe, or people, still quietly go about their business today at the same location. (I treasure a ceramic pot crafted and acquired there.)

From the Indies, several attempts were made to conquer "La Florida" which was a name for an indeterminately large territory extending into the wild green yonder north and west from the peninsula called Florida today. After a series of defeats inflicted by native resistance, a new *entrada* was organized by Fernando de Soto who landed on the west coast of modern Florida in May 1539. De Soto seems to have been better financed and equipped than Cortés, and he certainly was every bit as terroristic, but he found no empire among the populous communities he battered through. Instead, there were "chiefdoms" (a term invented by anthropologists to describe a political structure under authoritarian personal rule that had not developed into bureaucratic state form). The "Gentleman of Elvas" who is our chief source for de Soto's campaign mentioned cacique lords being carried in chairs or litters on the shoulders of their nobles, and these caciques had such great authority that they could order their men to probable torture and certain death as hostile messengers to de Soto, with confidence in being obeyed. (In Mexico, Moctezuma had been carried in such a litter to meet Cortés.) But there were many chiefdoms rather than one central authority hated by tributaries as in Mexico. Though many enmities prevailed among them, de Soto never managed to gain a steady ally as Cortés had won in the city of Tlaxcala in Mexico. De Soto forced hundreds, even thousands, of defeated persons into slavery, and treated them as disposable cattle, but he never eliminated the will to resist by the people farther on, and his force was steadily whittled down despite its ability to inflict massive destruction.

After much fighting and slaughter, de Soto reached the Mississippi River by a winding path still open to argument. There he died and his corpse was stealthily hidden in the river's depths so as to keep his death secret from the Indians. His men crossed the river to some distance farther westward. Theoretically they arrived at a relatively short distance from Coronado's most eastern penetration, but were unaware of the circumstance and retreated to the Mississippi down which they floated through fierce attacks from canoe-borne enemies. A remnant reached the Gulf to make their way eventually to refuge in Mexico.

De Soto's *entrada* was a disastrous failure for a few hundred conquistadors, but it was catastrophic for many thousands, perhaps hundreds of thousands, of Indians. Slaughter, massacre, and the introduction of epidemic diseases destroyed the persons of the leaders of Indian resistance. As they were also the governing chiefs of the tribes, death for them and their most loyal companions produced disintegration of communal fabrics already weakened by population loss. Europeans who later followed in de Soto's wake found desolation and abandonment where large communities had once thrived. Gulf Coast Indians never fully recovered from the holocaust inflicted by de Soto.

Considered overall, Spanish military conquests and failures permit several inferences.

Armed conquest was not new to either the Mexicans or the Spaniards. We have already noticed the Aztec conquests and their implications. For the Spaniards, conquest in Mexico was a continuation of the 700-year reconquest of Spain from the Moors. But the Mexicans were not Moors, and their country was many thousands of miles away from the Iberian peninsula. It followed that what happened in the Americas evolved along its own historical pattern rather than repeating what had happened in Spain.

In the Americas, as in Spain, the conquistadors fought as religious fanatics in a holy war, and their resisters were equally fanatic, but religion was not the motive that drew the conquistadors to the campaigns. Very plainly, they were moved by hope of personal gain. We should not be astonished by this, considering what is now known about the motives and practices of Crusaders to the Holy Lands. Spain's conquistadors in America, regardless of their zealotry, were mercenaries who fought for pay and plunder. Religion bound them together, but the conquistadors themselves made no visible effort to win Mexicans to their own faith. Their motives must not be confused with those of the handful of priests and friars, sworn to poverty, who accompanied them. (Even these, according to Las Casas, were long uninterested in converting natives.)

This distinction as well as others must be preserved. All Spaniards were not the same. This fact is as essential to comprehension as the salient, now-accepted fact that all Indians were not the same. Racist theory requires homogenization of conquerors and conquered alike into imagined patterns of mythology. In an older tradition, conquerors become heroic demigods, the stuff of saga and epic. The conquered become nonperson demons or brute beasts of predation (so powerful is myth). After centuries of domination by this myth, some homogenizers, in romantic revulsion, have turned it about so that the conquered victims emerge as heroes and the conquerors assume the forms of unvaried monsters.

Neither version of the myth is true. Conquerors and conquered alike were human with all the characteristics of humanity diversified by culture rather than inherent, unchangeable nature. It is true that much of their behavior was horrific to modern eyes, but the sixteenth century did not invent the ovens of Dachau, the Gulag Archipelago, the "gangrene" in Algeria, nor the bombing of Hiroshima.

To balance understanding of the Aztecs, we have remembered the mass of peasantry as well as the flamboyant warriors and gory priests. To balance understanding of the Spaniards, we need to take note of the missionary priests, the royal bureaucrats, and the immigrants who came after armed conquest to settle and colonize in the image of their homeland.

Missionaries and colonizers could go only where warriors had broken native resistance and imposed Spanish power. Beyond the limits of military conquest, the tribesmen of America continued to live by their own means and according to their own desires, but with this difference, that for the future they would have to cope with Europe's invaders somehow, whether by conflict or accommodation.

In conquered New Spain, Spaniards dictated the terms on which the natives of Mexico would live while natives and invaders shared the land, but inconsistency and conflicting interests resulted in much confusion. The Spaniards were united only in maintaining themselves as a ruling caste.

CHAPTER 15

Transformation

> The voice of history . . . is often little more than the organ of
> hatred or flattery.
> —EDWARD GIBBON, *Decline and Fall of the Roman Empire.*

Destruction of Aztec military power achieved opportunity for more substantial conquest. In itself it merely substituted new rulers for old, a situation with which the Mexicans had long been familiar, and perhaps the conquistadors would have been content to let it go at that. During the long centuries of the reconquest of Spain from the Moors, Castilians and Aragonians had often gotten along comfortably enough with Muslims in local situations so long as the infidels accepted them as overlords. But other forces came into play, in Mexico as in Spain, and these required conquest to go deeper than substitution of one ruling elite for another.

In the abstract we know these restless powers as Church and State. To churchmen it was unthinkable that all those millions of Indians should be left in idolatry. Though they differed among themselves about means, the churchmen agreed wholeheartedly that the Indians must be persuaded or compelled to reject their old gods and embrace Roman Catholic Christianity, the national church of Spain in alliance with the international confederacy directed by the Papacy. Thus the confrontation between conquistadors and Indians acquired significance that ramified far beyond the immediate parties involved. A late echo of the Crusades is perceptible.

A couple of centuries earlier, the Crusading knights who settled in Outremer—another land beyond the sea—had tried to accommodate with conquered natives of varied religions, and had often cooperated with surrounding Muslim rulers for mutual benefit. Always, however, unrelenting pressures from distant Europe forced the local colonists into expansionist hostilities that they would often rather have foregone. Similarly in the Americas, direct and indirect pressures from Europe never relaxed. Colonists continued to come and to demand shares of the conquest. The crown required vast treasure to fight its European wars. The church hierarchy insisted that all Indians must become Catholic Christians, and that vast estates must accrue to the church. Under such pressures in addition to their own greed, the conquerors of the Indians could not possibly settle into a live-and-let-live mode with the Indians. Pressures for exploitation increased constantly and were magnified immensely by Indian depopulation from many causes. What an Indian once had to produce as his own tribute became merely a fraction of what was demanded from survivors to make up the tribute of their fallen brethren. And as more Indians died more colonists added yet more demands.

In Spain the State manifested itself as a bureaucracy and armed forces ruled by a scion of the Hapsburg family which had interests also in the Holy Roman Empire and the Netherlands, and was feared by other rulers as the strongest power in Europe. Throughout their possessions the Hapsburgs were constantly embroiled in contests with powerful hereditary noblemen who sometimes ignored, sometimes challenged royal demands. From the beginning of conquest in the Americas, the kings of Spain were determined to prevent an insubordinate aristocracy from arising there. However, they faced the undeniable fact that the only agency of power on the scene was precisely the body of conquistadors who also constituted the nascent aristocracy. For the State, therefore—i.e., the Spanish crown—the great goal of conquest was not to substitute a conquistador ruling elite for the Aztecs, but rather to substitute reliable royal servants for the conquistadors.

An additional motive loomed large. If the crown were to clash openly with the mass of conquistadors, large expense would be required to put down the rebels, and the Americas were supposed to provide much treasure, not to drain it off. Spain's European entanglements and expensive militarism at home precluded thought of dictatorial policies in the Americas.

There, as elsewhere, Church and State worked hand in glove. Churchmen high in the hierarchy had three characteristics recommending them strongly for royal favor: they were under double discipline, from the princes of the church as well as those of the crown; they were literate, and therefore competent for administrative tasks; and they were formally celibate and therefore incapable of passing power on to descendants in the fashion of secular lords. Churchmen of lower status were useful for their zeal as missionaries, both to the Indians and to the conquistadors whose Christianity left much to be desired, even by the standards of that day.

Church and State had to proceed cautiously, slowly weaving legal webs of power strong enough to contain the men who held military power. In both institutions, differences arose concerning the means to be employed for agreed-upon ends, and these differences became complicated by the personal interests of office holders whose relatives had settled as ambitious permanent colonists in the Americas. Such colonists, though arriving long after military conquest, tended to side with the conquistadors against royal authority exerted by officials who came and went on brief tenures.

Everyone knew by whom the conquest had been made. *For* whom was another matter. In little and in large it became the subject of a thousand disputations. Only one assumption won unanimity: the source of benefit was to be the Indians. A case of raid and plunder would have been simple; complexity arose because the Spaniards came to stay, to colonize as lords over large servile populations. This was the core issue of power. If those millions of Indians were to come entirely under control of military freebooters whose loyalty to the crown was uncertain, Spain might find whole new nations arising in the Americas, capable of defying any force available to the crown. To buy off the conquistadors was out of the question for a perpetually leaking treasury, but they had to be compensated. The crown's solution grew naturally out of the circumstances; it was an institution called *encomienda*.

In theory, the tribute of a given number of Indians was commended or granted for services by the *encomendero* to the crown, but the Indians themselves remained free persons rather than slaves, vassals of the crown rather than of the grantee. In theory, the grant was revocable at royal pleasure and, though lifelong, was not hereditary. In theory, the Indians labored under their own chiefs in order to produce their granted tribute.

These distinctions were more important to the crown's hairsplitting lawyers than to the Indians. In practice, the encomendero did what he pleased with "his" Indians regardless of their technically free status, and, as often as not, he passed them on to his heirs. In practice, encomenderos were willing enough to let Indian chiefs sweat labor out of their peasants so long as they produced as much as was demanded. In practice, also, the treatment of Indians under this system was brutal and exploitative in the extreme. As Charles Gibson has observed, "Between the individual and the law in Spanish America there was always a certain irrelevance."

To the encomenderos there seemed at first to be an infinite supply of Indians, so they squandered Indian lives without even the minimal care given to other forms of property. Horses and dogs were much better cared for. A consequence of overwork, malnutrition, and physical brutality was the death of victims on a large scale. Given opportunity, Indians fled to the mountains where they died also of privation and exposure, and often from being hunted down like wild animals. In 1498, as noted earlier, Bartholomew Columbus conducted a census that numbered about one and a half million tribute-paying Indians on the island of Hispaniola. Within decades there were none visible. Of all the dense pre-conquest populations of the West Indies, there are left today only two communities of Caribs and "Black Carib" Indian-Africans, numbering in all less than a thousand persons.

(One must not overlook the possibility of descendants of Indian women and Spanish men having been assimilated among the Spaniards. Recently, and surprisingly, Fidel Castro claimed Taino ancestry.)

It is usual today to attribute the depopulation to epidemic diseases introduced involuntarily by the Spaniards to "virgin soil" peoples lacking resistance to these new pestilences. (I have done so in an earlier book.) There can be no doubt of the catastrophic effects of disease. Nevertheless, this harsh fact does not exculpate the conquerors from guilt for the merciless behavior that resulted in much murder independently of the epidemics—as, for instance, when men wagered they could behead a living Indian with a single stroke of the sword, and casually made the stroke—and certainly brutal conduct magnified the effects of disease by exhausting and demoralizing its victims.

Bartolomé de Las Casas is the most famous of the friars who described the outrages, but he was not alone. What he and his colleagues reported came to be known as the Black Legend, and it was adopted by Englishmen to excuse their own atrocities in Ireland. ("How terrible if the Spaniards were here.") In revulsion, some scholars have decried the Black Legend as mere propaganda, but it was true. That it was not the whole truth does not mitigate its horrors. The strongest reason for believing it is that Las Casas's outraged denunciations were convincing to the hard-nosed, unsentimental realists at the Spanish court.

Hernan Cortés, who was probably the most intelligent and rational of all the conquistadors but no more humane than the rest, realized that destruction of Indians was waste of his conquest. For him, massacre was a means to victory, but victory's fruits were to be provided by living laborers—and no Spaniard had come to the New World to be a laborer. Cortés could not control his men completely, but he welcomed to New Spain the friar-protectors of the Indians, and he rewarded with titles and privileges the Indian nobles whose alliance had been indispensable to his triumph.

His policies differed from those that had prevailed in the West Indian islands, and the difference in policies seems to have made a difference in historical results. The natives in one place were as susceptible to disease as those in the other, and disease raged in Mexico as well as on Hispaniola and Cuba, but some Mexican Indians survived. Few though they were in comparison with their pre-conquest population—they seem to have been reduced to 5 percent—their decline finally bottomed out in the nineteenth century, and their numbers grew again. (Today, Mexico City is more than twenty times the size of Tenochtitlán. Some call it the largest city in the world.)

It is beyond the scope of the present book to follow the post-conquest history of Indians south of the Rio Grande, but some general observations may be useful.

The Spaniards of that era were strongly class conscious. Besides distinctions among themselves they recognized upper and lower classes among the Indians; and, especially in the early years of conquest when Spanish women were in very short supply, the conquistadors were willing to marry upper-class Indian women. Such unions, sanctified by church and law, were recognized for social status denied to the commoner illicit variety, and the children of mixed licit marriages were accepted at first almost as peers of "pure blood" Spanish children. But not quite, and not for long.

As more Spanish women arrived and married, they and their children assumed a position of social superiority to ethnically mixed persons who were designated as *las castas*—"the castes." The term is more accurate and illuminating than its functional equivalent, "colored races," in the English language because *las castas* identifies a social category whereas "colored races" identifies the same thing in fact but describes it mythically. Spaniards were certainly "race conscious." They had a long tradition and a variety of pejorative terms for distinguishing Catholic ethnic stocks from Jews and Moors; and in New Spain they categorized *mestizo* (Spanish-Indian), *mulato* (Spanish-African), *zambo* and *coyote* (Indian-African). Regardless, however, of the kind of mixture, these were all *castas*. Class structures existed above and below the caste line, but the line became impermeable.

Something of the same sort was to happen all over the Americas. Where European women were scarce, men accepted the females who were available, but as European communities grew in size the offspring of mixed unions were consigned to a lower caste. Perhaps this process was not unique to the Americas. That is a problem for comparative history.

Below the caste line in New Spain, one criterion of Indian status derived from pre-conquest noble ancestry. Scions of princely Indian families enrolled as students in the Royal College of Santa Cruz where Fr. Bernardino de Sahagún questioned them in order to compile his *General History of the Things of New Spain*. His research was peripheral to the college's purpose which was to train Catholic Indian leaders to take charge of the big battalions of laborers in encomienda and to set an example of conversion to Catholicism. Charles Gibson has remarked that "encomienda allowed a thin surface of dominant, class-conscious Spaniards to spread over Spanish America" which is true enough, but encomienda could not function without Indian intermediaries between Spaniards and the peasantry. Especially in the allied city of Tlaxcala, which had made victory possible for Cortés, Indian aristocrats were compensated with privileges such as exemption from tribute and permission to flaunt rich costumes. They even possessed land and laborers of their own. But these privileges were transient. The successors to Cortés did not feel his sense of obligation, and the Indian aristocrats never breached the line of caste. Privileges and possessions eroded under pressure until the aristocrats became merely foremen of sweated labor, or were reduced themselves to laboring.

Thus the native social structure not only sank under a superposed layer of Spaniards; it was effectually destroyed and remade in a new mold. Regardless of efforts to collaborate with the conquerors, the old Indian aristocracy gradually disappeared, either by succumbing bodily to epidemic disease or by losing the wealth and privilege necessary to maintain high status.

In religion the process of transformation took several turns. Regardless of their own disregard for Indian humanity, even the most callous Spaniards were horrified by the human sacrifices and cannibalism of Mexican idolatry, and they razed the pagan temples as soon as they could. In a ritual as old as recorded civilization, they built churches of their triumphant god on the foundations of the temples of the defeated gods, and they pragmatically used stone from the demolished edifices in the walls of the new churches. (This went beyond practices in Spain where Muslim mosques were let stand but converted into Catholic churches.)

Indian natives had their own methods of adapting old materials to new functions. Scholars have rediscovered what missionaries suspected—the survival of pagan ritual traditions within Indian Catholicism. By anthropologists the adaptation is called *syncretism*. The missionaries called it blasphemy, sacrilege, and other hard names. Fray Diego Durán wondered whether Indians attending mass in the Cathedral of Mexico did so "in reality to worship the old gods, because their stone images have been used to build this Christian temple: the columns of the cathedral are actually standing on the plumed serpent." (Paraphrase by Tzvetan Todorov.)

Still today, great pilgrimages wend to the hill devoted in pre-conquest days to worship of "our mother" the goddess Tonantzin. Now the shrine of the Virgin of Guadalupe stands on that hill. The situation is reminiscent of the survival of the pagan gods in Christian iconography in Mediterranean lands.

In the end the Spanish Catholic god did conquer the Mexican pagan gods, but did not destroy them utterly. The Catholic religion of Mexican Indians today, though dominant everywhere, is not quite the same as the religion exported from Spain in the sixteenth century.

Not all the Spanish clergy concerned themselves about whether Indian souls might go to Hell or Heaven. In the early years of the conquest, zealous missionaries such as Sahagún, Las Casas, and Durán fretted and labored in the struggle to make Christians out of idolaters; but when the Inquisition inevitably came to New Spain in 1571, the inquisitors paid little attention to Indians. They concentrated, as at home, on Spaniards guilty or accused of heresy; and also, as at home, they confiscated much property from their victims. The zealous and self-sacrificial early missionaries must be distinguished carefully from successors whose greatest concern was the building of big churches and the creation of large estates of land and tributary laborers.

One more subject requires notice, inadequate though that must be: the economy of Mexico, as well as the country's social composition and organization, was transformed by the conquest. One might well approve the introduction of work animals to relieve human beasts-of-burden, but the conquerors brought more than domestic helpers; they bred great herds of sheep, goats, and cattle, besides swine, and let these animals run at large to forage as they might. The fast-multiplying herds destroyed the hillside forests. As soil eroded, the extensive pre-conquest arrangements for water control were ruined. Plow agriculture, replacing Indian methods of labor-intensive cultivation, contributed further to erosion. In that arid country, the effects on the land were disastrous.

Aztec downfall ended the system of royal patronage and controls of commerce. In its place, Spanish merchants brought entrepreneurial capitalism that turned away from the networks of intra-Mexican trade to concentrate on linking New Spain to the markets of old Spain. In brief, the Indians of Mexico were drawn into the world market from which they previously had been apart; and, in due course, they changed from barter and self-support to immersion in a money economy with all its institutions of capital, wage labor, banking, and so on.

As we shall see in North America, the introduction and growing domination of the world market would have a powerful transformational effect on the pre-existing great networks of trade in Indian America.

Whether the accumulation of all these changes was progressive may depend a little on a viewer's perspective and definitions. Most Mexican Indians seem to be as poor today as during Aztec times, and large numbers labor as peons under conditions not notably superior to their ancestors'. In one respect, however, there can be no doubt of improvement: contemporary Indians will not be reduced to slavery and delivered to the temples for sacrifice. Even a skeptic must appreciate that gain.

On the other hand, the skeptic must remember how great were the ravages of conquest. Otherwise, how should he evade the terrible judgment of Fray Toribio de Motolinía: "The avarice of the Spaniards did more to destroy and depopulate this land than all the sacrifices and wars that took place in pagan times."

Every historian knows how American silver and gold affected Europe by creating monetary inflation and empowering the Spanish Hapsburgs' wars, but the conquest went deeper to revive in Rome a Papacy that had sunk to the bottom of its temporal and spiritual authority. Schism, corruption, and sin, not to speak of the seizure of powers by secular authorities, had so reduced grandeur that Rodrigo Borgia, Pope Alexander VI—he who had grandly divided the western hemisphere between Spain and Portugal—fearfully fortified the ancient tomb of Hadrian as a refuge. Thereafter the Castel Sant'Angelo protected popes when condottieri or kings made the Vatican too uncomfortable. By 1415, papal authority in the city of Rome had become almost invisible. Wolves roamed the cemetery of the Lateran. The city was sacked in 1527 by unpaid imperial soldiers, and reduced to less than 30,000 inhabitants.

As Hugh Trevor-Roper has remarked, "The pope [was] faced with the religious defection of half of Europe." The Protestant Reformation exploded. In 1517, Martin Luther attacked papal indulgences. The unity of western Christendom that once had launched crusades fissured into pietist, Lutheran, Reformed, Anglican, and Catholic remnants. Despite the great losses manifested by such fragmentation, Rome grew again to 100,000 inhabitants by the end of the sixteenth century. Shorn of income and support in so much of Europe, whence did the papacy draw its new strength?

It came from the same source as in the Church's early centuries—from missionaries and their zeal. As they had once converted the pagans of Europe, so now they turned to transatlantic fields of work. In the sixteenth century and afterward, the missionary orders sent their members in astonishing numbers to the Americas under the benign patronage of Spanish and Portuguese kings whose general policy was to entrust care of the Indians to the orders, and who (as noted above) were readier to entrust royal authority to churchmen than to uncontrollable conquistadors.

As Catholicism prospered in the Americas, tribute to Rome revived the papacy, and the missionaries provided the wealth, manpower, and energy for the Counter-Reformation. Purportedly, when Alexander VI rebuilt the basilica of Santa Maria Maggiore, he restored the ceiling "with the first gold, as it is generally believed, ever yielded by America."

If not for conquest and missions in the Americas, the giant Roman Catholic Church might today be just another squabbling sect. It owes its eminence not only to the dedicated labors of the religious who went out to teach, preach, and rule, but even more to the toil and tribute of the Indians of their "flocks."

Of the many frontiers of Indian America, Rome was not the least significant.

CHAPTER 16

Transformation II.
Resource Accounting

Besides human society, the natural environment—earth, plants, animals, and fishes—also was transformed by conquest. It is worthwhile to pause a moment to assess the changes without limitation of chronology—to get an overall balancing of accounts. Although one may argue that conquest alone should not be held responsible for the effects of nineteenth- and twentieth-century industrialization, the rise of machine culture did not so much introduce novelties to the environment as it accelerated processes already underway.

We must consider human beings as components in the total population of the continent's animals. Overwhelmingly important has been the growth of human population, its urbanization, and its density everywhere. Our base line must be the numbers of persons on the land before 1492. As mentioned earlier, scholars are still debating estimates ranging from five to eighteen million Indians north of the Rio Grande. My hunch would be about ten million. Here, it is not necessary to be exact; we need only note that all of these figures are low compared to what happened when Europeans repopulated the continent.

Repopulation did not happen all at once. As we have seen in earlier chapters, native populations plummeted after invasion. However, the ships from Europe constantly added to the natural increase of colonists so that, after about two centuries, the continent probably held about as many human occupants as before 1492. From that time forward, numbers multiplied astonishingly. If we add the 1990 totals of Canada and the United States, we get something approaching 300 million persons, most of whom live in cities or metropolitan areas. The implications for consumption of natural resources, and for population, are obvious.

Other animals also underwent transformation. What happened to wild animals—the Indians' animals, so to speak—did not show clearly in Mexico because few wild creatures lived in that densely urban country in

152

1492. The change showed up in more northern latitudes where interso-cietal trade between Indians and Europeans sharply reduced populations of beaver, bear, sable, and other animals whose pelts fetched good prices in Europe. Herds of deer were also slaughtered to make soft, pliable leather.

On the prairies, horses introduced from Spain transformed Indian lifeways as erstwhile sedentary tribes remade themselves into mobile hunters of bison, but all changed again in the nineteenth century when American "sportsmen" killed vast numbers of these beasts and left their carcasses to rot. In some instances the killing was motivated by desire to deprive Indians of their subsistence so as to clear the land for ranchers and homesteaders. These introduced new herds of domesticated cattle and sheep which took over the ranges evacuated of bison.

Domesticated animals not only replaced wild ones, they transformed the land itself from the very beginning of invasion. When Cortés's Span-iards occupied the Valley of Mexico, they brought along cattle, sheep, goats, and swine, as well as horses, and let them find forage on the hill-sides surrounding that famously productive valley. The results were disastrous, as any of the "discoverer" sea captains could have foretold. Those mariners had a technique of dropping off pairs of goats on deserted islands in order to have fresh meat available on return voyages; but they found that the goats had multiplied and stripped formerly verdant lands of every leaf and grass blade. The same thing happened very quickly in the Valley of Mexico, aggravated and accelerated by careless cutting of firewood. The denuded hillsides eroded and became sterile.

Similar processes occurred all over the continent. William Cronon has described how the pasturing of cattle and sheep wrought havoc by ero-sion in New England. "Wherever the English animals went, their feet trampled and tore the ground . . . and eventually lowered the soil's car-rying capacity for water. . . . Ironically, then, an additional effect of woodland grazing was to kill many of the plants on which livestock depended for food." Over the long run, the animals were saved by the introduction of highly nutritious timothy grass and clover (which were also importations from Europe), but the effects of erosion could not be easily reversed, if at all.

Again, Henry F. Dobyns has related how stretches of Arizona's Gila River were "killed" by a series of introduced processes that counteracted former erosion controls. New livestock trampled trails that became chan-nels of erosion. An observer noticed that "when the storm becomes heavy each one becomes a miniature torrent." Early in the nineteenth century, American "mountain men" trapped off all the beaver along the Gila and its tributaries, with the result that the beaver dams gradually disinte-

Indians have dwelt in many climates and varied physical surroundings. As these pictures show, they adapted with a variety of shelters utilizing available materials in efficient shapes and sizes.

Chetro Ketl in Chaco Canyon—a reconstruction model. It is unusual for Pueblo architecture because the upper storeys are flush with the lower instead of being set back. Painting by R. Coffin.

Caribs understand hurricanes. A house on Dominica braced against the big winds.

Eskimo shelter, winter. COURTESY OF THE NEWBERRY LIBRARY.

Eskimo shelter, summer. COURTESY OF THE NEWBERRY LIBRARY.

Interior of a Mandan chief's earth lodge. This was a type built also by Hidatsas and Pawnees. Painting by Karl Bodmer. COURTESY OF THE NEWBERRY LIBRARY.

Interior of a (Northwest) Chinook Lodge. COURTESY OF THE NEWBERRY LIBRARY.

Encampment of the Piegan Indians. Such multitudes preceded the ravages of epidemic disease. Painting by Karl Bodmer. COURTESY OF THE NEWBERRY LIBRARY.

"A skin lodge of an Assiniboin Chief." The woman at center front is arranging a dog-drawn travois. Painting by Karl Bodmer. COURTESY OF THE NEWBERRY LIBRARY.

In a Great Plains village of earth lodges, spectators of ritual had good seats. COURTESY OF THE SMITHSONIAN INSTITUTION MUSEUM OF AMERICAN HISTORY.

Zuñi pueblo in 1879. Photograph by John V. Fillers. COURTESY OF THE SMITHSONIAN INSTITUTION MUSEUM OF AMERICAN HISTORY.

Seminole chickee on stilts. An adaptation to frequent flooding, and protection against snakes and insects. COURTESY OF THE SMITHSONIAN INSTITUTION MUSEUM OF AMERICAN HISTORY.

An early French portrayal of an Iroquois Longhouse. One such has been reported as 400 feet long, but most ran to about 120 feet in length. COURTESY OF THE NEWBERRY LIBRARY.

Wichita shelters. Cookhouse on left; bedroom in middle; and tepee frame for buffalo hunts. COURTESY OF THE SMITHSONIAN INSTITUTION MUSEUM OF AMERICAN HISTORY.

grated and allowed flood waters to roar unobstructed, taking topsoil with them. Later in the century, miners cut wood for houses, hearth fires, and charcoal burning; in doing so, they destroyed trees and brush whose roots impeded erosion. The combined effects made the lower and middle sections of the Gila and the lower Salt into "complete desert." Where Pueblo Indians had lived comfortably for centuries by contriving extensive irrigation systems, and where abundant fish and waterfowl had flourished, stretches of the river have now sunk underground and become functionally useless.

Not all the new animals were large. Rats jumped ship and proliferated in numbers like those of Browning's Hamelin town, with no Pied Piper for relief. Among other contributions, the rats brought fleas that brought bubonic plague, which is still latent in the rodent populations of the American West.

Fish abounded in American waters generally—and still do in some unpolluted places, but unfortunately those places are few. When the English "Pilgrims" landed at Plymouth, herring swarmed up their creeks in such numbers that they broke the nets; neighboring Wampanoag Indians had to give instruction for suitable devices. When Connecticut men founded Wilkes-Barre on the upper Susquehanna in the eighteenth century, they subsisted during their first spring season on fish running upriver from Chesapeake Bay. Salmon were a staple on the north Atlantic coast of the United States where they have almost vanished today; and half of Europe was fed from the Grand Banks of Newfoundland on days of religious fasting from meat. Change began instantly with the first European settlers who built weirs and dams that blocked upriver spawning of anhydrous fish coming in from the sea. Waste from industry and cities polluted streams and lakes, and even the ocean, to the point where what fish do survive are often toxic in human diet. Overfishing creates havoc in the Grand Banks and elsewhere.

On a more positive note, the honeybees introduced by Englishmen in the 1620s have spread everywhere, to the great benefit of agriculture and the economy.

On the whole, traffic in animals between the continents was one-way. American creatures taken to Europe did not go wild and spread unchecked like European animals brought to the Americas. The wild turkey, for example, when taken to Europe became merely another domesticated fowl.

Exchange of plants was more nearly reciprocal, but still generally to Europe's benefit. Clover and forage grass, as noticed above, became superior fodder for large herds of browsing animals, and clover renews nitrogen in the soil. On the other hand, as Alfred W. Crosby has reported, destruction of forests and ground cover invited a variety of European weeds to move in on the unsettled soil. He proposes a list including ferns, thistles, plantain, nettles, nightshade, sedge, "and so forth." Their mere names are enough to give heartburn to a gardener. In return, Europeans took home maize, potatoes, tomatoes, chilis, yams, and so forth. Of these, maize is the most productive cereal ever domesticated, potatoes became the basic staple for poor people from Ireland to Russia, and tomatoes took over the cuisines of Italy and Spain. (We may notice also that cornmeal mush feeds poor people in Italy and is now enjoying acceptance in haute cuisine, but under the disguise of *polenta*.)

It is not my purpose here to lay blame. Even lack of foresight can hardly be faulted among peoples who had no previous experience of what their adventures in the New World (and the succeeding new industrial world) would bring about. Some moralists are inclined to denounce greed, and there certainly was plenty of that, but greed by another name is ambition, sometimes creation; and many of the changes noted here were unintended happenstance.

In fact this chapter hardly scratches the surface of the immense transformations that resulted from contact between the continents. The event has been called the greatest in history. One special change, not so easily visible, needs special attention. "Colonists were moved to transform the soil," writes William Cronon, "by a property system that taught them to treat land as capital." They were thus moved to reproduce a type of culture which was still somewhat novel in most of Europe. (The process masquerades in our histories as "the transit of civilization.") Capital, like other cultural features, has evolved from its simple beginnings so that one may find it hard to recognize in ownership of a family farm worked by family members; but its essence is the amassing of wealth to make more wealth, and the family farm produced for markets as well as subsistence.

Europe was transformed by the reverse transit of capital. (Of civilization?) Wealth pouring into Europe from the Americas, whether in the form of precious metals or of valuable crops, created a positive explosion of capital on that side of the Atlantic, and with it the recreation of European society on a new model in which moneyed classes superseded landowners in dominance—not without violence. Subsequent revolutions in culture and politics cannot be explored here, but we may venture that they would have been much delayed and would have taken different forms if not for the riches brought from the new found lands.

Capitalistic organization and financing have resulted since 1492 in unprecedented exploitation of natural resources: on the ground and under it, and equally on the seas. Until quite recently, general knowledge of the environment and social controls over persons were inadequate to make much difference in planned controls over nature; and we are still a long way from a desirable balance. We need all the help we can get. It would be very foolish to forget what happened when the continents came together in what earlier generations liked to call "the conquest of the wilderness."

PART FOUR

New Frontiers

CHAPTER 17

The Sixteenth Century

SPAIN

We must narrow our focus to exclude Mexico from this point onward. Quite different sorts of historical processes evolved north of the Rio Grande. It was during the sixteenth century that France and England became interested in North America, and they immediately encountered Spain's claim to own the whole continent. In 1493, Pope Alexander VI, who was a native of Spain, "granted" the continent to his good friends at the Spanish court "out of the fullness of our apostolic power, by the authority of Almighty God." This was supposed to fend off poachers on Spain's preserves, but the Catholic monarchs in France and England were more impressed by the size and abilities of Spain's armed forces.

During the sixteenth century, the toughest challengers to Spain's monopoly were the Indian natives of the continent. The chiefdoms of the Gulf regions ruined and killed de Soto (at terrible cost), and Coronado's followers returned dispirited from their campaign, full of complaints. Not until the end of the century did Spain renew its explorations north of Mexico, the most substantial of which was led by Juan de Oñate in 1598. This penetration followed generally along Coronado's trail into the midst of the Rio Grande Pueblos (which probably had been an Indian trade route) and by 1610 enough colonists and missionaries had distributed themselves to justify establishment of a central administrative "capital" at Santa Fé de San Francisco. That was the limit of Spain's expansion for more than a century to come. As David B. Quinn has observed, the region governed from Santa Fé "remained only marginal in relation to the greater empire to the south."

Yet the effects of that presence were profound throughout a vast region, especially because of the introduction of Spanish livestock. Adjacent to the colony, the Pueblo Indians took up the herding of sheep and weaving of wool, and they in turn were herded into Catholic missions, not always willingly. Horses escaping from Spanish corrals throve and proliferated in the ideal environment of the Great Plains. Horses either stolen from the Spanish herds or redomesticated from the wild appealed strongly to the Indians living in the Plains—so strongly, in fact, as to stimulate revolutionary cultural change from sedentary horticulture to the mobility of hunters and raiders of "horse Indian" fame.

In the East, several Spanish expeditions dabbled ruinously in conquest. Everyone learns in elementary school that Juan Ponce de León searched for the Fountain of Youth in Florida, though the children are not often told that he went armed to the teeth. But the Indians of Florida had learned about Spanish cruelty in the West Indies, so when Ponce de León landed on Florida's west coast in 1521 he encountered stiff resistance and got an arrow wound that proved fatal. His project ended with himself.

Other ambitious conquistadors worked up the Atlantic coast with equal lack of success. An official effort was made to establish a mission in Chesapeake Bay in 1570. Seven Jesuits guided by a converted captive Indian called Don Luis de Velasco founded an establishment that quickly came to grief and martyrdom when Don Luis sided with his own people against the missionaries. Spaniards retaliated bloodily for the murder of the Jesuits, and the episode created a climate of opinion at Chesapeake Bay that was not at all favorable to the later English colonists of Jamestown.

One Spanish colony on the east coast survived like Santa Fé in the West, as a sort of capital of smaller settlements scattered in its vicinity. This was San Agustín, founded in 1565 by Pedro Menéndez de Avilés as a strategic base from which to destroy the French Huguenot colony of Fort Caroline farther north. Menéndez's policy was also Spanish crown policy, and there was reason for it though Menéndez's execution of the policy was atrocious as well as efficient. French Fort Caroline had been founded to prey upon shipping between New Spain and the metropolis. Menéndez furiously and treacherously massacred the "infidel" French, and thereafter maintained a garrison at San Agustín to prevent new intrusion by any of Spain's competitors. Along with the garrison came a mission and the beginnings of extensive reorganization of native society and culture in the vicinity. So early also began the recruitment of tribal allies by the French and Spanish contestants for attacks upon each other, about which the tribesmen were notably hesitant.

In summary: along the southern and eastern rims of modern United States, the conquistadors operated in the same fashion as earlier in the West Indies and in Mexico. An ambitious man—rich or with rich investors—obtained chartered permission from the crown for a campaign of conquest intended to make him richer still. He hired soldiers, bought provisions and equipment, and smashed into tribal territory. Usually priests accompanied or soon followed the first attacks. (The priests who ventured by themselves to Chesapeake Bay were exceptional, and their fate discouraged emulation.) However, the eastern tribes lacked Mexico's centralized institutions of government, and they were not compelled by a hostile environment (as in the Southwest) to stay in place when attacked. They had an option to disperse and regroup. In consequence, Spanish military tactics could not guarantee sudden and enduring conquest in the East, and Spain's colonies reached limits beyond which the gains were not worth the cost.

Spain's European competitors observed, and devised new tactics.

FRANCE AND ENGLAND

At a prudent distance from Spain's bases, French and English fishermen, and Basques and apparently Spaniards and Portuguese also, frequented the teeming waters off Newfoundland. Though England claimed all of Newfoundland (and much else) by virtue of John Cabot's voyages in the 1490s, and Sir Humphrey Gilbert tyrannized briefly over the fishermen in 1583, no efforts were made to colonize during the sixteenth century. The fishermen landed only to dry their catch. When their ships were full, they sailed home. There soon were an astonishing number of them. "Shortly after mid-century," writes David B. Quinn, fishing at Newfoundland "was already amongst the largest European enterprises." Quinn estimates that by A.D. 1580, 500 vessels per year took part in the fisheries.

In 1534, Jacques Cartier sailed around the coasts of the Gulf of St. Lawrence, and traded knives and trinkets for the furs of a party of Micmac Indians. The first such exchange on record, it was initiated by the Micmacs who perhaps had had earlier unrecorded experience with Europeans, and certainly had traded with other Indians. In 1535, Cartier sailed up the St. Lawrence to the Iroquoian village of Stadacona in the area of the modern city of Quebec. He followed this remarkable feat—the St. Lawrence is treacherous for navigation—by ascending the river still farther to *Hochelaga* where Montreal now stands. It is a pity that Cartier's diplomatic skills failed to match his seamanship on the hazardous river. When he returned in 1540, after having kidnapped Indians who later died in France, he encountered "Savages which went about dayly to annoy him." He does not explain their attitude. Cartier departed while he could. Troubles mounted for his successor, the Sieur de Roberval, who lost a fortune on a colony that lasted only until 1543.

One great benefit emerged from Cartier's wintering among the Canadian Indians in 1535–36. They showed him how to cure and prevent scurvy, the terrible killer of millions of Europeans who did not understand the necessity for diets including Vitamin C. The Indians made a brew by steeping the needles of an evergreen tree, probably spruce or white cedar. Cartier described its magical effects, but the "savage" remedy was disregarded and Europe continued to suffer until a British naval surgeon took Cartier's account seriously in the eighteenth century. After research, he found lemons to be effective antibiotics. The British navy then fed lime juice to sailors on long voyages, thus nicknaming Englishmen "Limeys."

We have seen already the fate of the Frenchmen of southern Fort Caroline who were killed by Menéndez in 1565, ending that brief enterprise. It seems worth noting that the only Frenchman to return home after escaping massacre and enslavement was one who had been captured by Indians.

European politics and internal tumults distracted the French from further efforts at American colonization until the seventeenth century.

England, like France, made grand claims and kept discreetly distant from Spanish might except for the hit-and-run raids of "sea dogs" like Francis Drake. Walter Raleigh's Roanoke colony was managed badly from its beginning in A.D. 1585 by commander Ralph Lane, a viciously bellicose man who suspected enemies everywhere and created them to fit his suspicions. His treacherous ambushes and general brutality left a legacy of ill will among the Indians that guaranteed the disappearance of the Roanoke colony as soon as it was left to its own resources. No one knows precisely what happened to Roanoke; the details hardly matter. Lane's murderous conduct made survival impossible in the midst of overwhelming numbers of Indians whom he had turned hostile. We do have a different sort of legacy from Roanoke in the descriptions by the scientist Thomas Hariot of the Carolina Algonquian Indians. Hariot observed carefully, and his report is still valuable.

He gave details of Indian horticulture, including special attention to maize, "a graine of marveilous great increase; of a thousand, fifteene hundred and some two thousand fold." Hariot did not use the language of *savagery*. In his eyes the natives were "a people poore," but, "considering the want of such meanes as we have, they seeme very ingenious." He is especially renowned for observing the effects of epidemic disease though he failed to understand its causes: "Within a few days after our departure from everie such [hostile] towne, the people began to die very fast, and many in short space; in some townes about twentie, in some fourtie, in some sixtie, and in one six score, which in truth was very manie in respect of their numbers. This happened in no place . . . but where wee had bene." Nothing of the sort had ever happened before, "time out of minde." Hariot thought it was divine punishment for "wicked practices."

His book appeared in 1588, after which English accounts were slight until the founding of Jamestown in 1607.

In a word, European approaches to the Americas (excepting Spain's establishments) were episodic rather than the products of rational policy. France and England were torn by religious and feudal struggles. The Netherlands were fully occupied with their rebellion against Spanish rule. Italy and Germany did not exist as political entities. Portugal showed no interest in North America except for fishing at Newfoundland. Catholic and Protestant Christians aimed more seriously at conquering (and sometimes exterminating) each other than in converting Indians to any type of Christianity. Only Spain had a crown and church hierarchy in control of an organized nation with pretensions north of Mexico, and the Spanish crown busied itself subverting and "destabilizing" other countries. (At its own cost eventually: Philip II's rage for conquest in Europe lost Spain all the advantage of its early start in America.)

Nevertheless, European influences and effects had already penetrated to the tribes at the very core of the continent. We must accept the anthropologist's distinction between macrocontacts and microcontacts. The jargon is unfortunate, but the distinction is genuine. Microcontacts occur when actual human beings come into touch with each other, face to face. Obviously, in A.D. 1600, such encounters had not yet happened between Europeans and Indians in the Mississippi Valley or around Lake Superior, much less in Alaska. But far in advance of European persons ran their epidemic diseases transmitted through the all-too-hospitable flesh of native carriers. Long before most Indians ever laid eyes on the exotic strangers, tribesmen may have suffered from the macrocontact of disease, although demographers have not yet found positive evidence of a pandemic sweeping over the whole continent.

This matter of population change is so full of irony that it can hardly be believed. Diseases from Europe brought down Indians like blight in a forest; but an Indian remedy, when finally adopted, saved untold numbers of Europeans from lethal scurvy. Europeans made great nutritional advances when they adopted the maize and potatoes from the Americas, a treasure greater than all the gold of the Aztecs and Incas. These new foods gave sustenance to European millions. More irony: the introduction of maize to Africa resulted in such a population increase there that it brought gladness to the hearts of slave traders.

In North America, the sudden terrible loss of population so weakened all Indians that armed resistance to European intrusion became unfeasible. Never again did the invaders face swarms of enemy Indians such as bedeviled and finally ruined Hernán de Soto. Instead, weakened tribal chiefs commonly sought European allies against enemy tribes in the beginnings of a system of patron-client relationships that was to become widespread in the seventeenth century.

Such relationships were still tentative and experimental in the sixteenth century when Indians still kept some freedom of diplomatic maneuver. Full-blown clientage, with its many implications, did not develop until the proliferation of permanent European colonies in the seventeenth century.

Macrocontacts occurred also through rumor and trade. The great networks of intertribal trade that had operated for thousands of years served to convey information as well as goods. Much of the information undoubtedly became garbled after passing through series of middlemen, but it hit upon essentials well enough to warn the Indians of Florida (for example) about Spanish treatment of West Indians, and served thereby as a death warrant for Ponce de León.

On the other hand, Indians everywhere were fascinated by the products of European crafts and manufactories. They often converted articles to functions other than what was originally intended; as, for instance, when, in the early days of trading, they wore utilitarian metal tools as body ornaments. For whatever reasons, the desire for European objects carried them through the hands of many middlemen thousands of miles into the interior.

Close attention must be given to chronology as well as geography when speaking of this *intersocietal* trade. Indians who had been newly introduced to European goods might wear small hatchets as jewelry, but longer familiarity led them to use the hatchets, as intended, for chopping. One must beware of well-meant scholarly efforts to show how *different* those Indians were by portraying them as perpetual primitive innocents locked into rigid conceptual systems. Like everyone else, those Indians learned, adapted, and changed. Otherwise none would be alive today. The issue is not really arguable; the source documentation is massive and explicit.

Trade with the Indians, instead of expeditions of military conquest, became the instrument favored by Frenchmen and Englishmen (and later by Dutchmen and Swedes also) for acquiring domination over the Indians. At first the trade was simply a means to profit. By A.D. 1600, most trading was still done from anchored ships, as a sideline of fishermen or as the objective of merchants cruising along the Atlantic coasts. When feasible, these merchants also kidnapped Indians for extra profit in the slave marts.

By A.D. 1600, European powers began to sort themselves out. With the help of an opportune storm, England and the Netherlands destroyed Spain's "Invincible Armada" in 1588. Philip II died in 1598 and was succeeded by the saner, lazier Philip III. In France, Louis XIV began his long reign in 1661. Plenty of religious and dynastic brawling still continued, but the greater powers had acquired control of enough resources to turn purposefully toward the Americas, and Spain could no longer deter them.

Within a relatively few years, new colonies splashed upon the ocean and river coasts of the continent, and many Indians had to find ways to cope with an entirely new situation. The vast interior of the continent remained as tribal territory, and most of it remained so until the nineteenth century. Geographically, the Europeans were nibbling, so to speak, at the edges of North America. The tribesmen who lived at such places were compelled to devise responses to preserve life, liberty, and the pursuit of happiness.

As the sixteenth century beyond Spain's sprawl had been an era of chance encounters between Europeans and Indians, so the seventeenth saw the formation of intersocietal frontiers. These were regions of interaction—sometimes armed conflict, most of the time some variant of accommodation—that seemed to repeat the intertribal trading networks of pre-Columbian times. But these new frontiers were different in quality because of the cultural differences of the trading partners.

We need not—should not—repeat the hypocritical cant that Europe brought *civilization* to its side of a single, mythological Frontier where civilization faced *savagery* on the other side. That sort of slush amounts to retrospective excusing of conquest such as the conquerors themselves rarely bothered to concoct. What happened on the real frontiers was a mingling of peoples of distinct continental origins during which all cultures were modified by the contacts. As populations of colonial Europeans and their enslaved Africans grew, while native Indian populations declined, the nature of their frontier regions transformed, evolving traumatically through three more centuries.

CHAPTER 18

Fallacies of "Frontier History"

The conceptualization of all Europeans as a single undifferen-
tiated whole labeled "the whites" cannot be sustained, and neither
can the notion that these whites adhered to a single monolithic belief
system labeled "Christianity." The Europeans varied among themselves even more than the Indians, and it follows that contact situations were structured differently in various areas.

—LYDIA T. BLACK

In the chronological Part III we attended to the sequence of events
beginning with Columbus's voyages and the Spanish conquests. In the
present chapter we take up another myth—the doctrine laid down by
historian Frederick Jackson Turner that *civilization* encountered *savagery*
at the east coast of the English colonies that became the United States,
and after epic battles marched westward across the continent to the Pacific
Coast. Turner failed to define what he meant by his abstract terms so a
student must try to see what they identify and how they fit into recorded
events. There is no doubt that *civilization* meant Europeans or, more particularly, Englishmen; and *savagery* meant simply Indians—all Indians.

Turner, like most English-speaking historians, adopted the point of
view of the sixteenth- and seventeenth-century English invaders. For them,
as a wit has observed, God was an Englishman. They held themselves to
be possessed of qualities superior to all other peoples, even such as
Frenchmen, not to speak of "savage" Highland Scots and Irishmen; and
they conceived the natives of America as natural candidates for subjection. Their objective was to "reduce" the Indians "to civility" which in
plainer terms meant conquering them. Turner adopted this point of view
so completely that he waved aside the entire human population of North
America by word magic. In his writings the land became simply wilder-

ness, more specifically "free land," which a disciple correctly translated
into "land free to be taken." Yet it held creatures who could not be denied
to look like human beings. Word magic was equal to the problem. Turner
deprived these ostensible persons of human status by classing them with
animals of the wild; they were creatures of the wilderness which was
woodland, and an English word existed, derived from Latin *silva* for woods,
so Turner called the Indians by the English word *savage.* Thus, as wilderness creatures they lacked the humanity of persons with *civil* government who were the only civilized peoples and, by inference, the only
truly human persons. This magic was already old by the time Turner
practiced it in the late nineteenth century, but we must reflect that Turner
kept the terms alive into the twentieth century, and he achieved great
renown. He wrote the common understanding of persons descended from
Anglo-Americans.

The logic of the Turnerian tradition is reproachless so long as human
beings and their doings are submerged in abstractions that can be made
to perform as desired. This logic falls apart only when real people and
factual events are matched against it. Then it becomes absurd, but this
task remained undone until after the middle of the twentieth century, so
Turner's "frontier history" was accepted as standard.

Many things are wrong with it. For the moment let us concentrate on
the notion that civilization came from Europe to North America's east
coast and marched westward. A few factual data show a different picture.
The European discovery of America occurred on islands in the Caribbean
Sea rather than along the continent's east coast. Spaniards first invaded
the mainland from a base in Cuba, driving northward through Florida
and then westward to the Mississippi, and leaving havoc in their wake.
They sailed across the Gulf into Mexico which they conquered (1519),
then spread southward into Peru and north into the Pueblo country of
present-day New Mexico. Long before the Pueblos knew of the existence
of Englishmen, and centuries before "Americans" existed at all, the Pueblos fought a fierce war of liberation in which they first succeeded in expel-
ling the Spaniards but finally went down to defeat and military occupation.
By the eighteenth century, Spaniards had established colonies in California, and they founded a mission at San Francisco when the American
Revolution was beginning 3,000 miles away.

Fifty years before Sir Walter Raleigh experimented with a short-lived
English colony at Roanoke, Virginia, France's Jacques Cartier had voyaged up the St. Lawrence River (in a southwestern direction) to attempt
a colony at Quebec. He, too, failed, but he was followed by other
Frenchmen, most notably Samuel de Champlain who established New

Major Paths of Entry by Europeans

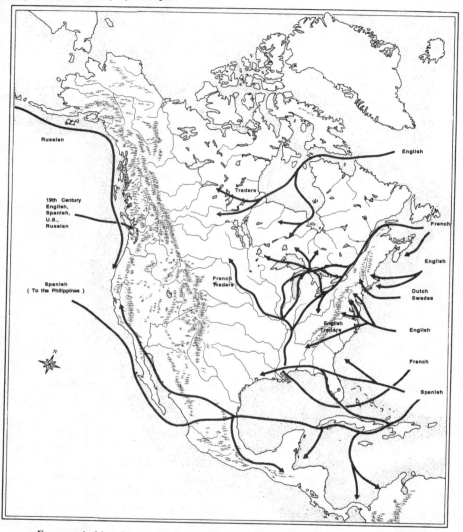

Eurocentric historians write that "civilization" moved from east to west across the continent, and they identify civilization with the cultures of Europeans. In contradiction, Europeans invaded in many directions.

France. Champlain and his successors set up chains of trading posts and forts that reached across the top of the Great Lakes and eventually down into the Mississippi Valley where they were met by other French settlements extending north from New Orleans. During all this time—more than a century and a third—English colonies were confined east of the Appalachian mountain range. Before the English could bring "civilization" to the Mississippi Valley they first had to conquer the French who were already there, and most Frenchmen were under the impression that they already possessed civilization. Their resistance to British conquest was the basic issue in the great Seven Years War of the mid-eighteenth century which spread conflict all over the world.

We must notice also that seventeenth-century Englishmen set up trading posts in Hudson Bay but were blocked from southern expansion by French interposition. And in the nineteenth century Russians complicated the pattern still more by invading Alaska and spreading southward to challenge Spaniards coming north from California, Britons making beachheads from the sea, and a motley lot of traders claiming jurisdiction and protection from the United States. Spaniards in Florida and Frenchmen on the coast of the Gulf of Mexico organized resistance to expansion westward from the English Carolinas and Georgia. Frontiers of competition and conflict surrounded the continent: Europeans invaded from every direction, closing in from south, east, north, and west, and Europeans struggled on *both* sides of the frontiers. As for civilization, the English founded Jamestown, Virginia, in 1607 and the Spanish founded Santa Fé, New Mexico in 1609. If civilization traveled westward from Jamestown to Santa Fé, it flew by jet plane. The National University of Mexico was founded in 1551 by Charles V, Europe's most powerful monarch, and cows did not begin to browse in Harvard Yard until 1636.

When such data are taken seriously into account, the east-to-west doctrine becomes ridiculous. Examined more closely, however, it discloses a political message masked by its abstractions. (Word magic again.) What did travel was the sovereignty and political administration of the British crown followed by the government of the United States. Some Europeans may doubt that such arrangements are equivalent to civilization. Quite a few Indians have reservations.

Putting aside the direction of civilization's travel, let us look at the line that separated it from savagery. No map shows that line. Historical atlases draw boundary lines between contesting European nations in America, and color the areas according to the claims of those nations. The Indian tribes and their territories disappear from these networks of lines and splashes of color, but we may use them as clues to understanding "frontier history." They represent boundaries between Frenchmen *with their tribal allies* on one side, and Englishmen with their Indian allies on the other. The point must not be ignored. French and British diplomats argued strenuously that their national sovereignties in America depended to a considerable extent upon the aboriginal or purported conquest rights of their Indian allies who were usually mentioned for this purpose as "subjects."

In this indirect fashion we penetrate the lawyers' myth of sovereignty to find the acknowledgment in practice of tribal rights to bounded territories separate from each other and also separate from colonial jurisdictions. No matter what the statesmen of Europe claimed, the Indians in these tribal jurisdictions governed themselves. Their boundaries do not appear in our historical atlases, but they can be found in the treaty documents and deeds of cession of lands from tribes to European colonies and empires. In such sources, boundary lines are carefully specified in graphic detail along with the compensation provided for land given up by the tribes. These boundaries were pulled together to form one continuous line by the British Royal Proclamation of 1763 that banned colonial settlement in "lands reserved to the Indians," and that is the reality behind the line between civilization and savagery.

Perhaps, however, we should view early frontiers as social relations between peoples instead of legal relations between governments. In that case we must abandon the concept of lines of division because the Indians and Europeans of early America eagerly mixed up with each other in commerce and politics, and sometimes just in sociability.

My favorite story about how friendly they could be when greed and power let them be concerns a Quaker family in Bucks County, Pennsylvania. Father and mother determined to attend Yearly Meeting of the Society of Friends some distance away at Burlington, New Jersey. As it would keep them away from home for several days, they provided a supply of food and left their children to look after themselves. A passing Delaware Indian warrior was shocked by such negligence. He moved in and baby-sat until the parents returned. (Without fee.) Such happenings are not the stuff of which "frontier history" has been written. Yet even the most bloodcurdling accounts of war and captivity mention friendliness between particular families of Indians and particular back-country colonials; and traders were received hospitably in Indian villages, often marrying into the tribe—sometimes into more than one tribe.

Another sort of line is enforced racial segregation. English colonizers in Ireland had experienced bloody uprisings by Irish natives living within their plantations. The colonists in America included men who had lived through Irish rebellions, and they did not intend to make the same mistake in America. Colonial rulers enacted laws in Virginia, Massachusetts, and Connecticut to keep their subjects apart from Indians and to keep Indians out of their plantations. These laws were enforced. When starving commoners of the Jamestown colony fled to Indian hospitality for food and freedom, they were seized by the Jamestown governors and brought back to be tortured horribly to death. The danger was real in all of the colonies that some of the common folk, especially bond servants, were inclined to go off to an easier life among the Indians (and were welcomed when they did). This could not be tolerated, even on grounds of security. When New Plymouth and Massachusetts Bay launched offensive war against the Narragansett tribe, they found a turncoat Englishman who had been advising the tribe how to fight back effectively. He was put to death. Even in New France where official policies encouraged ethnic intermixture when it occurred under control, unauthorized persons were forbidden to journey back into the woods to trade with Indians; the free-enterprising *coureurs de bois*, so famous in history and romance, were smugglers.

For the most part, despite mutual suspicions, Indians and colonials wanted to exchange goods with each other. The single most comprehensive and most influential institution promoting mixture was intersocietal exchange. "Fur trade" is a misnomer for this commerce which involved many varied commodities, extended over the entire continent, and sometimes proceeded without a fur in sight. What is important about it here is its factual refutation of the dogma about a frontier line between Indians and Europeans. In terms of populations, what existed were communities of Indians separate from colonial communities, and broad frontier *zones* or *regions* where the diversely ethnic peoples mingled in systems of exchange that required them to behave themselves in ways expected of business associates.

To the great scandal of white-supremacist historians, these frontier inhabitants exchanged genes as well as goods, and did so to an extent that is only lately being recognized. Their many children, and the children's children, too frequently have been dismissed as "half-breed" persons of no historical significance. This is utter fallacy. These synethnic "people in between" became cultural brokers between tribal traditionalists and the colonials who adhered to different traditions. Though they sometimes despaired of being fully accepted in either camp, they came to exert great influence in intersocietal diplomacy and intratribal politics and cultural evolution. New France's rulers recognized their practical value and employed numbers of them on official business; as civil servants in the field, so to speak, they were largely responsible for the remarkable success of New France's administration of Indian affairs. Among the French the descendants of mixed parents became known as métis, and as their numbers grew they formed communities of their own kind in western Canada and along the Mississippi River down to Louisiana. Scholars have only begun to examine their distinctive cultures and histories.

It should be evident from even so cursory a review that Turnerian "frontier history" is a myth that must be rejected and ignored by students of history. Instead we must attend to many sorts of frontier and unique regional identities at various places and times. We have already noticed intertribal frontiers existing before European invasion. These continued from the classic era into post-Columbian times—into what may be called "modern" Indian history. Intertribal frontiers were altered, but not ended, by the addition of frontiers with European colonies. Intertribal contacts and arrangements are very much alive still today.

We must not neglect "macrocontacts": i.e., effects that take place before face-to-face "microcontact." Besides lethal diseases, Spaniards introduced horses, sheep, cattle, and swine which also had a way of running ahead of colonial habitation. The horse frontier transformed the lives of Indians on North America's Great Plains.

Where natives of Europe came in contact with natives of America, the resulting mixture depended much on the particular subcultures possessed by each side. For example, in the Southeast, the feature of "civilization" called chattel slavery—a feature that also involved persons from the third continent of Africa—was adopted in modified form by Cherokees and Creeks, but not by Shawnees, who gave sanctuary to runaway slaves. On the issue of slavery, northeastern tribes also varied: Iroquoians enslaved war captives, but I have seen no reference to slaves of any sort among the Delawares. The frontiers of slavery must be studied individually. Among other reasons, slaves of Indians were treated differently from tribe to tribe and usually quite distinctly from plantation chattels.

When eastern tribes were forced westward, they were required to come to terms somehow with other peoples preceding them on the scene. In the Old Northwest, familiarity bred of previous trade and treaty arrangements permitted negotiations leading to uneasy condominium which was facilitated by shared hostility to American expansion; but in the nineteenth century when the United States literally dumped large numbers of eastern Indians into the territories of tribes west of the Mississippi, conflict resulted. In these situations, as in many others, intertribal frontiers were inextricably entwined with the intersocietal kind.

Long ago, writers noticed the differences between Spanish, French, and English relations with tribes bordering their colonies. Lately some students have begun to compare United States policies with those of the other imperial powers instead of treating them in isolation. Such comparisons reveal that many Indians became sandwiched *between* frontiers rather than placed "on the other side" of one. In the seventeenth and eighteenth centuries, tribes in New England dealt variously with New France, Massachusetts Bay, and New-York; tribes of the Southeast had to face on one side to the French in the Mississippi Valley, the Spaniards in Florida, and English rivals in Virginia and South Carolina. North of the Great Lakes, French traders based at Montreal, Michilimackinac, and Detroit strove to win tribes away from Englishmen who sailed in to "factories" on Hudson Bay. Early in the nineteenth century, the West Coast became an arena for Spaniards, Russians, Englishmen, and Americans, all competing for tribal trade and alliance—and ultimately for tribal lands.

Accordingly, the rest of this book must notice not only the variety of Indian societies and the variety of European societies, but also the complex combinations of the places where they mixed. Fortunately for understanding, patterns recur in the seeming chaos. Most of those patterns originated in the seventeenth century.

CHAPTER 19

Plantation and Accommodation

Of all Europeans colonizing North America, Englishmen migrated in greatest numbers. They brought a fleet full of immigrant families to Massachusetts Bay in 1630 following after several smaller ventures, and they quickly sprawled to the Connecticut River and Narragansett Bay.

We need not trace the growth of these colonies except insofar as it confronted indigenous Indians with exigent requirements to respond. Naturally, the first tribes to engage in microcontacts were those who lived near the new colonies, which, for the English, meant near the shore. Historians have rightly observed that English expansion in the seventeenth century was seaborne and coastbound. Cant phrases invented long after the facts motivate the English with desires for "an errand into the wilderness" or an intention to "conquer the wilderness." These myths flout all the recorded facts. Early English colonists were scared stiff by the wilderness. They clung tightly to the harbors and navigable streams at the termini of their lifelines to Home across the ocean. Frenchmen, though they migrated in only a fraction of the numbers of the English, were much more adventuresome. Following the example set by Champlain, they roamed far into the interior between the Great Lakes and Hudson Bay; but consideration of these *voyageurs* or *coureurs de bois* must be reserved for respectful treatment a bit further on.

As a general rule, the Indians received colonists hospitably except where predecessor Europeans had soured attitudes by kidnapping natives for sale in slave marts or by flaunting power with abuse and pillage. The mere display of such power caused Indians to think hard. Some wanted to fight back and did, generally disastrously. Others tried to accommodate to the newcomers; they engaged in trade, ceded territory for colonial habitations and farms, solicited patronage protection against their enemies, and accepted Christian missionaries.

All of these accommodation techniques forced traumatic and disintegrative cultural change upon the tribes in the long run, and in the background—often in the foreground—was the drastic steady loss of native populations from European-borne epidemic diseases. When the century opened, the Indians in their thousands and ten thousands far outnumbered the few hundreds of Europeans; but through the span of less than a hundred years the ratio was reversed. The regions near European contact were first depopulated of Indians, then repopulated by constant European immigration and natural increase. This was the reality behind the myths of America as a "virgin land" offering Europeans "land free to be taken."

Nevertheless, during the first half of the century, colonists depended heavily upon their neighboring Indians for subsistence and exploitation. It is another fact of life that the costs of colonization were paid by Indians. However muted this fact may be in the attention given to the details of proprietary grants and joint stock companies, *all* of those noblemen and merchants adventurers intended to profit from their investments. Most did, either through profit in trade with Indians or through seizure and sale of Indian lands. However unknowingly and involuntarily, Indians financed the creation of the America we know. Europeans had no interest in true wilderness. They were attracted by opportunities to dominate and exploit the indigenous peoples who had prepared the way—the true pioneers. For accuracy, it must be added that as Indian numbers dwindled, much of their contribution was made up by other people of lower caste who had originated in Africa.

In North America beyond Spanish controls, Europeans began to exchange goods with Indians in what was called "fugitive" trade, so named because it was transacted from ships that sailed on after business was completed. The crews of fishing boats learned to bring along tools and trinkets when they went ashore to dry their catch. Natives who had been watching for the opportunity would emerge with furs from nearby woods for a session of haggling that often culminated with the Indian stripping himself (or herself) of the robes he was wearing in order to acquire much coveted steel knives or equally coveted glass beads.

The next step in this "fugitive" trade was taken by merchants who loaded a ship with trade goods and cruised along the coast to seize opportunities, which sometimes meant seizing Indians also. In the seventeenth century, few Europeans had compunctions against lucrative traffic in *different* human beings. Or, for that matter, in persons like themselves except weaker.

Fugitive trade gave way eventually to the establishment of permanent trading posts at strategic places. These posts sheltered and implied far more than persons simply exchanging goods. They were the meeting place, in conditions of peace, of two distinct cultures whose representatives brought, along with their goods, quite different motives, customs, and expectations.

It appears that Indians originally conceived trade as ritualistic present-giving between groups or peoples at peace with each other, the exchange being controlled by the chiefs on each side. Some scholars suggest that certain European trade objects were desired by Indians for their supernatural significance which did not exist for the Europeans. Older writers were puzzled by the special interest of eastern Indians in wrought copper and glass beads, things which to Europeans were merely toys or ornaments. Now, however, we begin to realize that for Indians such objects were analogous to crystal and native copper, and George R. Hamell notes that they, together with shell, "had ancient and widespread magico-religious uses throughout the Great Lakes and Northeastern Woodland areas."

In due course, however, the inventories of goods traded show that Indian values became more materialistic, and the exchange procedures became less ritualistic and more simply "commercial." We shall see that in their Northern colonies, the English were required to conform to Indian customs in diplomatic negotiations, but in commerce the European way prevailed. Already, at the very beginning of contact relations, market economics showed its power.

We are accustomed to think in capitalistic analytical terms which do not appear plainly in exchange relations with noncapitalist societies, but the factors of capital formation *for the Europeans* can easily be found in the intersocietal exchange.

Land was contributed by the Indian who had not learned how to charge rent. (Indians did not hire labor though sometimes they accepted employment at wages.) The Indian provided raw materials in an extractive industry. He hunted or trapped animals for pelts valued in Europe. He expertly skinned those animals and carried the pelts back to his village where his wife engaged in the cottage industry of dressing the skins to add value. Husband carried the products of his industry—usually a mix of dressed and undressed skins—to the trading post with the expectation of bartering them for European products at standard, fixed equivalents, often including a binge on French brandy or English rum. It is worth notice that this Indian's journeys to the hunt in one direction and to the trading post in another might extend for hundreds of miles each way, though usually either the post was set up close to the Indian's village or the village moved closer to the post. In European cost accounting, the

Indian's labor in transporting freight would be a heavy factor, but at the trading post it was ignored.

The trade was more powerful than any of its participants realized. On the surface, a simple exchange of goods benefited both sides—each had what the other wanted, so they swapped—but the process had implications that were not so simple. Perhaps the most important of these in the long run was the European traders' linkage to world markets. A beginning trader wanted food and some land as a base of operations, but in many colonies he soon began to produce his own food, and Indians who had already conveyed surplus lands would not readily trade what they needed for their own subsistence. (That came later when Indians were fewer and Europeans more powerful.) Animal peltry became the staple of the trade from the Indian side. Markets in Europe demanded furs and hides in almost unlimited amounts, and Indians who wanted to trade had to hunt or trap for their part of the bargaining.

Thus the first implication of the trading process was a gradual transformation of Indian cultures along the Atlantic seaboard. Men who formerly had hunted part-time to provide meat in the family kettle now began to hunt for an omnivorous market. Commercial hunting, far more intensive than subsistence hunting, required most of the Indian man's time and much of his wife's. Formerly self-sufficient Indian families were absorbed into a system of industry which differed from that of formerly self-sufficient Yorkshire weavers in that the Indians had to supply their own raw materials; but like the Yorkshiremen they obtained their tools from merchant suppliers.

On the one hand, these Indians became dependent to greater or lesser degree on the European market beyond the trading post. If prices for fur fell in Amsterdam, Indians in Appalachia would have to hunt harder and longer.

On the other hand, as hunts intensified, the populations of desirable species dwindled, and the hunters had to march farther and farther into the backwoods for their game. They left their villages, like sailors, for long periods of time so that they were often not on hand when needed for labor or defense. Worse, the farther they hunted, the more likely they were to be intruding on territory belonging to alien tribes—an offense that could bring instant punishment or tribal war.

Europeans and Indians engaged in trade with different cultural preconceptions and different goals.

When the Indian returned to his village, he showed his merit and acquired status by distributing to kinfolk the surplus beyond his own family's needs. This Indian hunter-freighter-businessman might join with colleagues on the hunt or in convoys to the trading post, but he was individualistic in his work; he kept his own score and traded his own take. There were no tribal companies with shares in combined products. A good worker obtained for himself the tools that represented operating capital, but he did not accumulate investment capital. For his decrepit old age he depended on his children as his "social security," so he was careful not to alienate them. In short his business was permeated by kin relations, just as his politics were. However, without violating the principle of individualism, some tribesmen acted as middlemen between distant hunters and the trading posts. Hurons and Crees, for example, became specialists in this role.

At the trading post, the Indian dealt with a European who had different ideas. French, English, Dutch, or Swedish, the European trader obtained his merchandise for intersocietal exchange by first making exchanges within his own society. This trader worked at the end of a long line of operations extending through his importing merchant supplier who dealt with exporters overseas in Europe. These then faced in the opposite direction to buy trade goods from European craftsmen or factories and to sell skins and furs to European consumers. The range of European trade goods was wide. It often included luxuries such as beads, ribbons, and liquor; but its staples were woolen blankets and shirts, copper kettles and steel needles, knives and hatchets, and firearms and ammunition. Indian demand for such goods became an important factor in the prosperity of certain European communities; for example, England's Stroud Valley, Flanders's Duffels (near Antwerp), and Germany's Osnabrück.

The trader dealing directly with Indians often was a hired hand, but both employee and employer shared an attitude toward commerce. They wanted it to make them rich. They wanted to create capital to become even richer. They wanted to acquire means for fine clothes, great houses, and showy carriages and teams. Such desires are so integral to European culture that it is necessary here to emphasize how different they were from American Indian attitudes. And, of course, Europeans did not always succeed in business; the traders especially had high casualty rates.

The European or European colonial trader was not merely desirous of wealth; he measured it in *money*, and he kept written records, both of which procedures were novelties to Indians. Both also offered considerable opportunities for maximizing profit, as our modern phrase goes, because the Indian did not understand what was happening when calculations were reckoned up on paper. Money of account and books of record also made credit easy for the European. It seems that simple credit arrangements had existed among some aboriginal tribes; but in the intersocietal trade, credit developed elaborately as surviving account books reveal. When an Indian had a bad year in his hunting, the trader who knew him would provide equipment for the following year, knowing that he thereby secured the Indian's trade for that new year. Naturally, credit was chancy then, as it still is, but its gains more than offset its losses.

Among the effects of credit, in America as elsewhere, was the development of debtor dependency. The same process that sank England's Stroud Valley independent weavers into the status of hired hands worked also to make Indians dependent on traders for advances of guns and ammunition necessary for the hunt—or for war—and for clothing in the winter. The process did not work identically on both sides of the Atlantic because the Indian debtor preserved a degree of political independence through membership in his tribe. He could seldom be jailed for debt. Sometimes, of course, he evaded duns by vanishing into the woods, but there seems to have been remarkably little of that.

Dutchman Adriaen Van der Donck summarized simply and concisely why Europeans engaged in the trade with Indians: "The Indians, without our labour or trouble, bring to us their fur trade, worth tons of gold, which may be increased, and is like goods found."

CHAPTER 20

French and English Missions

One of the most potent instruments of creeping conquest was the religious mission. This should not surprise anyone familiar with church history in Europe, the Mediterranean periphery, and the "Near East." Medieval missionaries converted entire kingdoms by promising the kings spiritual salvation along with temporal alliance. Church and state were allies against internal heathen as well as the external infidels of Islam. The Roman Pope summoned western Christendom against Muslims, and his agents led the barons' assault on the Byzantine Emperor and Patriarch who were as Christian as the Pope. Theologies were crafted to fit political needs.

Yet, with all this in the substance of church history, the variously Christian missions of North America have often been presented as altruistic efforts to do good for the poor benighted Indian pagans. Indisputably, certain missionaries conceived themselves as bringing eternal salvation to the Indians at great sacrifice to themselves, and it is equally plain that some met martyrdom heroically. These noble souls have been given due praise in many books, and will not be denigrated here; what is at issue here is not hero worship, but rather an account of an institution.

Most missions were supported by their several governments and attacked by rival governments. Historians and political scientists have a maxim that governments have no morals, only interests. The governments' interest in saving Indian souls was to acquire rule over Indian bodies. Like war, missions were politics by other means. This purpose of rule was the very reason for which nations set up their home establishments of religion, a fact well understood by the eighteenth-century libertarians who insisted upon a Bill of Rights in the Constitution of the United States. The first words of their First Amendment were: "Congress shall make no law respecting an establishment of religion, or prohibiting the free exercise thereof." As will be seen in a later chapter, the Founding Fathers excluded Indians from this protection. In the seventeenth century, protection for Indians was wholly inconceivable by the overseers of conquest. (This thought should be noted by mythologists who insist that Indians strongly influenced the writers of the United States Constitution.)

Until nearly the middle of the seventeenth century, the Roman Catholic Church held a monopoly on missionary work in America. Two great religious societies, Franciscans and Jesuits, poured resources of men and money into missions founded as fundamental obligations, and they acquired experience from activities around the world. This chapter can notice only a sampling of their North American activities. As with all great institutions, enthusiasm waxed and waned, and where success occurred it transformed prophets into administrators; but the early Catholic missionaries were true zealots who ventured unarmed into the midst of unreceptive or hostile Indian villages far from familiar comforts and companions. Several met horrible deaths, sometimes because Indians held them responsible for outbreaks of epidemic disease that seemed to accompany them. Jesuit Father Bressani reported about Huronia: "With the Faith, the scourge of God came into the country; and, in proportion as the one increased, the other smote them more severely,—almost, indeed, to the ultimate destruction of this poor nation . . . [and] in the families in which the Faith was greatest, the trials were also greatest."

Opposition to the missionaries sometimes arose from opponents of the political alliances sponsored by them. English-allied Mohawk chiefs hated the "Black Robes" for drawing off converts to New France. In the Southeast, English-allied Creeks despised the Timucuans in Spanish missions. In the eighteenth century, Delaware converts in the Moravian mission at Gnadenhütten were attacked by their own traditionalist kinsmen who had gone into alliance with the Iroquois Six Nations. Indeed, so much hostility manifested itself that any sort of success may well arouse wonder, but far-sighted European sponsors understood what they were doing and were willing to pay the costs.

Indians who responded favorably to the missions did so for at least three distinct reasons identifiable in the sources. Some were genuinely moved by the missionaries' teachings. Tribal Indians were and are deeply religious, whether upholding traditional faiths or turning toward new gods. Many listened attentively to the missionaries and meditated seriously on their doctrines. Other Indians perceived the missions as sanctuaries offering protection against belligerent countrymen of the missionaries. And still other Indians were dragooned into the missions by main force as in Florida, among the Southwestern Pueblos, and in Massachusetts Bay. No general rule of method applied everywhere. Each mission system must be examined distinctly. All, however, were intended, and functioned in their various ways, to establish colonial domination over the Indians involved.

No matter what theology was involved nor what agency operated the mission, it was generally a divisive force in Indian society. Aboriginal cultures provided many rituals of worship that united the entire community, some of which, especially the Green Corn Ceremony, were to be found all over the continent. To the missionary, these were diabolical. His first objective was to withdraw his converts from participation in such rites and to incite them to denounce the participants as evil. This sort of activity persuaded traditionalist Indians that the Black Robes of New France were demons aiming to destroy the tribe, an understanding that had much truth in it. Regardless of each side attributing demonism to the other, the missionaries wanted only to destroy the *tribe*, not the people; they converted their charges not only to new faiths but also to new and different communities. These missionaries not only led; they also governed.

When an entire tribe allied to New France, there was no need to set up a mission distantly separate. A priest could simply move in and establish himself in competition with the tribe's medicine man, as happened among the Hurons before 1649. Even in that situation, however, the competing religious bodies acted as political factions whose antagonisms became bitter when French authorities permitted firearms to be sold to converts but denied to traditionalists. In its politically disintegrated and poorly armed state, the Huron Confederacy succumbed to Iroquois attacks culminating in the winter of 1649–50. The people fled in many directions. The largest group of survivors surrendered to the Senecas and became a fiercely anti-mission adopted village of that tribe.

The Onondagas—the middle tribe of the Iroquois Five Nations—had observed the prestige that French alliance had conferred on the Hurons before the debacle, but apparently did not appreciate the alliance's negative aspects. (The Onondagas had not joined in the Seneca and Mohawk attacks on Huronia.) Striving to achieve preeminence among the Five Nations, the Onondagas thought to acquire favored status from the French by requesting a trading and missionary settlement at Onondaga. Because the French urgently needed an important ally among Iroquoian speakers after Huron downfall, they quickly accepted Onondaga's proposal, and cemented the new alliance in 1654 by providing weapons for Onondaga's war against the Eries (Cat Nation). In 1656, four Jesuits and fifty retainers set up a new mission near Onondaga as requested.

Whereupon the epidemic pattern of Huronia repeated itself in Onondaga. Within two years, as Father Ragueneau reported, "more than five hundred children, and many adults" died, "most of whom died after Baptism." Such a price must surely have been too high to pay for the French alliance, but the Onondagas were spared the bitter intratribal strife of Huronia. In 1658, their Iroquois League brethren, the Mohawks, took decision out of their hands by marching to destroy the mission near Onondaga. Forewarned, its personnel fled. Significantly, Onondagas failed to resist the Mohawk onslaught, even though loss of the mission meant loss of status as special clients of New France. It also meant reversion to an older situation in which the Mohawks were "the head and the Leaders" of the Iroquois League.

Though frustrated in these experiments, French rulers would not abandon missions as instruments of policy; they made an occasion to force a mission upon its most intransigently hostile opponents, the Mohawks. To stop Mohawk ravaging of New France's backwoods settlers and Indian allies, the ministry in Paris sent over a regiment of veteran troops under Marquis de Tracy. In 1666, de Tracy marched against Mohawk villages and burned them, destroying food supplies for the winter as well as houses and crops in the field. The people had fled, but they could not ignore their damage nor the French capacity to repeat it at will. Grudgingly, the Mohawks sued for peace and were granted it on conditions, one of which required them to accept missionaries in their villages.

Again, the missions spawned factions, but this time the Black Robes adopted a new strategy. They withdrew converts completely from the tribal community and sent them to distant mission reservations near Montreal where the converts were free from the pressures of traditionalist kinsmen, and, incidentally, were completely under missionary control. The strategy was very successful and highly infuriating to traditional chiefs who saw the strength of their tribe being drained away. By 1680, the new mission villages had at least 400 Indian residents, most of whom were Mohawks. In the sources, they came to be called Caughnawaga Mohawks, and they came to act as some of New France's most dependable allies. (The community still exists, spelling itself *Kahnawake*.)

The missionaries adapted to circumstance, but some new refugee communities can be identified that followed the Caughnawaga pattern. In the seventeenth century, refugees from Mohawk wars and later "King Philip's War" came to Odanak (or St. Francis) where the St. Francis River joins the St. Lawrence downstream from Montreal. In the eighteenth century, many Iroquois abandoned the League's warring against New France by putting themselves under mission protection at Oswegatchie (or La Présentation) where Ogdensburg, New York, now stands. Still others fled to the Susquehannock homeland at Conestoga (Pa.) which was free of missions.

Many more missions were established, in varied forms, usually close to trading posts or armed garrisons (which were often the same) but all had in common that where they carried the Christian cross they also carried the French fleur-de-lys; and, where missionaries were set upon by resentful Indians, revenge would quickly be inflicted by French soldiers or allied convert Indians. The picture of the single Black Robe striding heroically into the wilderness needs more than a little adjustment.

After the disastrous end of Father Jacques Buteux's journey in 1652, French missionaries do not seem to have accompanied the northern hunting tribes of Canada on their seasonal rounds. The most successful missions targeted tribes with permanent villages north and northeast of New England and New-York. In Acadia (modern Nova Scotia) there was little need for separate mission establishments because intermarriage between Micmacs and French *habitants* created a population in which the same priests attended to both.

In the dark and bloody ground directly between Massachusetts and the St. Lawrence Valley—a land inhabited by Algonquian-speaking Western and Eastern Abenakis—French missions became sanctuaries for refugees from New England. Here the missions acted as *unifying* factors, joining religious sanctions to the obligatory hospitality of Indian custom. And here the motives of French statecraft were readily accepted by Indians who had been hounded out of their homelands by Puritan wars of aggression. It was not hard to persuade these refugee warriors to pursue revenge. Along with the Abenakis, Sokokis from the Connecticut Valley and Pennacooks from the Merrimack became crusading if somewhat syncretic Roman Catholics always in the fore of France's wars against Protestant heretics.

As the Reverend Thomas Charland writes about missionary Sebastien Rale who was killed and scalped in a raid by New Englanders, "Rale shared the fate of many other missionaries of this era who, willingly or not, found themselves and their work caught up in the larger colonial struggles of France and England in the New World." The Indians who were the objects of missionary work, and participants in it, were equally "caught up" in those colonial struggles. Many an Indian was handed a musket along with the cross.

In the English Protestant colonies, mission activity had none of the planned organization characteristic of Spanish and French Catholic effort. Regardless of phrases in colonial charters that spoke resoundingly of saving souls, English colonists were more intent on getting rid of Indians than on adopting them into Christian brotherhood for any purpose. Protestantism had developed no sort of organization like Franciscan and Jesuit missionary orders. In the seventeenth century, Protestant missions hardly existed except in the very special case of Massachusetts.

Early on, the Virginia Company was permitted to solicit donations from churches in England to support a missionary "college," but this was, in plain words, a racket. No attempt was ever made to build or staff the college. The money received was diverted to various businesses and purses, none of them sacred except to Mammon; and after the Powhatan uprising in 1622 even the pretense of converting the "savages" was dropped.

Massachusetts' charter also spoke grandly of bringing the light of salvation to the poor benighted natives, and Massachusetts' Puritan colonists long followed Virginia's Anglican example by pursuing other interests. A political crisis jolted Massachusetts' ruling oligarchy into action. In the midst of England's Puritan Revolution, powerful men had come to question the purity of New England's Puritans, so that a need for counterpropaganda appeared. In response to it, the General Court created a mission in 1646, and put its pastoral care under the Reverend John Eliot and its governmental administration under Colonel Daniel Gookin. To assure success, the General Court enacted the death penalty for "any person or persons whatsoever" for "wilfull or obstinate deniing the true God," and it outlawed all the rituals of traditional Indian worship. In John Eliot's words, "Religion would not consist with a mere receiving of the word. . . . Practical religion will throw down their heathenish idols and the sachem's tyrannical monarchy."

As in New France, Eliot and Gookin armed their converts and engaged them in various ways with other Indians. By a mere show of force, six "new towns" of Nipmucks were persuaded to accept mission supervision. (None of their inhabitants accepted baptism.) But when the "praying Indians" went to war against the Mohawks in 1669 they were handled roughly.

Like Virginia earlier, Massachusetts appealed to England for financial support for its mission, and received substantial sums for which substantial accounting was never made. However, the contributions from England seem to have been the only source of support for the mission and missionary. There is no record of appropriation from the colony's government, nor of contributions from individuals. Few historical records show more sanctimonious piety in words with less piety in performance, but the praying Indians did become, under direction, a force in intertribal politics; and in the circumstances of the time they necessarily affected decisions by neighboring colonies as well. Eliot's mission came to traumatic crisis during "King Philip's War" when the Nipmucks who had been "converted" by force joined Philip in the uprising—were indeed the first of Philip's allies.

(Family traditions have surfaced lately by which a number of living Indians charge that Eliot illicitly sired their ancestors during his visits to the mission village at Natick where he maintained a private apartment. In view of his documented lapses from truthfulness, such accounts must be respected as much or as little as family traditions of non-Indians, and certainly as much as the idolatrous gush by which Eliot has been almost deified as "the Apostle to the Indians." These Indian traditions are unproved, but not incredible. An Eliot family reunion would be an interesting affair.)

Eliot's was the official mission of Massachusetts Bay, and he came to be the special protégé of the English Society for the Propagation of the Gospell in New England. In the neighboring colonies of New Plymouth and Martha's Vineyard, separate missions were undertaken by devout individuals without official sponsorship, and before Eliot began. On Cape Cod, Richard Bourne went beyond preaching to accumulate a landed estate for the Mashpee Wampanoags which he tried to insulate against encroachment by a trust forbidding alienation of any part of the land without the consent of all the tribal members. It held good for a remarkably long time, serving to keep the tribe together even through the devastations of "King Philip's War" and the American Revolution. What distinguished Bourne's mission most sharply from Eliot's was total voluntarism. The Indians who came to Bourne came of their own accord.

Similarly, on Martha's Vineyard, a voluntaristic mission began in 1643 through the efforts of Thomas Mayhew, Jr., and a native named Hiacoomes. These two made headway against the usual opposition of traditionalist chiefs, and, when John Eliot started up, he pretended that their success was his doing. By accident the truth came out so that Eliot was forced to invent a lame alibi, but by that time he had become established.

There were good reasons for voluntarism on the Vineyard. A few score Englishmen dwelt among an estimated 3,000 Wampanoag Indians at a considerable distance from seaborne succor in case of conflict. Besides this potent consideration, Professor Jack Campisi's recent research has disclosed a legal situation that "Governor" Thomas Mayhew, Senior, kept well hidden during his lifetime and that his heirs were in no hurry to expose. Mayhew posed as proprietor of the island when in fact he had merely bought the right to *settle* from lords with conflicting charters. When Mayhew acquired Indian land rights, they were his only valid rights, but he sold tracts to other settlers as though he owned the whole place by charter.

This anomalous situation came to a head in 1682 after Thomas Mayhew died. Governor Thomas Dongan of New-York presented the claim that Martha's Vineyard was properly part of New-York, thus putting all land titles under a cloud. Missionary Matthew Mayhew, grandson of the colony's founder, struck a deal with Governor Dongan. Together, they put great pressure on sachem Joseph Mittark of the much-reduced Vineyard Indians who had consolidated and retreated to the western end of the island at Gay Head. Against the expressed wishes of his people, Joseph Mittark signed a deed conveying the Gay Head tribal lands to Thomas Dongan personally. Dongan set them up as his Manor of Martha's Vineyard on which the Indians became rent-paying tenant peasantry. Dongan sold his Manor in 1711 to the Society for the Propagation of the Gospel for £550, a satisfyingly large sum. It seems that the Society continued to collect rents. What it did for the benefit of the Indians is not apparent.

The other partner to the deal, missionary Matthew Mayhew, reaped his reward through appointment by Dongan to lucrative offices among the island's colonial towns. Dongan made him sheriff, chief justice, and clerk and register for Dukes County, besides steward of administration of Dongan's manor.

(I am so plain on this matter because I wrote rather naively about the Mayhew mission in an earlier book. For these improvements in understanding, I owe thanks to Professor Jack Campisi, an indefatigable researcher.)

In sum, the New England missions were variously successful in converting Indians to Calvinist Christianity; but, except for Richard Bourne's on Cape Cod, they functioned to divest the tribes of recognized rights in property. As for the "middle colonies" of New-York, the Jerseys, and Pennsylvania, no missionary effort was expended there in the seventeenth century except, perhaps, for an occasional sermon preached to Indians in language they did not understand. Dutchmen and Swedes in those colonies lacked interest. Quakers believed in setting an example of good conduct rather than compelling it, and they disdained organizations of clergy whom they condemned as "priests."

Jesuits in Maryland founded a mission simultaneously with the founding of the colony, but it soon came to grief in a quarrel between the missionaries and the lord proprietor over land rights derived from Indians instead of the said lord. He waxed wroth and they waned hastily, withdrawing from his immediate vicinity and concentrating their energies on colonials rather than Indians. Maryland's Protestant colonial settlers took a very

King Philip's throne. According to legend, this is where Wampanoag sachem Metacomet ("King Philip") presided over his people. The seat has a grand view across Mount Hope Bay in Narragansett Bay. Historical mythology proclaims that Indians "retreated" westward from Euramerican expansion, but Metacomet's resistance did not end until he was killed within a few yards of this spot. If he had gone to the mouth of Narragansett Bay and headed east, he would have had to swim to Europe. Wampanoag tradition reveres the place, as shown by the Naming Ceremony photographed there in 1969.

Naming Ceremony, May 30, 1969 at the King Philip Chair, Mount Hope, Bristol, R.I. Seated in the chair is Chief Mittark (Lorenzo Jeffers), Gay Head Wampanoag; Wamsutta (Frank James) stands in the foreground and Sweet Grass places her hands on Chief's shoulders. COURTESY OF THE HAFFENREFFER MUSEUM OF ANTHROPOLOGY, BROWN UNIVERSITY.

dim view of Jesuit work among the Indians which they suspected of being a conspiracy to turn the "savages" against themselves.

We have noticed already what happened in Virginia. South Carolinians were positively deadly to missions. During the seventeenth century, the Roman Catholic Black Robes had the missionary field almost exclusively as their own. Maryland's negative example demonstrates by its exception that success in that field depended largely on strong support from government.

CHAPTER 21

Partners and Rivals

> Trade was the lens through which Indians viewed Anglo-America, a lens that provided a distorted image of colonial society and encouraged natives to risk war. It was the loss of trade that then forced them to give up the fight, and the promise of trade's return that helped restore amicable relations. But even as Indian and colonist hammered out a new framework of exchange, it became clear that native independence was a thing of the past; the days when Indians could take trade or leave it were over. Trade was king.
> —JAMES H. MERRELL, *The Indians' New World*

Methods of trade varied according to circumstance. The "fugitive" trade from ships took place any which way and warily. Frenchmen resentful of chartered monopolies in Canadian trade beat the system by plunging deep into the interior to trade with hunters in their own villages. These famous *voyageurs* or *coureurs de bois* were tough men, capable of enduring many dangers and hardships, but it must be understood that they were not alone in a great wilderness. They traveled along Indian trails with Indian guides from village to village, often receiving hospitality, sometimes settling in for a year or more and joining an Indian family. These men had no "racial" aversion to Indians. Like sailors, they might have a sweetheart in every port, and the natural consequences included synethnic children. (*Synethnic* = of mixed genetic and ethnic stocks.)

New France benefited greatly from its licensed *voyageurs*. Quite apart from the great cargoes of peltry they brought to Quebec, their wandering ways created a network of political relationships, cemented by kin relationships, that multiplied the power of the small population of ethnic Frenchmen. It would be false, however, to leave an impression that liaisons between them and Indian women were always casual and fleeting. Many of these entrepreneurs in trade with Indians settled down with an Indian wife and her kinfolk, and adopted their tribe in preference to "civilization." This was especially true in the Mississippi Valley and in the Hudson Bay region where Englishmen also married Indians. (But few, if any, Englishmen stayed permanently with a tribe. Good family men while on duty at the Bay, they eventually returned to Britain leaving their Indian wives behind.)

We must guess about procedures of peripatetic smuggling *coureurs de bois* in Indian villages. Those who settled in would have had to behave themselves, but the wanderers might be tricky. They seem quickly to have picked up a technique of treating customers to a drink of rum or brandy before getting down to business and the sale of more drinks became part of the business, but the trader had to be a little careful about that because Indians who felt badly cheated could turn violent, and in their home villages no one would interpose. Apart from such hazards, which could be forestalled by a little common sense, the safety of traders in Indian country was phenomenal. They marched without escort through thousands of miles of trails and towns in far less danger than in the streets of a modern city. (In the Far West, however, and as time went on, hazards increased. Nineteenth-century homesteaders' seizure of lands embittered Indians into violence.)

Business at the more permanent European trading posts required formal arrangements of a political or diplomatic nature. "Peace and trade we take to be one thing," summarized one Seneca. Unlike Dutchmen who traded with Spaniards at the height of the Netherlands' rebellion against the Spanish crown, or colonials of varied nationalities who smuggled lucratively with enemies of their crowns, Indians would not permit trade until peace had been arranged beforehand. Such treaties between tribe and tribe, or between tribe and province, might be a barely minimal nonaggression pact or might extend to full defensive-offensive alliance. Each treaty, when available, must be read with as much care as treaties between European states. When Europeans formed one of the contracting parties, one must remember that the parties understood a treaty from the viewpoints of their different societies. Indians regarded such bicultural negotiations as agreements between sovereign peers, but most Europeans clearly regarded them as arrangements of necessity and convenience, to be dispensed with when circumstances would permit. New-York's Colonel Caleb Heathcote succinctly expressed the British conception in a letter to the ministry in 1715. He recommended an invitation to the "Heads of the Indians in their respective governments" to treat about complaints and grievances, "assuring them of redresse" so that "we may if possible keep the Indians quiet and in temper till we have our country better settled and secured and the French rooted out, and then we may expect to have the heathen on better terms." He added, "altho' justice ought forever to be done 'em."

Because Indians lacked literacy, we must conjecture the contents of intertribal agreements by interpretation of events. A major feature seems to have concerned access to one part or another of the trading cycle. Tribes competed over access to the trading post, and the tribe in whose territory the post was located exploited that advantage by demanding tribute or privilege from more distant tribes. Along the way a tribe might demand a toll for passage through its territory. (The classic example is the Allumettes on the Ottawa River who stopped canoes until they were paid off.) At the interior, the tribes possessing good hunting territories guarded them jealously. Especially when desirable furbearing animals had been hunted to near-extinction near a trading post, which happened rapidly, the resident tribe had to make terms for access to distant stocks of animals beyond its own bounds. Through variations on these themes, with complex interventions by Europeans, the notorious Iroquoian Beaver Wars came about. Similar hostilities broke out near Hudson's Bay Company posts between Crees and Assiniboines on one side, and more distant opposing Sioux tribes seeking direct contact with the posts.

Competition was also a major fact of life for European traders and commercial nations. Marylanders insisted that their war with the Susquehannock Indians came about because of the Indians being instigated by Virginia's William Claiborne. Rivalry between Hurons and Mohawks was at the same time competition between New France and New Netherland. Struggle between Susquehannocks on one side and Onondagas, Oneidas, and Cayugas on the other was supported and instigated by New Sweden against New Netherland. In due course, England took over the roles of Swedes and Dutchmen in order to face the French of Canada from New England to Virginia, but this frontier was not a line; it was a vast region inhabited by the tribes allied to both empires.

In absolute contravention of myths about hunting Indians "retiring before the advance of civilization," D. W. Moodie has found that when fur traders stretched their lines of communication too far, a band of hunting-and-gathering Ojibwas moved to the south shore of Lake Superior and took up farming to feed the traders. As a business, of course. An odd sort of "transit of civilization," but on record.

James R. Gibson's studies of the Russian fur trade stress that Siberia's climate handicapped the Russians by requiring them to ship provisions from home while American traders had the great advantage of living off the country—more precisely, off the produce of the country's native residents.

Sooner or later, however, as colonial populations grew, newcoming European immigrants established farms and towns of their own near the trading posts, and pushed the Indians farther west: or north or south, but away.

The statement must be qualified in the case of New Orleans where some Indians were welcomed for what Governor Bienville called "the abundance of provisions that they have furnished us." As historian Daniel H. Usner, Jr., remarks, in the eighteenth century, "provisioning early New Orleans with food, more than any other activity, integrated Indians into the social and economic life of the town."

Exclusion of Indians—in effect a form of segregation—was especially true for the British colonies between the Atlantic Coast and the Appalachian Mountains, where immigration was heavy and land hunger intense. Much nonsense has been written about "racial" differences between the British and the Frenchmen and Spaniards in the colonies. In this mythology, Englishmen supposedly possess inherent antagonisms toward Indians contrary to the psychic makeup of Frenchmen and Spaniards that permits them to accept Indians as neighbors. (The whispered hint is that they can do so because they are not equal to the British in civilization.) The real differences between these peoples arose from history, policy, and circumstance. Without digressing too far, we may note that at Hudson Bay the Company's agents were uninterested in acquiring landed estates.

Another frontier region came into being between the bellicose colonists of South Carolina and the Spaniards of Florida as each side vied for the trade and clientage of the tribes between; and later, when France founded Louisiana in 1698, this southern frontier extended through a broad swath from the Atlantic Ocean to the Mississippi River. It was deadly for the Apalachee and Timucuan Indians in Spanish missions. Carolinians organized and led great raids by Cherokees and Creeks against the missions for plunder in the form of captives to be sold in West Indian slave marts.

There was no such thing as "racial solidarity" in the seventeenth century. Even national identity flickered in various forms. South Carolina's management of Indian commerce and diplomacy varied widely from what was done in New-York, even more so from Pennsylvania. The "Goose Creek Men" of South Carolina resembled New France's *coureurs de bois* in eager willingness to carry trade goods deep into Indian country instead of waiting until Indians brought commodities to piedmont trading posts. When Frenchmen founded Louisiana, they discovered that Carolina traders had already reached tribes along the Mississippi and had made alliances.

René Robert Cavelier de La Salle dreamed of a great French empire in the vast Mississippi Valley, and initiated France's imperial outreach by cruising southward down the river in 1682, negotiating with tribes all the way. The French crown responded slowly and hesitantly to La Salle's urging. Meantime, South Carolina's Thomas Nairne and colleagues coveted the same great valley for England and penetrated it from the east, also negotiating with the tribes.

French ministers countered the Carolinian thrust by founding Biloxi in 1698 as the first settlement / fort of Louisiana, after which the Carolinians accelerated their challenge, assisted by Creeks and Chickasaws. Louisiana Frenchmen opposed them with Choctaw allies. The tribes of the lower Mississippi were drawn into a bloody maelstrom of vicarious imperial conflict.

A hypothesis seems tenable that the distinct northern and southern regions of the future United States developed in part from the northern and southern frontiers that got English colonials into the habit of facing away from each other toward their separate northern and southern antagonists. There was no common frontier of Europeans versus Indians, much less one of such abstractions as civilizations versus savagery. Seventeenth-century frontiers invariably involved a partnership of colony and tribe facing against a similar opposed partnership.

It is well, however, to recognize that the partnerships varied in their objectives. In earlier chapters, I have stressed the great variety of Indian societies and cultures. Despite natural tendencies to homogenize Europeans of any given nationality simply for the convenience of dealing with miscellaneous persons under one rubric, it is clearly apparent that the violent expansionists, such as the Carolinians, Virginians, and New England's Puritans, acted historical roles very different from those of Rhode Islanders or Pennsylvanians, who preferred gradual advance by cooperation above sudden conquest. Yet all were English. Equally, on the French side, imperialists like La Salle seem to have been cast from a mold different from that of the Acadian peasantry who labored incessantly to make productive farms and big families. As with the English, the motives were conquest for the one type and cooperation for the other. In categorizing according to nations, we unconsciously adopt use of power as our organizing theme.

A quite different sort of history would result if we categorized *across* national lines according to the eternal struggles between conquest types and cooperating types. One manifestation of such struggles is smuggling which was at the very heart of the intersocietal / intertribal / international trade. For Indian traders, the desires and edicts of rival crowns were far less important than the desires and offers of English or French traders; and when the colonial traders ventured to Indian villages, no means existed to control them from Europe.

Looking ahead, we may see that the major region of contention between French and English empires became the Northeast. Not by coincidence, their armies followed long-established trade routes in two directions: between Albany and Montreal on a north-south axis, and through the mountain passes that linked Albany and Philadelphia in the East with the Ohio country and Detroit in the West. Control of these routes became a major preoccupation of imperialists, traders, and tribes. Even in the late seventeenth century, the route between Montreal and Albany, through Lakes Champlain and George (the Mahican Channel) was used by French campaigners, and in the eighteenth century it became the central arena of imperial combat. Until the middle of the eighteenth century, the east-west route did not seem so important to planners in London and Paris, partly because its traffic was left to use and control by tribes along the way.

Special notice must be given to the smuggling along these routes, which was the dominant type of trade conducted there. *Smuggling is a form of accommodation.* In defiance of official decrees from both sides, traders and merchants and their associated Indians carried furs from Montreal and Detroit to exchange for manufactured goods from the markets of Albany and Philadelphia. This was highly illegal and highly prosperous "trading with the enemy." In the seventeenth century, imperial controls had not yet been developed enough to do much about the smuggling, but the crowns made it a serious issue later.

British colonists founded Charles Town, South Carolina, in 1670. Spanish soldiers promptly raided toward it, provoking retaliation and initiating an undeclared war that lasted thirty years. In this, the chief sufferers were the Catholic Indians of the missions who were raided again and again by Protestant English slave traders organizing war parties of traditionalist Creek Indians who shared in the booty. Neither racial solidarity nor the humanitarian creeds of the varied religions were much in evidence. By 1708, as many as 10,000 to 12,000 Catholic Indians had been seized and sold into West Indian slavery. Survivors fled to refuge near St. Augustine where a remnant of the mission system was re-established. The rest of the missions ceased to exist. Their destruction was not the outcome of infidel hostility; it was effected by opposing Christians.

In the wake of Carolinian destruction of the missions, the whole Spanish system of administration through "two republics" collapsed. (See chapter 22.) In the ensuing chaos, vassals rebelled, brigandage broke out, and many Indians fled to what they thought were safer regions. "In the eighteenth century," as Professor Bushnell tells, "little was left in the provinces to remind one of the time of the two republics or of the rulers who had shared sovereignty with Spaniards. It was the English system that survived."

CHAPTER 22

Some Effects of Trade

The fur trade, from the earliest settlement of Canada, was considered of the first importance to that colony. The country was then so populous, that, in the vicinity of the establishments, the animals whose skins were precious, in a commercial view, soon became very scarce, if not altogether extinct. They were, it is true, hunted at former periods, but merely for food and clothing. The Indians, therefore, to procure the necessary supply, were encouraged to penetrate into the country, and were generally accompanied by some of the Canadians, who found means to induce the remotest tribes of natives to bring the skins which were most in demand, to their settlements, in the way of trade.

—Sir Alexander Mackenzie (1801)

Wherever intersocietal trade developed, it caused transformation of social relationships among eastern tribes. In the sixteenth century these tribes subsisted by a mix of planting, hunting, and fishing, with well-established sexual division of labor and duties. Men hunted and fished and did heavy work of felling trees and breaking sod. Women planted and weeded, and attended to domestic duties around the house. (Among other things they developed sewing and beadwork into an art form much admired in museums and craft shops today.) In principle, the products of the chase and fishery were male property while crops belonged to the women, but the constraints of property were ameliorated by custom which required sharing of everything except very personal articles; and Indian hospitality was given so freely as to excite wonder among European observers. Children and infirm old people were looked after by kin networks, and the elders' crafts produced small surpluses for trade between villages and tribes.

Change became noticeable when able-bodied men began to specialize in hunting for trade with colonials. This sort of commercial hunting differed from previous hunting for subsistence by requiring more time from the hunters, and as game dwindled in numbers near the villages the men had to spend yet more time traveling long distances to good territories, often disappearing for months at a time. Women also labored harder. Besides the extra chores necessitated while men were away, the women faced the prospect of still more work on the men's return with skins for the women to "dress." (In industry, such processes are called tanning.)

While the men were distant, their villages lay open to attack by enemies and rivals who often took advantage of such undefended communities. The trade multiplied motives for attack as rivals strove for advantage, and their colonial patrons pursued their own interests by instigating intertribal raids.

One result of this situation was a new series of migrations by villages and bands moving from former territories to the vicinity of colonial trading posts (and missions, about which more below). Crees settled around the Hudson's Bay Company's "factories," Shawnees first traveled to join La Salle's posts in the Midwest, then trekked east to settle near James Logan's establishment on the Susquehanna, and Creeks moved closer to South Carolina's trade. These examples are chosen to give an idea of the range of the process; they could be multiplied. Indians involved heavily in the intersocietal trade saved much fatiguing travel by living near the posts; they could negotiate bargains and gain a degree of protection from colonial garrisons stationed in or near the post.

At Hudson Bay, the trade was almost a world apart. In 1660, two French *coureurs de bois*, named Groseilliers and Radisson, made a very successful trading journey to the vicinity of Hudson Bay and returned with a great cargo of the finest quality furs, the kind grown by animals in cold climates. The trip should have made the traders' fortune. Instead, because they had gone out without authorization from the chartered monopolists at Quebec, our hapless adventurers were fined and punished and forced to pay heavy duties on their great haul. As they watched the anticipated fortune vanish through hazards greater than any they had faced among the Indians, Groseilliers and Radisson bethought themselves of ways to get even. They went to London.

Important men in English court circles were much interested in their account of friendly Indians willing to trade very valuable peltry, and accessible by seas circumventing the French barrier along the St. Lawrence River and Great Lakes. On 2 May 1670, the crown issued a charter to the Governor and Company of Adventurers of England Trading into Hudson's Bay. Large territories were "granted" under the name of Rupert's Land, but the merchant adventurers long restricted their activities to trade at posts or "factories" around the rim of the Bay. (The Company still exists, but it operates department stores now.)

Almost immediately, the Company's posts attracted bands of hunting Crees who settled nearby and provided food and natively crafted equipment as well as furs. These clients were the "Home Guard" in Company jargon. Their women provided entertainment for the Company's lonesome employees during the long winter months despite the home office's strongly worded instructions to the contrary, and the natural result was a crop of synethnic offspring. In the mythology of race, Britons were not supposed to descend to this sort of thing, but the myth went into a deep freeze at Hudson Bay.

Very genuine advantages accrued from liaisons with Cree women, quite apart from sexual satisfactions. E. E. Rich, the official historian of the Company, acknowledges that "on the trail a squaw was not a luxury but a necessity; she took an essential share of the duties of travel, both on the canoe and at the portages." (Oxford Professor Rich's "squaw" terminology unfortunately displays the condescension native to Oxford for every ethnic group beyond, and sometimes including, Cambridge, where it is shared and reciprocated.) Canadian Sylvia Van Kirk says it better. "In the Canadian West . . . alliances with Indian women were the central social aspect of the fur traders' progress across the country . . . The marriage of a fur trader and an Indian woman was not just a 'private' affair; the bond thus created helped to advance trade relations with a new tribe, placing the Indian wife in the role of cultural liaison between the traders and her kin." And she was needed for very practical reasons: she made moccasins for her man, sometimes at the rate of a pair each day, and snowshoes without which a man could not even venture out to collect firewood in winter. "There is no stirring without them," wrote one famous trader. Women performed other necessary chores also—stress *necessary*—which need not be itemized here.

In such remote places as Hudson Bay, people got along with each other regardless of racial and cultural taboos, and in defiance of the strictures of government and clergy. Indians did not fight Europeans except under instigation of other Europeans. Rather, Indians fought other Indians, and British traders fought French *coureurs de bois* for economic advantage, while Indians and Europeans peacefully exchanged goods and genes. So it was in the seventeenth century in places where racial conceptions were irrelevant to the business of living. Change came in the eighteenth century, to be sure, with sad effects.

From the frozen Arctic to subtropical Florida, differences went deeper than climate. Spaniards concentrated their colonizing efforts in the northern parts of present-day Florida and along the coasts of Georgia and even, for a while, as far as Santa Elena on today's Parris Island, South Carolina (where U.S. Marines train now). Spanish colonists were few in those parts. The crown established *presidios* with garrisons of soldiers, but surrounding Indians far outnumbered them. The crown's chosen instrument for subjecting and assimilating Indians was the mission.

Some Indians were attracted to the Spaniards' powerful God. Regardless of theology, other Indians came in and subjected themselves to mission discipline as a way of participating in economic benefits and escaping intertribal war as well as the displeasure of Spanish troops. Here also, as in the far north and in the "middle," Indians were attracted to the colonizing Europeans rather than motivated to withdraw from them. The attractions must have been powerfully seductive, for mission discipline was strong and often unpleasant. Among the Spaniards, caste distinctions, conceived in racial and religious terms, were strong. The mission friars held it their duty to transform pagan Indians into mirror images of Catholic Spaniards, segregated in the missions. This motive required a head-on attack on tribal cultures and sometimes on Indian persons. Men must have only one wife, no matter how great their chiefly dignities. All traditional rituals of worship must be abjured and rejected. "Nakedness," defined broadly, must be covered. Hair must be worn at approved lengths and styles—and on and on. Above all else, the missionary friars must be obeyed in everything. The Indian convert in the mission experienced change more traumatic than the Spaniard who crossed the Atlantic.

Uprisings occurred, but rarely, and were suppressed by the soldiers. One must remember that though the missions were peaceful and the priests unarmed, the threat of force was never out of sight or mind. Nevertheless, it seems that during the times of their success the missions did bring stability and peace to northern Florida. Many came and went after only brief stays—a scholar has identified more than 130 separate locations—but others took root. "At the height of its development in the late seventeenth century," writes Jerald T. Milanich, "the Franciscan mission system included 40 churches and 52 missionaries."

But the Spaniards in sixteenth and seventeenth century Florida adopted still another agency to facilitate rule. Amy Turner Bushnell comments that "besides the secular and church officials, a third power existed in the provinces of Spanish Florida, that of the region's Indian chiefs, who survived the foreign invasion to become integral to the governmental system that developed out of it." The system evolved by experiment. After failure in the sixteenth century of an effort to integrate Indian and Spanish populations, the crown separated them in two "republics" territorially and governmentally apart though under the crown's general suzerainty.

Indian chiefs who converted to Catholicism and swore allegiance to the king were accepted as allies and recognized as vassal seigneurs. They were exempt from labor, tribute, and corporal punishment. Some of them even resisted Christianity and got away with it as long as they performed their duties as vassals.

Exceptionally among European colonials, crown officials allowed Indians to sue Spaniards in court, and even appointed counsel in the person of a "defender of the Indians." Astonishingly, Professor Bushnell reports a case which was decided in favor of Indians suing against a mission friar. Nothing like it ever happened in the colonies of England or France.

If the Indians gained a measure of peace and stability from the missions, they paid for it. John H. Hann observes that St. Augustine had a chronic shortage of food and labor early in the seventeenth century, and that this was "an important consideration" for the Spanish authorities in launching a permanent mission among the Apalachee Indians. Milanich remarks that "the mission system was intertwined with Spanish ranches for which missionized natives could serve as laborers and transporters of food and goods to St. Augustine for sale or export."

Once more, the terrible ravages of epidemic disease must be noticed. Even at the height of mission success in mid-seventeenth century, plague and pox claimed multitudes of victims. In 1659, 10,000 Indians died in a single epidemic of measles. More "wild" Indians were brought in to restore the missions' numbers—the methods of persuasion are not mentioned—and the institution might have survived except for unrelenting attack by human (and Christian) foes.

CHAPTER 23

Wars in the East

Warfare was "so integrated into the whole fabric of Eastern [Indians'] culture, so dominantly emphasized within it, that escape from it was well-nigh impossible."

—ALFRED LOUIS KROEBER

Indian warfare is "farre lesse bloudy and devouring than the cruel Warres of Europe."

—ROGER WILLIAMS

As we cannot openly oppose the English ventures, I think that we cannot do better than to incite the Indians to continue warring on the English.

—ABBÉ JEAN-LOUIS LE LOUTRE

Informe yourself of the process of the Warre [between the Susquehannocks and the Five Nations] and if you finde them slack in itt, to press them discreetly to a vigourous prosecution of it.

—Maryland's governor and council

Because histories of Indian–colonial relations are usually dominated by intersocietal violence (often called interracial war or savage resistance to civilization), I have deliberately chosen to concentrate in the foregoing discussion on means and institutions by which the peoples got along with each other. But, of course, there was fighting also. It would be very foolish to ignore the violent conflicts, if only to note the variety of proximate causes and the circumstances of their occurrence. The great underlying cause needs no long disquisition; it was simply the determination of Europeans to become masters of the continent and its inhabitants. This should come as no surprise to anyone even slightly acquainted with the history of Europe. It sometimes becomes a little confusing because the Europeans, in America as well as in their home continent, could not agree *which* of them should be masters, and so they locked in struggle with each other, often clandestinely by means of surrogate Indian allies. In terms of status, however, those allies were always regarded as tributaries or clients, never as full peers no matter how useful they might be. In North America as in Spanish America, the relation between the two societies, so far as Europeans were concerned, was one of caste. Full conquest is not necessary to create castes. Caste relations were the product not only of conquest, but also of the effort to conquer; and this was so whether the substance of caste was conceived in terms of religion, race, or civilization / savagery.

The desire for mastery over persons was by no means exclusively European. Indians had it too, but they learned rather quickly that they could not master the Europeans. Accordingly, their efforts became limited to trying to conquer other Indians. The first three-quarters of the seventeenth century saw much intertribal conflict for tribal purposes. Until 1675, a number of tribes set goals for themselves and pursued their own objectives. There were even instances of a strong tribe compelling a militarily weak colony to collaborate in the tribe's plans. For instance, in 1658, a Mohawk delegation needed a French-language interpreter from the Dutch at Fort Orange in order to negotiate at Quebec for the return of a hostage. When Dutch magistrates demurred, the Mohawks overbore them with an implied joint promise and threat, and they got their interpreter. Situations like this changed as inverse changes in population brought alterations in real power. During the seventeenth century, European colonials grew to outnumber the constantly diminishing Indians along the eastern seaboard, and as colonial numbers increased, colonial cockiness inflated.

After 1675, only the Iroquois Five Nations still held, or rather had regained, some power of initiative in the Northeast. That became possible through carefully modulated cooperation with the province of New-York, in return for which the Iroquois were allowed considerable latitude of self-determination so long as they did not interfere with New-York's purposes.

But this is to run ahead of events for the sake of perspective. Let us return to the century's beginning.

The episodes of Indians taking up arms against European colonials early in the seventeenth century can be dealt with briefly because they were few in number. In 1597, the Guale Indians led into the new century by rebelling against their Franciscan missions in what was then "Florida" (off the Georgia coast). They were quickly suppressed by Spanish destruction of their villages and crops. The missions were rebuilt and maintained until final destruction later by English raids from South Carolina.

In 1622, the Powhatan Indians at Chesapeake Bay surprised the colonists of Jamestown and massacred more than five hundred before being beaten down. (That this was a massacre cannot be disputed, but as has been noticed elsewhere general usage has Indians *massacring* Europeans though other terms are used when Europeans kill Indians or other Europeans. In the Jamestown incident, it is worth remembering that more than 18,000 English persons had died of neglect and cruelty by the sponsoring Virginia Company before the Indians struck.)

In revenge of the Powhatan attack, Virginians summoned the Indians to a treaty and poisoned their water. There are no statistics on the number of Indians who died in this sort of "incident."

In 1644, the Powhatans rose again, and again were put down bloodily. Thereafter their spirit was broken. Virginia's Indians coped with colonial power by taking initiatives within tolerated limits. It cannot be said without this qualification that the Indians made their own policies. The pattern repeated itself so regularly in other regions as colonial powers grew that it may be accepted as a rule of historical development.

In 1658 and 1664, the Esopus Indians of the Hudson Valley rose against New Netherland. Notably, Mohawk warriors aided the Dutch troops to defeat and disperse the Esopus resisters. Some scattered to refuge with other tribes; some descendants survived into the twentieth century at a hideout called Eagle's Nest near Kingston, New York. These latter ceased to have any political or diplomatic significance.

In 1656, Florida missions were upset again by rebellion of the Timucuas of the northwestern region of the colony. Disease and the military repression that followed the rebellion reduced Timucuan numbers so greatly that Indians from other tribes had to be drawn in to repopulate the missions. We are never sure about survivors of such disasters who may have fled to sanctuary elsewhere, but the Timucuan polity ceased to exist.

In short, the history of the uprisings is a catalogue of unrelieved disasters.

This is not to say that all the conflicts were started by Indians. In 1603, Samuel de Champlain suggested to his Algonquin and Montagnais allies on the St. Lawrence that they should combine against the Mohawks, and he promised to aid them. He kept his promise in 1609.

In 1636, Massachusetts Bay picked a fight with the Pequot Indians to acquire their tribute and territory. Connecticut forestalled Massachusetts by burning the Pequot women and children in a lightly defended "fort," thus obtaining legal grounds for claiming "rights of conquest" in Pequot lands and surviving persons. Notably, Massachusetts had Narragansett allies, and Connecticut had Mohegan allies in this action. (Mashantucket-Pequot descendants now have a reservation near Norwich, Connecticut, and Narragansetts live nearby.)

New Netherland's bellicose governor Willem Kieft thought the massacre technique was a good idea, and in 1640 he imitated it at the patroonship of "Pavonia" (Jersey City) thus igniting a series of Indian uprisings that got out of control until he hired some colonials from New England to help. (More deviously than the Indians, they became even less controllable.)

Maryland's authorities were annoyed by Susquehannocks trading with competitors and perhaps raiding Indians allied to Maryland. (The records of this time are vague and unreliable.) In 1642, the colony sent out troops who triumphed easily over the poorly armed Susquehannocks; but a follow-up campaign in 1643 came to grief because the Delaware Bay Swedes, who did not intend to lose their best trading partners to Maryland, had meantime armed and trained the Susquehannocks.

In South Carolina, colonists became annoyed by their allied Westo Indians whom they regarded as altogether too independent. As Verner W. Crane remarks, "From 1674 to 1680, the Westo Alliance formed the cornerstone of the South Carolina Indian system" but friction developed between the colony's traders and its proprietors because the chief benefit of Westo trade went to the proprietors. These traders were notorious, even among other colonials, for their belligerence. They found, or made, excuses for war in 1680, gained allies among the Savannah (Shawnee) Indians, and soon took Westo captives for sale into West Indian slavery, just as the Westos themselves had earlier joined in capturing and enslaving Florida's mission Indians.

By and large, however, colonials preferred not to provoke beyond patience the surrounding Indians who still, in the first half of the seventeenth century, greatly outnumbered the colonials. It was not the part of wisdom to stir up so great a potential enemy. Among other things, the English crown frowned on Indian wars that might jeopardize its colonial possessions. The Virginia Company lost its charter after the Powhatan rising. Besides, such wars were downright foolish commercially. Trade with those Indians, which paid much of the colonies' bills, stopped completely in wartime.

During this era, Indians digested the lessons of unassisted military confrontation and generally avoided it when possible. While colonial populations remained relatively small, and colonial land hunger remained relatively restrained, the tribes preserved enough political independence to undertake initiatives of their own against other tribes.

Intertribal conflicts generated out of struggle for advantage in inter-societal commerce. Of these the best known were the so-called Beaver Wars between Iroquoians. As noted in chapter 5 above, the Huron Confederation developed a great circuit of intertribal trade in aboriginal times; and when Frenchmen appeared on the St. Lawrence River, the Hurons added the French to their preexisting arrangements. This was highly satisfactory to the parties concerned, but exasperating to the outsider tribes of the Iroquois Five Nations and more than slightly annoying to the Dutch allies of the Five Nations. The cause of their irritation was very simple: enormous quantities of furs gathered up by tribes on the Huron circuit went to French merchants at Montreal (founded in 1642) instead of passing through the Five Nations to Dutch Fort Orange.

At first the Mohawks tried to deal themselves in to this lucrative business. They treated with New France at Trois Rivières in 1645 in a conference that enraptures anthropologists with its description of native ritual, but this did not have the effect intended by the Mohawks who were still kept outside the Huron-French circuit. Changing strategy, the Mohawks demanded guns from the Dutch to settle the issue by force. Since the Dutch had a fair notion of which way those guns would point, they resisted only feebly and supplied 400. The records say they sold the guns, and probably they did, but one suspects a discount price.

Guns in hand, Mohawk warriors picked up Seneca allies, and a thousand men descended on Huronia in the winter of 1649–50. There had been earlier raids by the Senecas, but never anything on this scale and never before with firearms. In a manner of speaking the Hurons were prepared for defeat in advance by intrusion among them of French Jesuit missions. (A priest was always accompanied by an entourage of lay assistants.) With the missions came epidemic diseases that reduced Huron numbers from 30,000 (Champlain's count) to 10,000 (according to a missionary), and the survivors were torn into factions of Catholic converts and traditionalists. Factionalism became embittered as missionaries taught their converts to heap scorn on traditional ways and the French supplied firearms to converts but withheld them from traditionalists. When the Mohawks and Senecas struck, the demoralized Hurons repulsed them briefly, but gave up the struggle afterward. They broke up into bands and scattered far and wide, taking terrible casualties from exposure and privation as well as continued raids from exultant Iroquois. Of the survivors, most ended as an adopted village of the Senecas.

The Iroquois sent colonies of their own into the broad peninsula of Ontario that sticks down between Lakes Huron, Erie, and Ontario—

formerly territory controlled by the Hurons. Scholars have debated whether the Iroquois wanted to acquire the Hurons' former role as middlemen in the trade, but there seems to be agreement now that the Iroquois wanted access to hunting territory because game in their own lands had been hunted to the point of inadequacy for commercial purposes.

The Iroquois confirmed their victory by subsequent attacks on remaining tribes of the old Huron circuit: Wenros, Eries, Petuns, and Neutrals. By 1655, the Iroquois had cleared out their Iroquoian enemies from the east shore of Lake Huron and the north and south shores of Lake Erie. Full of triumphal pride, they aimed at expanding their domination into New England, the Susquehanna Valley, and the Illinois country of the Mississippi Valley; but they had reached their limits. Though their opponents suffered heavy casualties, the Iroquois were turned back on all sides. Algonquian-speaking Western Abenakis on the east, Iroquoian Susquehannocks on the south, and Algonquian Illinois in the southwest had found their own sources of firearms, and their resistance was tough and effective. There is no truth in Cadwallader Colden's fable that the mere mention of the Mohawks' name caused other tribes to tremble. Equally groundless is the myth that the Iroquois conquered a vast empire from the Mississippi to the Atlantic. In fact, Iroquois war parties suffered losses as great as their enemies, and when the tide of battle turned against them they were forced to withdraw to their original homeland along the Finger Lakes region and Mohawk Valley of upstate New York.

They, too, suffered from epidemic disease, just as their enemies did, but they had a technique for partially restoring the numbers lost by war and pox. They spared young captives and women, and inducted them in rituals that combined adoption into families with naturalization into the families' tribes.

Having challenged the alliance of tribes under French patronage, the Iroquois acquired New France's unremitting hostility. In 1666, a regiment of crack French troops marched under the Marquis de Tracy into the Mohawk homeland. Most of the inhabitants had fled, but de Tracy's men destroyed everything in sight, and the loss was not negligible. Without help from friends and allies, the Mohawks would have starved. Their attitude toward New France became considerably more subdued.

Maryland armed Susquehannocks to invade Iroquoia from the south. Massachusetts' John Pynchon armed Mahicans from his Springfield trading post to attack from the east so ruinously that in 1672, Mohawks pled with the English and Dutch at Albany to make peace for them. By 1673, the Iroquois anxiously and futilely appealed to New France's Governor Frontenac to rescue them. In short, the Mohawks seemed on the verge of extinction.

We must veer aside for a moment to notice that New Netherland, the Dutch ally of the Iroquois, had disappeared under conquest by England's duke of York. That happened in 1664. Though the Mohawks rushed to ally with the new province of New-York, its rulers were incompetent novices in Indian affairs, easily diddled by experienced neighbors and not much use to their clients. By 1674, however, New-York got a brilliant new governor, Edmund Andros, who used tribal alliances to build New-York into a great colonial power despite its small European population. Like the French, Andros understood that power could be built on Indian populations. When in 1675 some tribes were provoked intolerably to fight back against colonial attacks, Andros saw the wars as both menace and opportunity. He aborted the menace and seized the opportunity with the aid of his clients among the Iroquois.

In 1675, Marylanders and Virginians jointly attacked the Susquehannocks whose survivors fled to the woods and retaliated on backwoods colonials. In the same year, New Plymouth, Massachusetts, and Connecticut attacked the Wampanoags. As the Indian chief Metacomet was called "King Philip," the attack against his people is miscalled "King Philip's War." (The name reverses responsibility by making the victim into the aggressor. It was a necessary propaganda technique to avert the wrath of the English crown whose ministers took a very dim view of the war; and the name as well as the propaganda has been accepted and adopted by most American historians.)

The Puritan New Englanders (as opposed to heterodox Rhode Islanders) quickly expanded their war to an attempted conquest of the Narragansetts whose misfortune was the possession of valuable land. Once again, "rights of conquest" were in the wind. It is worth notice that both Wampanoags and Narragansetts lived on the Atlantic Coast and were far from "retreating westward before the advance of civilization." This writer has sat in King Philip's "throne" at Bristol, Rhode Island, and gazed across the bay and ocean toward Europe, without any land to obstruct my gaze except the islands of Narragansett Bay.

The desperate Indians fought back. They gained some tribal allies and negotiated for more from among the tribes allied to New France who could have supplied arms and equipment as well as manpower. A horrible prospect loomed before Governor Berkeley of Virginia and Governor Andros of New-York. Suppose a grand alliance should form of all the tribes from Maine to Virginia? Berkeley was immobilized by Bacon's Rebellion, but Andros moved decisively.

He armed the Mohawks to intercede in "King Philip's War" *against* the tribes of New England, and when the latter were shattered, Andros offered refuge and protection to such of them as could escape to his jurisdiction in New-York. (Others fled to New France, and some traveled as far as what was to become Pennsylvania.) Andros fended off vengeful New Englanders and compelled them to accept peace with the victory he had made possible. (They did massacre the Indians they could get their hands on.)

Southward, Andros offered the same sort of peace and protection to refugee Susquehannocks, and he similarly frustrated bloodthirsty Marylanders and Virginians. In the sequel, a new institution emerged: the Covenant Chain. The refuge arranged by Andros was continued by William Penn when his new province of Pennsylvania was carved out of New-York in 1681, with the consequence that from 1677 until 1755 a long peace prevailed in Pennsylvania where there was no war between Indians and colonists. In the Delaware tradition recorded by Moravian missionary John Heckewelder, many Indian refugees from wars elsewhere found Pennsylvania to be "a last, delightful asylum." The province's Susquehanna Valley, especially, became sanctuary for tribal remnants from all quarters of the compass.

CHAPTER 24

The Covenant Chain

About two Years after the Arrival of the English, an English
Governor came to Albany, and finding what great Friendship subsisted between us and the Dutch, he approved it mightily, and desired
to make as strong a League, and to be upon as good Terms with us
as the Dutch were, with whom he was united, and to become one
People with us: and by his further Care in looking into what had
passed between us, he found that the Rope which tied the Ship to
the great Mountain was only fastened with Wampum, which was
liable to break and rot, and to perish in a Course of Years; he therefore told us, he would give us a Silver Chain which would be much
stronger, and would last for ever. This we accepted, and fastened the
Ship with it, and it has lasted ever since.
—ONONDAGA CHIEF CANASATEGO, 1744

This name requires a word of explanation because none of our standard
histories has noticed the Covenant Chain's existence, preferring instead
to blather about a great, imagined savage empire ruled by the Iroquois.
The Chain was the reality behind this myth. (I am constantly being surprised and amazed at how much of Indian history is the product of super-
heated imagination bent toward making the plain facts of the sources fit
into preconceptions.) Among other reasons for the consignment of the
Covenant Chain to limbo is the influence of legal conceptions and terminology created for purposes of government rather than history. These
conceptions deny the possibility of such political entities as the Chain on
the grounds that there could not be independent entities within a sovereignty. Minds formed on such conceptions were blinded by conquest
logic against the plain evidence of recorded facts.

What made the Covenant Chain invisible was its composition and
functioning. In form it was a confederation between Indian tribes and
English colonies. The tribes were allied together in a system headed loosely

by the Iroquois League. They violated the legal dogma against an *imperium in imperio* by regarding themselves as sovereign in their own territories though they might accept clientage status for practical purposes. English colonial negotiators, united loosely under their common crown, accepted the tribal self-definition, also for practical purposes, and with mental reservations. In the *form* of Covenant Chain treaty negotiations, the parties were peers, and this was so because the Iroquois had contrived the form out of rituals of their own rather than from those of Europe; and so far as the Iroquois were concerned they were "a free people uniting themselves to the English." If the English were to have any dealings at all with the Iroquois, they would have to defer to this form, and they did.

In contrast to this form, the Chain functioned substantively to make its allied tribes clients of England, despite much abuse and insult, partly because of French policies that kept the Iroquois constantly at sword's point. Iroquois chiefs understood well that when they could not get backing from the French, they must have English patrons. Their formal independence could exist only as circumscribed by actual power. In very fundamental terms, Iroquois military power depended entirely on the tribes' access to firearms that could be obtained only from one or other European colony.

The Iroquois wanted to be spokesmen for other tribes and thus, by a special relationship with European power, to derive power of their own. French governors would not permit this special relationship (certainly not with the Iroquois). The French insisted on direct dealings with all tribes, excluding intermediaries. English colonials, however, who lacked French finesse in Indian affairs, accepted Iroquois intermediation as a useful instrument of policy after 1677, and thus tacitly allowed the desired special status.

At its core, the Covenant Chain functioned by means of regular meetings between Iroquois chiefs and New-York's governors. They discussed issues, made agreements understood to be contracts, and returned to their respective peoples to implement the contracts. At intervals, other English colonies insisted on dealing directly with the Iroquois which Yorkers permitted only under supervision. Indeed, the Covenant Chain began when New Englanders insisted on face-to-face negotiation under Governor Andros's chaperonage.

In later decades, other colonies supplanted New-York at the core of the Covenant Chain, and, in 1755, the crown took charge directly, but the Iroquois League remained constantly at the Chain's center. Further

Cylindrical beads made from clam shells and strung together in strings and belts were called wampum, wampumpeak, or just peak. Their significance in earliest days in still an issue. Some scholars think it was purely religious.

Seventeenth-century New Englanders used wampum as money, and counterfeited it with glass beads, but its greatest importance came from its use in diplomacy.

Wampum certified the validity of treaty proposals. For Indians a belt was the proposal which had been "read into it" by the sending council. Handling wampum developed an elaborate protocol. In simplest terms, no treaty proposal was serious unless made by wampum.

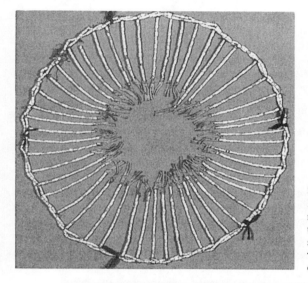

Symbol of the unity of the Iroquois League, fifty strands representing the fifty chiefly titles are twisted together in a sacred circle. COURTESY OF THE NATIONAL MUSEUMS OF CANADA.

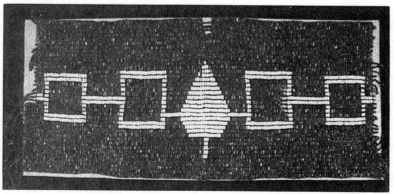

The Hiawatha Belt commemorating the foundation of the Iroquois League of five nations with the center at Onondaga. COURTESY OF THE NEW YORK STATE MUSEUM.

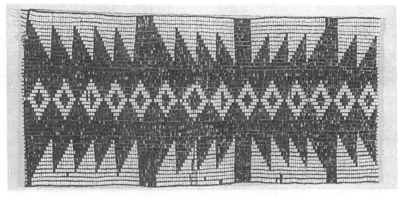

Ta-do-da-ho belt or Evergrowing Tree. COURTESY OF THE NEW YORK STATE MUSEUM.

Washington Covenant Belt symbolizing alliance between the United States (in center) and Indian nations. COURTESY OF THE NEW YORK STATE MUSEUM.

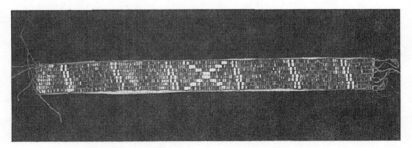

Penobscot Council Belt concerning treaty relationships of the Penobscot (non-Iroquois) Indians. COURTESY OF THE NEW YORK STATE MUSEUM.

details would be out of order here. It is advisable, however, to caution the reader once more to notice discrepancies between form and function. Descriptions of the Iroquois League as a great power between New France and the seaboard English colonies must be understood in relation to the sources and limits of that power.

A few words may be said in this respect about the Indians of the Delaware and Susquehanna valleys. In 1677, at the Covenant Chain's founding, those valleys were part of the province of New-York, and their Indians spoke to New York's governor through the intermediation of the Iroquois. (The Delawares were involved in the second Covenant Chain treaty, but did not speak for themselves.) In 1681, English jurisdiction in those parts passed from New-York to the newly chartered propriety of Pennsylvania which became a special place because of its government by Quaker pacifists.

Because of this change, the Indians of Pennsylvania and Delaware ceased to negotiate with New-York's governor and transferred their clientage to Pennsylvania's by whom Iroquois intervention was neither necessary nor desired. In the seventeenth century, Pennsylvania's "Chain of Friendship" was wholly distinct and separate from New York's "Covenant Chain."

Nevertheless, a tacit understanding existed between the Iroquois and Pennsylvania's successive governments, by which the Iroquois desisted from molesting "Pennsylvania's Indians" in return for unhindered passage through the Susquehanna Valley to war against southern Indians. The Iroquois needed this war because they could win bits of it at a time when French hostility defeated them in the East, North, and West. So there came about a special understanding between the most militaristic Indians and the most pacifist Europeans, a strange and unpredictable combination. (And one that infuriated Southern governors afflicted by Iroquois raids.)

In the seventeenth century, however, this understanding remained passive and tacit, so much so that when wandering Shawnees came from the west in 1692 to settle in the Susquehanna Valley, they chose that spot as much for Pennsylvania's protection from the Iroquois as for the advantage of trade.

Conclusively, William Penn bought land from Delaware Indians by a series of treaties in the 1680s, and in 1701 he purchased a large tract from the remnant Susquehannocks living at Conestoga. No Iroquois was anywhere in sight at the Delaware transactions. At Conestoga, Ahookasoongh, "Brother to the Emperor" of Onondaga, signed in behalf of the

"Emperor," but he signed well below the chiefs of the local Indians. Far from speaking in their behalf, he was only permitted to join them.

How Pennsylvania and the Iroquois became close allies (at the expense of local tribes) must be put off for consideration in eighteenth-century context.

CHAPTER 25

Frontiers in the Middle

Until roughly the third quarter of the seventeenth century, North American Indians generally still held much power to determine their own policies for their own aims. So early as mid-sixteenth century, de Soto had smashed the great chiefdoms along the southern rim of the continent, but after his men were driven out the surviving Indians, though crippled, managed their own affairs for more than another century. Only the Pueblos of the Southwest and the Indians of Florida wore the double yoke of garrison and mission.

This situation changed rapidly after 1675. As we have seen, the Puritan conquest called King Philip's War smashed the independence of Wampanoags, Narragansetts, and Nipmucks, and forced the Sokokis and other Western Abenakis into reliance upon New France for the means to resist further Puritan expansion into their territories.

The Iroquois Five Nations threw themselves against New France in the century's final quarter, sometimes on their own, and sometimes as allies of the English in imperial wars. The French summoned their allies—mission Indians, Western Abenakis, Ojibwas, Mississaugas, Potawatomis—and battered the Iroquois, forcing them to accept a treaty in 1701 that severely limited the scope and style of their operations.

Farther south, Virginia and Maryland attacked the Susquehannocks in 1675, destroying their polity and forcing the survivors to seek refuge among Delawares and Iroquois. In 1680, South Carolina destroyed the Westo Indians, and admitted a Shawnee band under strict supervision to play the Westos' former trading role.

In the midst of their Iroquois wars, the French extended lines of forts and missions across the top of the Great Lakes; and after Louis Jolliet and Father Jacques Marquette canoed downstream to Arkansas in 1673, the French sent their agencies down the Mississippi. René Cavelier de La Salle and his lieutenant Henri de Tonty established forts at the bottom of Lake Michigan, and went on to find a "short cut" to the Mississippi by way of the Illinois River where Tonty built Fort Crèvecoeur among the

Illinois Indians. Here, once more, the expansionist French clashed with the expansionist Iroquois, and the temporary victory of the Iroquois was soon nullified when they were driven back east. Despite much hullaba-loo, the indisputable fact is that in the many conflicts between the Iroquois and the French, the French invariably prevailed in the end, no matter their short-term setbacks. Diplomats with ulterior motives and historians with romantic imaginations have endowed the Iroquois with conquests over a vast wilderness empire, and there is reason to believe that the Iroquois aimed at something on that order, but New France and its tribal allies forced the Iroquois back into their homeland in upstate New York where they could maneuver but not dominate.

Surely it was mere coincidence that 1680 was also the year in which the Pueblos at the other end of the continent rose and drove out their Spanish masters, after which they held onto independence for a dozen years. But they, too, succumbed to renewed Spanish campaigns and their own disunity. Only the remote Hopis preserved complete self-rule and traditional religion. Indeed, when the Hopi-affiliated village of refugees at Awatovi accepted return of a missionary in 1700, the other villages rose in wrath and massacred all the Awatovi males. (The atrocity suggests that they understood the political functions of missions.)

The Spaniards suppressed the Pueblo Revolt with atrocities of their own, but they ruled with a lighter hand thereafter and the Pueblos never rose again. Indeed Pueblo warriors formed a militia that fought beside Spanish troops against marauding bands of Navajos, Apaches, Utes, and Comanches. As historian Marc Simmons remarks, "By 1800 the Pueblo Indians had gained a secure and comfortable place in provincial New Mexican society." His comment is pleasant, and it is all too rare in the history of American Indians, but independence had long ceased to be part of that security and comfort.

Already in this critical quarter-century, the colonies of France and England were seizing initiatives and compelling the tribes to respond. Beyond the military might of the Europeans, Indians of the Great Plains and the Northwest submitted only to King Trade, but even in the middle distance from the colonies, the Great Lakes and Mississippi tribes churned under rival thrusts. They continued to govern themselves, but within options set by European powers.

For the moment we may ignore the Englishmen at Hudson Bay (though the French never forgot them for a minute) to attend to efforts of New-York's ambitious Governor Thomas Dongan. In 1685 he sent out ten canoes from Albany, guided by French turncoats, all the way to Michil-imackinac where Lakes Superior and Michigan pour into Lake Huron.

A dugout canoe, still being made by Caribs in the West Indies in traditional fashion. Columbus and his men saw canoes like this one.

The art of beadwork. The intricate patterns sewn by Indian women can only be appreciated properly in full color, but this fine example gives some notion of the aesthetic imagination and patience required to create such beauty. This Iroquois beaded bag is photographed here by courtesy of the Mitchell Indian Museum, Kendall College, Evanston, Ill.

Another traditional craft. Hayes Lossiah making blow guns in Cherokee, Carolina (1962).

An expert Carib basket-maker's finished products.

First step in basket-making. The craft was practiced by Indians all over the Americas, and still is. This craftsman is a West Indian Carib.

Mrs. Joe English fleshes a moose hide. COURTESY OF THE BRITISH COLUMBIA ARCHIVES AND RECORDS SERVICE.

Finger weaving in the far Northwest. COURTESY OF THE BRITISH COLUMBIA ARCHIVES AND RECORDS SERVICE.

The French post there was the very hub of trade in what was then the Far West; it drew Indian hunters and controlled waterborne traffic in a vast region with a radius of hundreds of miles, and it was the key to French competition with the Hudson's Bay Company. If Dongan had gotten away with his penetration from the East, his men, combined with the Hudson Bay men, would have destroyed the French trading empire north of the lakes, and the political empire erected upon it. Dongan's men made a great impression on the Huron and Ottawa tribes, and they were escorted back to New York by Senecas who hoped to channel the trade through their territory.

This first expedition succeeded so well that Dongan and the Albany merchants planned two much larger ones for the fall of 1686 and spring of 1687. These came to grief as the aroused French pounced upon them. After that, colonial Englishmen left Michilimackinac alone. The Senecas paid for their aspirations by being forced out of Ontario after bloody attacks from Ojibwas and Mississaugas armed by the French. By the end of the seventeenth century, French sway north of the lakes was unchallenged except by those pesky Englishmen and *their* allies with a seaborne lifeline to Hudson Bay.

Like Dongan's Yorkers, a gang of South Carolinians based on Goose Creek (near Charleston) pushed into the interior. They wiped out the Westo Indians who had hoped to control the trade by blocking access to the tribes beyond them; and, worse, those Westos were dealing beyond tolerance with Virginians instead of Carolinians. It appears that the Savannah / Shawnees who took on the Westos' trading role were more cooperative.

After removing the Westo obstacle, the "Goose Creek men" plunged ahead. We have seen how they fattened in the slave trade with captives seized from Spanish missions. In doing so, they destroyed a main reason, in Indians' eyes, for the missions' existence. For Indians, life in a mission could be hard, but it was supposed to be protected. When the swarms of Indians armed and directed by the Carolinians ruined any possibility of protection, they eliminated the missions' prime function and made them no longer maintainable.

One inclines to imagine cutthroats like these Goose Creek men as lawless ruffians, but that conception is only partly true. They were important and respected men in their colony; one of them became governor. In fact, they were adventurous merchants, and their chief weapon was England's Industrial Revolution. As at Hudson Bay and Albany, the ships from England brought trade goods of better quality and at cheaper prices than anything at the disposal of Frenchmen or Spaniards. The

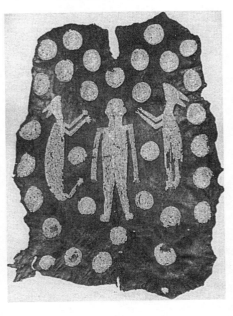

Reputedly this was the mantle or cloak worn by Chief Powhatan as a royal robe of state, circa 1608, ornamented by shells worked into patterns. By unknown routes, the mantle came finally to rest in the Ashmolean Museum, Oxford, England. REPRODUCED BY COURTESY OF THE ASHMOLEAN MUSEUM, OXFORD, ENGLAND.

Carolinians' competitors could not "meet the competition" so they lost the customers.

There is more than one way to compete. The Carolinians treated Virginia's traders almost as if they were enemies, and, in doing so, created a long-lasting feud between the two colonies. Virginians, of course, also peddled English goods. The explanation for the Carolinians' winning Indians away from Virginians may lie in the greater competitive ruthlessness of the Carolinian newcomers from Barbados. Life was very cheap on that West Indian island where pitiless planters treated slaves so badly that the overworked, underfed creatures averaged only seven years of life under the lash. Such brutal policies accompanied planter immigrants from Barbados to South Carolina.

Ruthlessness as an explanation gains credence from J. Leitch Wright's comment that "Westo, Guale, and Yamasee fugitives arrived among the Lower Creeks, describing poignantly what to expect should they not cooperate with the English. At the same time, Moore and Woodward (Goose Creek men) offered cheap goods." Club and carrot. The technique won over Lower Creeks, Upper Creeks, Mobilians, and Chickasaws, "among others," and the Carolinians marched west to the Mississippi.

Geography gave them an advantage. Unlike more northern English

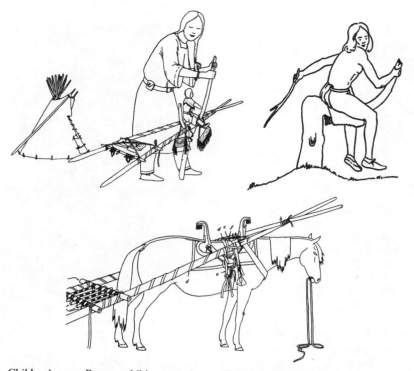

Children's toys. Because children are given so little attention in the literature, these sketches by the Piegan artist Calvin Boy are notable as illustrations of child training among Plains Indians. They are taken from John C. Ewers, "The Horse in Blackfoot Indian Culture," Bureau of American Ethnology Bulletin 159 (1955). Notice how the girl's travois faithfully follows the construction of the real thing above.

colonists who had to find ways through and over the Appalachian range, Carolinians could skirt the mountains' southern end. It was comparatively easy for them to walk through the Gulf lowlands, and Frenchmen who had followed La Salle down the Mississippi were alarmed by the presence of Carolinian traders in the midst of tribes supposed to be entirely within the French sphere of influence.

Such intrusion was beyond toleration by Louis XIV, "the Sun King," who had taken personal charge of his government in 1661, intending to conquer a great empire and to rule it absolutely. He was as aggressive in North America as in Europe (though a mite thriftier) and his government took steps to stop the advance of those rude Carolinians. Thus, missions were founded at Cahokia (1699) and farther south where the Kaskaskia River falls into the Mississippi (1703).

Most important in terms of long-range strategy, the ministry chose Pierre Le Moyne d'Iberville to campaign on the Gulf coast and in the Mississippi Valley to assure France's control. Iberville was a veteran of such frontier struggles in New France. He promptly built Fort Maurepas (1699) at Biloxi (Mississippi), and laid the groundwork for a new colony of Louisiana which flourished in the eighteenth century and did indeed thrust the Carolinians back east of the Appalachians.

If this chapter seems unduly attentive to European initiatives at the expense of attention to Indians, the reason is to show factually, regardless of argument and assertion, that the Europeans indeed held the initiative everywhere in the regions noticed, which was as far as their power bases permitted them to range. After about 1675, colonial expansion was aided by Indians rather than obstructed by them, *except* where opposing colonies supported Indian resistance. Caught between English, French, and Spanish colonies, tribal agendas were set by colonial thrusts and ripostes. It is sheer nonsense to speak of Indians being on "the other side." There was no line beyond which eastern Indians had freedom of action. Their frontiers were nets—webs spun in Europe. They could not spurn European entanglement in order to live their own lives in their own way. They could not run away, and they could not win a war of liberation. Their choices were limited, above all else, to which European power to go along with. In short, description of European imperial and colonial initiatives in this era is description by implication of the responses available to Indian tribes. They responded, certainly, in various ways, but the outstanding example of Iroquois experimentation proves the point.

PART FIVE

The Century
of Decision

CHAPTER 26

From All Directions

After William of Orange came to share the throne of England and to be effectively its executive, the rivalry between England and France which had simmered down through the Stuart dynasty came up once more to a boil. The series of wars that followed has no overall name, but it was bloodier and perhaps more far-reaching than what had started in 1066. The bare dates are eloquent.

1689–1697   King William's War
1701–1713   Queen Anne's War
1744–1748   King George's War
1754–1763   The Seven Years War (or "French and Indian War")

These are the names by which British colonists knew conflicts that were called otherwise in Europe. They were, as a sympathetic writer has called them, "storms brewed in other men's worlds." All of them originated in Europe's dynastic quarrels; all pitted Indians against each other and against the other side's colonists.

In addition, the brawls of Britain included the War for American Independence, 1776–1783 (which the French joined again in 1778); and, of course, the Napoleonic wars which the United States slid into in 1812.

None of these wars left North America's Indians unscathed in body or goods; and in reputation *they* became the "war lovers." From 1689 to 1815, men marched back and forth through tribal territories, and agents seduced and menaced the tribes into participation. For Indians the eighteenth century dragged out as a long agony east of the Mississippi. Excitable young warriors loved it until their turn came to die under the hatchet. Old chiefs, who saw authority and ancient custom being flouted and their tribes disintegrating, mourned the passing of the old days before European invasion and its "savage" consequences. (Scholars who attribute population loss to the Indians' "love of war" should take a look at the dates cited above.)

The great-power showdown took place between France and Britain, but Spain became involved from time to time, and even Tsarist Russia mixed into the fray after Napoleon's eruption. The Indians of the Far West beyond the Rocky Mountains were no longer able to stand by and mind their own business as Spain (or New Spain) resuscitated its expansionist energies and pushed north through California to be met by Russians coming south from Alaska. English and Yankee trading ships put in at Northwest harbors, Franco-Canadians pushed up the Missouri Valley, the Hudson's Bay Company and North West Company roamed through western Canada and south into the Rockies, and the Astoria Fur Company of the United States came from the East early in the nineteenth century.

The Northwest and the Rockies were the last great preserves of trade in furs taken by Indian hunters and trappers, and each of the European and Euramerican merchants was determined to get his share before that resource ran out. (Restraint for the sake of conservation was incomprehensible in the competition of their free-market economy.)

From 1701 until its expulsion from the continent in 1763, France tried to contain British colonies east of the Appalachian Mountain wall; and, incidentally, Frenchmen remained behind in the vast transmontane region after French governments were evicted. Even during the heyday of France's American empire, the ethnically French colonial population was only one-twentieth the size of the ethnically conglomerate colonials under British rule. In the empires' competitions, the French had no option but to use available manpower regardless of ethnicity, and there were many more Indians allied to France than there were Frenchmen in the colonies. This was well understood. From Acadia and Maine, through the Great Lakes country and along the valleys of the Mississippi and its tributaries, French policies undeviatingly aimed toward winning tribal allegiances and turning the tribes against the British. Militarily rational, these policies were as unscrupulous as most statecraft of the time, and their effects were what the British called savage. The French, rather contentedly and sanctimoniously, agreed. ("We had no choice.") In the event, the Indians were denounced by both sides.

Thus came civilization to North America's Indians. The process took longer than the conquest of New Spain, mostly because so many European nations contended against each other and got in each other's way. Until one empire came to stand alone, tribesmen had a smidgen of room for maneuver between them in a sort of unplanned divide-and-survive strategy. But for every maneuver a tribe had to pay a price which was cumulative.

In the context of this book, it has been necessary to select certain dominant phenomena from the multitude of actors and events. Regret-

European Empires in North America

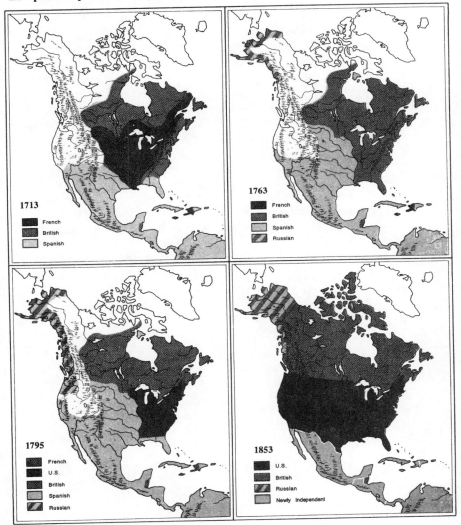

1713: French, British, and Spanish
1763: British, Spanish, French, and Russian
1795: United States, British, Spanish, and Russian
1853: United States, British, Russian, and Spanish successor states

tably, many tribes have not even been mentioned because taking them all up would require more books; indeed, it has done so already in overwhelming quantities. To keep the present discussion manageable and comprehensible, it has been focused on selecting and describing a variety of frontiers and their effects.

For convenience and clarity, this section begins in the United States Southwest, runs up the Pacific Coast to Alaska, and turns into the vast Canadian and U.S. territory probed by the Hudson's Bay Company and the North West Company. (It is not otherwise to be compressed into a phrase.)

The section then takes up the Mississippi Valley peoples as they were affected by New France's giant pincers movement from the Great Lakes and New Orleans. It proceeds from there to the Southeast and up the Atlantic Coast to the Northeast. In all, a sweeping figure eight.

Time sequences vary in the treatments of the different regions because the processes of the "eighteenth century" developed for Indians at different points on the calendar. A chronology has been provided to keep all in order.

CHAPTER 27

The Southwest

The American Southwest is the most complex cultural region north of Mexico, and its native Indian populations exhibit a bewildering variety of social structures.
                                                    —FRED EGGAN

The general structure [of contact] was that of a number of small, politically autonomous, and mobile societies meeting the more heterogeneous and more politically and economically powerful European society. The latter, with its formal political-administrative system, eventually became dominant and directed much of the contact processes in accordance with its own goals, while the Indian groups had to react and to adjust to this dominance.
                                                    —WILLIAM B. GRIFFEN

In the Southwest, the eighteenth century was marked by acceleration of action between peoples—between sedentary Pueblo communities and semi-nomadic Apaches, Navajos, Utes, and Comanches; between the empires of France and Spain; and between the European colonials and the Indians. Their actions and interactions heightened in commerce, religion, war, diplomacy, in the learning called acculturation, and in sexual and social mixing. As with molecules in a pot of water, added heat speeded motion. In this century, heat and action increased from three main sources: more pressure from incoming tribes; more Spanish colonials; and more competition between the empires.

To understand the variety of the Southwest's peoples, one must first take account of the region's landscape. Arid everywhere, it was less so on the mountains which are so prominent throughout the Southwest. Rainfall varied from almost none in the great Sonora desert to as much as fifteen inches annually in the hill and canyon country, and Indians were amazingly ingenious in adapting everywhere.

Political boundaries are irrelevant to these natural features. Desert and mountain alike sprawl across the artificial line between Mexico and the United States. When certain Pima Indians settled in the Sonora—nobody knows when—their concern was with sources of water, however intermittent or temporary they might be, and these Pimas could not possibly maintain dense clusters of population. The Colorado River at the western edge of their range was the only permanently flowing stream, and its valley was occupied by other Indians. The "Sand Papagos" or "No-Villagers" were food collectors rather than producers, whose extended family bands never exceeded ninety members. They were "No-Villagers" because they could not settle long in one spot. Necessarily they walked great distances to particular places where water welled up at special times from rain in the mountains. Though without permanent habitation, they knew where those water holes were and how to get to them. Even so bereft a people managed to find a commodity to trade with. Precisely because water sank into the sand it left a residue of salt which the No-Villagers collected and traded for pottery and the harvests of planters on the lower Colorado.

The No-Villagers became extinct as a people as a result of the pressures created by converging peoples on their very fragile adjustment to their harsh environment. Some died of the diseases that no Indians were immune to. Others scattered and assimilated among better-established distant neighbors.

In the foothills of the mountains lived the "Two-Villagers," so called because they moved cyclically from a village in the mountain to another in the valley. Here also, as everywhere, water was the reason. By channeling and damming runoff from summer rains to particular canyons, the Two-Villagers could get enough irrigation to grow some crops at arroyo mouths. When the water stopped and the harvest had been brought in, they moved back up the slope to the alternate village where springs ran perpetually. Basically these people were hunters, but their small crop harvests provided what might be called a gourmet supplement to their diet.

Where there was still more water, though never in the abundance of the East, Pima-Papagos settled down to be "One Villagers"—true sedentary horticulturalists who lived along the banks of rivers that flowed perennially along at least part of their courses. Some of these Indians used canal irrigation before the advent of Spaniards. On their rivers they were fortunate enough also to have a source of fish. Compared to their brethren of the desert, they were highly prosperous. One wonders why those desert people did not sooner leave their bleak surroundings. The attachment of people to even the least rewarding homelands is mysteriously strong.

The villagers, both Two- and One-, kept cultural identities under Spanish rule, but with modifications imposed by their new circumstances and opportunities.

At the center of the Southwest lived the Pueblos in what, comparatively speaking, were mansions. Their still-surviving villages, though not so extensive as before Spanish conquest, stretch from the western Zuñis eastward to the Rio Grande and upstream to Taos, with the separate Hopis off on their mesas north of Mount San Francisco. As we have seen, the Pueblos took the first brunt of Spanish conquest. Like all other Indians they suffered from introduced diseases. Additionally they took casualties from Spanish retaliation for violent rebellions, and from raiding Apacheans, yet their way of life has endured in essentials, apparently because of their strong religious traditions and institutions. Loss of population and attacks from outside caused some Pueblos to abandon outlying villages in order to concentrate in stronger places, but there was no inducement for Pueblos to migrate elsewhere; they already had the most water and best land in the Southwest, which they carefully cultivated. In those parts, they were regarded as rich and attractive to would-be conquerors long before the Spaniards came.

From the Far North—the Mackenzie Basin of west-central Canada—came the Apacheans who spoke their dialects of the Athapaskan language family. (Their closest kin in Canada seem to be the Sarcees.)

At about A.D. 1300—that portentous date again—the Apacheans began to separate into the seven tribes now recognized (and perhaps more). These are known as the Chiricahuas, Jicarillas, Kiowa-Apaches, Lipans, Navajos, and Western Apaches, of whom the Navajos have become by far the most populous. (Sometimes called the largest Indian tribe or nation in the United States, their pride of rank is disputed by Ojibwas in the North, but the Ojibwas are spread over into Canada. The contest depends on definitions.)

For purposes of this chapter, the Apacheans will be treated as one migratory people who began appearing in the Southwest sometime after 1300 and certainly before Spanish invasion. A.D. 1525 is generally accepted as the probable date. Wherever the Spaniards arrived in the region, they found Apacheans already in the vicinity. Some of these Indians pushed down into Mexico, but they were eventually repulsed by combined forces of Spanish regulars and militias embracing both colonists and Indians who were targets of the Apacheans. There is nothing like a worrisome enemy to unite people otherwise at odds with each other.

*A*bout 300 B.C., *some Hohokams migrated from Mexico to the Gila and Salt River valleys. Already well-acquainted with the essentials of irrigation, they immediately began construction on a system of deep canals (not just ditches) and installed devices to control water flow. Constant maintenance kept the systems operational for more than a millennium, but they eventually filled up for reasons we do not understand. Careful archaeological digging (with modern machinery) has reconstructed some of them and plotted others. For details see Emil W. Haury,* The Hohokam, *pp. 120–51.*

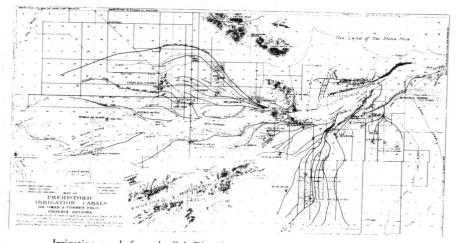

Irrigation canals from the Salt River in use a thousand years ago or longer. COURTESY OF THE ARIZONA STATE MUSEUM, UNIVERSITY OF ARIZONA.

Hohokam "Expressway." Junction of irrigation canal 6 with canal 5 (looking west). The great size of these canals suggests a large population, both for construction and for service. Photograph by Helga Teiwes. COURTESY OF ARIZONA STATE MUSEUM, UNIVERSITY OF ARIZONA.

Hohokam irrigation canals from the Salt River (Arizona), seen from the air. To compare size, note that the white "line" from lower right to upper center is a dual-lane highway. COURTESY OF ARIZONA STATE MUSEUM, UNIVERSITY OF ARIZONA.

Papago use of mesquite for food. Juanita Ahill crushing mesquite beans on mortar. Photograph by Helga Teiwes. COURTESY OF ARIZONA STATE MUSEUM, UNIVERSITY OF ARIZONA.

An important, long-lasting trade in seashells was conducted by the Hohokams of the Gila River valley. From their home in Snaketown, they made a trail to the northern shore of the Gulf of California to collect shells, and probably also dealt with middlemen of the Trincheras Culture of Northwestern Sonora. For the Hohokams, shell was "the basis for an industry in which some craftsmen seem to have achieved the level of specialists." The craft-worked products were then traded great distances throughout the Southwest. See Emil W. Haury, The Hohokam, *pp. 304–6.*

Hohokam petroglyphs marking water hole on trail to source of shells for trade. Photograph by N. M. Simmons. From U.S. Fish and Wildlife Service. COURTESY OF ARIZONA STATE MUSEUM, UNIVERSITY OF ARIZONA.

Prehistoric shell trade trail, Sonora. The omnipresent rocks have been carefully cleared off. Photograph by B. Fontana. COURTESY OF ARIZONA STATE MUSEUM, UNIVERSITY OF ARIZONA.

The Apacheans were not homogeneous in culture although they shared political structures in which leadership authority was weak, dependent on ability to persuade, and removable. They lived in separate nuclear families clustered in bands related by blood and marriage, without strong allegiance to a tribe. They were highly mobile and hard to pin down, but gradually they came to identify with particular territories. Originally hunters and gatherers, some of them (not all) picked up crop cultivation from the peoples they moved in with, and especially the Navajos adopted sheepherding as a major occupation.

Their neighbors were most concerned about the Apachean predilection for raiding. It is not to be confused with innate love of war or a desire such as Plains warriors had to gain prestige by counting coup (i.e., by touching an enemy boldly and riding away without killing him). If the Apacheans had lived in Europe they would have been called brigands or pirates. They raided for plunder, and like sensible plunderers they avoided combat as much as possible. When caught in a raid, they fought and fought well, but they preferred evasive tactics above holding out to the bitter end. Running away was not shameful. Apacheans conducted real war only to avenge casualties previously suffered.

As Apacheans swarmed in, they gradually surrounded the Pueblos on three sides, while the Spaniards moved in from the southern fourth front. Standard military doctrine forbids getting caught in a two-front war, but the Pueblos were completely surrounded by fronts. Fortunately their opponents were not all vengeful enemies. Even the Spaniards, who were implacably determined to conquer and exploit, softened their rule after the Pueblo rising of 1680 showed harshness to be self-defeating. Contrary to the rude maxim that "the only good Indian is a dead Indian," the post-conquistador Spaniards believed that dead Indians were no good at all. Dead Indians didn't work. When the Pueblos showed an inclination to accept conquest on reasonable terms, the Spaniards tacitly met the terms.

No such arrangement was possible with the Apacheans because they were too individualistic. Spain's conquests came to a stop at the Apachean barrier. The Apacheans refrained from attempting to conquer the Pueblos from the other side. Although they, too, wanted to exploit the Pueblos, they had no political structures for managing subject peoples. (They could hardly manage even their own.) They liked having those rich Pueblos handy to raid and trade with, and the Pueblos set up regular annual fairs at Taos and Picuris to encourage the trading and distract from raiding.

Pueblo captives from the raids, and Pueblo refugees from the Spaniards, taught farming to their Apachean hosts, utilizing irrigation from the streams along which Apacheans established their rancherias. Pueblo potters and weavers traded the highly valued products of their crafts in return for bison hides. And Pueblo herds of sheep and horses tempted raiders beyond resistance. Some Apaches recognized the Spaniards as their real enemy so that they joined the Pueblos in the 1680 rebellion and were forced to flee when Spaniards marched back in force.

In general, however, though Pueblos and Apacheans interacted variously, exchanging cultural traits and products, it appears that the Pueblos objected so strenuously to Apachean continual raids that many of them enlisted in Spanish militias involved in erratically successful search-and-destroy campaigns.

Then, just to complicate these frontiers more, the Apacheans acquired Indian enemies on their "backs," so to speak. Utes attacked Apachean Navajos from the north, and fierce Comanches rode in from the Plains to drive the Jicarilla Apaches westward, closer to Pueblos and Spaniards. The Comanches were armed by Frenchmen in the Mississippi Valley.

In all this welter of violence by surprise, the only permanently stabilizing factor was the imposed partnership of Pueblos and Spaniards that maintained a degree of territorial integrity despite constant assaults.

Perhaps the strongest agency maintaining the partnership was the mission system. If Spanish troops conquered by naked force, the friars mediated between the two peoples to make conquest bearable; and some, at least, of the governing officials had good sense enough to go along with the mediation. As the missions grew in numbers and acceptance, troops were withdrawn except from outermost frontier posts.

However, an erroneous notion is common, similar to that of "happy darkies" among the magnolias, that missions were places of sweetness and light. In fact, they were not so intended. The purpose of the mission was not to make Indians happy; it was to make them Catholics. This could be done only by changing them from traditional lifeways and "idolatry." Missionaries received training at special colleges before going into the field, and among the precepts stressed was the need for discipline. It appears that whipping was one of the means taught for enforcing discipline, as it was ubiquitous in all the missions, French as well as Spanish. It was also totally alien to Indian culture everywhere, and it became a great cause for rebellion and running away.

We tend to think of whipping as chastisement administered to small boys on the seat of their pants, but the whipping of Indian neophytes had more in common with flogging of troops for military offenses. It varied, of course, as the friars varied in personality, but one case that resulted in the victim's death shows how severe that punishment could be.

In 1655, Father Salvador de Guerra accused a Hopi named Juan Cuna of an "act of idolatry." The friar whipped him in public, took him inside the church and beat him again, then doused him with turpentine and set fire to him. Cuna died, and the Hopis protested vigorously enough to force a hearing. Father Guerra was transferred, but not discharged, much less punished for murder. One must wonder how many of these priests were motivated by something other than solicitude for Indian souls. Power corrupts.

Edward H. Spicer, who was a foremost student of southwestern frontiers, has remarked, "Missionary discipline by the whip was a factor in the resistance of Indians, and the missionary control which whipping sanctioned was resented by Indians . . . [but] systematic and regulated corporal punishment, together with forced labor" were standard sanctions of the Spanish legal system "and also of their religious training system."

Thus, conquest in America meant something more profound to the Indian peasantry than the same sort of experience in Europe where the conquered peasant (if he minded his business) simply turned his taxes and corvée labor in to his new lord. Indians were not permitted to mind their own business. They were to be remade in the image of their conquerors, by whatever force seemed to be necessary—or gratifying.

Missions were not equally successful everywhere. The friars could not gain acceptance among the mobile Apacheans (all the more mobile after they acquired horses). The Catholic message could be assimilated syncretically to Pueblo religions that had complex idea systems and rituals maintained by elaborate priesthoods; but such things did not exist among the Apacheans. In a manner of speaking, they had no soil for the missionary seed. The missionaries concluded that conversion would work only among sedentary, agricultural peoples, and they aimed always to pin Apacheans down to farming at fixed places, but this was usually a losing battle.

(Syncretism is still highly visible among the Pueblos. When I visited Santa Clara, everyone went to mass on Sunday morning; and in the afternoon, when their priest tactfully disappeared, they all celebrated the traditional Green Corn Dance.)

At the outermost limit of New Spain's frontier, which had become also the Pueblos' frontier as they were gradually organized under the Spanish administrative system, the Apacheans proved to be unconquerable. They were too mobile, too decentralized, and too good at fighting. In 1786, New Mexico's Governor Bernardo de Galvez inaugurated a new policy of making peace treaties with the Apacheans, band by band, and bribing them to keep the peace. By encouraging them to develop appetites for goods obtainable through trade and presents (and by keeping them sodden with liquor), Galvez calculated on making them dependent on the Spaniards who could then settle in Apachean territories and gradually gain control.

For a while, the policy worked. By 1800, Apachean raiding had become minimal. As Edward Spicer notes, "A symbiotic relationship between Spaniards and Apaches slowly developed, with considerable disorganization among those Apaches of the southern part of the region who became involved." But the policy broke down after 1811 because of tumults in Mexico that must be reserved for later consideration.

CHAPTER 28

California Missions

Even so late as mid-eighteenth century, the Indians of California were practically untouched by European invasion. A couple of Spanish exploring expeditions had sailed northward along the coast in 1542 and 1602, but their landings were few and far apart. Francis Drake's booty-laden *Golden Hind* stopped off, probably at Drake's Bay near San Francisco in 1579, but the Indians did not interest him as much as the cargo already in his hold. After 1564, trading galleons sailed annually from Mexico to the Philippine Islands and returned southward with the currents along the California coast, but after being so long at sea their crews were in a hurry to get back to port; they did not stop along the way.

Not much exists of documentary information about pre-invasion times. A historian must depend once more on archaeology and anthropology with some imaginative extrapolations backward from records made in the eighteenth and nineteenth centuries. Generally it appears that the California Indians differed from others throughout North America by preserving a way of life largely dependent on gathering wild plants. They hunted some small animals and fished and collected shellfish, but their staple foods were acorns, properly leached and pounded into powder or paste, supplemented by dried salmon and nuts. It seems clear, therefore, that they had escaped the culture of Mexico's Indians with its stress on maize cultivation.

One must not conclude that California's Indians lived perpetually on the verge of starvation. The great natural plenty of their environment permitted comfort and multiplication.*

From linguistic evidence, it appears that the Californians included many spillover groups from migratory tides that swept past. On average,

---

*Even Alfred L. Kroeber, whose condescension allowed only an estimated million Indians to the whole continent (north of Mexico), put a tenth of them in California alone. Kroeber based his estimate on professional authority (mostly his own) which he did not hesitate to throw against recorded evidence. His slapdash methods (now in disgrace) did not satisfy Sherburne F. Cook, who concluded, after thirty-five years of innovative research, that the California region had held about 310,000 Indian persons in aboriginal times.

they were smaller in stature than Indians farther east. Their weapons were inferior to those of the peoples who lived largely by hunting, and the subsistence systems of California were sharply distinctive. Communities were small and independent; they have been called "tribelets." Families consulted each other and engaged in mutual religious rituals, but they kept authority in their own hands. This decentralization produced no less than 135 regional dialects and perhaps more that have escaped linguists' notice.

These Indians neither produced nor amassed wealth, and got along mostly peacefully without it. No urgent reasons existed among them for extensive warfare or centralized government. Pressed hard, they would fight back, but they did not go to war just for the fun of it, and they did not torture prisoners. (Some scalped dead enemies.) Theirs was a quiet sort of life varied by the tantrums of California's volatile earth and climates, and by many ceremonial festivities.

New Spain began to intrude with the founding of mission San Diego in 1769 as the first of a series extending along the coastal lowlands northward to San Francisco Bay and a little beyond. Their general supervisor was Franciscan Father Junipero Serra who has achieved great renown and has been proposed for beatification for his great accomplishments. These were indeed remarkable. In the short span between 1769 and 1782, he presided over the founding of nine missions spaced at intervals from San Diego to San Francisco Bay, a distance of 514 miles, and he is regarded as the founder of the cities that grew up in the missions' vicinities. Serra died in 1784, but the momentum of his energy carried on to the founding of twelve more missions. The buildings of all twenty-one have survived intact or have been restored to impress visitors today.

But the praise lavished on these missions is equivocal in regard to their relations with the Indians who were their reason for existence. A eulogist confesses that they were not founded until after the Spanish crown became worried about England's rise to power in North America, and Russia's rumored expansion southward from Alaska. The publication *California's Missions* remarks, "Again the Crown looked to the missions . . . and plans were made for extending the Spanish domain into Upper California by use of the mission system."

To be brief, this purpose signified that Indian welfare necessarily was subordinated to the crown's welfare, a circumstance that the Indians quickly came to understand. Where the friars went, their soldier comrades went also, and what the friars decreed, the soldiers enforced.

There is general agreement that California's Indians were friendly and hospitable at first, but (inexplicably) within two years the Ipai-Tipai "reluctant hosts" of mission San Diego attacked the mission and were fought off by its protecting troops. A modern Cahuilla Indian explains the situation simply; Edward D. Castillo states "the California missions were coercive, authoritarian institutions."

His judgment is confirmed indirectly by Father Francis F. Guest, O.F.M., with a distinction: "The reasons why the Spanish captured and imprisoned whole rancherías, or the remains thereof, were judicial and military. They were not necessarily religious." Another modern member of his order mentions that "the instruments of punishment [at Santa Barbara] were the shackles, the lash, and the stocks." Professor Castillo itemizes particulars as "whipping with a barbed lash, solitary confinement, mutilation, use of stocks and hobbles, branding, and even execution." A missionary who protested such treatment to the viceroy in Mexico was seized, declared insane, and hustled out of California under armed guard.

One should not condemn the missionaries in the same terms as the conquistadors because they were generally not the same sort of vicious brutes. They were men of their age and culture, and the disciplinary measures they imposed on their converts were the same as Spaniards in authority used on other Spaniards of low degree, though less arbitrarily. Why should "savages" be treated any better? One of Father Serra's successors justified the discipline by writing, "We use the authority which Almighty God concedes to parents for the proper education of their children." Another friar in charge was explicit: "It is evident that a nation which is barbarous, ferocious, and ignorant requires more frequent punishment than a nation which is cultured, educated and of gentle and moderate customs." My point in mentioning these attitudes and punishments here is that many Indian converts did not relish such treatment, and they left.

But that was forbidden. According to most sources, no Indian was required to accept baptism, and *un*baptised Indians were free to come and go, but converts *must stay*. (The sources are not wholly unanimous: compare Father Guest's remark cited above.) When a convert fled, which happened frequently, he was allowed eight days in which to return voluntarily. After that grace period, he was pursued (for "judicial," not religious reasons) by a friar with reliable converts and/or troops. The free Indians among whom the refugee had sheltered observed his pursuers and acquired a distaste for the converts. Sometimes this manifested itself violently. In short, missions here as elsewhere were a divisive force in Indian society.

Nevertheless, they succeeded in accomplishing what the crown wanted done. They created a Spanish presence and authority, with a scattering of troops, all along the coast to San Francisco Bay, and at very small cost because labor was performed by unpaid Indians whose time and energies were diverted from traditional activities to work as the friars directed.

Cheap labor makes wealth, and the missions became rich. The editors of *California's Missions* note that "at the height of its prosperity, Mission San Diego possessed 20,000 sheep, 10,000 cattle and 1,250 horses" and embraced 50,000 acres." This was wealth of a sort literally undreamed of by the Indians, to whom domesticated animals were unknown until the advent of the missions. And, of course, it never became the Indians' wealth.

The fact demonstrates also that the friars were remaking the environment as well as the people, and the results in California repeated the results in Mexico. The animals ate up the available forage and trampled the earth. In California's arid conditions the damage was heavy, and it required the mission flockmasters to expand their range eastward from the coast. Free Indians lost *their* usual range for subsistence gathering, and gradually lost the land as well. Allowed few options, some retreated into the mountains where life was hard while others surrendered to the seemingly inevitable and capitulated to the new religion with its new restrictions. The voluntariness of such conversion is semantically a little obscure. It certainly magnified bitterness between the missions and the holdouts.

The greatest price paid by the Indians must be reckoned in human lives, both within and outside of the missions. Despite growth from natural births and recruiting of new converts, mission Indians fell from a total of 72,000 to only 18,000 in 1830, shortly before the missions were secularized. The net reduction can be reasonably calculated at about 54,000. The same authority, Sherburne F. Cook, figures that for California as a whole, the Indian population fell in the same period from 310,000 to about 245,000. If his calculations are valid, they point to a rate of death within the missions much greater than that outside.

On the surface this seems incomprehensible. Unarguably, the friars had taken in "wild" Indians living to all appearances from hand to mouth, had given them shelter and a disciplined daily routine, and had taught them the crafts of rural science as it was then known in Europe. In logic, the mission Indians should have fattened and multiplied. In fact, however, the mission environment was unhealthy and the Spanish soldiers attached to it had not reformed their morals or behavior. Dr. Cook remarks that the California Indian "was driven from his home by the thousands, starved, beaten, raped, and murdered with impunity."

Three basic reasons for depopulation emerge from the data: reduction of the food supply (which went to animals instead); diseases, both endemic and epidemic, introduced by the mission entourages and abetted by poorly heated and badly ventilated buildings; and "social and physical disruption."

The worst was yet to come. Pain and loss caused by intrusion of the missions and their auxiliary presidios were mild compared to what would happen in the nineteenth century when California was thrown open to waves of get-rich-quick adventurers submitting to no restraints of religion or conscience.

CHAPTER 29

The Northwest Coast

The history of Russia is the history of a country being colonized.
—V. Kluchevsky, quoted by James R. Gibson

While western Europeans crossed the Atlantic to invade North America from south and east, Russia extended its empire across Siberia to the Kamchatka Peninsula. Much of that conquest was unofficial, being effected by merchant adventurers and their employees, many of whom were native Siberians. In consequence, reports of events have survived erratically, especially when circumstances might have made them embarrassing to the participants. Among those not written at all was the 1648 voyage of an illiterate Cossack called Semen Dezhnev who proved the separation of Siberia and Alaska by sailing from port on the Kolyma River (which flows into the Arctic Ocean), southward through the strait which was to be called Bering, to the Anadyr River, which flows into the Pacific. As illiterate Dezhnev was not strong on written reports, the fact of his voyage has had to be pieced together from other sources amid considerable controversy, but it is now generally accepted.

Vitus Bering, a Dane working under direction of Russia's Emperor Peter the Great, set sail from Okhotsk on the Siberian coast and made the Strait passage from the south in 1728. He was literate and did write reports, so the Russians back home learned of his voyage before they picked up Semen Dezhnev's. The passage therefore became Bering Strait.

But Bering deserves all honor for his later accomplishment and sacrifice. In 1741, he sailed again from Okhotsk, stopped at Kamchatka, then followed along the Aleutian Islands to mainland Alaska. He skirted Kodiak Island, ran along the coast to Kayak Island, and came to grief when his ship was wrecked on Bering Island where he and many members of his crew died during the harsh winter. The survivors salvaged enough timber from the wreck to fit out a small vessel that carried them back to port in Kamchatka.

Although Bering's triumph cost many lives, including his own, he discovered more than a land mass. Word came back to Russia that the "Americans" willingly exchanged valuable furs for cheap bits of metal and trinkets. Russian merchants had been conducting this kind of business all the way across Siberia. They understood it and its potential well. By 1744, some of them extended their trade to the Aleutian Islands and began working eastward to the Alaskan mainland.

Beyond commerce, the Russian crown understood how claims to sovereignty could be flung at a continent on the basis of a sighting by an official "discoverer." Other crowns also understood this.

Spain's Russian embassy sent home an alarm that galvanized Madrid into ordering expansion of the Spanish presence northward along the California coast. Thus the California missions came into being as far north as Solano and San Rafael north of San Francisco Bay. Soon the Spanish crown realized that more would be needed to maintain its claim to the entire Pacific seaboard than Balboa's performance in 1513 when he waded into the ocean at Darien, waved his sword, and shouted at the surf.

(The legalities of these situations are incredible to a nonlegal modern mind. Yet the United States still solemnly bases its claim to own Indian territories all over the continent on the fact that some European "discoverers" intoned certain phrases at the water's edge. Our judges accept the "discoverers' " mere words as establishing sovereignty over the native inhabitants. For the validity of this procedure, imagine throwing open the courthouse door and yelling, "I claim this place for the Mafia.")

As Russians and Spaniards moved toward each other, British adventurers and the great East India Company joined the contest, supported in principle by their crown. (In practice, the British government was somewhat distracted by its rebellious colonists and the French Revolution.) Britons had been stimulated by the 1778 voyage of Captain James Cook which landed at Nootka on Vancouver Island and explored farther north. Like the Russians earlier, Cook discovered fur. Commercial ventures soon followed.

Russian, Spanish, and British claimants converged on Nootka in the 1780s, and shortly they were to be joined by Yankees. Within that one decade, ships sailed to the Northwest Coast around Cape Horn from London and Boston; eastward across the Pacific from Bengal, Hong Kong and Macao; through the Baltic Sea and Atlantic Ocean from St. Petersburg, around the Cape of Good Hope and through the Indian and Pacific oceans; through the Arctic Ocean for transshipment across Siberia; and northward along the California coast. These long voyages took a terrible toll in human lives, especially from the scurvy which was still the sailor's bane, but sailors were cheap and expendable. The voyages made large profits from very advantageous trades: cheap goods taken to the Northwest for sable and sea otter furs; thence to China to sell the furs for fantastic markups and to take on cargoes of tea; and home again for another fat profit on the tea.

The prospect of immense riches invigorated all the merchants to aggressive assertion of their nations' "rights," and their claims came to climax in 1789 when ships of four nationalities anchored at Nootka. Tempers flared. The Spanish commander, Esteban Martinez, seized control, and British captains went home to complain to Parliament. War was averted by diplomacy that gave Britain what it wanted, which was freedom to trade at will; and eventually Vancouver Island, after abandonment and reoccupation, became part of Britain's Canada. In the meantime, however, Russians and Yankees continued to busy themselves in that lucrative fur trade which was, of course, trade with the native peoples.

The foregoing is intended to give some notion of how suddenly the lives of those native peoples were transformed. As along the California coast where missions sprang up in a single decade, so also, farther to the north, Indians were exposed to the impact of European cultures within an astonishingly short time. The agency here was trade, rather than missions as in California, but the Russians moved in to stay—and kept on moving southward to within thirty miles of San Francisco Bay. The name of Russian River reminds us of their farthest advance.

Potlatch celebration, Duncan, B.C. COURTESY OF THE BRITISH COLUMBIA ARCHIVES AND RECORDS SERVICE.

In some ways, the Northwest Coast Indians were plunged into colonialism even more complex than their brethren of the Atlantic Coast. In matters of religion, for example, Spanish Catholics denounced the Russian Orthodox as heretical (and vice versa), and British Protestants were outside the pale of real Christianity for both Spaniards and Russians, an attitude which the British reciprocated fervently. Matters quickly became even more confusing when traders from inland appeared—ethnic Frenchmen from the Missouri Valley, and Britons of a mixed assemblage of ethnicity from Hudson's Bay Company and its rival North West Company. That additional intrusion, however, must be noticed as of the nineteenth century.

On one thing, the Europeans all agreed, and the Yankees too: there was money to be made from furs. Operationally this meant that the money would come via exploitation of the Indians who hunted and trapped for the furs; and that logic, when carried one step further, decreed that the most money would come from the most control of the most Indians.

Indian response to all this varied considerably. The Aleuts of the islands were fragmented in bands that the Russians dominated easily. Some Aleuts responded positively to trading partnerships and baptism in the Russian Orthodox Church. This process began almost immediately after Bering's pioneering voyage. A historian observes that patron-client relations were thus established "with individuals who often served their godfathers loyally." He adds drily that "the newly baptized natives represented a reliable labor force . . . [during] a labor shortage." On the favorable side for these new Christians, Russian law accepted them as citizens (or subjects) nominally equal to ethnic Russians. As usual in such colonial situations, the crown's law diffused in transit to its outposts where local powers ruled in fact, so everything depended on those patron-client relations.

These involved more than labor. Ethnic Russians, like ethnic Spaniards, Frenchmen, and Englishmen, practiced divide-and-rule. The Aleutians for them were "but an extension of an ongoing enterprise" of conquest through Siberia. When they encountered fierce resistance in their advance to Alaska, they used sea power at the coasts and their baptized native warriors farther inland. Russians never emigrated to Alaska in substantial numbers. (Vastly greater numbers migrated to America later via the Atlantic Ocean.) Like Englishmen in India, the Russians used forces of natives against opposing natives, a technique made possible by longstanding intertribal hostilities.

As distinguished from primarily commercial types, the first Russian empire builder was Grigori Shelikhov who made a "swift and brutal" conquest of Kodiak Island. By 1786 he had built fortifications on Afognak

Island and the Kenai Peninsula. He imported cattle and poultry, experimented with agriculture, and built a school. In 1790 he hired Aleksandr Baranov who soon became the dominant personality in Russian America. Shelikhov and Baranov were iron-fisted men whose brutal practices caused concern in distant St. Petersburg.

As with other colonial empires, men on the scene intended to build their own power and wealth quickly at any cost to the natives, while central government wanted to preserve the natives for long-term growth and power. Yet concern for native welfare did not move the crown to discharge the colonial despots who were, after all, doing the empire's work. In this quandary, St. Petersburg quickly acquiesced when Shelikhov requested missionaries. They arrived on Kodiak Island in 1794.

Conflict developed at once. The missionaries served the state rather than the local bosses, and they perceived their duty to involve protection of the state's subjects and their church's converts. They protested vigorously against harsh treatment of the natives instead of justifying it, and they worked for amelioration. The modern scholar Lydia Black comments, "This stance was one of the major reasons why the Orthodox Church gained strength and adherents so that today it is perceived as *a native institution*, the primary marker of Aleut identity." [Italics added.]

But, tragically for the natives, most of the staff of the mission died in a shipwreck in 1799. In the same year the Russian American Company was granted a monopoly of commercial activity and was appointed the official representative of the Russian State. And Aleksandr Baranov was put in charge.

In colonial societies discrepancies always exist between official policy and actual practice. Russian citizenship for natives meant something different from the same legal status for Russians as is clearly demonstrated by the rule promulgated early in the nineteenth century. It stipulated that *only* half the native males might be impressed to hunt for the Russian American Company at any given time, and it further required that they must be paid for their labor at a minimum wage—not less than one-fifth the pay of a Russian. (Historically such discrepancies have been widespread, perhaps universal. For example, in mid-twentieth century, United States citizens working in the Panama Canal Zone were paid on the "gold" payroll; Panamanian natives doing the same work were on the "silver" payroll.)

Regardless of imperialists' dreams, lack of manpower and the attraction of sea-mammal peltry kept the Russians close to the coast. The restriction is reflected in modern maps by the long, thin strip of Alaska extending between Canada and the sea. Though the presence of Russians anywhere on the Pacific coast alarmed Spain, Baranov and the Russian American Company kept headquarters at distant Kodiak Island during the remainder of the eighteenth century.

But the Spaniards were indeed disturbed, so much so that after evicting the British from Nootka Spain reoccupied the place in 1791. Not for long. A book title concisely describes the affair as the *Flood Tide of Empire*, and the tide soon ebbed. By the end of the eighteenth century, Spain's power was on the decline.

Nootka long remained the focal point of international competition in the Northwest, and Nootka was in the territory of the Tlingit Indians, one of the strongest tribes in the region. The Tlingits were also clever about playing one European power against another through much of the nineteenth century. In consequence they maintained their aboriginal culture substantially intact until waves of newcomers arrived from the United States after Russia sold its colony in 1867.

Tlingit language connections suggest an origin inland among the Athapascan peoples as long as 5,000 years ago. (Much more recently, Athapascans migrating southward became Apaches and Navajos.) In the eighteenth century, when the Tlingits were first recorded by European observers, they still maintained what the Indians called "grease trails" of trade to the interior, but they had come to live mainly from the sea, exploiting five species of salmon as well as shore birds and their eggs, and sea mammals. (This plenty is another reason to believe that prehistoric migration from Beringia had moved southward along the coast.)

When European traders arrived, otter and seal furs became especially important, but the Tlingits kept their independence from trader domination. Shrewdly acquiring firearms from transitory New Englanders, they fought the Russians who had come to stay. Tlingits not only raided Aleuts hunting for the Russians; they attacked and destroyed settlements of the Russians themselves, ruining New Archangel (Sitka) in 1802, and Yakutat in 1805. Their sizable numbers, and especially their firearms, prevented vengeful retaliation such as Russians inflicted on weaker peoples.

No central control existed among the Tlingits. Even within a local community, government was by clans whose members might feel closer identification with matching clans in other localities than with different clans in their own neighborhoods. The sea and shore were bountiful, and the Tlingits became rich Indians who flaunted wealth. As among other peoples throughout the continent, their motive for acquiring possessions was to gain status by giving them away or ostentatiously destroying them. The famous "potlatch" ceremony was important to the Tlingits. By it a man could raise his rank and demean his competitors or enemies by aristocratic largesse greater than the rivals could hope to match.

The potlatch was practiced generally by the Indians of the Northwest Coast. Though natural resources were plentiful and European traders were lucratively competitive, the redistribution principle of the potlatch effectively prevented riches from becoming capital. Equally it forestalled the development of state-form polities based on property. In the long run, the intrusive state proved abler than the clan to amass and wield power.

Is it fated that power must always suppress altruism?

No account of Northwest Coast Indians, however condensed, may properly omit to mention the powerfully dramatic style of artistic creation that evolved there. Having seen it once, any observer recognizes it instantly at the second experience. The artists wove symbolic designs in cloth garments, and carved them into wooden totem poles and door frames, displaying much versatility in combining and interweaving the conventionalized forms of mythic creatures. Today their creations are recognized by critics as one of the great artistic traditions, as individual and coherent as the traditions of ancient Egypt or medieval India, and for the same reason: i.e., because religious belief infused and controlled the figures. Whether this traditional art can long survive exposure to the dominating culture called "Western" must be decided by time.

NOTE: DEZHNEV AND BERING

For a fascinating account of how academics got wrought up over Semen Dezhnev's voyage, partly because it became entangled with conflicting claims of the great powers, see "The Recovery of a Discovery," chapter 1 in *The Voyage of Semen Dezhnev in 1648: Bering's Precursor*, by Raymond H. Fisher, Works Issued by the Hakluyt Society, 2nd series, no. 159, London, 1981. The matter was still in dispute when Fisher published.

CHAPTER 30

The Vast Middle Northern Sector

In this chapter, the "Middle" includes regions from Hudson Bay and the Great Lakes extending to the Rocky Mountains and southward to the Missouri Valley. Its unity for present considerations was determined as an arena in which English and French fur trading companies, and multitudes of *coureurs de bois*, competed—and also cooperated on occasion—amidst Indians who had been trading with each other for centuries, but came to vie with each other in the eighteenth century for special privilege in trade with Europeans. In functional coherence, this "eighteenth century" begins before the calendar's, and it continues until the Seven Years War, 1754–1763.

In the 1660s, the Northwest opened up to European activity in the hazy way usual to such penetrations of strange territories. It is apparent that many entrepreneurial *coureurs de bois* had spread about the countryside north of the Great Lakes and had discovered that trading Indians congregated where Lakes Superior and Michigan pour into Lake Huron, in the vicinity of Saulte Ste. Marie. As most of these traders were engaged in illegal business, they were not eager to attract official attention, so documentation is sparse until Jesuit missionaries joined the crowd and began to send reports back to Montreal.

Light began to dawn after the founding of mission Saulte Ste. Marie in 1668 by Fathers Claude Dablon and Jacques Marquette. In 1671, Father Marquette founded mission Saint-Ignace on the straits of Michilimackinac. This was a momentous year. The Hudson's Bay Company set up its first "factory" and sent a governor over its claimed territory (called Rupert's Land). According to Peter C. Newman, a recent student of the Company, its chartered territory embraced an area ten times the area of the ancient Roman Empire at its maximum extent. (He may have been as generous with his calculations as with his lush rhetoric, but we get the idea.) In any case, the Company's influence and trade soon extended in various directions beyond its formal, rather vague boundaries.

The French were not laggards in the claims business. They had had ample warning because the *chartering* of the Company in 1670 was very public. In New France, Intendant Jean Talon responded to the English advance by sending Simon-François Daumont de Saint-Lusson to Saulte Ste. Marie where, on 4 June 1671, the emissary staged a ceremony. Before representatives of fourteen Indian nations, he intoned a proclamation that the immense territory, discovered and to be discovered, stretching from the seas of the north and west to the sea of the south, belonged to the king of France. A sod of earth was lifted in the air three times, a cross was erected, and a cedar post planted bearing the king's arms. The crowd, including the Indians, cheered lustily, "Long live the king." In records of this sort of bombastic nonsense, the Indians are always presented as delighted to have their lands taken away from them by fiat; however, the Hudson's Bay Company had a different feeling, and in practice the Indians shuttled between the grand claimants for their own advantage.

In brief, the events of 1671 mark the beginning of frontier war between England and France for empire in the great Northwest. When the English Company established a permanent post on the Bay, the French set up a competing post distant one week's travel away, and both sides soon made more posts. When relations worsened between their far-off crowns, competition became combat.

Their commercial strategies differed significantly. The Company's men sat tight in their trading post "factories," depending on Indians—mostly Crees and Assiniboines—to bring trade in. Their attraction was superior goods at cheaper prices, the products of the nascent Industrial Revolution in England.

French strategy, deprived of advantage in quality and price, resorted to "hard sell." Instead of waiting for Indians to come in to their posts, the French traders went out to Indian villages, and French agents mingled with chiefly families to influence tribal diplomacy. In retrospect it is difficult if not impossible to distinguish the traders from the political agents; they performed the same functions.

The arena of competition, so far as can be seen, was the broad "isthmus" between the Great Lakes and Hudson Bay, where activity quickly heated up. Geographically the Company had advantage by sailing directly to its posts from England, whereas Montreal's merchants were required to trudge and paddle to Michilimackinac. That distinction, however, had a reverse French advantage in diplomacy by involving arrangements for travel through tribal territories.

Both sides moved aggressively. In 1681 the French crown chartered the Compagnie de la Baie D'Hudson, and in the following year the French took prisoner the crews of English ships in the Bay. The English expanded from one post to three.

In 1686, French voyageurs and troops seized all the English posts on Hudson Bay but one, and for the rest of the century French attacks made life miserable for the clerks sent out from England. Though many of the lower echelon Company employees were Highland Scots accustomed to hard life, they were tenderfeet in comparison with the forest entrepreneurs of New France inured to the hazards and hardships of wilderness travel. Yet the Hudson's Bay Company managed to stay in business and make profit.

Intermittent English warships are one explanation, but not a sufficient one. Tribal concerns must be taken into account. The Indians had learned how to play the trading competitors against each other. Among other things, they discovered the variations between English and French business practices concerning price. The Company set standard prices in London, using a unit called "made beaver" as a sort of money of account. Good, bad, or indifferent, the price for a particular sort of fur was the same. The French, however, negotiated each transaction individually, adapting to markets, persons, and circumstances. When the market was favorable, many Indians took their finest furs to French traders for top prices, then peddled furs of less quality to the English for the pre-set standard prices. In reverse, when the French were handicapped by unfavorable markets, the Indians could take advantage of English standard prices. It was greatly to Indian advantage to keep the competition alive, and I think they took pains to do so. Neither side was ever able to eliminate the other completely.

Tribal diplomacy and statuses were also highly involved. Although most northern tribes were allied to New France, the Cree and Assiniboine "home guard" of Hudson's Bay Company were English clients who simultaneously abetted trade with distant western tribes and interposed themselves as middlemen. Another important middleman tribe was the Mesquakies, about whom more later. Probably most important in terms of balance of power were the Iroquois Five Nations allied to the English of New-York and the bicultural confederation called the Covenant Chain. Toward the end of the seventeenth century, New France and the Iroquois competed bitterly for control of the trade in the Great Lakes country. The French claimed it by right of discovery. The Iroquois claimed it by right of conquest over Hurons, Wenros, Eries, and Petuns. The French led several inconclusive, though punishing, invasions of Iroquoia, but the issue remained unsettled until they armed Ottawas, Ojibwas, and Mississaugas to reconquer Ontario from the Iroquois. Thus, what had been a "right," actually more substantial than that of "discovery," was nullified, but English diplomats pretended that the reconquest never took place. They recognized an Iroquois "empire" and insisted that England was sovereign over it because the Iroquois supposedly were England's "subjects."

By 1701 the beaten Iroquois treated for peace and obtained it on terms of standing neutral between the French and English. It was an odd sort of victory for New France. If the Iroquois had been forced into the French system of alliances, all of New France's Indian allies would have had an open path to Albany and English trade, with subsequent ruin for Montreal. The French needed the Iroquois as antagonists of other tribes to prevent free trade with Albany. Under the leadership of a master diplomat among the Onondagas, the chief called Teganissorens by the French and Decanisora by the English, the Iroquois adapted their strategy to the new situation by resorting to commercial diplomacy with French allies, offering special terms and free passage through Iroquoia to Albany's trade, which was precisely what the French did not want. They kept French agents very busy intercepting and nullifying the work of Iroquois negotiators.

Meantime the trade reached out from the bases on the Bay and the Lakes far to the west, and Indians traipsed all the way from the Missouri Valley to do business. René Cavelier de La Salle led an official expedition down the Mississippi, building forts along the way, each of which immediately became a base for the highly unofficial and omnipresent *coureurs de bois*. When the Iroquois tried to conquer the tribes of this "Illinois country," the French forestalled them.

The *coureurs de bois*, men of inextinguishable initiative, were true arbiters of imperial destinies in the Far Northwest—they and the missionaries who accompanied and sometimes preceded them. Odd couple though they were, they established patterns of culture that prevailed until the tidal wave of immigration from the east overwhelmed them in the nineteenth century.

The traders may be noticed in five aspects: they carried trade in the eighteenth century up to the very walls of the Rocky Mountains, long preceding the expedition of Lewis and Clark; they rediscovered routes of travel that had been set between tribes in pre-Columbian days; they mixed constantly in tribal politics to the general advantage of France though their patriotism was come-day, go-day; they smuggled without scruple for their own advantage against all the policies and laws of New France; and by their sexual and social activity they engendered a new population, neither wholly Indian nor wholly French, but deriving genetic and cultural features from both sides of their parentage. Offspring of the Scots and Englishmen of the Hudson's Bay Company mingled with and added to this new people whose uniform component everywhere was Indian ancestors.

This new people has suffered from the racial biases of historians who regarded synethnics as mere "half-breeds," neither true Europeans nor true Indians. It has not until recently occurred to scholars that the third alternative deserved respect in its own right. The French called them *métis*, meaning "mixed," and that term has become fixed especially on the community that came together around Red River near Winnipeg, but these mixed peoples grew up everywhere throughout the vast Mississippi basin and the regions drained by Hudson Bay and the Great Lakes. Their fathers were not exclusively French; lonely Englishmen also sired children born of Indian women, especially around Hudson Bay.

No matter how imperialists might plan and scheme, their policies had to suit the mixed peoples who policed themselves out beyond the reach of imperial arms. There was a large discrepancy between precept and practice, particularly notable in regard to "trading with the enemy." When the traders of the backwoods could get better bargains from merchants under a different flag, they hesitated only long enough to see if an official was watching. Sometimes the official played the same game. It is doubtful whether the important English trading centers of Albany and Philadelphia could have grown and prospered without the help of smuggling French traders and conspiratorial Indians.

French officials were able to intercept Thomas Dongan's effort to make direct contact with Michilimackinac, but they could not stop the illegal process by which western furs went first to Montreal's merchants, then to Albany's in exchange for English trade goods. When the merchants were squeezed by officialdom, they used Mohawks and "French Mohawk" Caughnawagas as middlemen. No official, French or English, could forbid trade with Indians.

So early as 1691, an expedition set out from Burlington, New Jersey, on the Delaware River near Philadelphia. Under command of Jacques Le Tort, a Huguenot gentleman of some standing, it followed tributary waterways to the Ohio River and the Mississippi, then up the Missouri, making friends with "over forty" Indian nations along the way and succeeding prosperously in trade. Le Tort's voyage did not achieve the fame of La Salle's north-to-south penetration of the Mississippi Valley (it was unofficial), but it had similar historic importance by introducing those far-off Indians to English goods and prices.

About the same time, and perhaps after joining Le Tort's party, a *coureur de bois* named Pierre Bisaillon (who became "Peter" in Pennsylvania) came to the vicinity of Philadelphia and began to work for merchants trading with Indians. Bisaillon had four brothers strategically placed in the Carolinas, the Illinois country, and at Lachine near Montreal. It is fairly plain from scanty documentation that they set up a sort of family syndicate that paid little or no attention to official edicts. Even more plainly, the Philadelphia merchants asked no embarrassing questions about how or where Bisaillon acquired the furs he so lucratively delivered.

Sometime in the 1690s a party of Minisink Indians (from the upper Delaware Valley) journeyed to the Mississippi and persuaded a band of Shawnees, right under the nose of La Salle's lieutenant Henri Tonty, to come east. With the Shawnees came Martin Chartier, a *coureur de bois* who had married one of the band. Chartier, who was in trouble with the law at Montreal, settled with his band on the Susquehanna River near Conestoga. Another band settled with the Minisinks. These Shawnees had friends and relations out west, and they became important in the trade of both Pennsylvania and New-York.

These are examples of persons who left some traces. We may confidently assume that they had many anonymous counterparts, for which the best evidence is what happened after the founding of Detroit in 1701. Yorkers urged the Iroquois to attack this strategic new post that guarded the strait between Lakes Erie and Huron, but the Iroquois had had enough punishment from New France and its allied tribes. They told the Yorkers to go take Detroit themselves—which was not attempted. Nevertheless, the English hung on in pretense. They pretended that the Iroquois owned Detroit "by right of conquest," and they took a "deed" from the Iroquois for a vast territory around the Great Lakes, west to the Mississippi. This scrap of paper became a sort of diplomatic time bomb to be exploded in mid-eighteenth-century negotiations between Britain and France.

More immediately useful, the Yorkers found the commander at Detroit to be a very cooperative gentleman. He was Antoine Laumet La Mothe Cadillac who amply earned the honor of having Detroit's twentieth-century luxury car named after him. A former commander at Michilimackinac, Cadillac well understood English desires to trade with the western tribes, and the results show that he knew whom to work with, and how. Historian Yves Zoltvany remarks that under Cadillac "Detroit had practically been transformed into a satellite of New-York's trading system." This, in effect, implicated the Iroquois who "missed no opportunity to exploit the Detroit Indians' eagerness to obtain English trade goods."

With knowledge of the Bisaillon brothers and the Shawnees of Martin Chartier, we may add that Philadelphia, as well as New York, probably had a substantial share in Detroit's trade. In 1718, brother Michel Bisaillon, who had worked with Cadillac at Detroit, visited merchant James Logan in Philadelphia and provided him with very detailed information about the entire region between the Lakes and the Ohio. Some of his data extended even into the Missouri Valley. His disclosures were worth a death sentence if they had been discovered in New France, and for good reason.

When reported to the Board of Trade and Plantations in London, Michel's information became the foundation for an aggressive new campaign to penetrate French domination of the Lakes country and Mississippi Valley. This failed, however. For the time being, it seems that French and British colonial merchants and their attendant traders and tribes had arrived at mutually satisfactory arrangements that resisted imperial policies.

When the system threatened to break down in the 1740s, its upsetters were primarily Indians—"Mingo" Iroquoians from the Five Nations homeland and the Susquehanna Valley, and Delaware Indians from the Schuylkill Valley and upper Delaware Valley. These displaced tribesmen migrated westward to the "Ohio country"—the valleys of feeder streams to the Ohio River and Lake Erie—and they were followed by traders especially from Pennsylvania. Under threat of eviction from the entire Ohio Valley, the French reacted violently and an imperial showdown ensued.

In the Far Northwest, Indians were long able to deal with the introduction of European trade goods without having to cope with the Europeans. Indians of the grasslands managed by simply continuing trading networks they had been operating for 5,000 years. They had, however, one special problem, and, throughout the seventeenth century, one special solution. The problem was the Sioux, a semi-nomadic people who shuttled back and forth, sometimes preferring the forests of northern Minnesota and Michigan's northern peninsula, sometimes attracted to the prairies of the Dakotas. Restless, decentralized, and fierce, their tribes were unpredictable and terroristic, especially to village peoples who could not simply get out of their way. Each component Sioux tribe made its own decisions for its own reasons so an agreement with one had no effect on the others.

To keep the Sioux under some sort of control, the trading Indians adopted the same policy as that of colonists farther east; the trading middlemen denied guns to the Sioux and thus maintained stability. Hudson's Bay Company's "Home Guard" of Crees and Assiniboines carefully maintained their profitable monopoly of direct access to the Company's factories. They were equally careful to keep on terms of profitable alliance with the traditional Mandan-Hidatsa trading centers on the Missouri River which exemplified one more "frontier in between." Though no Europeans except Le Tort's ephemeral party from Pennsylvania is *recorded* as visiting them before 1738, their villages handled trade from Pueblo country and Spaniards in the Southwest, from Frenchmen after the founding of New Orleans in 1718, and from tribes farther west all the way to the Pacific Coast. Still more middlemen were involved, many of whom traded at the Shoshone rendezvous in Wyoming.

William R. Swagerty passes on the observation of John C. Ewers that this giant trading network was "an elaboration of native patterns rather than . . . a European innovation." Numerous tribes were able "to acquire Spanish, French, and English trade goods a generation or more before they actually glimpsed a White trader." Our special attention here is with the Middle Missouri system focused on Arikara villages near the mouth of the Grand River (South Dakota) and the Mandan-Hidatsa villages near the mouth of the Knife River (North Dakota). The tribes who traded at these villages were many and varied: Crow, Assiniboine, Plains Cree, Cheyenne, Arapaho, Kiowa, Kiowa-Apache, and Comanche of the Plains brought goods to Mandan-Hidatsa. Teton Sioux came in to Arikara. They brought horses, dried meat, deer hides, bison robes, crafted leather goods; they took away Knife River flint, maize, and other produce of the village gardens, and trade goods carried down from Hudson Bay and Michilimackinac.

Later observers noted with grudging respect the commercial perspicacity of these tribal tradesmen. Guns that changed hands at the Bay for fourteen beaver pelts were passed on for fifty. Hatchets that cost the Crees three beavers at the factory were retailed for nine. Crows sold horses to Mandans at double their cost from the Shoshones, and the Mandans doubled the price again when selling to the Crees who had, of course, marked up their Company trade goods in the same manner.

The Mandans were redoubtable businessmen who used techniques that seem made for hard-selling corporations of the twentieth century. They staged special dances at fairs, and they offered women to customers (call girls, yet). They lived in large earth lodges in compact villages, and were renowned as rich people. But we may observe the likelihood that they still fell short of European business practice by never converting wealth into capital. (This judgment must be based on the universal Indian custom of redistributing riches. Confirmation was forestalled when catastrophe befell the Mandans in the nineteenth century and erased them as a political entity.)

Western Indians maintained their great trading network as long as Europeans kept their distance—the English at Hudson Bay, the French at Michilimackinac, and the Spaniards in New Mexico—but dreams of imperial glory by France's Louis XIV became troublesome reality in the Mississippi Valley that gradually pulled apart the traditional Indian trading network.

King Louis' American policies were only part of the flamboyant aggressions with which he drained France, but they added to the cost. He wanted to prevent the populous English seaboard colonies from breaking through the Appalachian Mountain barrier into the Mississippi Valley. To that end his ministers planted forts *with community settlements* at Detroit in 1701 and Mobile in 1711. With their settlements, these forts became something more than trading posts; they were colonies in reality. Detroit was supposed to prevent New-York's traffic through the Great Lakes. New Orleans was intended to prevent English entrance to the Mississippi and to foil the intrigues of traders from South Carolina. As we have seen, smugglers prevented Detroit from blocking English trade, but the fort there functioned efficiently nevertheless as a control and as a threat against overt English colonization. New Orleans became a base for French traders and missionaries along the Mississippi and up into the Missouri hub of the traditional Indian trading network.

The giant pincers operation along the great waterways—the Mississippi and the St. Lawrence–Great Lakes—was essentially a military conception that ignored demographic and economic realities. By it, the French tried for half a century to hold back British colonies that came to have twenty times the French number of ethnically European persons. The French necessarily resorted to help from Indian allies. This required provision of trade goods of ample quantity and quality, and the British had advantage there also. The French had no choice but to try to prevent contact between their Indian allies and British traders and agents.

Policies made in Versailles were at the mercy of those uncontrollable *coureurs de bois* in Indian villages, and they threw the tribes into turmoil. The first *official* Frenchman to reach the Mandan country was Louis-Joseph Gaultier de la Vérendrye who arrived in 1738 looking for a route to the Pacific, but he noted that unofficial *coureurs de bois* had preceded him. He gave no details. What became immediately at issue was the willingness of some of those Frenchmen—whether from Detroit or New Orleans is not clear—to sell guns to the aggressive Sioux who had been deprived of them in preceding intertribal trade. With firearms, Sioux bands hit the trading tribes as the Iroquois had earlier smashed the trading Hurons in the Lakes country.

The effects of Sioux raids were not as immediately catastrophic as the destruction of Huronia had been because the Sioux were not following a concerted plan as the Iroquois had done. Rather, in their pursuing resources from woodland to grassland, particular Sioux tribes or bands would descend upon particular villages in processes that were calamitous enough for the victims and gradually erosive for the region.

CHAPTER 31

War against the Foxes

We shall have to return to the West in the nineteenth century. Here we must notice once more that the Iroquois turned to diplomacy after 1701. Attempting a pincers movement of their own, they allied with the Mesquakie Indians (Outagamis, Reynards, Foxes), many of whom were drawn from Green Bay (Wisconsin) by Cadillac's invitation to settle near Detroit after 1710.

What happened then exposes the fallacy that the French generally "embraced" the Indians. Different sources slant the events in a variety of ways, but the substantial fact emerges bright as day: to wit, the French government authorized or organized repeated massacres of the Foxes in an attempt to exterminate them entirely. One must distinguish. Both *the French* and *the Indians* are misleadingly homogenizing phrases. It is true that French *coureurs de bois* mingled with and lived with Indians of particular tribes, and that French officialdom allied with particular tribes; but both traders and officials joined *their* tribes in a demonstration of the classic aphorism that the enemy of my friend is my enemy. Both traders and officials fought fiercely against their tribal enemies. As embraces go, this was the hug of a grizzly bear.

We have seen the implacable French enmity for the Iroquois nations, tempered only by the need to keep the Iroquois existing as an obstruction to trade with Albany. We shall see again in chapter 32 how Frenchmen wiped out the Natchez nation in the South. Here let us look at the French and the Foxes.

Underlying Montreal's hostility was the belief that the Foxes were harming trade rather than contributing to it. Cadillac had invited them to Detroit, but Cadillac was a smuggler to the English (and known as such) and Montreal's very well informed merchants disliked other smugglers who interfered with their own arrangements. They saw rapprochement between Foxes and Iroquois as an extension of Albany's trading network to their own cost. They contrived to get Cadillac transferred to New Orleans. His successor was Jacques-Charles Renaud Dubuisson, whose policies were the opposite of Cadillac's.

It was only a matter of time until friction should develop between Dubuisson and the Foxes. For their part, they contributed to tension by what the French called a haughty, "insolent" attitude toward neighboring tribes as well as Frenchmen. All sources agree that those Foxes were independent and tough. Crisis came in 1712 when a party of Mascoutens, who were Fox allies, fled to Detroit from a war party of Ottawas and Potawatomis who were strong French allies. Fox chief Pemoussa offered protection to his allies, and French commandant Dubuisson joined the French allies who besieged their enemies for nineteen days.

This brawl ran deeper than a frontier episode. Pemoussa offered peace terms twice, but Dubuisson rejected them. What he wanted was not just the Foxes' capitulation, but their destruction. When they escaped the siege, they were pursued and forced to surrender, whereupon, as Dubuisson's biographer remarks, "most of the male captives were butchered, and Dubuisson reported the total losses as 1,000 enemy, 60 allies, and 1 Frenchman." In consequence, "This victory established Dubuisson's reputation both at Quebec and among *the Indians*." (My emphasis.) Here are *the Indians* again. It seems likely that the Foxes surviving farther west held different views from *the Indians*.

Thus began the "Fox Wars." The Foxes still at Green Bay were aroused instead of terrified by the massacre near Detroit. As their raiding parties kept trade in an uproar, the French launched new campaigns against them, futilely in 1715, apparently more successfully in 1716. Interestingly, the army of 1716 was composed of 400 *coureurs de bois* and 400 Indians of various tribes. One of the traders was Michel Bisaillon who had been denounced by a missionary as smuggling to the English (accurately enough). He redeemed himself officially by recruiting a party of Illinois Indians against the Foxes. (After which, he joined brother Peter in Philadelphia.)

Under command of Louis de La Porte de Louvigny, this expedition arrived at what seems like a surprisingly amicable peace settlement with the Foxes under chief Pemoussa who had survived the Detroit massacre. Perhaps Pemoussa's influence was part of the reason, but another becomes apparent when we turn from Canadian writers to the Wisconsin historian Louise Phelps Kellogg: "Reading between the lines, one recognized that this was a vast trading expedition, disguised under a show of war in order to deceive the court in France." It is not so strange, after all, that an army of traders should prefer business to fighting. They took Pemoussa as a hostage back to Montreal where Governor General Vaudreuil relied upon him to maintain the peace. How Pemoussa could have managed his tribesmen from that distance is puzzling, but he died in Montreal of smallpox in the winter of 1716–17. The Foxes continued to be independent.

From their home base at Green Bay, they followed the Iroquois pattern of alternation between diplomacy and war. They fought bitterly with Illinois tribesmen who were close allies of the French, and they interfered constantly with French trade in the Mississippi Valley. At the turn of the eighteenth century, the French had not yet developed traffic south of the Great Lakes and down the Ohio River; they still used and depended on a route that took them into Wisconsin and westward to the Mississippi, but the Foxes stood athwart that route.

Fox Chief Kiala resembled the Iroquois also in grandeur of conception. He aimed to create a giant confederacy stretching from the Abenakis and Iroquois in the east through the Foxes, including even their traditional enemies the Sioux, and farther west to the Missouri and Oto tribes. If successful, Kiala would certainly have made French occupation precarious, and he might have driven them out. He failed because the Sioux defected and the French struck first.

In one decisive feature, the Foxes differed from the Iroquois. Whereas the French needed the Iroquois as an obstruction to trade between their Indian allies and Albany, the Foxes were an obstacle to trade between western tribes and the French. This the French neither needed nor would tolerate. Foxes pulled a trigger by wiping out a party of eight French soldiers from Fort de Chartres. A new governor general promptly decided on a final solution to this problem. Governor Charles de Beauharnois de La Boische, Marquis de Beauharnois, organized an army of about 1,500 tribesmen and Frenchmen to attack the Green Bay homeland of the Foxes in 1728, but they were forewarned and escaped in time. Although this French expedition failed of total victory, its display of power frightened Fox confederates into hastening to make peace, which meant abandoning hunting parties of the Foxes to punishing raids from French allies.

Isolated and menaced, the Foxes asked for asylum among the Senecas. This was offered, and the Weas gave permission for passage through their territory. The whole Fox nation began the long trek to the east in 1730.

French officers learned of the plan. Hastily mustering their forces, they pursued the migrating Foxes, caught up with them, and repeated the massacre of 1712. French forces and their allies killed between 400 and 600 men, women, and children, and enslaved about as many more. Once again, those who escaped fled back to their old home in Wisconsin where French mission Indians fell upon them still once more, killing or capturing 300, but even this was not enough to satisfy Governor Beauharnois. Though only fifty warriors still lived, and Chief Kiala begged for mercy in Montreal, Beauharnois ordered the utter extermination of the tribe. He sent Kiala in slavery to Martinique where the chief soon died.

As it happened, Beauharnois' plan went awry in a way not anticipated. He was to learn that "the Savages have their policy as we have Ours, and they are not greatly pleased at seeing a nation destroyed, for Fear that their turn may come." French troops sent to complete the genocide of the remaining Foxes found them refuging among Sauks who refused to give them up. The French, as well as the Indians, lost heavily at the ensuing battle of Butte des Morts in 1734. They retreated.

Sauks and Foxes united firmly thereafter. Although they retain individual identities, they are known today as the Sac and Fox tribe. Other tribes unsympathetic to Beauharnois' policy sent Fox captives back to join their people, and the battered but bellicose allies retreated into Iowa where they enforted themselves. When Beauharnois exhorted his allies to attack them, he met with refusal. He sent French troops who were misdirected by Kickapoo guides and beaten by their intended victims.

In the historical literature, the Foxes are usually portrayed as arrogant brutes hated by all the other tribes, but this image originates as war propaganda from French enemies, and it is at odds with Fox ability first to create a wide confederation, later to win protection from so many neighbors. Events force a conclusion that the arrogance imputed to them by the French scribes might better be interpreted as refusal to take French orders. The same attitude, as shown by individuals, is often termed *insolence*. Scribal semantics require careful comparison with demonstrated facts.

Sioux bands briefly stayed allied to New France, probably because of their ancient enmity to the Foxes, but they too turned hostile in 1736 when they massacred a party of twenty traders and a missionary. All in all, what had seemed to be a great triumph over the Foxes had turned to ashes. Even in the southern range of the Mississippi (as will be shown) Frenchmen lost control to the "savages." When a delegation of western chiefs came to Montreal in 1737 to ask for mercy for the Sauks and Foxes, Beauharnois interpreted their request as a demand he was powerless to refuse.

Whereupon—such are the ironies of history—the new peace policy produced the benefits for French trade that the assaults upon the Foxes had been supposed to achieve. Communication routes were reopened, and French western settlements grew.

Yet one more irony: the policy of conciliation that brought this new prosperity was administered by Paul Marin de La Malgue, the officer who would soon help to bring on the Seven Years War with Britain by his own imposition of force in the Ohio Country.

CHAPTER 32

End of the Natchez

> The Commandant, upon the [Natchez Sun's] arrival at the fort, told him, without further ceremony, that he must look out for another ground to build his village on, as he himself resolved, as soon as possible, to build on the village of the Apple, that he must directly clear the huts, and retire somewhere else. . . . But he knew not that the natives of Louisiana are such enemies to a state of slavery, that they prefer death itself thereto . . .
>
> —ANTOINE LE PAGE DU PRATZ

By the turn of the eighteenth century, the trading frontier in the Southeast had become very complex. It included Spaniards based in Florida, *official* Frenchmen at Mobile and others descending the Mississippi, Indians of a dozen important tribes, and Englishmen from Carolina. We must make distinctions among traders and fit them into their semantic and political contexts. Frenchmen out among the Indians were *voyageurs* if licensed, *coureurs de bois* if they acted independently of authority. The *voyageurs*, naturally enough, cooperated with military authorities in conformity with official policies. *Coureurs de bois*, however, were laws unto themselves. According to Marcel Giraud, thirty to forty of them in the Southeast "claimed to be independent of any government" and rejected proffered amnesty conditioned on return to Conada. "They reached Carolina by way of the Tennessee [River] and returned with English goods." Prominent among them was one Jean Couture who deserted from New France sometime before 1696 and acquired special influence among the Shawnees. The Bisaillon family network was linked to the region by brother Richard and apparently also by brother Michel in the Illinois country.

It is equally necessary to distinguish different types of traders on the English side. The "plantation" type waited on their estates for skins to be brought to them. Such men, who easily developed into import-export merchants, existed in Carolina as well as in New-York where they predominated. To some extent this type of trader was dependent on the policies of nearby tribes who controlled access from more distant Indians. A new type of independent trader emerged in Carolina after the Westos were ruined in 1680. Like the Frenchmen, he took his goods out into Indian villages, and it is not surprising to find him getting along swimmingly with those Frenchmen (with the *coureurs de bois*, that is, not with licensed *voyageurs*). They were birds of a feather—but not precisely the same feather. What distinguished them from each other, besides ethnicity, was different relationships to political authority. The *coureurs* were outlaws, whereas the Carolinian traders often controlled the assemblies that supposedly regulated them. It was easy, therefore, for them to draw the Frenchmen into fraternal relations of commerce just as something of the same sort had stimulated a trading system in Pennsylvania based on the Bisaillons and other independent Frenchmen.

Out in the Indian communities, these independent traders carried more weight than the agents of state power. They carried on their own diplomacy based on private armies, and they acquired great powers among the Indians because they brought directly to the villages what those Indians wanted, especially guns. Official Frenchmen withheld guns from their tribal allies during this era. Carolinians and *coureurs de bois* observed no such restriction, and the tribes they armed were able to loot and enslave other Indians.

We may remember that Iroquois with guns had ruined Huron traders who lacked firearms. So also in the Southeast, firearms became the key to success by Carolinians and their allies. They armed the Chickasaw tribe and instigated it to attack Choctaws who were allied to official French agents. Unarmed and populous Choctaws made easy prey for the slave markets. To call this sort of process the "fur trade" is clearly a misnomer. Besides being a trade *with* Indians, it was a trade *in* Indians. That it was a frontier phenomenon is beyond question, but the most cursory thought reveals it as inconsistent with the dicta of Frontier Theory. This frontier was one more of many regional frontiers-in-the-middle in which Indian peoples lived among and contended with Europeans pressing in upon them from several directions. A "line between civilization and savagery" cannot be found in it.

What can be found is an explicit expression of English policy to use trade, particularly trade in weapons, as means to subjugate Indians. James Merrell has dug up an instruction in 1681 by the True and Absolute Lords Proprietors of Carolina to the colony's governor and council which leaves no possibility of ambiguity: ". . . furnishing a bold and warlike people with Armes and Ammunition and other things usefull to them

. . . tyed to soe strict a dependance upon us . . . that whenever that nation that we sett up shall misbehave themselves towards us, we shall be able whenever we please by abstaineing from supplying them with Ammunition . . . to ruine them." The device was simple and easy to administer, and it was highly effective. It still is as twentieth-century great powers provide complex arms to lesser states dependent upon the providers for replacement parts.

In 1700, Pierre Le Moyne d'Iberville noted that "allies of the English . . . were armed with muskets," and he appealed to Choctaw and Chickasaw chiefs to end their warfare in their own interest. Because of English incitement, he declared, the Chickasaws had killed more than 1800 Choctaws and had taken 500 Choctaw prisoners. During the same span of eight or ten years, the Chickasaws themselves had lost 800 men in their raiding. Iberville threatened that if the Chickasaws failed to oust English traders he would arm their Choctaw opponents as he had already started to do with other tribes. Peace settled temporarily, but Iberville was no pacifist. Having stalled Carolinian advance for the time being, he concocted a grand scheme to reverse the direction of march by mobilizing Indians and Floridian Spaniards to conquer Carolina, but this got nowhere. Spaniards were not about to become catspaws for the French.

It seemed to English gentry of that era that they could do anything they pleased in America. The court physician, Dr. Daniel Coxe, was one of the projectors who thought *big*, and his schemes acted powerfully on the Indians of the lower Mississippi Valley although Coxe never left England. This busy, busy man owned a trading center in Burlington, New Jersey. About 1687 or 1688, he sent a party led by Huguenot Jacques Le Tort up the Missouri River. In 1698, having acquired a dubious sea-to-sea charter for "Carolana," Coxe negotiated with Huguenot refugees in England to establish a colony west of Apalachicola River, and he "transferred" 500,000 acres to them in anticipation of quitrents to come.

It is amazing to read of the casual way that such gentlemen disposed of airy empires and their Indian inhabitants by simply drawing some lines on vague maps. (After the first American spacecraft reached the moon, a jokester printed up "deeds" for lunar lots and sold them to persons who shared his sense of humor. But Coxe was serious!)

And he was taken seriously by the French because his proposed settlement constituted an escalation of the conflict simmering between French and Carolinian traders. It was one thing to let the traders conspire among the tribes in their customary ruthless style of competition. It was quite another thing to sit quietly by while the English took possession by planting a settlement. This being intolerable, the French pricked Dr. Coxe's bubble by planting their own settlements first. Coxe publicized his project in 1698. In 1699, Pierre Le Moyne d'Iberville built Fort Maurepas at Biloxi (Mississippi) by direction of the French ministry, and he laid the foundations of a Louisiana intended to dam the English behind the Appalachian Mountain wall.

As also elsewhere, French celerity was possible because it was state-directed and militarily executed. In contrast, Coxe's Carolana project was that of private persons accumulating resources by negotiation. The result showed how much more efficient the military procedure could be—Iberville did foil Coxe. But the efficiency of an episode is not the same thing as advantage over the long term. The factor of expense must be weighed into this balance. Coxe's project cost the English crown the price of paper and seal for his charter; and had it succeeded it would have added income to the royal treasury. Louisiana, on the other hand, never paid its way despite the advantages it created in trade with Indians. Trade's profits were private; the cost of the infrastructure (to borrow a modern term) was public. Maintaining the Appalachian dike against the British flood looked better on a military map than on a financial report. Louisiana became and remained a drain on the royal treasury of France. Here as in Canada, Frenchmen settled sparsely in numbers that did not begin to compare with the immigrants pouring into Britain's colonies. In the long run, population created more power than militarization. Unfortunately for the French, the tribal populations on which they depended for manpower continued to decline from epidemic and war while British colonials increased. What must be added is that some Frenchmen did their bit to reduce Indian numbers.

We have seen how that happened in the Fox wars. In Louisiana, however, conflict had to be postponed for a while as Carolinian aggression impelled the French to seek friendship among Indians wherever they could find it.

Louisiana stayed in French possession, not so much by reason of frantic French effort, as by the self-undoing of the English whose excesses raised up enemies in their own back yards. In 1712, Virginia suddenly had to cope with aroused Tuscaroras. When beaten down, many of the Tuscaroras fled north to temporary refuge in ever-hospitable Pennsylvania, later to continue on to Iroquoia as the Sixth nation of the Iroquois League. Apart from other considerations, their migration was a dead loss to the traders from Virginia and Carolina who had competed for their business.

Carolina's comeuppance came in 1715 with the Yamasee War. Brutal-

The beginning of Louisiana at Biloxi. Photographed courtesy of the Newberry Library from a large print hanging there.

ity, fraud, and debauchery among the Carolina traders had strained Indian patience beyond the breaking point. Creeks broached an uprising, and Yamasees touched it off with massacres of traders and destruction of border settlements. French officials would not mourn over the richly deserved fate of Thomas Nairne who had played so much havoc in Louisiana. Because he had been as ruthless with the Indians allied to Carolina as with those of Louisiana, the Yamasees burned him at the stake over a slow fire. In a situation where no Indian could prefer charges in court against any Englishman, the Yamasees brought Nairne to justice in the only way open to them. So doing, they eliminated one of the most potent

leaders of anti-French aggression, and one of the most vicious men in all the colonies.

Other tribes joined the fury—Choctaws, Cherokees, Yuchis, Apalaches, Shawnees, Catawbas, Saraws, Waccamaws, Santees, Cape Fears—until, in Verner W. Crane's words, "around Charles Town was drawn a menacing circle of fire and destruction." Charles Town got some help from Virginia, but it seemed that Virginians also saw opportunity to take over parts of Carolina's trading system. Between the two colonies, though both were English, much antagonism existed. The Carolinians, who were experienced in backwoods war, resisted their Indian attackers with considerable success. Diplomacy won the war when they succeeded in detaching the Cherokees from their enemies, a feat that caused the Creeks to move farther back into the mountains and the Yamasees to retire into Florida.

This war produced various results. Louisiana became secure to the French. Florida regained a significant Indian population. The British crown rescinded the charter of South Carolina's proprietors and made the colony royal. (All of Britain's chartered colonies lived under this threat of loss of charter for failure to keep their Indians quiescent.) For a while, the Carolinians were reined in.

The aggressions of Louis XIV in Europe had provoked so much opposition that he had little money to spare for Louisiana, so he tried to get glory, English fashion, on the cheap; but he lacked the knack. He turned the colony over to the financier Antoine Crozat who pumped men and money into the place, but the object of financiers is profit rather than glory, and Crozat lost interest when he saw how little return his investment would bring. He delivered the charter back to the crown. Next it went to John Law, the Scottish big speculator in France, whose "Mississippi Bubble" inflated and burst, leaving many investors bitterly broke, and Louisiana once more royal. It is perhaps superfluous to mention that no Indians were consulted in all this tossing about of their homelands.

Still the colony managed to survive, squeezed between Spanish competitors on both sides and the ever-threatening English of Carolina reinforced after 1733 by the founding of Georgia. Small subsidies came from the French treasury, but Louisiana could not have endured without its trade with Indians of the vast Mississippi Valley. Traders who had picked up a cargo from as far away as the upper Missouri Valley found it far easier to float it down to New Orleans, founded in 1718, than to go laboriously upstream to Michilimackinac or across to Detroit. Indeed, New Orleans came to be considered in Montreal as a competitor. Trade with Indians was never simple.

One might assume that Louisiana Frenchmen would feel some gratitude for the hospitality of the particular Indians among whom they had thrust themselves, but such an assumption does not fit the mentality of the militaristic colonialists in charge of Louisiana. These were a very different lot from the *coureurs de bois* who assimilated to Indian customs and married into Indian families. Those troops were not placed amid Indians because of officialdom's love for the natives; they were there to exert control. To the soldiers, marooned by orders in a godforsaken outpost thousands of miles from civilization's familiar amenities, the Indians were at best a necessary evil, otherwise just a damned irritating nuisance. To the Indians the soldiers were an arrogant, swaggering lot of presumptuous, thieving bullies. It was only a matter of time until such incendiary materials should blaze up.

So long as trouble came mainly from clashes of personalities, it could be smoothed over. In 1724, a local commander of Fort Rosalie in the midst of the Natchez country failed to discipline one of his men who had shot an elderly Indian who was walking away from an altercation with the soldier. Thus provoked, Natchez warriors took to arms and killed two Frenchmen, but they were talked out of war by a French planter whom they trusted and by their own chiefs who were not ready for full-scale combat with the French.

These Natchez were extraordinary among the Indians. By their own tradition, they had come originally from Mexico, and their culture was wholly unrelated to the lifeways of the Indians surrounding them. It is evident that they descended from the "Mississippian" Mexican colonials whose commercial empire had sprawled over the entire Mississippi Valley and most of the Southeast. They were still a numerous people who commanded respect from all the tribes of the Southeast. They were also, in the estimate of French military men, in a position to wipe out the French amidst them by surprise.

Once more the local commandant at Fort Rosalie started trouble. In 1729, he demanded that the Natchez abandon their head village so that he could take its lands for himself. By that time, they had had enough. Like the Foxes in the north, they organized a wide anti-French conspiracy of the tribes. Fighting started prematurely with a Natchez massacre in 1731 of one French settlement. Warned, the others defended themselves, organized an anti-Natchez alliance, and prosecuted a retaliatory massacre. Natchez survivors fled to the Caddo territory of Natchitoches, but the garrison of a French fort there exterminated them; others sought refuge among the Chickasaws upstream on the Mississippi, where they were accepted and defended against French campaigns led by Governor Bienville himself. Most of his 500 Natchez captives were sold into West Indian slavery.

The Natchez nation ceased to exist. As with the Foxes, however, its fate was remembered among other tribes at least as long as the refugees lived, and the memory did not conduce to trust of French agents.

One yearns for source materials from the Indian sides of these conflicts. How genuine were those giant intertribal conspiracies so dear to the imaginations of Europeans in Indian country? Some scholars will rise in passionate defense of Indian abilities to organize widespread alliance systems, and they may be right up to a point, but the real question concerns the capacities of tribes rather than motives of "Indians." Given the conditions of tribal cultures, with their strong emphasis on local independence and their lack of the nation-state's institutions for coercion, how could the members of a wide conspiracy have been held to the same policies for any length of time? It seems foreordained that they would subordinate the general interest to their particular goals. The strongest argument for such an inference is the historical record: the alleged conspiracies always broke up at times of crisis.

CHAPTER 33

The Northeast

The Northeast region of the United States is a place of intertwined river systems originating in the Appalachian Mountains and flowing from north to south into the Atlantic. The parallel Connecticut, Hudson, Delaware, and Susquehanna rivers, with their tributaries and some smaller streams, drain the territory, and before being dammed they provided means to travel upstream to the interior. Their direction of flow naturally drew a traveler's attention to what awaited him *in the North* beyond the watershed. Western interests were slower to attract British colonials.

In the eighteenth century their interior was Indian country, and the Indians paddled busily downstream as well as up. There was as much intercommunication through the multiple river valleys of the Northeast as in the more obvious great basin of the Mississippi.

The Susquehanna's extension in Chesapeake Bay linked Maryland and Virginia to the Northeast though Englishmen in those colonies thought of themselves as southerners. Regardless of that self-conception, when Virginians at mid-century launched a campaign of expansion they aimed toward the northwest. South of the mouth of Chesapeake Bay was unquestionably the southeastern region; as we have seen, expansion there aimed toward the west and south.

In both eastern regions, Indians lived in the middle. In the Northeast they were boxed in by a row of British coastal colonies facing north and west to New France which spent much energy to push the British back. The Indians of this frontier-in-the-middle were speakers of Algonquian and Iroquoian languages, with the strategically important Iroquois Five Nations occupying the middle of the middle, the highland watershed from which great waters flowed in every direction but due east. Some Iroquois nations were clearly in the Northeast region as it then existed, but the Iroquoian Senecas sat on top of the "Ohio country" which was considered western in the eighteenth century.

In the eighteenth century the Northeast became the region of show-down between Britain and France, culminating finally in the Seven Years War of 1754 to 1763. (The dates make it nine years, but the name is less chauvinistic than "The French and Indian War.") After Britain's victory in that war, the Northeast became also the region of that decisive conflict between Britain and her colonies which culminated in the foundation of the United States of America.

Histories of these tumults ordinarily relegate Indians to minor roles, unimportant and subsidiary to the main events. This approach can have some justification in histories of nation-states—the big battles were won, after all, by European-style armies—but a history of American Indians must attend more seriously to what the Indians did or refused to do, and certainly to the effects of the great wars upon tribal peoples who could not possibly be merely passive spectators.

As everywhere else, commerce was the key to intertribal and intersocietal relations. Goods moved up and down the Connecticut River between Canada and New England; and up and down the Hudson River–Lake George–Lake Champlain–Richelieu River "Mahican Channel" between Canada and New York. The Iroquois had access to both these routes, and used them. A little farther west, the headwaters of the Delaware and Susquehanna rivers originated in Iroquoia. The Susquehanna, especially, might well be called the Mississippi of the East. Besides carrying freight, its valleys delivered Iroquois war parties "behind" the British colonies of Maryland, Virginia, and Carolina, where they created incessant turmoil.

Certain arrangements were needed to make these Iroquois raids feasible. Officials in New York and Pennsylvania turned blind eyes to them despite furious protests from governors of southern colonies demanding punitive action against the Iroquois. Officials in the "middle colonies" were acutely conscious of dependence upon the Iroquois as a bulwark against French aggression, and the Iroquois were an especially desirable military defense because they paid their own way in profitable trade as well as in manpower that the colonials regarded as expendable.

Pennsylvanians were determinedly incurious about the destinations and purposes of Iroquois war parties marching southward across the colony's claimed jurisdiction, and the astute Iroquois took pains to preserve the colonists' lack of curiosity by carefully keeping beyond the areas settled by immigrants from Europe. The tacit understanding was even confirmed by secret treaty in 1710, but the manuscript record of that event was kept out of Pennsylvania's official records and away from prying outsiders who would have been very curious indeed if they had been permitted to see it.

Traffic along the Susquehanna Valley became so heavy that the route has been called "the warriors' path." Demography as well as geography made it attractive to the Iroquois because the pacifist Quakers of Pennsylvania avoided the use of armed force against Indians which had become horrifyingly familiar elsewhere. The Susquehanna Valley early in the eighteenth century had become a sanctuary for Indian refugees who could feel secure there. Fugitives had settled there from New England's second Puritan conquest (called "King Philip's War"), from "back country" Indians of Maryland and Virginia, from La Salle's Fort St. Louis on the Illinois River, and from war-torn Tuscarora villages in North Carolina. They were joined by Delawares dispossessed from their Brandywine lands at Delaware Bay, and by Susquehannocks and Senecas fleeing from the incessant pounding of Iroquoia by French allies. All settled along a short span of the Susquehanna River near the trading post at the mouth of Conestoga Creek which was secretly owned by provincial secretary James Logan.

By 1710 there was a thriving Indian population along the river. It consisted entirely of fragments of whole tribes or nations, without unitary government. They were held together and in order by the covert policies of the Iroquois league and Pennsylvania's government, and by the trade available at the Conestoga store. The Iroquois were happy with this arrangement on several counts. The communities near Conestoga fed and rested those Iroquois war parties on their long marches southward, for which reason the Iroquois called them "props" of the League. Young men of the Susquehanna communities who yearned for distinction as warriors would join the Iroquois parties. When the returning raiders were pursued by revenge-bent Catawbas or other southern tribes, the Susquehanna Indians took the brunt of their fury while the Iroquois warriors went home, safely beyond reach.

This situation contradicted the promise of peace and security that had attracted Indian immigrants to the locality. For immigrants from Europe, however, the promise held good until mid-century, and its very validity became the undoing of the Indians. Beginning with "peace people" newcomers from Switzerland and the Rhine Valley, and increased in numbers by whole congregations fleeing the rack rents of absentee landlords of Ireland, a tide of immigrants poured into Pennsylvania, beginning about 1712 and accelerating year by year. They were almost all country people hungry for land, and they soon began pushing at the edges of Indian villages.

The pressures on Pennsylvania's Indians mounted seriously. The colony was proprietary, its lands having been granted to William Penn by royal charter. Penn sincerely desired to "do good" for the Indians and he recognized their original right to the land, but he died in 1718 leaving his property rights and huge debts to his sons. In their eyes, and as so common elsewhere, Indians receded from human status to that of nuisance. John, Thomas, and Richard Penn liquidated their debts by selling land in large lots (5,000, 10,000, 20,000 acre "lots"), and when some "Forks of Delaware" Indians protested that the land belonged to them, *these* Penns arranged to have the nuisances removed.

They were smoother than the bloody desperadoes of Carolina. The younger Penns made a deal with the Iroquois league whose chiefs allowed themselves to be persuaded that they had conquered the protesting Delawares. In return for recognition as exclusive spokesmen for all of Pennsylvania's Indians, and some more substantial immediate benefits, the Iroquois menaced the protesting Delawares into leaving their land. By a fraudulent device called the Walking Purchase, the Penns put a face of legality on the transaction that fooled historians nearly 200 years. (Its details are in my books, *Ambiguous Iroquois Empire* and *Empire of Fortune*.) The Delawares were shoved off their land without bloodshed or compensation, and the Penns kept their charter, unlike other proprietary lords whose Indians fought back against dispossession.

Actually, this squalid transaction only climaxed a process that had been operating without much publicity for several decades. As Pennsylvania's immigrants grew in number, they founded an arc of new towns north and west of Philadelphia at a radius of about forty miles away—Lancaster, Reading, Allentown, Bethlehem, Easton—and the immigrants muscled the natives aside. The Brandywine Delawares who first migrated to Conestoga made a further retreat over the mountains to the "Ohio country." They were joined by "Schuylkill Delawares" pushed out by the Germans who founded Reading. Later some of the "Forks of Delaware" Delawares went west also as Moravians, Germans, and Scotch-Irish planted Bethlehem, Allentown, and Easton. Farther upstream, the Shawnees at Minisink were ordered west by Iroquois chiefs intending a new warriors' path toward Detroit, but these Shawnees double-crossed them by settling instead under the protection of New France. When immigrants breached the Susquehanna River boundary of Indian territory, the motley natives who had settled along the river went further west or up north into Iroquoia.

The net result of all this was a growing Indian population in the formerly empty hunting territory of the Ohio country—a region that included the valley of the Allegheny tributary of the Ohio River as well as the upper Ohio itself. The new residents were all Indians who had suffered dispossession from ancestral homelands, and who were determined not to be evicted again. For them the Appalachian Mountains were a dam to hold back British colonials. Coincidentally, this was just how Frenchmen felt about those mountains.

The Iroquois, however, were more ambivalent. Like the banker who gambles with other people's money, they had learned a trick of selling other tribes' lands to the British. (The French refused to play that game.) Realists that they were, the Iroquois understood that they could not stop colonial expansion. They aimed instead at guiding and controlling it as much as might be, and to that end they manipulated the tribes of the Covenant Chain. By their management, Iroquoia held firm against thrusting Yorkers and Yankees while the Susquehanna Indians were made to allow expansion from Pennsylvania. It was expertly, if somewhat ruthlessly, done; but west of the mountains could not be managed as easily. Delawares and Shawnees there had congregated under more unified leadership than they had had in the East. The French were not far away. And hard times in Iroquoia had attracted young warriors from that land to become neighbors of the other tribes at the Ohio. Together with Iroquoian migrants from the Susquehanna, they made up a substantial population of "Mingos" who paid little attention to orders from the old league centered on Onondaga. Altogether, by about 1740, there were more Indians in the Ohio country than in Iroquoia, and they were very restive under Iroquois leadership in the Covenant Chain.

Into this new population came a catalyst—traders from Pennsylvania who followed their old customers with pack horses to set up new trading houses, and who attracted Indians from the west as well as the east. Frenchmen were greatly distressed. Pennsylvania's traders offered better and cheaper goods than Montreal's, so Frenchmen found their business drying up. French officials saw that British traders had breached the mountain dike, and assumed correctly that British colonists would soon follow. The rock foundation of French strategy, for which much blood and treasure had been spent at other times and places, seemed to have been destroyed. The same tide of immigrants that had pushed Indians over the mountains would push Frenchmen out of the Mississippi Valley. Something had to be done, but what?

For a while, French governments in Canada and France did nothing as their western position gradually eroded. Far from being in control of vast armies of Indians, their strength had narrowed down to reliable allies among the western "Three Fires" of Ottawas, Ojibwas, and Potawatomis, and in the east the mission Indians, the Abenakis, Algonquins,

Micmacs, and other northeastern tribes beyond the reach of British trade or seduction. Gains by traders from Pennsylvania and Carolina made it seem that Britain's allies might soon outnumber France's.

In 1750, some Virginia gentlemen forced the French to decision. Forming the Ohio Company of Virginia, they laid plans to build a fort and found a settlement at the junction where the Allegheny and Monongahela rivers form the Ohio. For the empires it was a highly strategic position. Whoever held it would be able to control all traffic feeding into and moving along the Ohio River, and British superiority in trade goods was already attracting tribes in the Ohio Valley to Pennsylvania's entrepreneurs. Control of the river had easily visible implications for regions beyond.

Virginia's project seemed entirely feasible. The Indians living at and near the forks of the Ohio were Delawares, Shawnees, and Mingo Iroquois, all of whom had long been accustomed to treat with British agents rather than French, and all of whom were already involved with Pennsylvania's traders. Virginia would need their agreement. That would require some softening up with presents, and a good deal of deception, but the Virginians felt confident of managing it, and they arranged for a big treaty conference at Logstown (Ambridge, Pa.) in 1752 where they proposed to stagger the Indians with £1,000 worth of presents—a previously unheard of amount. (The presents had been wangled from the royal treasury, which was also unprecedented and showed the crown's interest in breaking into the Ohio country.)

Up to that point the Ohio Company's most serious problems emanated from Pennsylvania rather than Canada. That province's Quaker-dominated assembly rejected proposals to expand past the mountains, but Proprietary Thomas Penn believed (accurately) that the forks of the Ohio fell within his chartered grant, and the traders on the scene were linked to Philadelphia's merchants by financial arrangements as well as provincial loyalties. When Virginia's commissioners showed up at Logstown, the effect of their ostentatiously displayed present was lessened somewhat by suspicions sowed among the Indians by traders and Penn's personal agent. The Virginians had aimed at getting a huge cession of Indian territory, but the job became harder than anticipated.

To get their validating piece of paper, they had to play a swindler's trick on the Delawares, aided, sorry to say, by Mingo superiors in the Covenant Chain. The details were different, but the process echoed what had happened in the Walking Purchase fraud in Pennsylvania. Virginia's commissioners came to private understandings with the Mingo chiefs in a back room. After emerging, they reported to the Delawares their version of the treaty document that had been agreed on in that back room. However, the words on paper were very different from the oral report. The written document permitted the Virginians to go ahead with their project that would ultimately dispossess the Delawares once again. At least one of the Iroquois chiefs, Andrew Montour, was paid thirty pistoles on the spot by the Ohio Company, and granted a modest estate of 80,000 acres. Having swung the Iroquois chiefs into line, Virginia Commissioners assumed that after a settlement had been put firmly in place the Delawares' resentment could be disregarded. Had there been no Frenchmen about, the assumption might have been correct.

But there were Frenchmen, and they were nerving themselves to challenge all and sundry British colonials. As an experiment in bluff in 1749, Montreal had sent out Captain Céloron de Blainville with a company of men to demand that Indians of the Ohio country expel Pennsylvania's traders. The result of this was a sad revelation for France, and an even sadder for Céloron who barely managed to get back alive when the Indians at Logstown threatened his weak party. For New France, the terrible truth was that the traders had become stronger than the French among the Indians. If New France was to maintain any shadow of its claimed sovereignty, it would have to exert force.

The British were winning in commercial competition. France's only hope was resort to arms. In 1752 a new governor general landed at Quebec with instructions "to check the progress of the claims and enterprises of the English" in the Ohio Country, for "were they to succeed there, they would cut the communication of the two colonies of Canada and Louisiana." On this point, Frenchmen and Britons were agreed. The new French governor, Ange Duquesne de Menneville, Marquis Duquesne, set to work immediately.

Coincidentally, the synethnic French agent Charles Langlade led a party of Ottawas, Ojibwas, and Potawatomis in a bloody raid upon the Twightwee / Miami village of Pickawillany, headquarters of a tribe defecting from the French to join the Iroquois Covenant Chain. Langlade's raid was brutally successful, and the news came as a horrifying shock to members of the tribe sitting in at the Logstown treaty conference. Since British authorities did exactly nothing in response, though Pennsylvania and the Iroquois had accepted those Twightwees and promised them protection, the punished Indians subsided meekly back under French rule. (It may be observed that Langlade's force comprised warriors from the same tribal allies who had earlier smashed the Foxes.)

Duquesne thought Langlade's example an excellent one to emulate. In 1753 he sent out parties to chase Pennsylvania's traders back east of the mountains, and French traders moved in to fill the commercial vacuum. This change represented far more than an ordinary voluntary switch to competitors because trade monopolies functioned to create political dependency. Indians who refused to subject themselves to French authorities were cut off from necessities acquired through trade until they learned obedience. The longer they held out, the more hardship and hazard they endured.

In Virginia, the partners of the Ohio Company saw their fine project going up in French smoke. Like their French competitors, they concluded that clandestine war via traders had become outmoded; arms must now decide. They observed that Governor Duquesne was perpetuating French military tradition by building a new chain of forts west of the mountains, with the double purpose of controlling the tribes and barring the British. Virginia's deputy governor Robert Dinwiddie sent an emissary from Williamsburg to Fort Le Boeuf (near Erie, Pa.) to tell the French commandant to cease and desist. Young George Washington completed the arduous journey despite its many physical difficulties. He did not do so well with its major political purposes.

Washington was supposed to get an escort of supporting Indians from the forks of Ohio region, but when they questioned him closely about his aims and function he gave unconvincingly deceptive answers. His intended Delaware and Shawnee escort found other business more important, and disappeared. When Washington continued to Fort Le Boeuf, only four Mingo chiefs accompanied him, and they were uncomfortably inquisitive. At the fort he told the commandant to go back to Canada. The commandant politely poured him more wine and regretted being unable to comply.

While Washington thus officially represented the province of Virginia, the province's Ohio Company tried to block French advance by building its own fort at the forks of Ohio. Delawares and Shawnees observing construction were highly uncooperative, and they stayed conspicuously away when 600 French soldiers marched to seize the Company's unfinished structure. But then, to the Indians' dismay, the French completed building Fort Duquesne for which they had planned all along.

Aroused Virginians commissioned Washington as a colonel and sent him back to the region with a company of men and the impossible mission of dislodging experienced French forces that far outnumbered his small band of raw men. (As tactics, the procedure was so ludicrously stupid that one must wonder whether it was intended simply to create an incident to force the British crown's involvement. If that indeed was an ulterior motive, it succeeded brilliantly.)

Washington's Mingo ally Tanaghrisson created an international scandal by assassinating a French officer who had just been taken prisoner, and French propaganda twisted the affair to make it seem that Washington himself had been the assassin. Washington appealed to the local Delawares for help against the outraged French, and the terms of his appeal bear notice. "The only motive of our conduct," he assured the Delawares, was "to put you again in possession of your lands, and to take care of your wives and children, to dispossess the French, to maintain your rights and to secure the whole country for you; for these very ends are the English arms now employed." The Delawares were inexplicably unconvinced by this heartwarming utterance (which Washington himself recorded), and they were nowhere nearby when Washington had to surrender to the brother of the man who had been murdered while his prisoner.

It says something for the code of the professional soldier (when dealing with other European soldiers) that his French captor took no revenge. The surrender took place on 4 July 1754, after which the French shooed Washington back home, keeping only two hostages for his good behavior.

Now the fat was in the fire. Up to this point, French strategy was working perfectly. British efforts to break through the encircling cordon had failed completely. British traders dared not venture west of the mountains. But back in London, British "hawks" were determined to fight it out. *Their* strategy was working too.

The Indians who had wanted to create a frontier of the kind enshrined in myth, with themselves on one side and "civilization" on the other, found reality instead. Delawares and Shawnees had wanted to keep the mountains as a dike against further British expansion. Frenchmen performed that task for them, but at what a price! Stopping invasion at the front door had only let it in the back. Instead of being encroached upon by British settlers, the regional Indians became acutely aware of French forts and garrisons that dictated the limits within which they could thereafter govern themselves—and incidentally forced terms of trade upon them far less desirable than they had known before. In modern terminology, we might say that they had become an occupied people living under repression and a reduced standard of living. They were in a genuine frontier region—a frontier-in-the-middle. It was not a recipe for contentment.

CHAPTER 34

Savage Empires

While Virginia went through its charade, well-informed members of the Board of Trade and Plantations in London realized the necessity of lining up Indian allies. So far, they were correct, but they chose the wrong Indians and the wrong approach. Lord Halifax, who presided over the Board, wanted the Iroquois league on Britain's side, under the false impression that the Iroquois could dictate conduct by other tribes in the Covenant Chain, such as the Delawares. Halifax also knew that New-York had alienated the Iroquois by cheating and abuse. He therefore instructed the governors of the colonies to send commissioners to Albany for a great joint treaty with the Iroquois in the king's name instead of New-York's.

What resulted was farce. New-York's Governor DeLancey seized control of the Indian negotiations by trickery and simply repeated the same sort of funny business that had alienated the Iroquois in the first place. But the Albany Congress of 1754 has been seen by historians through a haze of nationalist delusion because some of the delegates, under Benjamin Franklin's leadership, proposed a Plan of Union that seemed to foreshadow emergence of the United States. It was a chimerical scheme (despite Franklin's great reputation), rejected by every colony and the crown; and the ministry concluded that Indian affairs could no longer be trusted to colonial management. They appointed a *royal* superintendent, independent of colonial governments.

Washington's surrender of his emergency-built Fort Necessity arrived as news during the Congress's sessions and was duly forwarded to London where it had far more impact than anything done by the Congress. The Iroquois chiefs accepted the Congress's presents and did nothing to halt French advance. Instead of the Albany Congress being a forerunner of colonial unity, it was the last gasp of the traditional system of colonial administration of Indian affairs. The forerunner myth was born as part of the larger myth of *The Frontier*. Neither has any relation to the reality of the times.

Highly placed men in both England and France wanted to settle differences by diplomacy, but "hawks" outmaneuvered them. By a kind of tidal current, the countries were swept toward the vortex of war. Still hoping to isolate the conflict as a bush war without European involvement, British ministers sent an army under General Edward Braddock to retake Fort Duquesne, and Braddock committed every conceivable mistake. A statesman's descendant has called him "the last man in the army . . . for that command."

Braddock had every possible advantage. Franklin used his personal credit to hire heavy farm wagons to carry the army's masses of equipment. One of Washington's hostages at Fort Duquesne, at the risk of his life, drew a plan of the fort and described the garrison, which information he smuggled out by Delaware Indians uncomfortable in the French embrace. The Delawares offered to capture the fort for Braddock by a subterfuge possible because they had the run of the place, but they wanted first to know his answer to a vital question. When the French and British finished fighting, what of the land? Where would be the Indians' land? Idiotic Braddock told them bluntly that "no savage should inherit the land." It was one occasion when truth was not a virtue. (Delaware chief Shingas told of this encounter which did not appear in official reports.) The offended Delawares withdrew and stood aside as Braddock, on Washington's advice, and made confident by the information in hand, violated military rules by splitting his forces and rushing forward with the advance guard. The honor and glory of capturing Fort Duquesne were to be his own, not a plum for lowly savages.

Were it not for the lives sacrificed by his arrogance and stupidity, one might say he got what he deserved. The French fort's garrison had been reinforced by a large contingent of "Three Fires" Indians—those reliable French allies from the distant west whose lands were not yet threatened. When Braddock came closer, a small number of French troops and a large number of Indians sallied out and utterly routed the British army (lacking Indians) which was much larger than the French and their Indian allies combined. Braddock died in that battle which was won by tactics he could not comprehend nor cope with. Death was the kindest reward he could have had, for when the panic-stricken survivors of his army (still greater in numbers than the enemy) fled all the way to Philadelphia, they met more contempt than pity. Said Benjamin Franklin after he watched them trudge through the city, "This whole Transaction gave us Americans the first Suspicion that our exalted Ideas of the Prowess of British Regulars had not been well founded." It did not escape colonists' notice that those regulars had been ruined by Indians. (Nor did it escape the

Indians' notice.) From that time forward, defiance of the British crown was no longer irrationally incredible.

Franklin's observation about the retreat of Braddock's army was much closer to reality than his Albany Plan of Union had been. The Plan had been conceived by Franklin as British imperialist. Braddock's defeat edged Franklin's imperialist vision closer to being purely American.

Fort Duquesne became a base for terrorism. Unlike the French wars against the Foxes and the Natchez, but very much in the pattern of former raids on New England, the new victims were British colonials. They could not be wholly exterminated, but French purpose remained much the same— to create panic by killing and torturing persons without regard to sex, age, or condition. Ordinarily these atrocities have been blamed on Indian "savages," and it cannot be denied that the hands that lifted hatchets and torched cabins were Indian, but it is equally on record that each raiding party was led and commanded by a French officer, and the officers acted under orders and definite policies of the governor general of New France. By 1755 he was Pierre Rigaud de Vaudreuil de Cavagnial, Marquis de Vaudreuil, a man whose name alone would seem to dictate chivalrous conduct, but Vaudreuil's nobility derived from status rather than attitude. After a year of purposeful terrorism, he boasted to Versailles that he had caused a hundred British casualties to one of his own. He did not spell out the noncombatant character of those British casualties, nor did he need to. Official propaganda boasted of *"beaucoup de ravages."*

Notwithstanding pious denunciations by British officers, one must not think that they were above that sort of thing; they were just not as good at it. As early as 1755, General William Shirley organized a company of Stockbridge Indians as "rangers" and instructed them "to distress the French and their allies, by sacking, burning, and destroying their houses, barns, barracks, canoes, battoes, &c. and by killing their cattle of every kind; and at all times to endeavour to way-lay, attack, and destroy their convoys of provisions by land and water, in any part of the country." Obviously such instructions could not be carried out without eliminating the persons associated with all that, and equally obviously most of them would be noncombatants. British officers were not morally superior to the French; they were only technically inferior. French raiding parties were led by men experienced in backwoods war of a kind strange and fearsome to the British who took good care to keep their distance and their skins.

Without constant prodding, Indians stood aside, frequently suggesting that the imperials should fight their own war. General Montcalm's senior aide complained bitterly about how hard and expensive it was to launch Indians on the war path. "It is a long job to get them to make up their minds. It requires authority, brandy, equipment, food and such. The job never ends and is very irksome"; but he too paid tribute to piety: "I shiver at the frightful spectacles which they are preparing for us."

When General James Wolfe undertook a "ravaging" assignment in the Gaspé peninsula, he performed it energetically without scruple, and he ordered the same grisly business when he commanded at the siege of Quebec (besides mercilessly cannonading the civilians of the lower city because he could not reach the military defendants in the fort above.) For such officers on both sides (as some demented football coaches like to say nowadays), "Winning is the only thing."

For a change and for a while, all the Indians seemed to be fighting for the French. Besides their usual allies they now had Delawares and Shawnees based on Fort Duquesne, who had joined up after the rout of Braddock. Even the Iroquois contributed warriors to raids southward. Although other Iroquois formally professed British loyalties, the Grand Council of their league waffled in an obvious desire to be on the winning side whichever it should be. Iroquois war aims were primarily advantages for themselves. Some Iroquois were identified as helping French parties scourge colonial settlers out of the region variously called New-York or Iroquoia. The Covenant Chain of alliance became a sad wreck of its former self.

This urge to run settlers out of tribal territories also motivated Delawares and Shawnees. When they raided into Pennsylvania, it was remarked that their first targets were the areas from which they had been forced to emigrate. This difference between tribal objectives and French goals must not be overlooked. When setbacks forced British leaders to think about what they were doing, they found that fault line between French and Indian purposes, and eventually the British won the war by cleaving eastern tribes away from the French armies.

CHAPTER 35

The Forty Years War

> The profound difference between the treaty system that was
> established by 1796 and the system of the early 1760s lay in the dis-
> parity of power between the participants. . . . The Indians had lost
> their freedom of maneuver and thus their negotiating leverage. The
> great disparity of power between them and the United States could
> not help but skew the treaty relationship into one so unequal that it
> can only be called colonial.
>
> —DOROTHY V. JONES

The Seven Years War will not be fought again in this book, but certain
features of it concerned Indians especially, and established dimensions
for their future history. Ever foremost in Indian minds was the question
put to Braddock: "Where will be the Indians' land?" Braddock's response
and fate had clarified the issue in one respect: the Indians would have to
determine for themselves where their lands would be—and fight to enforce
their decision.

This understanding imposed a stern requirement on the eastern tribes.
They could not simply shrug off the empires' war as not their own. Instead,
they must define their own war, independent of the empires though necessarily involved with them. Princeton student Stephen Auth has correctly sensed that Indian hostilities should be dated by actual Indian
participation rather than by conflating them to the empires' wars. Instead
of the Seven Years War of the textbooks, he saw Delaware Indians fighting from 1755 to 1765 in a Ten Years War. His insight opens a wider
vista; those Delawares did not stop fighting, except for truces, until 1795.
Their experience crosses traditional historiographical classifications, but
when the textbook divisions are ignored and the era is seen from the
Delawares' viewpoint, the period appears as one long agony that properly
must be called their Forty Years War.

During that time, Britain fought France and won, Britain fought its
colonies and lost, and the new empire of the United States fought the

tribes directly with mixed results. Through all the events the issues remained the same: sovereignty and ownership of the land. Through them all the Indians' cause weakened year by year, not through lack of dedication or military skill, rather because European immigrants rose in number every year while Indian populations continued to decline. In retrospect the end was predetermined, but the demographic, military, and political processes did take forty years of struggle.

It began when the Delawares were turned off by Braddock. They raided Pennsylvania to pay off old scores and with the hope that the mountains could still be kept as a dike against the colonial flood. For this, they needed the French at Fort Duquesne, but never became fond of them or of the fort. Realistically, however, the tribes lacked resources and skill to get rid of that fort by their own effort. Realistically, they would need British help. They sought it. Their search manifested itself at this time as a desire to make peace with the British.

In 1758, Britain sent a new army against Fort Duquesne. From the colonists' point of view, it appears that General John Forbes and pacifist (!) Quaker leader Israel Pemberton became partners in a campaign to get Delaware help. Whichever viewpoint one adopts, the result was a great treaty conference in 1758 at Easton, Pennsylvania, where promises were exchanged. The Delawares promised to abandon the French. The colonists promised to accede to Delaware demands for a boundary between Indian country and colonial settlements.

Thus originated the image of The Frontier, not as a mythical, ineluctable line between civilization and savagery, but rather as a political line drawn between Indian and British territories. It is necessary to stress the political-diplomatic nature of this line, for all the parties at that conference were well aware that Indians and Europeans would continue to do business in the frontier *region* spraddling across the line.

From these negotiations, General Forbes got what he wanted, which was the Delawares' abandonment of the French and the consequent French abandonment of Fort Duquesne. Regrettably the general's dispatches failed to acknowledge his dependence on the indefatigable aid of Quaker Pemberton (which has to be seen in other manuscript sources). More regrettably, the promise of a boundary, a frontier line, upon which the Quakers had staked their honor, was abandoned by officialdom as quickly as the French garrison had left Fort Duquesne. General Forbes's successors in command (after he died of a long illness) simply ignored the promise and rebuilt the fort, renamed Fort Pitt.

The Delawares understood the difference between Quakers trying to be decent and militarists aiming at command. Reluctantly, the Delawares concluded that the Quakers lacked power to fulfill their promise. Realistically, the Delawares found Fort Pitt to be even more obnoxious than Fort Duquesne. They consulted with allies and with their "uncles," the Senecas, in the reconstituted Covenant Chain. The Senecas also had a fort, Fort Niagara, dominating their territory, and there also the end of the Seven Years War in 1763 did not eliminate the French fort but merely transferred it to a British garrison who strengthened it. Delawares and Senecas agreed that they could not be independent tribes so long as their territories were occupied by British garrisons. The Senecas circulated wampum belts inviting the former tribal allies of New France to rise up and drive out the British garrisons.

An important factor in mobilizing the tribes and arousing them to belligerence was the influence of a Delaware "prophet" named Neolin who preached hatred of the invaders. Neolin understood vaguely how dependence on European trade goods had reduced Indians to political dependence on European colonies. His remedy was for the tribes to revert to aboriginal crafts in order to become independent of the enemy, and he proclaimed it as a direction from the divine Master of Life.

This revivalist idea was to recur in a number of tribes across the continent, each time stressing that salvation required return to the good old days in one way or another, not always in technology. Neolin's auditors listened respectfully to his diatribes against the colonials, but they had had much practical experience with weapons, so most of them did not abandon firearms for bows-and-arrows. Even so, they still lacked cannon, and muskets were not powerful enough against European fortifications.

The outcome of the political and religious agitation was a general tribal attack on British forts and supporting settlements which has been miscalled Pontiac's Conspiracy. Pontiac was an Ottawa chief who got credit for the war by leading the long siege of Fort Detroit, but he was a local chief with little respect from others. Britain's royal superintendent of Indian affairs learned worriedly of Seneca intrigues before the outbreak of hostilities, and in the east the Senecas besieged Fort Niagara while Delawares attacked hated Fort Pitt.

In the end, the forts demonstrated their efficacy as bastions of power by withstanding the Indians' best efforts. Of the major forts, only Michilimackinac fell. Detroit's siege lasted longest, but the garrison held out successfully. Niagara was relieved in short time by ease of transport across the lakes. Pitt rescued itself by infecting its besiegers with smallpox. The garrison presented negotiating Delaware chiefs with blankets from the smallpox hospital, thus starting a terrible epidemic among the Delawares. It will be observed that smallpox does not distinguish between warriors and noncombatants. Actually, there seems to have been a backwoods tradition of this sort of germ warfare. Although General Amherst sent word to authorize its use, the men in the fort performed the operation before Amherst's message arrived. (All thoroughly documented.)

The failure of "Pontiac's Conspiracy" did not imply conquest and surrender of the tribes involved. A truce followed. The forts stayed in place, but the ministry in London made a political concession. It revived the boundary that had been promised at Easton in 1758, and renewed that promise in the form of the Royal Proclamation of 1763. By the king's prerogative, a line was to be drawn down the "backs" of the colonies, with lands west of the line being denominated as crown lands "reserved" for the Indians "as their Hunting Grounds . . . for the present."

This was presented to the Indians with some embellishments and without the qualifications. The royal superintendents of Indian affairs conducted a series of treaty conferences to negotiate the surveying of the line. As the Indians were made to believe they had been awarded their great goal, they kept quiet for a while.

What sedated the Indians aroused the colonists. Their charters were curtailed to make that Proclamation line, and the act was performed by royal prerogative alone over the heads of Parliament and colonial assemblies. Other grievances combined to arouse the colonials to demonstrations and riots. Ironically, in so doing, they accomplished what the Indians had failed to do in "Pontiac's Conspiracy": they stimulated the British government to withdraw troops from western forts to suppress the eastern turmoils.

Still under the spell of the Proclamation line and its confirmation by Parliament in the Quebec Act of 1774, the tribes stayed quiet until the colonists rose in revolt. The Frontier so earnestly desired by the eastern tribes had lasted only from 1763 to 1776. When the new empire of the colonies-turned-States sprang into being in 1776, the familiar frontier-in-between came back to life, and just as in the old days the contending empires pressed the Indians to take sides. Again as in the old days, the Indians lost heavily no matter which side they took.

They had no more "racial" unity than the British empire and its secessionists. Most of the Iroquois stayed with Britain, but most Oneidas and Tuscaroras went over to the States. Delawares immediately lost the temporary unity formerly aroused by Fort Pitt. Some scented opportunity to shake off Iroquois domination and even to acquire ascendancy for themselves. At a treaty council with General Lachlan McIntosh in 1778, some Delawares proposed to support the States in return for creation of an Indian state with the Delawares at its head. (Congress ignored that treaty.) Others, farther west, joined the Iroquois and Britain. Still others tried to keep out of it and suffered the worst fates of all.

These neutralists were pacifists who had been genuinely converted by the Moravians of Bethlehem but had been forced to emigrate by the bellicose non-Moravian "Christians" of their neighborhood as well as brutal treatment by unconverted Delawares and Iroquois. They trekked out to what then seemed a safe distance west of the mountains, but the war caught up with them. British allied Indians demanded hospitality from time to time which the Moravian converts were powerless to resist whether or not they wanted to violate old custom. A party of Revolutionary soldiers interpreted the harboring of enemy Indians, no matter how temporarily, as savage enmity to themselves. They surrounded the mission village, killed its unresisting inhabitants and burnt their bodies. The Christianity of the Sermon on the Mount was not conspicuous during the American Revolution.

As an aside, we may also notice that the Quaker leaders who had negotiated peace at Easton in 1758 were seized by Pennsylvania's revolutionary Committee of Safety and sent into internal exile at Winchester, Virginia. They were old, its comforts in those days were few, and they did not long survive the ordeal. Their former ally Franklin, now prominent among the revolutionaries, made no protest. All other pacifists and neutralists were deprived of citizenship by a complex loyalty oath that religious principles forbade them to sign, and their religious and political enemies joyously seized control of the State. Democracy, as well as Christianity, went down under the new power in Pennsylvania.

(Loyalty oaths, then as now, have always required more than simple allegiance to the reigning sovereign, monarchical or republican. The function of a loyalty oath is to suppress dissidence rather than to guarantee loyalty.)

Among the northeastern Indians, the Iroquois fought most ardently and suffered most grievously. Something unheard of happened to the Iroquois nations. Their Covenant Chain broke up, but that had happened previously in the Seven Years War, and the Chain had been mended again. This time, however, there was no renewal. The confederation so carefully created at Albany in 1677, and tended through so many vicissitudes for a century, stayed broken. A new confederation in the Ohio country took its place as voice of the Indians, and postwar efforts by the Iroquois to take charge were positively rejected.

The worst calamity was disruption of the core Iroquois league that had been the source of the Five Nations' strength for at least 300 years and perhaps many more. Its unifying rituals were designed to achieve consensus, but that became impossible after British agents prevailed on most of the Iroquois, but could not win over the Oneidas and Tuscaroras who aligned themselves with the Americans. Actually there were also splits within the tribes on both sides. Crisis came in 1777 when the league chiefs "covered their fire." The disunity in the league was disastrous for British General Barry St. Leger as he marched eastward through the Mohawk Valley, planning to join General John Burgoyne's army marching southward down the Hudson Valley. The combined force meant to split New England from the rest of the American revolutionaries.

St. Leger's way was blocked by Fort Stanwix (Utica, New York). Aiming to seize the fort, St. Leger encountered an American force at Oriskany, New York, where a fierce battle took place. Mohawks and Senecas were with St. Leger, Oneidas with the American General Herkimer. For the first time within living memory, Iroquois fought and killed Iroquois, and their league shattered.

Students still argue over which side "won" at Oriskany. As to certain outcomes of the battle, argument would be foolish. St. Leger turned back and failed to make his planned junction with Burgoyne. Other problems also beset Burgoyne, but it seems reasonable to assume that St. Leger's absence contributed to Burgoyne's miring down in a situation so defenseless that he surrendered his entire army at Saratoga. This news persuaded France to ally with the States. At least some of the dominos in that sequence had been pushed over by the Oneidas.

The fighting in "upstate New York," which the Iroquois knew as their homeland, had only begun. Infuriated Iroquois warriors allied to Britain attacked and laid waste the Oneida town of Oriska. Oneida warriors continued firm in their American alliance. British Indian agents organized Indian raids into the Wyoming Valley of Pennsylvania (the North Branch of the Susquehanna) where their ravages were denounced as massacres although casualties were few and captives were not harmed. Joseph Brant, the sophisticated Mohawk leader allied to Britain, led a raid against Minisink on the upper Delaware River.

In retaliation, the Americans sent an army in August 1779, under Generals John Sullivan and James Clinton, to lay waste the towns and fields of Onondagas, Cayugas, and Senecas; and twelve Oneida and Tuscarora warriors were commissioned to accompany Sullivan.

Barbara Graymont's dry comment is apt: "Once the British had gotten the Indians into the war, the sad fact was that they had not the forces readily available to assist them in any large-scale invasion of their territory." After a half-hearted skirmish at Newtown (near Chemung), Sullivan's American army marched without serious opposition, destroying all that they reached. "The business of this campaign," remarks Graymont, was "a strange task indeed for men at arms—a warfare against vegetables." Strange or not, it was effective, as indeed it had been for centuries in wars between colonials and Indians. When the tribe's harvest was destroyed, the people had to seek provision elsewhere. In this case, *elsewhere* was British headquarters at Fort Niagara where food was already in short supply. By the end of September, more than 5,000 Indian refugees camped around the fort needing assistance of every kind.

Yet the war was not over, and the Indians angrily demanded revenge. It is unnecessary here to recount the succeeding horrors. After Oriskany, the damage was done, and it was perpetuated by the manner in which the war ended.

At Paris, in 1783, British and American commissioners signed a treaty that said nothing about Indians. In Parliament some opposition members denounced it as dishonorable, but Parliament is a center where unctuous excuses have been raised to a fine art. Lord Shelburne responded that "the Indian nations were not abandoned to their enemies; they were remitted to the care of neighbours."

Perhaps the Honorable Members could hear harps and dulcimers with that uplifting message, but the music did not carry across the Atlantic. Britain's Iroquois allies were aghast. We may imagine Oneidas saying, "I told you so." The "neighbors" from New England, who had for more than a century ached to get into the Mohawk Valley, now crowded in. (To the present day, that east-west valley is culturally and politically different from, even hostile to, the north-south, originally Dutch axis between Albany and New York City.)

Though Parliament and the crown were ready enough to toss their Iroquois allies to the wolves, their military commanders in Canada felt acutely uncomfortable at what they perceived as dishonorable conduct. General Frederick Haldimand tried to make amends for the loss of the Iroquois homeland to the States by providing a refuge for his allies in Canada. He bought a large tract of land from the Mississauga Indians who had driven an Iroquois colony out of Ontario during the latter's French wars of the seventeenth century. (The tract was part of the mythical Iroquois "empire.") Haldimand turned this tract over to his allies who recreated their league there.

But the original league continued to meet at Onondaga because many Iroquois chose to remain and make do in their homeland despite the inrush of Yankee settlers. Of course, Oneidas and Tuscaroras who had fought on the American side thought their position was secure until they, too, were disillusioned. This took a little longer.

If the statesmen chose to ignore Indians in their Treaty of Paris, the Indians chose to ignore that treaty. The Congress of the new United States understood that it would have to make a separate treaty with the Iroquois, but that necessity became entangled in a contest between the new nation (really a confederated empire) and its constituent States. Congress wanted Virginia to cede its chartered sea-to-sea claims to the nation. Virginia demanded a price so high that Congress boggled; but, if the cessions should abort, the western tribes might negotiate peace with Virginia instead of Congress. Pennsylvania forced the issue by proposing to treat with the Iroquois for purchase of its western territories, and the Congressmen realized that they could not prevent the purchase and they would lose all authority over Indian affairs unless they got to the Iroquois before Pennsylvania. Suddenly Virginia's demands seemed more reasonable and were granted. Virginia ceded its western claims, and Congress rushed commissioners to Fort Stanwix in October 1784 to treat with the Iroquois as Pennsylvania's superiors. It was the first of several contentions between the nation and the States for control of Indian affairs, echoing the former long struggles in that respect between the British crown and its colonies.

Except for Pennsylvania's purchase, what happened at Fort Stanwix can hardly be called negotiation. The United States commissioners dictated terms, demanded signatures from unqualified Indians, and seized hostages. The commissioners also formalized the end of the Iroquois Covenant Chain. When Mohawk Aaron Hill assumed the former role of Iroquois spokesman for the western tribes as well as the Six Nations, the commissioners refused to recognize him in that capacity, and Seneca Chief Cornplanter acceded that the westerners would have to treat for themselves (for which he was criticized by his tribal council). The great Iroquois "empire," which had always been the imaginary creature of diplomacy, now died as it had been born. The commissioners dictated bounds for the individual Iroquois nations, and Congress turned its attention westward.

Congress had good reason to be concerned about the west because the transmontane National Domain was where Congress had most freedom of action—except for those Indians. Political bosses in the States jealously guarded their powers and patronage, but conceded that united action was necessary in the "territories." While its commissioners bullied the Iroquois, Congress passed a Resolution on the Public Lands, followed three years later by the famous Northwest Ordinance. This series of acts comprised one of the most remarkable political inventions of the nation-state, and it is notable for what it omitted as well as for what it included.

Unlike all other empires of the time, the United States provided for its colonies (called "territories") to become the peers of the founding States by peaceful and legitimate process. Given certain qualifications a territory could be accepted as a State on terms of full equality with its predecessors, and with this device the United States in due course would expand across the continent. What the Ordinance failed to do was to provide for Indian participation in that process except by purchase of their lands. "Their lands and property shall never be taken from them without their consent" recited the Ordinance, and "they shall never be invaded or disturbed, unless in just and lawful wars authorized by Congress."

It was as highminded an utterance as the 1776 Declaration that all men are created equal, and, so far as Indians were concerned, nearly as irrelevant to events. The lands delineated by the Ordinance were understood by Congress to be available for conversion to statehood when the tribes occupying them should give their consent. When the Indians in question withheld consent, Congress authorized "just and lawful" wars. The United States sent two armies against the confederation of tribes in the Old Northwest (the country's Midwest today), and the tribes, to everyone's astonishment, trounced the armies in Harmar's Humiliation, 1790, and St. Clair's Shame, 1791. Power and realpolitik began to seem ambiguous.

Looking over their shoulders at troubling international problems arising from the French Revolution, President George Washington and Secretary of War Henry Knox concluded that the Indians must be dealt with politically as well as militarily. In 1794 they sent a third army into the Indian country, commanded this time by veteran General Anthony Wayne who understood politics as well as combat. Wayne defeated the confederation at Fallen Timbers in 1794 but knew better than to proceed as though this one battle made a conquest. In the Treaty of Greenville, 1795, with the full approval of his government, Wayne reversed the assumption made by the commissioners at Fort Stanwix in 1784. They had operated on the principle that the United States had acquired rights of conquest over all the Indians resident under Britain's former sovereignty, and they had dictated terms to the Iroquois as to a fallen foe. Wayne at Greenville in 1795 acknowledged tribal rights and *negotiated* peace instead of trying to dictate it.

He also negotiated a boundary between tribal territories and the lands that "Americans" were permitted to "settle"—in fact, to colonize. Thus ended the "forty years war" that began in 1755 when Delawares raided

Pennsylvania; and there were Delawares treating with Wayne at Greenville.

We know that it was the end of a long episode rather than the end of expansion by the United States, but its significance must not be underrated as it has been, for example, by omission of the Treaty of Greenville from the standard *Documents of American History* edited by Henry Steele Commager. Such omission subtly underscores an assumption still prevalent today that Indians have been and are a lower caste in American society and irrelevant to its political processes.

Those Indians of the Old Northwest forced the United States, as they had previously forced Great Britain, to recognize territorial rights that could not legally be brushed aside by the doctrine of "rights of conquest." In case after case, that principle is still being adjudicated in American courts of law, generally with benefit to the tribes concerned. Though American expansion continued, and the tribes were dispossessed and dispersed time after time, yet their situation is markedly better than that of the aborigines of Australia where rights of conquest have been promulgated as the law of the land.

A further thought is prompted by the Greenville treaty. Here, in the boundary line between the tribes and the United States, we find substance behind the myth of the Frontier "line between civilization and savagery." There was a line, not one imagined between abstractions, but rather a line on the map between the territories of tribes and those available for development and colonization by the United States. Its significance has been obscured by the lawyers' flimflam of sovereignty doctrine, but the negotiating parties understood the importance of that line, and so should we.

PART SIX

The End of Independence

CHAPTER 36

"Manifest Destiny"

I have been long impressed with the absurdity of entering into
Treaties with the Indian tribes residing within our territorial limits,
subject to our jurisdiction and to such laws as Congress may pass for
their security, happiness, and safety.

I have constantly observed that in Indian treaties the Chiefs are
fattened and the common Indian left to starve.

Another and very important reason for adopting the policy I have
recommended, is the great obstacle which will otherwise exist to the
surveying and bringing the public lands into the market, which I
presume is intended to be done as speedily as possible.

—GOVERNOR ANDREW JACKSON to the Secretary of State,
6 October 1821

We are at the threshold of the nineteenth century, the epoch of the rise
of the empire of the United States, and of the crushing of the Indian
tribes everywhere. Let there be no quibbling about calling it an empire.
The men who governed it made no secret of their intended creation and
its "manifest destiny." Invoking the sacred obligation of democracy, they
drove Spain out of Florida, bought France and Russia out of the Louisiana Territory and Alaska, seized Texas, California, and the Southwest
from Mexico, and were restrained from taking Canada also only by the
power of Great Britain.

They defined democracy as a caste system organized by conceptions
called race. In this system, the mixed immigrants from Europe were arbitrarily declared "white" regardle f the multitudes who had hacked and
spawned their ways through Europe from Asia and Africa in centuries
gone by. Rare is the European, even today, who can pass the test imposed
by legislatures in South Carolina and Louisiana which required that if
even one of a person's ancestors, no matter how far back, was identifiably
Asian or African, that person could not be "white"; he was "colored."
(Louisiana recently reaffirmed the rule.) By that rule, most Europeans

should be Huns as those raiders had not been chaste. In fact, biology was irrelevant to the system; caste was socially determined, not genealogically. As time would show, the possession of large amounts of money erased the taint of race, but this was not easy to come by.

Democracy meant parity among whites. (South Africans of the twentieth century called the system *Herrenvolk* democracy. This term is not easily translatable. Literally it means democracy among the people of the lords. More freely, democracy among the ruling caste.) Africans were enslaved; later, after manumission, they were segregated from whites as far as was feasible. Indians had been segregated from the days of Jamestown colony, but theirs was separation in tribal communities rather than as individuals, and they liked it that way.

In 1848, the French student Alexis de Tocqueville observed what was happening to Indians. "In its dealings with the North American Indians, the European tyranny weakened their feeling for their country, dispersed their families, obscured their traditions, and broke their chain of memories; it also changed their customs and increased their desires beyond reason, making them more disorderly and less civilized than they had been before. At the same time, the moral and physical condition of these peoples has constantly deteriorated, and in becoming more wretched they have also become more barbarous." (It may be noticed that de Tocqueville said *European* rather than *white.*)

Despite this horrendous bill of particulars, de Tocqueville saw also the inextinguishable survival of the "Indianness" that nobody has been able to define: "Nevertheless, the Europeans have not been able to change the character of the Indians entirely."

The tribes were beaten down and forced or menaced into little islands of territory, enclaves called reservations, within their former lands, and even these were whittled at by various processes, legal and otherwise. Reformers approved transplantation of the peoples against their will "for their own good." Invaders who cared nothing for Indians' welfare seized their lands for the invaders' own good. All this, in the mythology of standard American history, constitutes the "transit of civilization" from Europe.

There could be no doubt about the power of the nation–state–empire as compared to the scattered powers of tribes at odds with each other. Benevolently, the conquerors took the subjected peoples under their wing as wards of the state, and interpreted that high-sounding legal phrase to mean that the wards must henceforth do only what they were told. To assure the success of this magnanimity, the philanthropic empire sold Indian lands and appropriated a small portion of the proceeds for the benefit of its wards. To assure that the money would indeed be used for the benefit of such "childlike peoples, incompetent to manage their own affairs," the appropriations were entrusted to reservation agents who usually identified their own benefit as surrogate for the wards'. This political patronage became so notorious that it aroused a reform movement especially strong among churchmen.

All the while, the empire fattened on hordes of voluntary immigrants from Europe and, during half of the century, of involuntary immigrants from Africa.

In contrast, the Indian peoples dwindled in numbers until nearly the end of the century. Was it more than coincidence that the mythic Frontier was proclaimed dead by its historian inventor at just the moment when Indian populations began to recover from their centuries of catastrophe? Frederick Jackson Turner ended his Frontier in 1890.

The nineteenth century hiving-off of Anglo-Americans to create new communities of their own kind in the trans-Appalachian West was a landborne repetition of the seaborne colonizing of the seventeenth and eighteenth centuries. Continental colonization does not differ in essentials from beachhead colonization. Less controlled and more individualistic, this landborne colonizing nevertheless aimed at the same goals of seizure of the land from Native occupants and transformation of it to the colonizers' uses and possession. In the process the Natives were to be either expelled or subjected. We may properly recognize that that result comes only from colonizing, regardless of whether the colonizers come by land or sea or whether they arrive in a trickle or a flood. That the colonizers surround and overwhelm the Natives instead of forming an island within a surrounding Native population does not change the relations of power and process except in possible implications for the long run.

Distinctions must be made between macrocontact and microcontact phenomena. On the macrocontact scale, many Indian tribes of the trans-Appalachian West preserved their independence and a degree of freedom of mobility well into the nineteenth century, long after most eastern tribes had been brought under political control and forced into reservations. Seen in this perspective, the phenomena of "the moving frontier" lie along a range of the processes of colonizing from initial intrusion to ultimate domination.

The means used by Euramericans for achieving domination were only intermittently violent, often because the threat of force was efficacious in itself. Peaceful intercourse, however, established patterns of social process that led inexorably to the economic and eventually political depen-

312 · *The End of Independence*

dency of Natives upon the colonizers. It hardly mattered that the Europeans understood the effect of these processes and helped them along; the processes worked in consequence of interaction between societies whose technologies were sufficiently alike to create the basis for commerce, and sufficiently different to create a powerful demand, with the advantage in the market on the side of the Europeans.

Neither the people nor the government of the United States intended to respect treaty contracts with Indians longer than the Indians could enforce them. Recognition of this very plain fact requires some painful revision of the pleasant myths we all learned in grade school. These portrayed an "honest yeomanry" (Andrew Jackson's phrase) bravely setting out with their families to conquer the wilderness and create civilization. Pursuing the destiny of Progress, these sturdy, self-reliant, God-fearing folk endure all the hazards and toil of their mission, standing constantly at arms to fend off attack by savage denizens of the wilderness. Among other things, almost as a matter of course, they create democracy which conflicts with the old world oligarchies of the seaboard States and ultimately overcomes them under the leadership of that inspiring champion of the common man, Andrew Jackson.

Even just to recite it all at once like that sounds like parody. The myth is nationalist and racist propaganda to justify conquest of *persons* who happen to be Indians, and their dispossession. It has the further effect of vindicating bellicosity toward Britain, Spain, and Mexico, and of expressing contempt for the synethnic French heritage in the Mississippi Valley.

It will not be enough to assert the myth's falsity. The myth was an intellectual paradigm that cleared the consciences of persons acting in ways that would otherwise be denounced by their religions as immoral and sinful. Bits and pieces of it have been demonstrated by researchers as irrelevant to reality, but the whole paradigm was highly relevant to the purposes of the people espousing it. A different purpose requires a different paradigm.

CHAPTER 37

Over the Mountains

> Although the leaders of the American government had qualms of conscience, the frontiersmen saw no inconsistency in expanding the area of freedom across the land of dead or dispossessed Indians.
>
> —REGINALD HORSMAN

The South was not immune to the turmoils created by imperial wars, but events in the South responded to two special influences: the Gulf frontier between Britain's colonies and those of France and Spain, and the institution of plantation slavery. During the Seven Years War, southern planters hesitated to send manpower north to the main arena because of fears of invasion by tribal allies of Louisiana and Florida, and hesitated even more because of fears of slave uprisings. To aid General Forbes on his march to Fort Duquesne, the Carolinas and Virginia scraped up a contingent of Cherokee warriors, but the Indians grew dissatisfied with delays, and they went home before Forbes got within striking distance of the fort. If not for incessant activity by Pennsylvania's Quakers, Forbes might have suffered like Braddock without Indian help.

As for fears of slave uprisings, the southerners had reason enough to be concerned. Stephen Saunders Webb has told of intense slave response in 1676 to that demagogue for whom Bacon's Rebellion is named, and Herbert Aptheker has detailed rising after rising that required constant vigilance from the planters to forestall and suppress. Steady importation of Africans had changed the nature of the slave trade and the consistency of Southern colonial populations. The early trade involved seizure of Indian captives for export to the West Indies. By mid-eighteenth century, the British South imported more Africans than it exported Indians, and the surplus were put to work on plantations. The result was a proportion of Africans to Europeans that became especially worrisome in times of stress. In South Carolina, always the center of slave trade, Africans greatly outnumbered Europeans. In 1724, Governor Glen estimated the colony's numbers at 14,000 "white" and 32,000 slaves. The planters did not believe propaganda that their "chattels" loved life under the lash. Trustworthy guards were necessary. Instead of able-bodied men, the planters sent good wishes and some money to fight the war that Virginia had touched off. Virginia fielded troops of its own, but they were treated so miserably by Edward Braddock (and so negligently by Virginia) that Governor Dinwiddie confessed, "no person of any property, family or worth" could be induced to enlist. He filled up the ranks with immigrant Scots who, we may presume, did not know what they were getting into.

Indians as well as Africans constituted a perpetual menace to Southerners partly on their own account and partly because of escaped slaves being harbored among the tribes. It appears that Shawnees especially were hospitable to the runaways, whose influence upon them, as well as the financial loss, could not be overlooked. The tribes varied in treatment of escapees because some of them maintained their own systems of slavery, about which more later.

In 1776, Virginia was again in the forefront of belligerents, and again the twin menaces of Indian and slave uprisings acted as deterrents to southern valor. As in the Seven Years War, the major theater of operations long lay in the North (until frustrated British armies turned south to ravage in 1781).

British officials remembered the ethnic strains and cleavages in the South. These had become harsher between the wars. The boundary line decreed by the Royal Proclamation of 1763, supposedly to protect tribal territories, had become a bad joke. Though some British Indian officials strove to give the line validity, and thereby earned a measure of tribal friendship, colonials swarmed over it without serious restraint. The Creeks were forced into a new cession of territory in 1773, and in Kentucky the Shawnees faced a new menace that threatened to deprive them of livelihood as well as territory.

In 1769, after seven months of hunting that had filled his cabin with deerskins, one of the legendary heroes of American schoolboys was seized by the Shawnee band of Captain Will. Daniel Boone and his five companions had been poaching in the Indians' hunting lands and "stealing" Shawnee "cattle." To the Shawnees, Boone's crime was flagrant and serious. They depended on trading deerskins for their living, and every one taken by Boone's "long rifles" was one denied to a Shawnee; furthermore, Boone and his gang were far past the boundary line set by treaty. For the same sort of offense against property owned by a colonist they could have served much time in jail.

The Shawnees were far too lenient for their own good. Contenting themselves with confiscating the stolen goods and (by way of fine), the hunters' gear, they turned the culprits loose after equipping them sufficiently for safe return to their own people. (An aside on semantics: the Shawnee method of doing justice is described by historians as "robbing" the poachers.)

Boone had no gratitude for such clemency, nor did he intend to respect Shawnee admonitions to refrain from future offenses. His depredations, and those of his equally lawless companions, became the more serious as more "back country" settlers joined the hunting without any visible signs of restraint by colonial authorities. To these men, treaties were mere scraps of paper. To the Indians, treaties were their only means of regulation in frontier country short of war. If treaties could not protect, war was the only recourse, at whatever cost.

Let us reflect for a moment. The advent of Europeans had brought about a revolution in eastern tribal cultures, involving a new stress on hunting for the world market. Now Boone's men were depriving the Indians of their role as commercial hunters and traders. A second revolution was being imposed on the Indians—a change from commercial hunting to they knew not what—and this was being forced by outlaws violating the most solemn agreements between their own governments and the tribes. The semantic magic by which this situation is converted in the histories to heroic conquest of the wilderness by champions of civilization rests on a very simple device: the Indians are not permitted to be human beings with internally regulated communities; instead they are wild "savages" without control or restraint. By this magic the criminals become heroes, and the overlenient enforcers of law become rabid robbers.

So long as the Shawnees had only the likes of Boone to contend with, they could cope, but they lost their hunting grounds in Kentucky, totally and permanently, when a gang at the top of colonial society cleared the way for the gangs at the bottom.

Lord Dunmore, governor of Virginia, revived his province's claim to the forks of the Ohio in 1774, and when the British garrison left Fort Pitt to bring order to rioting coastal cities, Dunmore sent an agent to seize the fort. Incidentally, while proclaiming Virginia's jurisdiction, the agent went into the business of jobbing lands for Dunmore and himself. This did not set well with the tribes who had maneuvered the French out of the place and rejoiced at the British garrison's evacuation. Their protests promised to be more effectual than ordinarily because Pennsylvania's proprietary Penn family would not lightly accept such arbitrary dispossession. (In 1784, Pennsylvania purchased the region from the Iroquois at Fort Stanwix.)

Meantime, incidents proliferated in the woods. Seizing upon them as excuse, Dunmore declared war on the Shawnees in 1774 ("Lord Dunmore's War") and mobilized armies that defeated the Shawnees in the Battle of Point Pleasant after they ran out of ammunition. When they could get no more, they were at his mercy. He required them to give up their rights in Kentucky and to stay north of the Ohio River. Thus the conflicts in Kentucky merged with those of the Old Northwest. Shawnees were among the warriors facing General Anthony Wayne later at Fallen Timbers.

It is worth notice also that the intruders, high and low, were not defending themselves. From the beginning they were aggressors aiming to expel *all* Indians from Kentucky, the friendly Mingo Iroquois as well as the more independent Shawnees. The Iroquois Six Nations had sold all their assumed rights to Kentucky in 1788 (a sale not recognized by the Shawnees), but the worst atrocity of the war was committed on the family of a Mingo Iroquois allied and helpful to the British.

He was Soyechtowa, better known by the name he had taken in admiration for Pennsylvania's secretary James Logan. The Indian James Logan was son to Shickellamy, an Oneida chief who had contrived, with the Pennsylvanians, the treaty by which Pennsylvania joined the Iroquois Covenant Chain. In 1774, thirteen members of the Indian's family were murdered by means that even Lord Dunmore described as "marked with an extraordinary degree of Cruelty and Inhumanity." Following the requirements of justice prescribed by tribal custom, grieving Logan killed thirteen back settlers in retaliation. So far as he was concerned, that ended the matter, but the intruding Euramericans regarded his revenge as savagery rather than justice, confirming their belief that the only good Indian was a dead one. After wiping his crocodile tears, Dunmore sided with them.

Their belief gained currency in the southern backwoods, replacing the former attitude of the trading fraternity that Indians were their necessary partners in business. The land became more desirable than its occupants, and in order to acquire *it*, *they* had to be ousted by one means or another.

Like the Shawnees, Cherokees in the deeper South had been suffering from the same sort of encroachments and abuse, and acquiring the same bitter resentment. They were strengthened by British agents among them under the superintendency of John Stuart, the counterpart in the South of Sir William Johnson in New York. As tensions rose between the colonists and the crown, Stuart ordered his agents to recruit warriors to aid southern Loyalists. His brother Henry brought twenty-one pack horses loaded with ammunition into the Cherokee town of Chote, and discrepancy promptly arose between the purposes of the British and the goals of the Cherokees. The Stuarts wanted the Indians to sit tight until they could be coordinated into a British plan with specific military objectives, but the Cherokees' objectives were to get rid of intrusive settler communities called Watauga and Nolichucky. With ammunition on hand, Cherokee warriors could not be restrained. Once more, the conflicts of the Old Northwest merged with the South's as a delegation of Shawnees, Delawares, and Mohawks arrived to urge the Cherokees to fight. Accepting the war belts of these ambassadors, the Cherokees began to raid late in June 1776.

What would the populous Creeks do? South Carolinians assumed that the surest way to neutralize the Creeks would be to devastate the Cherokees before the Creeks could mobilize. They raised an army (with twenty Catawba scouts) and attacked early in August, burning houses and destroying crops in traditional fashion (as Sullivan's troops would do also in Iroquoia soon afterward). Virginia raised more troops and emulated the Carolinians' example. The alarmed Creeks did stay out of it, and Cherokee power was broken. As James H. O'Donnell, III, comments, "However one views Indian affairs in the South in 1776, the conflict with the Cherokee dominates. . . . Later British campaigns in the South could be opposed more effectively because the Southern tribes had been cowed . . ."

We may notice also that when Virginia joined the Revolution and sent Lord Dunmore scurrying to safety, he showed his loyalty to former colleagues in land larceny by calling upon their slaves to revolt. He guaranteed freedom to all slaves who would join the crown's cause. As he had few resources for his guarantee beyond the slaves themselves, his offer was nullified by the planters' precautions.

It goes without saying that waves of American "settlers" continued to cross the mountains into Cherokee country. In the histories, its previous Indian populations do not qualify as *settlers;* they are only inhabitants of the wilderness.

Whatever one thinks of them and their predecessors, the newcomers signified the wave of the future. Population ratios now changed very fast as land-hungry immigrants thrust themselves into territories where tribal peoples kept declining in numbers, and losses in battle did nothing to correct that situation. Where once masses of Indians had surrounded little groups of intrusive Europeans, the Indians soon found themselves surrounded by masses of people of European descent. From that time forward, no matter how ingeniously the tribesmen maneuvered, the power of decision had passed from them to the newcomers.

One of our more cherished myths is the notion of Frontier democracy. It holds that the sturdy settlers who took their families to conquer and civilize a wilderness learned in the process the arts of self-government and taught them to the effete East. Its falsity is the product of willful ignorance of two kinds. One center of such ignorance is the West itself where the dominance of wealth can be ignored only by refusing to see what is plain on the record. In that connection, "Frontier democracy" was mostly the rise of Western men of large property to share power with formerly dominant Eastern men of large property.

The mythologists also display appalling ignorance of what was happening elsewhere in the world. The men who mounted city barricades in France, Belgium, Austria, and Germany in 1830 and 1848 were not followers of Andrew Jackson. It is much to the point that German refugees from the repression of the '48 settled in St. Louis, Missouri; and when slave-owning "Jacksonian democrats" tried to seize the city and State for the Confederacy early in the Civil War, those German democrats shot them down and preserved Missouri in the Union.

The losses sustained by Shawnees and Cherokees opened the transmontane South to colonizing unobstructed by Indians; and when Great Britain ceded sovereignty as far west as the Mississippi River, the floodgates of immigration opened.

Then a new issue arose: how were these new lands and peoples to be governed? Numbers of them had already made clear that they had small respect for any governance except their own. If the new empire of the United States were not careful, its colonies might revolt as successfully as the self-proclaimed States, formerly colonies, had seceded from Britain. We have already noticed that Congress responded ingeniously with the Northwest Ordinance by which the new colonies were to become States through due process of law, having rights and powers equal to the founding States. Under that authority, Vermont acquired Statehood in 1791, Kentucky in 1792, and Tennessee in 1796, but the Indians of the Old Northwest prevented colonizing in that region until after Wayne's treaty at Greenville in 1795. New States in the Old Northwest were delayed until the nineteenth century.

Even after defeat the Indians retained importance because they held the key to whether the United States should be only a confederation of equal States or should become an empire with sovereign central jurisdiction. That issue long pitted nationalists against states-righters, and some leaders, like Thomas Jefferson, were ambivalent. All agreed that the tribes must be subjected, but agreement ended at the assignment of responsibility for dealing with the tribes.

Congress claimed it. So did various States. Massachusetts and New York State simply ignored Congress when treating with their own Indians, and Congress was powerless to punish them. Pennsylvania accepted Congress's supervision when purchasing Indian claims within its acknowledged boundaries. If the western colonies should treat with the tribes independently of Congress, they would gain powers of patronage greater than Congress's own.

The basic issue was land, and it was as old as the original colonies of England in America. Whoever had the right to obtain tribal cessions of land would have the right to convert that land into real property recognized by law. Whoever gained that power gained dependents among persons desiring property. All of Britain's colonies had enacted laws specifically invalidating purchase of Indian lands by individual persons. Now, in 1790, Congress forbade its own colonies ("territories") in the "National Domain" to interfere with Congress's right to treat with the tribes. Congress's Trade and Intercourse Act provided in its fourth section "That no sale of lands made by any Indians, or any nation or tribe of Indians within the United States, shall be valid to any person or persons, *or to any state*, whether having the right of pre-emption to such lands or not, unless the same shall be made and duly executed at some public treaty, *held under the authority of the United States.*" (Italics added.)

The founding States could get away with disregarding that law, but new applicants for Statehood had to accept it before being admitted to the Union. In a very real sense, even within the arbitrarily fictional domain of law, the empire of the United States has derived its authority from power over Indians.

The "conquest of the wilderness" had nothing to do with it.

CHAPTER 38

. . . And Tippecanoe Too

The purchase of Louisiana from Napoleon in 1803 was the event
which, more than any other, started the United States on its westward march.
—E. E. RICH, *Hudson's Bay Company* 2:241

"We were happy when he [the white man] first came," explained
the Flathead chief Charlot. "We first thought he came from the light;
but he comes like the dusk of evening now, not like the dawn of
morning. He comes like a day that has passed, and night enters our
future with him."
—Quoted in JAMES P. RONDA, *Lewis and Clark
among the Indians*

Not everyone believed that the United States should expand swiftly
westward. Some important Easterners, politically organized in the Fed-
eralist party, feared the loss of needed workers and consumers to the
West, but their party lost the national election of 1800 to Thomas Jefferson's Republicans who were hot to encourage western migration; and the
vagaries of European diplomacy unexpectedly stimulated their expansionist ambitions.

After losing the Seven Years War, France tried to keep some of its
American possessions out of British hands by the device of ceding territory west of the Mississippi River to Spain. In 1800, by the secret treaty
of San Ildefonso, Spain gave this giant tract back to France. In practical
terms this meant that Napoleon Buonaparte acquired it, and when Jefferson learned of that he became understandably alarmed. However, Napoleon's deepening involvements in Europe (as well as disaster in Haiti at
the hands of Toussaint L'Ouverture) reduced Napoleon's interest in
America. In a grandly imperial gesture, he offered to sell all of his Louisiana Territory in 1803, and did so for fifteen million dollars.

With this single coup, the United States doubled its own empire
(dubbed the expansion of democracy) and aroused frenzied imaginings

among persons desiring land—great speculators as well as little people yearning to homestead. In later years, the terms *virgin land* and *land free to be taken* were coined to make such appetites seem innocent, but the appetites' possessors understood very well that the lands they wanted had previous owners. History makes strange twists, and the semantics of historians contort even more oddly. The autocratic Federalists wanted to leave western Indians alone (for a time) while the imperialist Republicans thirsted for immediate conquest. In their dealings with their own people, the Federalists earned a reputation for being opposed to democracy, while their opponents became noted as favoring it. The scene makes sense when Indians are simply not allowed to be people.

Jefferson fed imperialist fantasies by sending the famous expedition of Meriwether Lewis and William Clark to explore and map the Far Northwest (1804–6), not just within the purchased territory but all the way to the Pacific Coast. Spaniards understood what lay behind that sort of curiosity, and they tried to intercept the expedition, but missed it. The explorers had the good sense to solicit help from friendly Indians—in their case, good Indians were not dead—and after making a base camp among the Mandans on the upper Missouri River, Lewis and Clark struggled to the top of the Continental Divide and down the other side, eventually following the Columbia River to the Pacific.

They had the indispensable guidance of Toussaint Charbonneau, a French-Canadian trader, and his Shoshoni wife Sacagawea who served together on the expedition for nineteen months. Without them, the expedition would have stopped dead at the Rocky Mountains, and the explorers might have stopped dead too; but Sacagawea's presence guaranteed to tribes along the way that intentions were peaceful because women did not accompany war parties.

Much mythology has grown up about the Lewis and Clark expedition, especially about Sacagawea. Facts reduce her from a superwoman heroic role to one of value as a respected part of a team, and a representative of Indians who were "active participants in exploration." As James P. Ronda stresses, "Exploration was a cooperative endeavor requiring substantial information and support from the Indians. . . . To a vast enterprise they lent their intelligence, skill, and nerve. . . . Maps, route information, food, horses, open-handed friendship—all gave the Corps of Discovery the edge that spelled the difference between success and failure."

This expedition displayed remarkably two sides of American character in that era: its dogged determination against brutal odds, to overcome all obstacles heroically, and its peculiar satisfaction in the conviction of being a chosen people superior by birth to all others. Lewis remarked in his journal that Toussaint Charbonneau had interpreted faithfully everywhere they went, but slurred the synethnic trader as "a man of no particular merit." For the couple's services during those nineteen months, Lewis laid out the princely sum of $500.33. (The thirty-three cents are intriguing.)

Spaniards had correctly intuited danger to themselves from this expedition. Russia and Britain also laid claims to territories in the Far Northwest, and the great trading companies doing business there were even more interested. However, for several decades after Lewis and Clark the Far Northwest remained a sort of jurisdictional no-nation-state's land in which the resident Indians continued to live and trade in accustomed ways. Basic decisions of power were being made farther east.

The Shawnees banished from Kentucky in 1774 had been led by Chief Cornstalk who served time afterwards as a hostage. Later, when the American Revolution broke out, some Shawnees sided with the British, and once again Cornstalk became a hostage, but this time he was murdered by a lynching party while in custody. No effort was made to punish his assassins.

One of the more gruesome discoveries of the research for this book has been the revelation of repeated lynchings of Indians who were supposed to be under government protection. It was more than an occasional aberration. It became as much of a pattern as the lynchings of Afro-Americans (so deliberately flagrant in the nineteenth century, and now performed more secretively) and the purpose was identical in both cases: to terrorize the peoples of the lower castes.

Sometimes lynchings arouse fury instead of terror. Cornstalk's assassination failed of its intended effect, partly because of a family of warriors who admired him, one of whom was named Tecumseh. There were plenty of reasons for these Shawnees to resent being crowded back into a corner of the region that had once been their own, yet Cornstalk had been a moderate while he lived. Though he had not shirked his duty to lead the fighting in wartime, his was a voice of conciliation, of compromise with the Americans. His death became a lesson for the young warriors that death in battle would be far preferable and more honorable than death at the hands of lynchers.

The Shawnees became the shock troops of the Indian armies that defeated Josiah Harmar in 1790 and Arthur St. Clair a year later. (St. Clair lost 600 men, three times as many as the better-publicized George Armstrong Custer.) The absolute routs of the two armies inflated Shawnee confidence in their ability to preserve their homeland, to a degree that lost sight of relative numbers and relationships of power. They were brought back to earth when "Mad Anthony" Wayne defeated them at Fallen Timbers in 1794, and in 1795 they accepted the Treaty of Greenville.

This treaty was noticed in an earlier chapter as re-establishing the principle of a recognized boundary between the Indians and the United States, but few Shawnees expected it to be honored, and they were correct. As R. David Edmunds remarks in his biography, *Tecumseh and the Quest for Leadership*, "The line of demarcation meant little to American frontiersmen. . . . By 1800, significant numbers of squatters were erecting cabins north of the Greenville line."

Not content with edging into Indian territory, they slaughtered the game on which the Indians depended. A witness unimpeachably hostile to the Shawnees commented, "One white hunter will destroy more game than five of the common Indians—the latter generally contenting himself with a sufficiency for present subsistence—while the other, eager after game, hunt for the skin of the animal alone." This, we may note, was the heritage of Daniel Boone, brought across the Ohio River from Kentucky.

The quoted observer was William Henry Harrison, governor of Indiana Territory. In his own person he represented the surging encroachers and their motives. His birthplace was Berkeley Plantation on the James River (still visible to tourists). He had made a military career and was among Wayne's victors at the Battle of Fallen Timbers. Thomas D. Clark comments, "No figure in the history of the American frontier was more a part of the events that resulted in the opening of the early West." Another way of saying this would be that Harrison became the Indians' worst enemy, making a career of conquest that finally elected him president of the United States.

He started in politics as the delegate to Congress from the Northwest Territory, in which capacity he sponsored an act to sell western lands in smaller tracts than before, thereby making them more available to less affluent purchasers. Congress highly approved of selling western lands because Congress was perpetually strapped for funds.

When the Northwest Territory was divided into Ohio and Indiana territories, Harrison set the capital of Ohio at Chillicothe. It was a gesture of utter contempt for the Shawnees whose capital the place had been; its name is a corruption of their word for "principal town." Their reaction is not hard to guess.

Wayne's victory at Fallen Timbers had opened most of Ohio to Virginian settlers who poured over the Ohio River after ascending the James and descending the Kanawha River. (An alternative was Braddock's road to Pittsburgh, then down the Ohio.) When the Shawnees were forced back into Indiana Territory, Harrison busied himself by imposing a series of treaties to cut still more deeply into Indian lands. In the single treaty of Fort Wayne (1803), he gained cession of 1,152,000 acres. Questions have been raised about the legitimacy of the Indians with whom Harrison treated. Whether or not they had valid right to sign away those lands, the overpowering fact could not be ignored that such cessions made a mockery of the boundary supposed to lie between Indians and the United States.

Reginald Horsman's comment summarizes neatly: "The victims of this advance were, of course, the Indians. Although some American leaders hoped to include the aboriginal population as equals within the expanding American state, they never conceived that this could be accomplished through cultural pluralism. Even those who hoped to save the Indian believed that this could be done only if the Indians became American farmers. Assimilation, extinction, or expulsion were the choices."

For simplicity, this narrative has focused on the Shawnees, but other tribes—such as Miamis, Kickapoos, Potawatomis, Wyandots, Ottawas, and Delawares—were also involved, and this diversity complicated the task of uniting the Indians in opposition to Harrison's aggressive policies. Two Shawnees rose to leadership in complementary ways. Tecumseh was one. He had taken part in all the major battles of resistance since growing into manhood, and had achieved renown as a great warrior. His brother Tenskwatawa, "the Shawnee prophet," preached a new intertribal religion of rejection of American culture, renewing the doctrines of Neolin, the Delaware prophet of "Pontiac's War," to revitalize the Indians' old ways uncorrupted by the changes that made them dependent on the invaders. Tenskwatawas' teachings won wide, but somewhat selective, support. The Indians did not forsake firearms to return to the bow and arrow, and they continued to get guns and ammunition by trade and presents from British troops and traders at Detroit and Michilimackinac, places not yet surrendered to the United States.

The charisma of the two brothers did not convince all Shawnees. Some wanted only to have peace and were willing to pay the price of adopting the Americans' way of life. In the winter of 1802–3, Chief Black Hoof went to Washington to solicit farm implements so that his followers could become "civilized" by adopting a sedentary, agricultural life.

Black Hoof was a chief of more than ordinary importance. McKenney and Hall's massive compilation of lives and portraits of Indian chiefs (1838–44) identifies him as "Principal Chief" of the Shawnees and praises him

Sauk Chief Keokuk. Recognized as tribal head by the U.S. after the Black Hawk war, he displaced the traditional sachem through control of annuities. COURTESY OF THE SMITHSONIAN INSTITUTION MUSEUM OF NATURAL HISTORY.

Shawnee Chief Black Hoof. Identified by T. L. McKenney as "principal chief," Black Hoof tried to accommodate to the invaders of his tribe's territory. He and his people gave up armed resistance and offered to adopt the culture of the newcomers. He accepted a missionary and requested assignment of land for his people to farm, but the federal government was alarmed rather than pleased by the promise of their success. Reproduced from Thomas L. McKenney and James Hall, *History of the Indian Tribes of North America* (Philadelphia, 1838–44). COURTESY OF THE NEWBERRY LIBRARY.

Tenskwatawa, the Shawnee Prophet. He taught that compromise with the advancing tide of emigrants from the east was impossible, and that it must be stopped by armed force. He and his brother Tecumseh led a resistance that went down under the greater numbers, unity, and power of a federal government determined to acquire tribal lands. Reproduced from Thomas L. McKenney and James Hall, *History of The Indian Tribes of North America* (Philadelphia, 1838–44). COURTESY OF THE NEWBERRY LIBRARY.

for two reasons: first, because Black Hoof was "one of the greatest warriors of his race." He had helped defeat Braddock in 1755 and had fought through all the subsequent wars "until the treaty of Greenville in 1795."

The second reason for praise was Black Hoof's change of mind. Unlike Tenskatawa and Tecumseh, he concluded that "submission alone could save his tribe from destruction," for which McKenney and Hall became lavish in praise of this chief's nobility and fidelity. There was never the slightest question about his earnest effort to reconcile his Shawnee people to the invading American "settlers," and to do it by adopting the American way of life.

His desire pleased War Secretary Henry Dearborn, but Black Hoof made a serious strategic mistake by also requesting a deed for Shawnee lands in western Ohio. Deeds for Indians were not on the agenda at Washington.

Black Hoof's people persevered. In 1807 they were granted a Quaker missionary for their village at Wapakoneta on the Auglaize River. Friend William Kirk understood farming. Under his guidance, which stressed "civilization" rather than conversion, the 500 members of Black Hoof's village cleared 430 acres, planted orchards, acquired breeding stock of swine and cattle, hired a blacksmith, and built mills—all in one year.

But missionary Kirk made a mistake, too, in dealing with Washington. He thought that real progress was more important than paper work. Worse, he did not understand that promise for the Shawnees was threat in Washington; the administration wanted the Indians' room rather than their progress. Officialdom seized happily on the excuse that Kirk had failed to make proper reports—it sounds very modern—and they ordered him away from mission Wapakoneta in 1808. Without his expertise and initiatives, the farm quickly fell into ruin.

We may note in passing that the praise lavished on Black Hoof's character by McKenney and Hall stopped short of reciting what happened to this accommodationist Shawnee when he tried to become a "good American." The episode of mission Wapakoneta is not to be found in these pages.

It is worth repeated emphasis that this destruction of high hopes was official. Though homesteaders were not often renowned as "Indian lovers," Black Hoof's Shawnees had made such a favorable impression that their "settler" neighbors petitioned in behalf of the mission! Ruin came from Washington. (In this respect, Andrew Jackson would later show himself to be a true Jeffersonian.)

Reginald Horsman summarizes neatly: "If the Indians became American farmers they would need land. . . . The Indians, like the animals, would have to go. In spite of all the hopes of assimilation the normal method of advance had been by military victory followed by supposed willing Indian land cessions."

With Black Hoof's example of failure before them, Shawnees listened attentively to Tenskwatawa and Tecumseh. Experiment had shown that adopting the Americans' way of life failed to win favor from the United States. Even more decisively, it had shown that the American government was faithless. The alternative was to revitalize their own traditions, and what seemed like trustworthy friends were available to help them. British trade and presents would enable a united Indian people to fend off the aggressors.

Ah, but there was the rub. How could unity be achieved?

Tecumseh could count. He had seen the size of his enemy's armies, and he reached out for more warriors to pit against them. He traveled southward to evangelize for his cause, and succeeded to an extent among the Creek Indians but was unable to gain coordination of Creek resistance with the Shawnees'. Nor did he win over all the Creeks, leaving instead a legacy of factionalism that would cost that people dear. He failed utterly with the Choctaws who plainly opposed him. R. David Edmunds remarks, "Many of the southern Indians were more suspicious of Tecumseh than of the United States. . . . Didn't Chickasaw and Choctaw scalps still hang in the lodges of some warriors who accompanied Tecumseh?"

Governor Harrison watched and worried about these agitations, and decided to strike before the brothers could achieve intertribal unity. From his point of view his logic was impeccable. Harrison persuaded the federal government which provided troops in 1811, and Harrison marched against Tenskwatawa before Tecumseh could return from the South. The result was the battle of Tippecanoe in which Tenskwatawa prayed and made medicine while his warriors fought. The medicine failed, the warriors scattered, and they cursed Tenskwatawa. Although Tippecanoe was not the stuff of great military triumphs—rather more like a hot skirmish—it succeeded politically beyond all expectations. Tenskwatawa was discredited and disowned, Tecumseh's confederation shattered, and Harrison became the Hero of Tippecanoe, a slogan that took him to the White House.

CHAPTER 39

Paths of Glory / Trails of Tears

At the end of the year 1831 I was on the left bank of the Mississippi, at the place the Europeans call Memphis. While I was there a
numerous band of Choctaws (or Chactas as they are called by the
French of Louisiana) arrived; these savages were leaving their country and seeking to pass over to the right bank of the Mississippi,
where they hoped to find an asylum promised to them by the American government. It was then the depths of winter, and that year the
cold was exceptionally severe; the snow was hard on the ground, and
huge masses of ice drifted on the river. The Indians brought their
families with them; there were among them the wounded, the sick,
newborn babies, and old men on the point of death. They had neither tents nor wagons, but only some provisions and weapons. I saw
them embark to cross the great river, and the sight will never fade
from my memory. Neither sob nor complaint rose from that silent
assembly. Their afflictions were of long standing, and they felt them
to be irremediable.

—ALEXIS DE TOCQUEVILLE

More than any other man, [Andrew] Jackson was responsible for
the removal of the Indians to the remote reaches west of the Mississippi River.

—ROBERT V. REMINI

By 1800, Indians between the Appalachians and the Mississippi had lost
power to resist the advancing Americans unless assisted by other powers,
and the incoming Americans understood keenly that their Indian antagonists had help from Britain in Canada, and Spain in Florida. There also
were still Spanish colonists effectively ruling in Louisiana despite paper
shuffling between Spain and France in Europe. Jefferson's government
managed to keep conflict in the West at the level of scuffles because Jef-

ferson wanted to avoid dangerous involvement in Europe's Napoleonic wars, but, as we have seen, he aroused the land-hungry with the Louisiana Purchase.

His successor James Madison was not so fortunate. Caught between Britain's seizures of American ships and seamen, and the importunate demands of western "War Hawks" in Congress, Madison had to preside over the War of 1812 in which a British fleet forced him to flee while it burnt his capital. In the West, however, American arms were more successful.

The War Hawks had planned to conquer Canada. Their thrusts toward Montreal and Niagara failed dismally, but their favored leader William Henry Harrison managed to penetrate Canada as far as Moraviantown on the Thames River where he defeated the British decisively. (Ironically, Moraviantown was so named because founded by missionaries of a "peace" religion.) Shawnee Chief Tecumseh died in that battle. The Americans were obliged to retreat south of the Great Lakes, but they had finally put a stop to British support of Indian raids in the Old Northwest. The region opened wide to floods of immigrants from the East who were not slow in coming. They called their new State "Indiana."

Something similar in effect happened farther south. Tecumseh had preached unity there, and Tenskwatawa's revitalization doctrine had made some headway. Young warriors became Indian "Red Sticks" whose enemies were the American "War Hawks." Among the Creeks, however, older leaders feared American power. When unrestrainable young men accepted Britain's hatchet, something like a civil war broke out among the Creeks, dividing them regionally between Upper Creek Red Sticks and Lower Creeks who were more temporizing. A rising Tennesseean seized the opportunity and defeated the Red Sticks at the Battle of Horseshoe Bend (1814) as decisively as Harrison had done at the Thames. Andrew Jackson forced the Creeks to cede twenty million acres to the United States, and it would be very strange if some of them had not ended up as possessions of his political patrons and himself.

Jackson has been puffed unrecognizably into an icon of Frontier Democracy. In actuality he had little feeling and less sentiment for common people. Jackson identified himself as a *gentleman* of substance and status above the common ruck. As a young lawyer he sided with creditors against debtors, with property against the poor. He soon acquired slaves. He allied with the richest man in Tennessee politics, Governor William Blount, who had acquired a million acres of land by speculation, and it was Blount who had appointed Jackson commander of the Creek War troops.

Jackson's victory over the Creeks began his rise to glory and power. When the British prepared to attack New Orleans, Jackson was sent in 1815 to organize the defense. Luck served him well. A pirate named Jean Lafitte offered help that included cannon and an intimate knowledge of the terrain, and Jackson shrewdly accepted. He adjusted his defense lines in accordance with Lafitte's advice, and set Lafitte's cannon among them. When British troops advanced, the partners mowed them down. Folklore attributes the victory to Jackson's backwoods sharpshooters, but most British casualties fell before grapeshot from the cannon. Nevertheless, folklore prevailed, and Lafitte dropped out of the picture reported back east.

Though the battle occurred after peace had been negotiated, it was decisive in two ways. It convinced British rulers that sea power could not penetrate the Mississippi, and it projected Andrew Jackson to national fame.

The War of 1812 guaranteed security to colonizers of the vast Mississippi Valley. What must be stressed now is that the Valley was *not* a wilderness. Before the Anglo-Americans flooded in, a mixed population inhabited and organized the region for their own purposes. "Frontier history" has chosen to ignore their presence and the culture they had created and lived by for more than a century, primarily because those facts are completely at odds with the assumptions and theories underlying racist Frontier history, but a new generation of scholars has arisen.

Among them, Daniel H. Usner, Jr., has identified and explored a "cross-cultural web of economic relations" that extended within "a network of coastal towns and interior [French and Spanish] posts stretching from the Alabama River to the Red River." He calls it a "frontier exchange economy," and its first feature to strike the eye is its complexity. It is an advanced development of the intersocietal exchange so prominent wherever Indians traded with Europeans. This network involved nationals of Spain in West Florida and New Mexico, Frenchmen along the Mississippi, and Afro-Americans, slaves and free, as well as American Indians in a number of tribes. An uncountable number of those "free" Afro-Americans were "maroons" who had escaped from slavery. The network depended heavily upon barter of food—crops and meat provided by Indian and African peasants for military garrisons and commercial and political Europeans. Extra quantities of some foods and many deerskins were produced for European markets.

Far from being the haunts of wilderness, the lower Mississippi Valley of the eighteenth century began to reassert the function it had performed as "main street" of trade under Mexico's earlier Toltec colonists, but only up to the point (geographically) where trading networks of the Great Lakes commercial system took over. (Competition was keen between merchants of Montreal and those of New Orleans.) By the nineteenth century, the southern system had acquired a maturity fully equal (at least) to the culture of backwoodsmen thrusting west from Tennessee. (Young Andrew Jackson did business at Natchez.) Interspersed among a multitude of small holdings were a few large plantations which became more dominating after the export market increased for cotton. Farms were fully agricultural including poultry, swine, cattle, and horses, many of which were imported from New Mexico. Entrepreneurs descended from every ethnic stock and used every traditional commercial device, including pilfering and much smuggling.

In short, when Anglo-Americans broke into the lower Mississippi in the nineteenth century, contrary to Frontier mythology, they brought neither "civilization" nor "democracy" to the region. What they brought must be recognized as conquest and domination which they exerted through imposition of their own system of economics, politics, and government. They strengthened and added to what Daniel Usner describes as a "colonial elite" which "worked steadily to enforce bondage upon black Louisianians and West Floridians, dependency upon Indians, and subordination upon a mixed lot of white settlers." The Anglo-American new social hierarchy and institutions acted to diminish instead of increasing personal freedom while introducing political democracy that functioned as such only for the *herrenvolk*. For lower castes and classes the new systems functioned as colonialism with increased emphasis on chattel slavery.

Before they could take over the lower Mississippi, the expansionists of Tennessee, the Carolinas, and Georgia needed to get rid of several obstacles, mostly Indian. Andrew Jackson increased his reputation as a military hero by seizing Pensacola, the capital of West Florida (1818) under pretext of attacking hostile Seminoles, refugee Red Stick Creeks, and "Maroon" escaped slaves; and he thus deprived hostile Indians of a major source of supplies. Under pressure, Spain ceded all of Florida to the United States, an action that sent Jackson's political stock soaring. Jackson became president in 1828 and was re-elected in 1832. In 1830 his administration picked up a suggestion previously made by Thomas Jefferson. It enacted the Indian Removal law to require the southeastern tribes to move west of the Mississippi.

A series of enforced treaties followed. In 1830 the Choctaws were summoned to the Treaty of Dancing Rabbit Creek. When they objected to the terms presented to them, United States Commissioner John Eaton gave an ultimatum: they must move west or consent to be governed by

Sequoyah. The Cherokee genius who invented symbols to represent all the sounds of Cherokee speech. With this syllabary the tribe published a newspaper. COURTESY OF THE NEWBERRY LIBRARY.

Mississippi law. Resistance would bring down upon them destruction by American armies. In 1831 the Choctaws started west.

Cherokee leaders considered their options carefully and decided that they could no longer sustain independence on their own terms—they must adopt the civilization of their powerful neighbors. Deliberately, the Cherokees transformed their system of government into a republic. Their genius Sequoyah invented a syllabary that enabled reproduction in writing of all the sounds in the Cherokee language, the people became literate (probably more so than their attackers), they published a weekly newspaper and they adopted the Anglo-American methods of agriculture and capped them with that crowning glory of civilization, plantation slavery.

The Cherokees also accepted missionaries, but chose the wrong kind. The State of Georgia ran their New England Congregationalist missionary off the Cherokees' land and jailed him. Supreme Court Chief Justice John Marshall affirmed the people's right to their territory and was ignored. A story is told, perhaps apocryphal, that President Andrew Jackson remarked, "John Marshall has made his decision, now let him enforce it." Whether or not Jackson actually said that, neither he nor anybody else enforced Marshall's decision.

Pressures on the Cherokees increased instead of lessening, and a party formed within the nation to seek an agreement with their persecutors. Georgians quickly caught on to the division. As Theda Perdue has written, "Governor Wilson Lumpkin of Georgia surreptitiously promised special consideration and some degree of protection to the faltering Cherokees who stood to lose the most in terms of material wealth." Offered this temptation, the "treaty party" signed the treaty of New Echota (29 December 1835) relinquishing all claims to land east of the Mississippi in exchange for five million dollars. The richer Cherokees took their slaves and portable possessions west in the spring of 1836, but the Cherokee nationalists who had had no part in the treaty arrangements stuck fast to their land until rounded up at bayonet point and forced onto the "trail of tears" under hardships and with casualties that few armies have had to endure in combat. Of the 13,000 Cherokees on that trek, at least 4,000 died of privation and exposure.

We may notice in passing that the Treaty of New Echota opened wounds of racism in Cherokee society. Partisans for and against the treaty were genetically mixed, but those in favor appeared to have more Euramerican ancestors than Cherokee, and were culturally the most inclined to accept American ways. Their approval of the treaty won them blame for the subsequent trail of tears and opened a wide gap between social classes and perceived races. The racism of the conquering Americans had the effect, here and elsewhere, of arousing feelings and divisions of race among the conquered peoples.

Like the Cherokees and Choctaws, the Creek Indians were forced west, but the Seminoles of Florida, who included many Creeks, went to war against the United States. Their great war chief Osceola, himself a Red Stick refugee, made the mistake of trusting to negotiations with military commanders who believed in opportunity more than honor. He and eighty-four other Seminoles were seized and imprisoned (October 1837). He died in prison four months later. Although deprived of leaders, the Seminoles fought on in the longest American war before Vietnam. They never accepted defeat though most moved west after being given a cash settlement in 1857.

The Americans were unable to find and remove all the Southeastern Indians, or perhaps they found that troublesome and expensive task not worthwhile. They achieved their main goal by destroying tribal polities and seizing tribal territories, and they ignored the Indians who hid away in mountains and swamps, often with the cooperation of sympathetic American neighbors. Such kindly souls did exist though the spotlight has been given to rampaging imperialists with power.

Nowhere is it clearer that rationalizations of "Frontier history" are irrelevant to plain facts. The conqerors did not bring civilization to the Indians, nor did they bring Christian religion; they actually stopped the mission among the Cherokees. The Indians did not "retire" before the advance of civilization; they were pushed, and pushed hard. The Indians did not require vast territories for their savage way of life; their conquerors wanted and took those territories that had subsisted the Indians from time immemorial. These are all alibis. Southern backwoodsmen had the same motive as German tribesmen forcing their way into the Rhine Valley in ancient times: more recently, the same as the Scots who crossed to Ulster in Ireland; they wanted the land and they had power enough to take it. That was enough for them. The alibis were concocted later by nationalist and racist historians.

Most Southeastern Indians were forced into Oklahoma Territory where they encountered new problems of adjusting to previously resident tribes who did not welcome newcoming competitors for limited resources. Even among the uprooted and transplanted, many survivors successfully regrouped and recovered. Richard Sattler, who has specialized in their history, believes that a minimum of about 10,000 each of Cherokees, Muskogees, and Choctaws preserve their native languages today.

Americans of the present day are apt to give undue importance to the mid- and late-nineteenth-century freedom struggles of the trans-Mississippi Indians. Worthy of respect though these are, they amounted in U.S. policy to repetition of patterns tried and tested in the East, and the odds were so great against the far western Indians that they never had a chance, regardless of valor. Some knew that and were careful to come to humiliating terms with the threatening colossus. Others fought on to honorable but foredoomed defeat.

The moment of fateful decision occurred during the War of 1812 when William Henry Harrison in the North, and Andrew Jackson in the South, destroyed the last chance of effective Indian resistance. Anthony Wayne's victory at Fallen Timbers and the subsequent Treaty of Greenville had established a system by which the tribes could co-exist with the United States, each managing its own affairs on its own side of a recognized boundary. Symbolically, Wayne returned to his estate near Philadelphia. But Harrison and Jackson were men on the make in the West, and they shattered the Greenville agreements.

Shawnee chief Tecumseh was the last hope of Indians to hold the tide of Euramerican advance to bilaterally negotiated agreements. After Tecumseh's death, government officials never had the slightest intention of honoring treaties with the tribes. Such arrangements were regarded as mere conveniences to keep the natives quiet until more resources could be mustered and organized.

Many scholars tend to absolve the government of fault by ignoring its actions in order to exclaim over the "resistless tide" of homesteaders. This is error. The homesteaders were resistless because the government intended them to be and took pains to smash opposition wherever it appeared.

From 1812 until the end of the century, official policy, no matter in what euphemistic terms expressed, was simply conquest. Its purpose was to reduce Indian persons to dependence and to seize tribal lands.

Whether anything else could have been done, given the circumstances of the century, I cannot even guess, but it seems worthwhile to single out individuals who were especially treacherous or brutal. Though history's horrors were widespread, violations of common decency become especially significant as indicators of how racist conceptions negated established standards of morality. Perhaps the most valid reason for penetrating hypocritical facades is just this: that the same racist conceptions, if not exposed and rejected by new generations, will produce the same urge to bloody and disastrous conquest. *Conduct condoned will be conduct repeated.* Anyone familiar with contemporary events can supply examples.

CHAPTER 40

Progress and Erosion

The intercourse of Americans with the natives of this continent
has always been of a hostile character, their object being to remove
the aborigine from the soil as the first step toward its occupation by
the whites.
—SIR GEORGE SIMPSON,
Governor of Hudson's Bay Company

In the Southeast, farming by backwoodsmen was generally more individ-
ualist than farming by Indians, but differences in technique were not
great between small holders in both cultures. Indians had learned about
plows and draft animals. The big difference came with large slave plantations created by the sort of capital formation that most Indians simply
did not understand. (Nor did most homesteaders.) Exceptions occurred
when some of the leading "civilized" Indians set up their own plantations—these men being of mixed ancestry and cultural inclinations—but
traditional Indians did not aim at wealth; indeed they have been charged
with laziness for being satisfied with subsistence production. (The same
charge is made against subsistence homesteaders in somewhat of a contradiction to Jefferson's praise of the independent yeoman.)

Another cultural innovation brought by the newcomers was acceleration of transportation by roadbuilding and flatboat freighting along the
Ohio and Mississippi. Roads speeded up resettlement of lands from which
Indians had been evicted (and helped the eviction process along); and the
cargo carriers turned subsistence farms into producers for export.

By and large, however, the Southeasterners' culture, though it bewil-
dered Indians by the speed of its buildup, was based on agriculture and
scattered villages in patterns that Indians could comprehend, and if most
Indians were illiterate, plenty of their new neighbors were also.

In the Old Northwest, however, something new was gestating in the
invading culture. Its precursor was the Erie Canal, projected in 1817 and

opened throughout its entire Albany-to-Buffalo length by 1825. More than coincidence is involved in those dates. William Henry Harrison and his Kentucky militia had finally ended Indian resistance in the Old Northwest by 1815. Ironically, these Southerners made fortunes for Northerners. When the last western resistance went down, New York's Senecas—already battered from the invading troops of the Revolution— gave up. The moneyed investors who financed construction of the Erie Canal knew that the way was open. One of them was the fur trade magnate John Jacob Astor.

They could foresee also what would result from a single communication system linking New York City to the outpost village of Chicago by way of the Hudson River, the Erie Canal, and the Great Lakes. Instead of isolated villages as in the Southeast, towns and cities mushroomed along the canal, and Chicago almost exploded as it became New York's largest and farthest satellite. If "civilization" may be said ever to have moved from East to West, it did so from New England through Iroquoia along the southern shores of the Great Lakes to Chicago where early arrivals bought land by the acre and sold to later comers by the square foot. Much history would be made by the sharp distinction between the migrants who raced westward from Massachusetts and Connecticut and those who threaded through the mountains to the Ohio Valley from Virginia and the Carolinas. Transplanted "freesoil" Yankees in the northern counties of the Old Northwest held to the Union and helped force it upon slaveholding secessionists in the nation's most bitter war, then just a cloud on the horizon.

From these Northerners would come a culture new to the earth, certainly fantastically new to American Indians. Railroads and factories and dense urban centers of population were just beginning to emerge when the Erie Canal aroused wild excitement about things to come.

Excitement, that is, for everyone but the Indians.

We have bypassed the Iroquois peoples in order to follow Shawnee battles and retreats from Kentucky to Indiana and to final defeat at Moraviantown on the Thames. In fact, the Senecas, the westernmost Iroquois nation, frequently participated in those conflicts and constantly consulted with the western nations until the 1795 Treaty of Greenville. After that crucial date, American garrisons were posted between the Senecas and the allied Indians of the Old Northwest; in the sequel, the Senecas of New York became contemptible to Iroquois in Canada who had continued in British alliance; and tribal "nephews" in Indiana spat defiance at

Seneca efforts to resume leadership as in the Covenant Chain. As A. F. C. Wallace remarks, "The war for the Northwest Territory was the rock on which the Six Nations finally foundered."

Hostility increased between Iroquois in Canada and those behind in Iroquoia until two separate leagues were organized with distinct council fires at Ohsweken on Canada's Grand River and Onondaga near Syracuse, New York. Pressures from Massachusetts and New York for the sale of tribal territory stimulated growth of a party among the Senecas similar in general motive to the "civilization" party among the Cherokees. The Senecas were vulnerable and had no place else to go. They fell to disputing among themselves until "the embers of the old confederacy guttered out in a welter of liquor, bribery, and high-pressure salesmanship." Within the demoralized and greatly reduced collection of "slums in the wilderness" tensions and violence increased between "progressives" and traditionalists. The time became ripe for a prophet of revitalization.

The man who heard the call was Chief Cornplanter's brother, an experienced warrior and diplomat in his own right, who had participated personally in many of the events of Seneca decline. His personal name was Connediu. We know him as Handsome Lake, a title belonging to one of the *royaner* titles of lordships in the Iroquois League.

Deeply depressed by the evils fallen on his people, Handsome Lake sank into drunkenness until a day in 1799 when he had a vision in which the Creator sent angels with a message of reform. More visions followed, and Handsome Lake accepted the duty to preach the new syncretic gospel of the Longhouse Religion, one that in the broadest sense was puritanical, demanding abstinence from liquor and illicit sex. He made such an impression that the Seneca council created an unprecedented office for him—"High Priest, and principal Sachem in all things Civil and Religious."

Handsome Lake moved fast to attack sin powerfully, even to the point of identifying and executing witches by his own authority. He differed from other prophets of revitalization (Delaware Neolin and Shawnee Tenskwatawa) by concentrating reforms on personal morality. In regard to agricultural technology, he accepted the examples of Quaker missionaries (who were also highly moralistic). They had scrupulously set up a model farm on land unclaimed by the Indians. Though the Quakers did not kill witches, their doctrines were close enough to Handsome Lake's so that communication was possible, and the Quakers must be credited with being careful as missionaries to take no advantage for themselves or their society at the expense of the Indians.

It appears that Handsome Lake did revive Seneca morale, but in doing so he also revived objections to his arbitrary methods and literal witch hunts. His political authority did not last long. Opposition reasserted itself on the one side in Seneca traditional councils, and on the other from what seems like a host of missionaries competing with the Quakers. (Even the Hicksite Quakers joined in the competition, to the great annoyance of orthodox Friends.) Nevertheless the heritage of Handsome Lake's charisma found warm acceptance among other Iroquois peoples as well as the Senecas, and the Longhouse Religion—a syncretic blend of Christianity with Iroquois traditions—is potent still today.

Notwithstanding religious belief, early nineteenth-century Senecas had to face some hard facts of life. Their tribal territory had sprawled over the easiest road from East to West—not quite the "water level route" that promoters dubbed it, but close enough to level so that heavy wagons could pass that way without having to cope with mountain passes. Came the Erie Canal and a tide of builders, many of whom stayed; and they were followed by an outpouring of land-hungry migrants. The Senecas had been Iroquois Keepers of the Western Door. Their very advantage of position became a heavy burden as the newcomers shoved them aside and chipped at the reservations that had been awarded by the Treaty of Fort Stanwix in 1784.

Connivery and crookedness became routine. For once, reliable source documents exist to picture events in honest detail. These are the reports of Quaker missionaries and visitors who could not be evicted like the Congregationalist missionary to the Cherokees. When in 1838 the Ogden Land Company bought the last remaining Seneca land, the proceedings have been characterized as "blatantly corrupt" and marked by bribery, forgery, and menacing intimidation. Even so, only about half the chiefs' signatures appeared on the deed. Opposition was so strong, aided by the Quakers as well as other decent people, that the deed had to be rescinded.

In 1842 it was replaced by another, a "compromise" agreement that gave up two reservations but retained Allegany and Cattaraugus. Of the Senecas who had previously agreed to remove to Oklahoma, only two remained there.

The "progressive" Senecas tried to cope with all this change by adapting to the newcomers' way of life. Gradually they changed from the traditional extended family and communally permeated subsistence system to nuclear families with particular tracts of land cultivated by plow agriculture and stocked with domesticated animals. Many Senecas hired out as wage laborers in the newcomers' enterprises. (In itself this was not new. Senecas had hired out to French garrisons in the eighteenth century; novelty came from increased scale.)

Finally, in 1848, the Senecas overthrew their old government by hereditary chiefs, replacing it with elected councillors and officers. This was too much for some of the traditionalists who managed to frustrate the Ogden Land Company's grab of their reservation at Tonawanda. To the present day, Tonawanda preserves government by a council of chiefs in defiance of the constitution and elected government of Allegany and Cattaraugus.

During the American Revolution, the Senecas had fought against the United States while the Oneidas had allied themselves with the new nation. The unhappy Oneidas were to prove once again the old adage that with friends like these nobody needs enemies. Guaranteed their territorial integrity at Fort Stanwix in 1784, the exhausted and faction-riven tribe was immediately pressured by New York State to cede the territory so guaranteed, and the supposedly protecting officers of the United States looked the other way. Within one year the first of a long series of treaties with the State began giving up land. Jack Campisi remarks, "The government of the State of New York, although pledged to protect the Oneidas, became their major exploiter and the federal government, with its attention focused on the west, ignored its obligations to the subjugated tribes of the east."

Campisi lists thirty-two transactions and claims only that they are "representative" of the "majority" of the State's manipulations. Some of these representative transactions were made with one or another faction of the Oneidas instead of the whole people. What is quite certain in the confusion is that the Oneidas lost almost all their land. As I write this, they are suing in federal courts for restitution on grounds of fraudulent spoliation.

By equally complex arrangements, they were compensated with a tract in Green Bay, Wisconsin, formerly part of the territory of the Menominee Indians. Beginning in 1823, most of the Oneidas *settled* in the new land where they have built a thriving, model community after many hardships. (I have underscored *settled* to draw attention to the rarity of its use in regard to Indians.)

Though the bulk of Oneidas moved to Green Bay and eventually prospered there, others remained in New York, and still others went off to Canada where their descendants still live among the Six Nations of Canada.

Like the Senecas, the Oneidas had no real choice but to adapt their culture to the pressures from dominant neighbors, and so they did, adopting nuclear families and American institutions of business as well as farming. Yet they cling to their Indianness. One expressed it this way: "From nine to five, I'm a good American businessman; but after five, I'm all Oneida." It is a remark that could be made by many an Indian among those who survived being uprooted and dispossessed.

Much of the mythology about pioneers settling America originated in the events of the early nineteenth century. Frederick Jackson Turner, whose middle name proclaims his outlook, summarized: "The existence of an area of free land, its continuous recession, and the advance of American settlement westward, explain American development." The semantics are wondrous. Turner himself noted Indian wars and Indian resistance at various points in his musings, but the land upon which the wars and resistance took place was "free," and what remained free kept continuously receding while the nearer regions were "settled."

Turner's frontiers (and Frontier as an abstraction) are always seen from the eastern side of a line—the line between "civilization" and "savagery"—never from the middle of real people mixing together. Turner's frontier hero is the individual *pioneer*, the "stalwart and rugged frontiersman" who led the wave of settlement by opening a space in the wilderness to make a farm. That such men and their families existed is beyond dispute; equally so, their labors and hazards were great; but Turner and his disciples have left out much. These vanguard pioneers were likely to be squatters whose advance was motivated by lack of enough money to buy land. So handicapped, they squatted on Indian land and became the "rednecks" and "crackers" of bigger men who followed. Until the hordes came after, the pioneers would be tolerated by the Indians, but when hostilities broke out, they were the first to suffer and to provide rationalization for counter-murders and massacres of Indians. (Incidentally, though Indians might tolerate a few squatters, land speculators did not. Those squatters were obliged always to keep moving on. In the mythology, they are "restless.")

Most homesteaders who came to stay arrived in organized groups. With or behind them was the great speculator in lands, sometimes a man who had bought up soldiers' bonus tracts and was selling them by the parcel. These organized communities put up rude but adequate fortifications and formed militias. When they got into deep trouble, an army was sent to clear their way. This was what caused the land to become "free," and as the speculators did "land office business" the area of freedom "receded."

Within this chapter and the preceding ones, which could be expanded many times, enough has been said to show that no matter what the Indians did, their invaders intended to push them out of the way and take over their land. If they fought to the death for independence—if they converted to one or another sect of Christianity—if they adopted the Euramericans' living patterns—it was all one. Promises extracted by force or pleas from the invaders were not fulfilled. Treaties were made to be broken. In dealings with Indians in the early nineteenth century, the governments of the United States and of the separate States were utterly cynical.

When once the Appalachian barrier had been breached by hordes of the land hungry—when the value of Indians as partners in trade had reduced to less than the value of their lands—when personal obsession acquired rationalizations of Democracy and Progress creating an empire for a people chosen by Divinity to enjoy, as that people was so assured by its highest religious and lay leaders—then Indians became nonpersons beyond the pale of moral obligation due to human persons, and their homelands became "land free to be taken."

Hopi bean planting ritual. In their difficult arid country, the Hopis take great pains to solicit supernatural favor. COURTESY OF THE SMITHSONIAN INSTITUTION MUSEUM OF AMERICAN HISTORY.

Subsistence adaptations of traditional practices. Poosepatrick eel fishing and decoys at Martic, Long Island. COURTESY OF THE SMITHSONIAN INSTITUTE MUSEUM OF AMERICAN HISTORY.

Subsistence as dependents. Indians assembled for delivery of beef rations at Fort Yates on Standing Rock Reservation in the nineteenth century. After their land was taken, insult was added to the injury when the newly dependent Indians were scorned as beggars. COURTESY OF THE SMITHSONIAN INSTITUTION MUSEUM FOR AMERICAN HISTORY.

Drying salmon in the far Northwest. COURTESY OF THE BRITISH COLUMBIA ARCHIVES AND RECORDS SERVICE.

Pole fishing on Arrow Lakes. COURTESY OF THE BRITISH COLUMBIA ARCHIVES AND RECORDS SERVICE.

Hunting the buffalo on the great prairies before and after horses were introduced. These paintings by George Catlin were lithographed for wide public consumption by Currier & Ives. COURTESY OF THE NEWBERRY LIBRARY.

CHAPTER 41

Indians Who Have Vanished

Not even the onrushing immigrants could immediately absorb all the lands in the vast American West. For varied reasons, some regions remained relatively uninfluenced for several decades, and the intersocietal commerce called the fur trade continued in its normal tumultuous course. In Thomas Jefferson's imperial vista, the Far Northwest was a distant reserve to be exploited when the United States could get close enough, so he instructed his Lewis and Clark explorers to encourage intertribal peace on the Great Plains, thus to stabilize and increase trade. Tribal unity was the very opposite of government's desire in the *Old* Northwest, as we have seen, for unity implied stronger resistance to expansion, but the great Missouri Valley still lay beyond the land business and was therefore a desirable place for business with Indians.

The vastness of the Hudson's Bay Company's hinterland also remained relatively undisturbed for the excellent reason that most newcomers were slow to appreciate its climates. To be sure, most of the Company's territory was claimed by Canada, but plenty of bellicose Americans were ready to agitate "54–40 or fight": i.e., an American boundary at latitude 54 degrees, 40 minutes, which would have reached up to Alaska and taken in half of the present-day province of British Columbia. Whatever the reason for the Bay Company's continuing privilege, it maintained the business with Indians that was its reason for existence. Indeed, the Company's greatest concern was competition from rival companies: first the North West Company which the Bay Company gobbled up in 1821, then the American Fur Company and Pacific Fur Company of John Jacob Astor, and always the enduring Russian-American Company in Alaska.

Overland migration of farmers on the "Oregon Trail" began in 1841. Until the new wave of western migration which then began, the Far Northwest remained Indian country, but with certain rearrangements. On the upper Missouri, the Mandans were weakened from successive epidemics of smallpox and the political error of too-confident antagonizing of Sioux bands drifting westward in pursuit of bison herds. The Mandan commercial reign came to an abrupt end in 1837 when the American

Fur Company's steamboat brought smallpox up the Missouri. By spring of 1838, the Mandan population of about 1,500 was reduced to 130, and the survivors have been assimilated among other peoples. Their picturesque culture as an integrated whole has disappeared.

In the sequel, the American Fur Company's men picked up the pieces of Mandan commerce. Sometimes disease struck Indians too conveniently for an inquirer's peace of mind. The present writer cannot forget the deliberate infection of smallpox that had occurred at Fort Pitt in 1763. Whether the Mandan epidemic occurred innocently or by design has been the subject of local rumors. Either way, the American Fur Company's ensuing monopoly produced such wealth for German immigrant owner John Jacob Astor that when he cannily invested the profits in New York City real estate he became the richest man in the United States.

The history of subsequent competition in the trade—a historically brief episode—is of concern here only in a demographic aspect. Homesteaders trundling along the Oregon Trail brought their women along, but traders everywhere in Indian country accepted their women where they found them. Nature took its course, and a new population was created.

Only recently have scholars begun to examine the conditions of communities so created. Preceding generations of historians skimmed over the (to them) shocking facts of "interracial" coupling which produced (to them) degenerate "half-breeds" and "mongrels." Genetic stocks and cultural traditions were slushed together in the cesspool of racial conceptions, but they are wholly different things, and they have mixed historically in different combinations. In the American East, some Indian women mated with men of African stock because of severe shortages of men of their own tribe. This happened, for example, among the Wampanoags of Massachusetts whose men had fought and died in the patriots' cause during the American Revolution. Today among the Wampanoags a range of skin color from white to black can be seen. It confused census takers who sometimes classed them as "Black," sometimes as "White," but the people never wavered in knowledge of themselves as Wampanoags. "Indians" come and go in the censuses. The people remain.

History worked differently in the Southeast where Catawbas enforced a rigid rule against marriage with Afro-Americans because of fear of violent discrimination from dominant Southerners. The Catawbas did not object to intermarriage with Euramericans.

In the Far West and Far North where commerce persisted in the early nineteenth century between Euramericans and Indians (rarely with Africans), family patterns varied. All Euramerican traders found advantage

THE UPPER MISSOURI MARKETPLACE

The Mandan-Hidatsa trading villages were the great commercial crossroads of the upper Missouri Valley. Their prime attraction for hunting Indians was the basic staple of farm products: corn, beans, squash, and tobacco. James P. Ronda remarks that these villagers "served as brokers in an international economic and cultural trade network that faced in three directions and stretched over thousands of miles."

Unlike Cahokia on the Mississippi, this Missouri center flourished well into the nineteenth century and adjusted effortlessly to business with French and English traders and their goods. In addition to their own crops, the villagers handled goods that included varied meats, fancily dressed leathers, horses and mules, guns and ammunition, axes, kettles, knives, and other European "trade goods."

The Lewis and Clark expedition wintered there in 1804, and both George Catlin and Karl Bodmer painted portraits and scenes. However, these important Indian peoples are given less historical attention than their due because of being wiped out as communal entities by Sioux enemies and more catastrophic smallpox that culminated in an epidemic of suspect origins in 1837.

By coincidence, the two finest portrayers of Indian persons and scenes visited the Mandans within one year—George Catlin in 1832 and Karl Bodmer during the winter of 1833–34. Thus we gained a rich pictorial record of the time and place. In a few instances we see the same subject through each painter's eyes.

A few Mandans survived the catastrophe but fled to refuge and assimilation among other tribes.

Mandan buffalo dance depicted by Karl Bodmer. The audience watches from roofs of great earth lodges in the background. Painting by Karl Bodmer. COURTESY OF THE NEWBERRY LIBRARY.

A crossroads market. The Hidatsa village allied to the Mandans, on the Knife River, a tributary of the Missouri, upstream from Bismarck, N.D. COURTESY OF THE NATIONAL MUSEUM OF AMERICAN ART, SMITHSONIAN INSTITUTION, GIFT OF MRS. JOSEPH HARRISON, JR.

Mandan Cemetery by George Catlin (1832). The dead were exposed on raised platforms. The circle of skulls and standing poles in the foreground held ritualistic symbolism. The lodge habitations in the village are in the background. COURTESY OF THE NATIONAL MUSEUM OF AMERICAN ART, SMITHSONIAN INSTITUTION, GIFT OF MRS. JOSEPH HARRISON, JR.

Mandan. Mah-to-toh-pa (the four bears): war chief of the tribe and one of the most celebrated chiefs known to have existed amongst the North American Indian tribes, in a very splendid dress of skins, trimmed with ermine tails and scalp locks. His headdress, made of ermine and war eagle plumes, descended to the ground and was surmounted with horns denoting his power as head war chief of the tribe. (This curious custom, met in all the American tribes, resembles a Jewish custom.) "The Mandans, now extinct (although they still survive as individuals living among other tribes), numbered 2,300 when the Author was amongst them—lived all in one village—upper Missouri, Latitude 50" [caption by Catlin]. (*Editor's note:* In Catlin's day, the notion was widespread that American Indians were descended from the lost tribes of Israel.)

Mah-to-toh-pa (the four bears) as painted by Karl Bodmer within a couple of years after George Catlin had depicted him. Such portraits by different artists of the same Indian chief are a great rarity. This pair may be unique. COURTESY OF THE NEWBERRY LIBRARY.

Mandan war chief. Mato-Tope (Mah-to-toh-pa) in a different aspect "adorned with the insignia of his warlike deeds." Painting by Karl Bodmer. COURTESY OF THE NEWBERRY LIBRARY.

Mandan. "Ha-na-tah-nu-mauhk (the wolf chief), head (civil) chief of the Mandan tribe, in a beautiful costume and holding two calumets (pipes of peace) in his hands" [caption by George Catlin].

Mandan earth lodges on a bluff overlooking the Missouri River. The boats in the foreground were made of buffalo hides stretched over wooden ribs. (Welshmen made similar craft with bull hides.) Painting by Karl Bodmer. COURTESY OF THE NEWBERRY LIBRARY.

in marriage to Indian women who belonged to important tribal families (which regarded the advantage as reciprocal), but traders of English or Anglo-American stock were less ready than French Canadians to make the connection permanent.

William R. Swagerty has identified a significant proportion of "mountain men" traders in the Rockies who kept their Indian wives after the trading era had passed (about 1840). The Anglo family men differed from their French counterparts by eventually taking their families out of the tribal milieu to join homesteading immigrant communities. The history of their synethnic children "is yet to be written."

We have noticed (in chapter 22) that men from the British Isles were sent out by the Hudson's Bay Company to staff the Company's factories—and that they acquired Indian consorts who were regarded sometimes as wives, sometimes as mistresses or concubines. Typically these men returned to Britain after their tour of duty. Usually they left their Indian mates behind. Children were mostly left with their mothers and with them went back to the arms of the tribe; but some boys were sent to Britain to be educated as gentlemen. Obviously such efforts were made out of a sense of paternal love and duty, but the outcome generally was tragic. Race feelings in Britain prevented acceptance of the synethnic youths as real gentlemen and sometimes drove them to despairing alcoholism. Others returned to their mothers' homes where they became round pegs in square holes, unfit for Indian cultural patterns and unable to find alternatives. Female offspring of the Company men fared somewhat better though scandalously in terms of Christian morality. Their physical appearance came closer than their mothers' to European ideals of beauty, so they were sought after as mates by the next generation of Company men. After which, of course, more children were born.

The French approach was sharply different. A distinction must be made between upper-class French Canadians who preserved pride in what they called purity of blood, and the men who went out into Indian villages and stayed there, as many did. The latters' children and grandchildren multiplied until they became dominant in some villages or founded new settlements of their own. The French called them *métis*, meaning "mixed," and they mixed cultural traditions as well as genes. Americans migrating westward found thriving *métis* communities at Detroit, Chicago, St. Louis, in Wisconsin, and in New Orleans.

Scandal raised its head in these places also, for many métis couples had married according to "the custom of the country," which meant that they had wedded by a tribal ritual or had simply publicized their union and maintained it in stable family life. This deviation from church doc-

This small sample of portraits drawn in the 1830s is best introduced by the artist in his own words. His hand-lettered title:

Souvenir
of the
North American Indians
as they were, in the middle of the 19th century
a numerous and noble race of
HUMAN BEINGS
fast passing to extinction
and leaving no monuments of their own behind them

Having become fully convinced of the certain extinction of the North American Native Races, I resolved at an early period of my life, to make and preserve for future ages, as far as my individual labours and personal means would enable me to do, a pictorial history of those interesting people; and with this view have, with great fatigue and expense, and with the most complete success, visited 50 Tribes, mostly speaking different languages. From amongst these Tribes I have brought home a very extensive collection of portraits and other paintings illustrating their modes of living and customs, the portraits of which collection are contained in these two volumes, reduced from the original paintings and copied, by my own hand.

Geo. Catlin
London, 1852

To which Catlin added a "Remark":

The best part of my life, and all my earthly means have been expended in thus recording the looks and customs of these vanishing Races . . . and in justice to the character of those abused and murdered Races, let it be as imperishable as these designs, that amongst more than two millions of these people where I have traveled unprotected, they everywhere treated me with hospitality and kindness.

Portraits and captions are reproduced from the unique copy in the collections of the Newberry Library, by courtesy of the Library.

Crow. Ba-da-ah-chon-du (he who jumps over every one): Chief of a band, in an extravagant costume. Shield and quiver slung—his lance in his hand, and his headdress made of War Eagle plumes. The Crow (Belantsea, in their own language) is one of the finest tribes in America and certainly the most beautifully costumed of all the American tribes. It numbers about 10,000. Rocky Mountains, sources of the Yellowstone River. Latitude 47 and 48.

Ojibbeway. I-an-be-wa-dick (the male caribou): a young warrior seated on the ground, in war dress and war paint, with his bow and arrows in his hands, his leggings fringed with scalp locks taken from the heads of his enemies killed in battle.

Ojibbeway. Ka-bes-kunk (he who strikes everywhere): a very distinguished warrior, in his war dress and war paint, holding his pipe and tobacco pouch in one hand, and his war club and medicine bag in the other. Medicine (mystery) bag is the Indian's talisman. It is made and carried by every male Indian, as his protection from accidents and disease in times of peace, and for his success in battles with his enemies. The skins of various animals, birds, and reptiles are made to contribute to the construction of these mysterious sacs, which are indicated to the Indian boy, in his dreams, as his medicine or mystery, when he hunts or traps for the animal and prepares the skin to be his companion and protector through life.

Konza. Meach-o-shin-gaw (the little white bear). One of the most noted warriors of the tribe, dressed, painted, and equipped for war.

Kiowa. A Kiowa young woman and boy, brother and sister, names not preserved.

Sioux. Toh-to-was-con-de-pee (the blue medicine): a medicine man (or doctor) with his medicine (mystery) drum and rattle in his hands, in the plight in which he visits his dying patients. Falls of St. Anthony, upper Mississippi. The physicians in all American tribes are eccentric persons, professing to deal in mysteries and to cure diseases by their magical powers, as well as by the vegetable specifics of their country, in which many of them are, no doubt, very skillful.

Sioux. A Sioux woman, wife of the chief, with her boy, four years old, at the breast: an occurrence not infrequent among the North American Indian tribes. This unnatural habit, and the premature age (12 and 14) at which the young women marry, are no doubt the principal causes of the paucity of children borne by the Indian women, who are very seldom the mothers of more than three or four. (*Editor's note:* Children five and six years old were suckled in Italy, at the time Catlin wrote, for the same "unnatural" reason the Sioux mothers had, i.e. to prolong the time between births.)

Mandan. Mi-neek-e-sunk-te-cah (the mink): a Mandan woman, the young and favorite wife of Mahtotohpa, the chief, in a very beautiful dress, and holding up and exposing the historical robe of her husband, with the battles of his extraordinary life painted on it.

Mandan. Mah-tah-ta-ha (he who runs through the middle): a distinguished young Mandan warrior, in full war dress, armed and ready for battle.

trines outraged sanctimonious officials among the incoming Americans. Jacqueline Peterson tells how a zealous circuit court judge forced the leading citizens of Green Bay, Wisconsin, who had maintained stable families for decades, to acknowledge "fornication" and "adultery" and to marry according to the judge's notions of propriety. He seems to have considered his personal crusade as bringing civilization to the wilderness. (This bigot was better versed in his church's dogmas than in his country's law or he would have known that common-law marriage had been recognized as legitimate in England as well as the United States for centuries. Benjamin Franklin and his Deborah are an example.)

Faced with the racial caste system of the immigrants, most métis and other synethnics "went underground" to escape discrimination, and became invisible. In Professor Peterson' words, "traditional American historians continue to show a remarkable myopia regarding racial mixture within the continental United States." For example, we have a statement by Frederick Jackson Turner: "In the crucible of the frontier *the immigrants* were Americanized, liberated, and fused into a mixed race." (Emphasis added.) (We may be quite sure, incidentally, that Turner did not mean to include the immigrants who had been brought involuntarily from Africa though it is undeniable that gentleman planters did fusing enough in the slave quarters.)

Canadian scholars have become conscious that "the fur trade was a socio-cultural complex which lasted 200 years," a realization that comes from their advanced researches in intersocietal exchange and mingling. Some American historians—Peterson, Swagerty, and Daniel Usner among them—have begun trying to mine that lode. It is an inspiring beginning, comparable in its own field to the revelations that followed publication of *Black Reconstruction* by W. E. Burghardt Du Bois.

Excitement at Fort Mackenzie, 28 August 1833. Artist Karl Bodmer witnessed an enemy raid on Indians camped outside the fort's palisade. COURTESY OF THE NEWBERRY LIBRARY.

Women of different tribes—Snake (left) and Cree. This painting by Bodmer is unusual because most of his subjects were men. COURTESY OF THE NEWBERRY LIBRARY.

Pehriska-Ruhpa: a "Minatarre" or Hidatsa Indian, painting by Bodmer. COURTESY OF
THE NEWBERRY LIBRARY.

Pehriska-Ruhpa: a second Bodmer portrayal of the Hidatsa warrior. This is the costume of the Dog Dance. COURTESY OF THE NEWBERRY LIBRARY.

Karl Bodmer's composite painting of *(left to right)* a Missouri Indian, an Oto Indian, and a Ponca chief. The chief wears a medallion signifying recognition of and friendship with the United States government. The small padlock attached to the Oto's necklace exemplifies how Europeans' utilitarian trade goods frequently were converted by Indians to personal ornamentation. COURTESY OF THE NEWBERRY LIBRARY.

"Horse racing of Sioux Indians near Fort Pierre," painting by Bodmer. COURTESY OF THE NEWBERRY LIBRARY.

Bodmer and Prince Maximilian meet Hidatsa Indians near Fort Clark. Painting by
Bodmer. COURTESY OF THE NEWBERRY LIBRARY.

Sac and Fox Indians painted by Bodmer in the 1830s. COURTESY OF THE NEWBERRY
LIBRARY.

A large encampment of Piegans (Plains Indians) on the move. Painting by Bodmer.

"Funeral scaffold of a Sioux Chief." Painting by Bodmer.

CHAPTER 42

The Golden West

> In years when Indians killed no overlanders, they were also not being killed by the emigrants.
>
> Thirty-four emigrants [were] killed between 1840 and 1848, 26 Indians [were] killed same period. In '49, figures jumped to 33 emigrants, 60 Indians. 1850—48 emigrants, 76 Indians. Total by 1860, 362 emigrants, 426 Indians.
>
> —JOHN D. UNRUH, JR., *The Plains Across*

> In 1974 there were a record 970 homicides in Chicago. At the current rate, the city could exceed that number this year, even though the population has dropped about 500,000 since then to 2.8 million. . . . Chicago is the fourth most violent of the nation's 52 largest cities, behind Miami, Atlanta and St. Louis.
>
> —*Chicago Tribune*, 29 August 1991

For a time, the Indians of the Far West had more immediate concerns than the approaching but still distant Americans. Mexico achieved independence from Spain in the years 1820 to 1823, and promptly eliminated the "Indian problem" by legally eliminating Indians. All Indians were converted, legally, into Mexican citizens. Government abolished both the status of Indian and the keeping of records of Indian persons and groups. As citizens, Indians were formally equal to all other citizens. Since these changes were reflected (more weakly) in Mexico's far north which was to become the American Southwest, a moment of attention is worthwhile here.

It is an open question whether the legal mind will ever learn that reality cannot be altered by giving it new names. George Orwell understood that in the egalitarianism of *Animal Farm* some pigs were more equal. In Mexico, the citizens who happened to belong to different tribes resumed age-old hostilities, and a series of rebellions against the new federal government were put down by force. Edward H. Spicer explains that "forcing the Indians to accept the new regime was a part of the general struggle for setting up the independent Mexican nation. The use of force was justified by the ideal of a unified nation, and Indians could not be permitted to stand in the way." In short, though details differed, nation-building in Mexico had much the same effect on Indians as nation-building farther north.

Indian unrest arose from the way the nationalists' grand ideals worked out in practice. Since no distinctions were to be made between Indians and others, no distinctions could be allowed in regard to land tenure or local government. Towns and territories formerly set aside for Indians were opened to infiltration by outsiders, and soon the tribes saw both their lands and their limited degree of self-government being whittled away. (Political feminists may notice what happens when legal equality precedes social equality.)

This process was accompanied and furthered by the growth of haciendas—great estates granted without requirements for protection of Indian welfare. These became powerful agents of detribalization and impoverishment of their Indian workers, especially through the device of what Americans know as the "company store." Employees of the hacienda, who were typically far away from alternative sources of supply, bought on credit from their employer's store. His close cronies kept the accounts which illiterate Indians could not correct. Law required the workers to stay on the hacienda until they were free of debt, which the company store guaranteed would never happen. These hacienda workers became peons whose citizenship was a nasty joke, and they lost even the minimal protection of tribal membership.

It seems quite plain that under the social and political conditions of the nineteenth century, the developing nation state grew everywhere by dissolution of tribes. Whether this had to happen, I cannot guess, but wherever one looks it did happen.

California, Arizona, New Mexico, and Texas were still Mexican provinces when the nation became independent. For the Navajos, the new regime became especially traumatic because Mexico opened the northern provinces to trade with the Anglo-Americans beginning to press westward from the Mississippi Valley. These sold large supplies of weapons to the creoles of New Mexico and their Indian allies, and the new weapons became means to capture Navajos for the slave trade. Considering the Hollywood image of Navajos, it is hugely ironic to read David M. Brugge's comment: "The tribe, suffering from the aggressiveness of the New Mexicans, as well as from drought, tried to avoid war, but with limited success. By 1833, warfare was rapidly escalating."

As for Texas, we have but to notice that Moses Austin got permission for Anglos to colonize in 1820. His son Stephen brought the first contingent of newcomers in 1821, and they brought slavery and Protestant religion. We must remember that, under Mexico's law, Africans as well as Indians had become free citizens, and, except for the hidden remnants of tribal religions, Mexicans were Roman Catholic. The newcomers promised to reject both slavery and Protestantism, and intended to give up neither. Fifteen years later, after their numbers had sufficiently increased, they established the independent Republic of Texas.

The depth of their loyalties is revealed by the dates: 1821, first colony; 1836, secession from Mexico; 1845, Statehood in the United States; 1861, secession from the United States. Not until after 1869, when Texas was readmitted to the American Union and further maneuvering became impossible, did Texas's citizens acquire the peculiarly fervent style of nationalistic patriotism for which they have become noted.

Immigrants to Texas brought along the policies toward Indians that were normal and accepted in the regions from which they had come. We have seen what those were. The usual results followed, including a long-lasting war with Comanches as fierce as the Texans—"horse Indians" from the Great Plains. Hostilities prevailed, on and off, until well after the Civil War (which they complicated). Smallpox epidemics, destruction of bison herds, and "total war" by the United States Army finally brought Comanche surrender in 1875.

Newly independent Mexicans wasted no sympathy on California's Indians. The citizenship supposed to have been granted in 1821 became hard to find. Missions continued to send out military expeditions to seize "wild" Indians for forced labor and prayer—a process deemed necessary because so many converts died young. Of 53,600 who had been baptized between 1769 and 1836, only 15,000 survived.

The missions were secularized by Mexico's government between 1834 and 1836. The central government intended that mission property should be divided between clergy and neophytes, but local officials took it as a windfall for themselves. Mission Indians were sent off in different directions, some returning to their homelands, others seeking work as domestics in Californian communities, still others to labor in great estate haciendas or ranchos. Edward D. Castillo remarks: "The hacienda-peon society was transplanted intact from Mexico to California. This peonage system was rapidly developed by the rancheros and maintained by methods ranging from economic persuasion to outright slavery."

As Mexican colonists came up from the south, they spread rapidly into the territories of the still-independent tribes of the interior. Despite having become much weaker, these tribes resisted the new intrusive pressures, and their resistance excused more military campaigns and more seizure of Indians. It made little difference to the Indians that they were being kidnapped for labor on ranchos instead of labor in missions. If anything, the missions had treated them more kindly on the assumption that they had souls to be saved. Souls were no concern of the rancheros.

In response, tribes that had formerly been peaceful turned violently hostile and developed guerilla tactics. Reciprocal raiding between tribes and rancheros continued throughout the era of Mexican control.

That era was brief, lasting only until President James K. Polk could manipulate his Congress to declare war on Mexico which, when done, ended quickly in Mexico's cession of its northern provinces to the United States by the Treaty of Guadalupe Hidalgo in February 1848. For California's Indians it was out of the frying pan, into the fire. Missionaries had sought the Indians for their souls, rancheros for their laboring bodies. The new crowd of Anglo-Americans had no use for Indians at all, and they started a program of systematic slaughter. Adam Johnson, an agent of the United States Commissioner of Indian Affairs, characterized the situation tersely: "The majority of tribes are kept in constant fear on account of the indiscriminate and inhuman massacre of their people for real or supposed injuries."

Hollywood's pictures of the great "prairie schooner" cavalcade to the Far West invariably concentrates on blood and thunder. In such portrayals the emigrants are heroic pioneers (as many were) and the Indians were treacherous, murderous villains (as some were, and as some of the emigrants were also). Plenty of books support this version which is drawn from a selection of sources written by emigrants who were certainly a minority in the early 1840s and may still have been even after their bellicose and arrogant conduct produced the kind of Indian response that such behavior has always stimulated everywhere.

We are fortunate today to have a magisterial history based on meticulous research in the writings of *all* the overlanders including those who understood that Indians were human beings with rights to be respected, as well as the chosen-people types who denied rights to Indians. John D. Unruh, Jr., who devoted his short life to this superb study, was a Mennonite—a member of a "peace religion"—who clearly believed in the brotherhood of man and rejected the dogmas of divine privilege for some of humanity to exploit the rest. What follows is based on his work.

A brief example will serve to show how this sort of history illuminates what the other kind masks. Bear with a brief comparison of texts. The first, from the *Readers' Encyclopedia of the American West* (a standard and often helpful work), mentions that "the Stephens-Murphy party [of emigrants], upon reaching the sink of the Humboldt River, elected to cross the Sierra as directly westward as possible. They thereby opened up the Truckee River route . . . (p. 155) Unruh tells of the same party who "were following the exact directions of a Paiute Indian chief who told them of the route and went ahead with the leaders." (p. 117) And the route was named by them after the chief. In the *Readers' Encyclopedia* version, the Indian vanishes and the party he guided become "discoverers."

Unruh was fully conscious of his corrective approach to the literature of the Wild West. He explained it tersely: "Trade and aid were extremely significant aspects of the almost infinite variety of emigrant Indian encounters. But they have been too often bypassed in the usual concentration upon pitched battles, scalps, and massacres." That violence did occur is not denied, but dates as well as other circumstances must be considered. From 1840 to 1844, not a single emigrant was killed by Indians. (Two Indians were killed by emigrants.) Many overlanders, in fact, were saved from natural death by Indians who showed them where to find water and which desert plants were edible, and who helped them cross raging streams. Even after hostilities acquired momentum, different tribes were distinguished by varied attitudes. Those near the jump-off points in Missouri and Iowa became quickly disenchanted by the masses of emigrants who killed and scared away game, overgrazed grass, destroyed timber, and used up scarce water, all of which resources were essential to the Indians' subsistence. Farther off, a correspondent reported to the Commissioner of Indian Affairs that Chief Washahaki's Shoshoni or Eastern Snake Indians had aroused the gratitude of over 9,000 emigrants who signed a paper stating "that they have been most kindly treated by the Indians."

Unruh did not deny the facts of hostilities; he studied them. Astonishingly, until he compiled data, most of the gallons of ink spilled on the westward trek had been based on hearsay embellished by emotion. When he had actually counted the numbers, Unruh made a table of verified killings, year by year, comparing emigrant victims to Indians in a parallel column.

The result is history in the guise of statistics. Incidents were few until the gold rush of 1849. In that swarm of get-rich-quick characters, the restraints of ordinary morality in any circumstances, including conduct toward other emigrants, were hard to find. Indians were in the way. Sixty of them were killed in 1849 compared to thirty-three emigrants; and in 1850, seventy-six Indians were killed as compared to forty-eight emigrants. The totals, 1840–1860, inclusive, were 362 emigrants killed, 426 Indians. An emigrant was safer from attack on the trek than he would be on the streets of any large modern city. Notably also, Indians suffered more than their invaders, but the Indians did not publish newspapers to rage against the emigrants as the frontier press whipped up fury against Indians.

Nor were Indians the only human hazards for the emigrants. In 1857, a gang of fanatic Mormons leading an Indian band massacred about 120 Missouri and Arkansas emigrants at Mountain Meadows in Utah. In that single episode, more emigrants were killed than during the first eleven years of migration. The Mormons themselves had arrived only ten years earlier. This was an aberration neither ordered nor condoned by Mormon leaders, but perhaps that sect's own experience of persecution and dispossession had made them sensitive to the Indians' dilemma. Their president Brigham Young was remarkably sympathetic: "It is hard to make an Indian believe that the whites are their friends, and the Great Father wishes to do them good, when, perhaps, the very next party that crosses their path shoots them down like wolves."

"White Indians" repeatedly were identified as robbers of the wagon trains and rustlers of their livestock, sometimes leading Indian allies. The "white Indians" who raided for plunder sometimes came from the ranks of the emigrants themselves, but more typically they were desperadoes of the sort who have formed outlaw banditti and pirates everywhere. Sometimes, but rarely, they were identified personally and dealt with. Usually they disguised themselves as Indians more effectively than in the Boston Tea Party, but blonde hair, blue eyes, and full beards gave them away. These outlaws were fully as atrocious as the wildest Indians when they struck, and they had the advantage of actually joining wagon trains in advance in order to direct them into ambush.

None of this should be understood to say or imply that Indians never troubled nor endangered the emigrants. If Indians traded horses for food, clothing, and weapons—and especially for liquor—they also charged tribute for trains passing through their territories, and they punished refusal to pay. They had little compunction and much skill at stealing from the emigrants, paying special attention to livestock. Some became expert pickpockets (a skill not usually associated with Indians). One even stole a neckerchief off its wearer.

Much depended on the attitudes of the individuals dealing with each other. There were some emigrants who started on their journey with the intention of killing Indians which they found opportunity to do and incidentally brought down upon their party's innocent members the revengeful wrath of the victim's tribesmen. Fortunately for all concerned, such murderous psychopaths were few. Most of the persons involved in the migration, Anglos and Indians alike, were sensible, practical people who made the best arrangements possible in the circumstances. Unruh's conclusion is worth respectful thought.

"The final outcome of the increasingly frequent interaction between the two cultures was not inevitable. Indians and overlanders did not have to be juxtaposed as enemies locked in mortal combat. In fact, most were not, even during the most dangerous periods of overland travel, since firmness and caution, together with a readiness to treat the natives with friendliness and respect, generally elicited reciprocation. . . . almost everyone did complete the trip safely, and this fact needs to be underscored. Nevertheless, it is indisputable that Indians posed a greater threat to overland travel by 1860 than they had in 1840, a situation for which the overland emigrants, especially those lured westward by the gold rush, shared, with their culture and their government, a major responsibility."

CHAPTER 43

The Way to Wounded Knee

> During the 1850s, the modern meaning of Indian reservation emerged, referring to land set aside under federal protection for the residence of tribal Indians, regardless of origin. By 1885 this meaning was firmly established in law and was intended in the Indian Major Crimes Act.
> —FELIX COHEN

> [The United States] for more than a hundred years has been a great colonial power.
> —ALBERT BUSHNELL HART, 1899

> In brief, assimilation would extinguish the red race as surely if not as speedily as extermination. With the Dawes Act's passage, the Vanishing American was more plausible than it had ever been in the darkest days after the War of 1812. For it was the Indian's culture, his way of life, which defined him as an Indian, and the allotment policy was designed to stamp out all vestiges of the past. It was, in Theodore Roosevelt's words, "a mighty pulverizing engine to break up the tribal mass."
> —BRIAN WILLIAM DIPPIE

President James K. Polk fulfilled the imperialists' dream of Manifest Destiny. He avoided war on two fronts by negotiating with Britain for an acceptable boundary with Canada, then prodded and led the United States into war with Mexico. The ensuing cession of territory from Mexican sovereignty filled out the American empire from ocean to ocean. Occupying Indians were doomed to lose independence as soon as the new government could get around to them, but first that government had a quarrel to settle within its own ranks.

The imperialists agreed that Indians must become subservient, and tribal culture must be transformed into "civilization." Difficulty came with the definition of civilization. Frontier regions of States facing divergently North and South had grown into separate centers of power based on distinct, incompatible cultures within the empire. At root of the difference were competing systems of labor—chattel slaves in the South versus legally free persons working for wages in the North—and from these systems had grown rival dominant classes—landed planters in the South and moneyed merchants in the North. These had clashing interests and goals, and each side stood to gain supremacy by increasing the territorial base of its power.

The vast acquisition of new territory from the Mexican War brought competition to crisis. It was clear to everyone that whichever side gained most of the new territory would become dominant in Congress and ultimately in the nation. Further compromise became impossible when each side came to consider it could concede no more without weakening itself irremediably in relation to the other. Extremists in Southern States seceded and formed the Confederacy to preserve and expand their power and culture; and extremists in Northern States determined to conquer the Confederates and subordinate them to the Union.

In the resulting Civil War, Indians were recruited to fight on both sides (as usual), and shared in costs and casualties (as usual), and gained nothing (as usual). Thereafter, they faced a tremendously more powerful "White Father" in Washington, D.C., whose power was multiplied by industrial revolution within the very culture that had just become supreme. Even the Russian Tsar looked askance at this rising empire. Rather than risk conflict, the Russians followed Napoleon's example and sold their American colony, but the climate and rugged terrain of Alaska long acted as deterrents to expansion in that direction.

One of the more ironical episodes of history occurred when France's Napoleon III decided to venture into Mexico after Spain had given up. Following the example of England's delicious name for Ethelred the Unready, let us distinguish this sequel Napoleon as the Incompetent. He installed as the puppet "emperor" of Mexico the Austrian archduke Maximilian, but had second thoughts when the American Civil War ended and an army of a million men intimated its desire for Europeans to get out. Poor Maximilian got a crown and a firing squad in rapid succession. Thus the Yankees, who systematically suppressed Indians at home, saved the independence of the nation governed by *mestizos*, men who would have been derided as *half-breeds* in the United States. Consistency is not the essence of racism.

The rate of dispossession of Indians in territory *formerly* Mexican was immensely accelerated by the speeding up of the Industrial Revolution in the United States. Wagon trains heading to California and Oregon had disturbed the tribes and territories through which they passed, but when railroads thrust through after 1850 they brought farmers and herders to stay and to seize Indian lands and transform them to purposes irreconcilable to Indian methods of subsistence. Towns sprang up along the railroads as they had previously risen along the Erie Canal and other engineering works. The newcomers aimed far beyond subsisting themselves. They produced vast quantities of grain and meat for export to the markets made accessible by the same railroads. Indians did not share in their surpluses. The newly introduced cultural trait of private ownership of property did not allow for communal sharing of subsistence needs except within sharp limits among kin and "objects of charity."

Indian options were limited to abandoning their traditional cultures and modeling themselves on the newcomers or resisting in arms. Pressure toward the first option increased as the newcomers quite deliberately slaughtered the great bison herds which were the mainstay of tribes on the plains. Ranchers rationalized that bison ate grass needed by cattle and sheep, so the shaggy wild beasts became a form of vermin to be exterminated. Some newcomers reasoned also that Indians could not live where there were no bison, so killing bison was a quick way of getting rid of Indians who were also conceived as vermin.

For the relatively few Indians who tried to adopt agriculture, the process was made exceptionally difficult by their being pushed into places where soil was poor and water scarce. It seemed that the only remaining option was to take up arms against the tremendous odds. Few Indians deluded themselves about ultimate victory in such war. They could count and reckon odds, and chiefs were sometimes taken to the East to see more people in single cities (and many cities) than there were Indians left in the whole West. But, as it seemed to those remaining Indians, no honorable alternative was left besides throwing themselves against the monster devouring them.

When, under Andrew Jackson's approving eye, the Five Civilized Tribes of the Southeast had been ordered across the Mississippi, they were "granted" reservations in what is now eastern Oklahoma, with hunting grounds reserved farther west. A difficulty with this benevolence was prior ownership of the territories by Osage, Comanche, and Kiowa Indians who needed the land for their own subsistence. Government solved the problem by the method that it came to depend on for the rest of the century: it sent in troops who laid down the law (in the guise of treaties) to keep the Plains tribes quiet.

Oklahoma became the Indian dump. Grants to the Five Civilized Tribes were ignored as blithely as the rights of prior occupiers. Wilcomb E.

Washburn itemizes Southern Cheyenne, Arapaho, Kiowa, Comanche, Kickapoo, Sauk and Fox, Kaw, Seneca, and Wyandot *re*settlements and summarizes that "by 1885 representatives of some fifty Indian tribes had settled on the lands once promised to the Five Civilized Tribes."

Railroads built through, from north to south, from east to west, and crosswise. Each railroad right of way typically consisted of a swath of land on each side of the tracks, sometimes extending miles wide. The railroads sold lots to get the money to lay track, and they sponsored towns to provide the traffic to make the railroad profit. Texas ranchers drove herds of cattle through "Indian" lands to railheads, and the cattle did not fast en route. (Sale of lands financed government.)

Finally, in 1889, President Benjamin Harrison (another scion of the imperialist Harrison family) opened a section of Oklahoma to emigrant homesteaders, and in 1893 the whole territory was thrown open. It quickly acquired a population of a million people.

Government agencies (called the Dawes Commission and Jerome Commission, about which more later) threw up a facade of propriety by "negotiating" with the tribes for them to give up their granted lands. In return, each man, woman, and child received a new grant of 160 acres of *personal* property. (By analogy, a trust might turn in a corporation's bonds for compensation in cash to the trust's beneficiaries of ten cents on the dollar.)

The quality of the "negotiations" by which ex-Senator Dawes accomplished this feat is illuminated by knowledge that they were not *treaty* negotiations. Although Indians will discourse fervently about treaty frauds and deceptions, in form the treaty constituted negotiation between peers which allowed some initiative and maneuver by the Indian parties. By the time of the Oklahoma "negotiations," this was no longer possible, chiefly because negotiator Dawes had earlier sponsored a law to abolish treaty-making with Indian tribes (1870). In his "negotiations" in 1893 with the Oklahoma tribes, he *told* them what was to be done. Their participation was to accept and obey. The troops stood ready. Government had many forts in Oklahoma.

A further word on the subject of treaties is needed to clarify a point of law. One may think (and it has been written) that substituting "agreements" for treaties meant only that Congress's House of Representatives became part of the ratifying process, and therefore part also of whatever patronage might be involved, whereas only the Senate ratified treaties. That much is true, but not quite all the truth because there is a legal difference between a treaty and an agreement.

Treaties override laws. Congress's agreements, however, are con-

374 · *The End of Independence*

tracts that the Federal government is not obliged by the Constitution to honor. (Article I, Section 10, provides that *"No State"* shall enact any law "impairing the obligation of contracts," but is silent about Congress.) Felix Cohen commented that agreements were "virtually" identical to treaties, but for Indians a real difference existed between negotiating as theoretically independent powers and pleading as wards of the State. Lawyers live on such fine distinctions, but nineteenth-century Indians had no lawyers. That has changed.

Perhaps I am making a distinction without a practical difference. It is common scandal that the United States has violated every single one of its treaties with Indians.

The reformers' first goal was abandonment of the treaty system. Overall they wanted to assimilate Indians to American society and culture, to make them just like other (rural) Americans. For this, it was necessary to destroy tribal organizations, to concentrate Indians in small reservations for better control. In process, the reformers wanted to eliminate the corruption scandalously rife in the government's Indian agencies, and to treat the Indians with kindness.

They were apt to be better informed about theology than about Indians. One of the most vigorous "friends" of the Indians was Episcopal Bishop Henry B. Whipple of Minnesota. He justified the demand to abolish treaties with the dogma that "they have no government of their own, and are to receive none from us." This good bishop's understanding was firmly grounded in the sixteenth century. But he caught on to one solid fact when he called Indians "a people whom *we will not permit* to exercise one single element of that sovereign power which is necessary to a nation's existence." (Italics added.) The contradiction between not having government and not being permitted to have government escaped Bishop Whipple and his cohorts.

Full of such conceptual contradictions, the reformers undertook to remake the whole structure of administration of Indian affairs. They became so zealous and fervent that historian Francis Paul Prucha calls the century's last third "the most critical period in the whole history of Indian-white relations in the United States." Some Eastern tribes might think that their own critical periods had long passed by, but much remained to be done in regard to the "horse Indians" of the Great Plains.

One thing was absolutely certain: the reformers intended to work *for* the Indians, not *with* them. The Indians were allowed no participation in planning their own welfare except to do as the reformers thought best. This required abandoning tribal culture as well as tribal government and territory, in order to cultivate small plots of ground, dress like Euramericans, go to church, learn English, and accept doles. The reformers' program for a brave new Indian world was startlingly like the demands of seventeenth-century missionaries.

Reforming philanthropists and land-hungry westerners joined in a curious alliance. Those hoping to "civilize" Indians wanted to take land away from the tribes so as to weaken and ultimately dissolve the tribes; thus the Indians would have to assimilate to the American Way. The Westerners were less roundabout; they wanted to take land from Indians in order to keep it for themselves. In the definitive *Handbook of Federal Indian Law*, Felix Cohen remarks, "The overriding goal of the United States during treaty making was to obtain Indian lands." It remained an overriding goal after treaties were abolished.

Reformers and land grabbers allied to pass the General Allotment Act in 1887, sponsored by Massachusetts Senator Henry Dawes, a sincere and righteous reformer who knew better than the Indians what was good for them. The act mandated allotment to each reservation Indian of specified tracts of land, varying in quantity and function according to successive legislation. These individual tracts were to be patented as private property and protected against encroachment. The protection supposedly was good for twenty-five years, after which the Indians were presumed to have learned enough to look after themselves. The presumption was wrong. Even during the protection period, sharp operators devised means of leasing lands perpetually, getting Indian owners into debt that could be foreclosed, and so on and on.

Lawrence C. Kelly recites staggering statistics: "Between 1887 and 1900, approximately 32,800 allotments of Indian land, covering 3,285,000 acres were made. During the same period the federal government forced the cession or sale of approximately 28,500,000 acres of 'surplus land' from tribes that were in the process of being allotted. The cession of these lands was, of course, the primary purpose behind the allotment program, for once the Indians were settled on their allotments, the remainder of their former reservations could be opened to White settlement."

Only a small portion of preceding tribal possessions was turned into such individual allotments. As for the rest, Felix Cohen remarks that "Indian reformers probably did not realize that allotment would be such an effective method of separating Indians from their lands." At a guess, it seems possible that Senator Dawes did that job more effectively than Andrew Jackson.

The sound and fury of the reformers signified little else in practice despite their activity. Perhaps some exception might be allowed for the

376 · *The End of Independence*

schools set up for a small minority of Indian children, often officially kidnapped from their parents.

The churches that were supposed to substitute virtuous religious men for crooked Indian agents cooperated for a while, but grew tired of the task. Virtuous men were in short supply, and those on hand were not all that eager to isolate themselves in the midst of "savages." Those who truly felt the missionary call wanted to go to far-off places where infidels were more exotic. Indians, though picturesque, were too familiar.

What the churches let drop, the military picked up. Indeed, the reformers' grants of duties had never been matched by grants of power from government. Power remained firmly in the hands of army officers who discovered many ways of "interpreting" reformer policies to suit themselves. The army had its own program for dealing with Indians, and when attempts to detribalize and concentrate particular groups came up against stubborn, sometimes violent resistance, the army took charge. Its program was simplicity itself—stamp out resistance—and its means were what the twentieth century came to know as total war. Considering that the army's head after the Civil War was General William Tecumseh Sherman (what irony in that middle name!) we should not be surprised. Any photograph of Sherman's Civil War devastation of Atlanta will reveal his style of war. Why should anyone expect him to be more merciful to alien Indians than to people of his own kind?

Walter L. Williams reminds us of a fact too often overlooked: to wit, that the acknowledged imperialism of American expansion across the Pacific was but an extension of official policies toward American Indians. It was acclaimed as such in the 1890s. The reformer Henry L. Dawes, whose "Dawes Act" had reduced tribal land by the fiat called "allotment," proclaimed that the same sort of benevolence should be used toward "other alien races whose future had been put in our keeping." His phrasing is interesting, suggesting as it does that some superior power had deputized the United States to receive what had in fact been seized in the Spanish American War. It is a positive trademark of imperialist propaganda that genuine goals and intentions are always expressed in mealymouthed euphemisms or sanctimony.

Arguing against citizenship for the newly conquered Filipinos, Senator Henry Cabot Lodge blurted out the harsh truth: "This Republic . . . has held subjects from the beginning, in the presence of those whom we euphemistically call the 'wards of the nation.' " But even Lodge, who was a Massachusetts man, did not care to recall the precedent set by the Black slaves who also had been held in subjection from the beginning.

When President Grover Cleveland denounced the subversion of Hawaii's government by American emigrants, and refused to accept the revolutionists' application to join the United States, they bided until he left office, then were accepted by a new administration desiring to bring light "to the people that sit in darkness." They brought so much light that by 1967, as Linda S. Parker has written, "seventy-two private owners held 47 percent [of all Hawaiian land] with seven owning nearly 30 percent." The reformers undoubtedly approved because that, too, is in the tradition of Indian policy—so direct an extension that the thousands of miles of Pacific Ocean seem like a mere hop, skip, and jump.

But this book is about North American Indians; we must not wander.

New statistics show that ninety percent of American property is now owned by one percent of our people. It seems that economic processes under political controls have converted all Americans into "Indians."

As Dee Brown remarks, "Out of that time [1860–1890] came virtually all the great myths of the American West." Of them all, the one that still fascinates most Americans, to judge by the publications devoted to it, was the 1876 "massacre" of Lt. Col. George Armstrong Custer and his cavalry troop at Little Big Horn creek in Montana. The simple facts do not penetrate public consciousness: that Custer was killed while on the way to perpetrate another in the series of his own massacres already on record, that he was bullheadedly disregarding warnings and defying orders, that the Indians who wiped out his troop did so in defense of their families, and that if the roles had been reversed the defenders would have been eulogized as heroes. Such is the power of race thinking that cruel and contemptible Custer, who had determined to slaughter Indians in pursuit of political ambition, and who sacrificed his own men to his unrestrained vanity, became a heroic martyr.

That episode unfortunately encapsulates the era. We need not join the cavalry in still another pursuit of fleeing bands, and some acknowledgment is due to army officers who performed horrid duties as decently as was possible in such circumstances. General George Crook won the esteem of Sioux Chief Red Cloud whose tribute was, "He never lied to us. His words gave the people hope." It is enough here to note that tribes with famous names—Navajos, Apaches, Sioux, Cheyennes, Nez Percés—were rounded up, marched about, and finally penned into reservations of lands set aside because homesteaders were not interested in them just then.

If there were decent soldiers, there were also deliberate terrorists whose methods included assassination of Indian chiefs (Sitting Bull, for example)

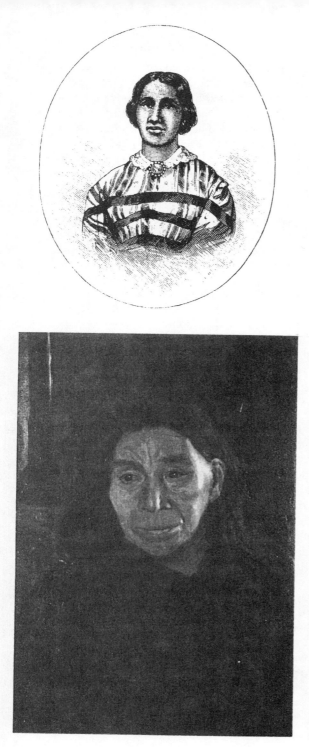

Esther, the last of the Royal
Narragansetts, circa 1879.
Nostalgic eastern Americans
in the nineteenth century
made almost a ritual of
mourning "the last of" various tribes. In fact, the Narragansetts are still a going
concern. COURTESY OF THE
RHODE ISLAND HISTORICAL
SOCIETY, PROVIDENCE, R.I.

Martha Simon, by Albert
Bierstadt, circa 1860. Bierstadt called her "the last of
the Narragansetts," but she
descended from Wampa-
noags. She died shortly after
posing for this portrait.
Henry David Thoreau had
visited her and made a long
entry in his journal on June
26, 1856. An extract: "The
question she answered with
most interest was 'What do
you call that plant?' and I
reached her the aletris from
my hat. She took it, looked at
it a moment, and said,
'That's husk root. It's good to
put in bitters for a weak
stomach.' . . . Its root is
described as intensely bitter.
I ought to have had my hat
full of plants . . ." PORTRAIT
AND QUOTATION COURTESY OF
THE MILLICENT LIBRARY, FAIR-
HAVEN, MASS.

These gentlemen represent opposing philosophies. Minnesota's Protestant Episcopal Bishop Henry B. Whipple aimed at reform by assimilation. Tlingit Chief Shotridge venerated his tribe's traditions. They were photographed within decades of each other at the turn of the century, each in formal finery. Bishop Whipple courtesy of the Library of Congress. Chief Shotridge courtesy of the American Philosophical Society.

and massacre of isolated villages. George Custer already had a history of massacre when he headed toward Little Big Horn. The era culminated, 29 December 1890, at Wounded Knee creek on the Pine Ridge reservation in South Dakota. A band of Sioux, under mortally ill Chief Big Foot, had been rounded up and were surrounded by the Seventh Regiment under Colonel James W. Forsyth. This was Custer's former regiment. The Indians in the center gave up their weapons except for one who clung to his expensive gun that went off when soldiers struggled to take it from him. The soldiers in the surrounding ring immediately opened a hail of fire with their carbines and Hotchkiss guns—predecessors of today's automatic weapons.

In the melee that followed, between 153 and 300 Sioux men, women, and children died of the total of 350. Figures are uncertain because many wounded crawled away to die elsewhere. Dee Brown itemizes, "The soldiers lost twenty-five dead and thirty-nine wounded, most of them struck by their own bullets or shrapnel." (How else could it be when most of the Indians had surrendered their guns?)

The event was so horrible that the War Department felt obliged to cover it up by converting the slaughter into a "battle." This was accomplished by issuance of no less than thirteen Congressional Medals of Honor with unspecified citations for "extraordinary gallantry," "distinguished gallantry," "bravery in action," "conspicuous and gallant conduct in battle," and so on.

The events of the era have been retold many times and from many points of view. For present purposes, only the outcome need be considered. "The end of the Indian wars," writes W. T. Hagan, "marked the conclusion of a long chapter of American history." By coincidence, the year of Wounded Knee was also the year when the Superintendent of the U.S. Census celebrated the end of the Frontier, defined as a *line* between Indians and homesteaders—a line that Frederick Jackson Turner converted into "the meeting point between savagery and civilization." Perhaps more significant for Indians in the long view, 1890 was about the time when the Indians' long decline in population bottomed out, and they began to increase in numbers once more.

With new vitality came cultural resurgence. It is not quite right to agree with Dee Brown that "the culture and civilization of the American Indian was destroyed." That smacks too much of what I call the ethnographic fallacy—the anthropological counterpart to the historians' "Golden Age" fallacy—which assumes that at some given time and place there was a "true" culture from which all subsequent changes are decline and degeneration.

The Battle of the Washita. This was an illustration for George Armstrong Custer's autobiography, *My Life on the Plains* (1874). It shows graphically, with his approval, his style of combat against Indians.

In fact, there have been many Indian cultures. As populations declined, cultures necessarily were adjusted to new situations, but the culture of a people is not what their ancestors had; it is what they make and remake for themselves. With the coming of the twentieth century, North American Indians revived in ways unforeseen by themselves or anyone else.

CHAPTER 44

Cultures within a Culture

The record of American expansions which closes with Alaska has
been a long one, and today we do but continue the same movement.
The same policy runs through them all.
— SENATOR HENRY CABOT LODGE, 1898

With all the native Indians under control, the exponents of Manifest Destiny raised their sights and looked overseas toward Asia. Already as early as 1854, Admiral Matthew Perry compelled the Japanese government to open its islands to "western" trade, but trade followed a different course in Japan than formerly among Amerindians. Unlike Indians, the Japanese people became adroit at accumulating capital. At the time of this writing, it appears that financial dependence may have reversed direction. The richest capitalist in the world is Japanese.

A more traditional pattern prevailed in the Hawaiian Islands where the opening of trade early in the nineteenth century exposed the "virgin soil" native population to epidemics for which the people had no natural immunity. Catastrophic death followed, wiping out 90 per cent of the people within decades. Missionaries were invited in from the United States, and they promptly helped themselves to large landed estates from the possessions of their charges. (In 1975, 97 per cent of the land was owned by some forty individuals.) With adaptation forced by circumstance, the Texas pattern of rebellion against established government, followed by an appeal for annexation to the United States, was repeated. The affair was so rank that President Grover Cleveland rejected the appeal, but after he left office Hawaii was accepted as a territory in 1900. It became the fiftieth State in 1959.

War between the United States and Spain in 1898 culminated in Spain's cession of the Philippines and the crushing by the United States of the native republic that had been founded in those islands. A guerilla uprising followed. Historian Walter Williams has traced how the conquest of the Philippine guerillas mirrored United States wars against Amerindi-

ans, but the pattern broke up when somewhat equivocal formal independence was re-established in the Philippines in 1946 by act of Congress.

During the twentieth century, the United States had internal peace,
but fought a series of formal and undeclared wars abroad: World Wars I
and II; Marines and mercenaries in Nicaragua; large-scale intervention in
Korea; invasion of Vietnam; "covert" military actions in Laos, Cambodia,
Africa, and the Americas; overthrow of governments in Iran, Indonesia,
Guatemala, and Chile; and large-scale war in the Persian Gulf. These
actions will not be characterized or evaluated here, but they did happen—the series conveys its own impression—and the list is not exhaus-
tive.

Numbers of Amerindian warriors volunteered for these affrays and
gained grudging respect from patriotic citizens for their services. Navajo
"code talkers," especially, became famous in World War II because their
complex language constituted a code unbreakable by Japanese experts so
the Navajos could transmit orders and information "in the clear" over
vast stretches of the Pacific. Ojibwa speakers, though less celebrated,
performed the same function.

The dreary patterns of the late nineteenth century continued for Indians in the earliest years of the twentieth. Enormous areas of tribal lands
passed from tribal possession. The movement to break up reservations
peaked between 1900 and 1910 when about 18,000,000 acres of tribal
land were "negotiated." Lawrence C. Kelly remarks, "In one way or
another most of the acts passed by Congress between 1900 and 1921 provided for the transfer of Indian lands to White ownership."

Having acquired most of the Indians' land, officialdom became anx-
ious to slough off the obligations that ostensibly had been assumed in the
process. These included health care for Indians and schooling for their
children, about which Congress became more and more grudging at
appropriation time. There was a more comprehensive and final way,
however, which had the advantage of seeming to be altruistic: this was to
take an Indian entirely out of wardship by making him a citizen. When
that happened, the civil rights and benefits of other citizens were conferred upon the citizen, and his champions could not complain that among
those benefits was eligibility to be taxed and personal responsibility under
State and local laws.

When Oklahoma "sooners" complained about the tax exemption of
the Five Civilized Tribes who had been dumped in Oklahoma before the
territory was opened up, Congress naturalized those Indians. As a special
reward for service in World War I, Congress naturalized Indian veterans.
Finally, tired of nibbling at the problem, Congress made all Indians citi-

A Cheyenne Indian policeman
in uniform. COURTESY OF THE
SMITHSONIAN INSTITUTION.

zens in 1924. As one might guess, their gratitude for this boon was
ambivalent. In other circumstances, the right to vote could have been
important, but at the time there were not enough Indians to constitute a
voting bloc of significance. A chief effect of citizenship was to put Indians
under hostile police and courts—and, of course, tax collectors.

Although training in schools of the Bureau of Indian Affairs (BIA)
gave many Indians some advantage toward employment, the manner of
that training was hateful. Agents with quotas to fill descended suddenly
upon Indian families and seized as many children as the quota required.
Parental protests were ignored and children's rejections were suppressed.
Corporal punishment was inflicted at the schools for a variety of offenses
that included the horrid infraction of speaking the child's own language—
they were all to confine themselves exclusively to English in all circumstances—and daily routines were rigidly regimented. Former students
remember that many teachers scorned the children and did not hide their
contempt. The school buildings were often unhealthy and needing repair.
Not strangely, this sort of benefit won few advocates among Indians. It
went far toward making the B.I.A. detestable.

It appears that Indian children encountered disease as well as training
in BIA schools. Mute testimony exists in Carlisle, Pennsylvania, in the

Indians complained much of being punished in the schools for speaking their mother tongues and other lapses into tribal customs, but their worst affliction in these schools was exposure to killing diseases. Are there any other schools in the United States with row-on-row of headstones like those for soldiers killed in combat far from home? The plaque of identification for this cemetery reads: "Buried here are the Indians who died while attending the Carlisle (Pa.) Indian School (1879–1918). In 1931 the graves were transferred to this site." The graves are neatly kept, but clearly visible on four of them is the single word "unknown." Photograph by A. Pierce Bounds, Carlisle.

Apaches from Arizona as they arrived at the Carlisle School. COURTESY OF THE SMITH-SONIAN INSTITUTION.

Apaches from Arizona after three years at the Carlisle School. COURTESY OF THE
SMITHSONIAN INSTITUTION.

Fort Peck Indian Fair, 1912. James Bad Marriage gained twenty yards in the Piegan–
Mandan game. Football was one BIA school innovation accepted by young Indian
men. PHOTO COURTESY OF MONTANA HISTORICAL SOCIETY, HELENA.

graveyard of the former Indian school, now the Army War College, where the crosses are lined up "row on row" as though for casualties in war.

All of this was part of the general assimilationist "reform" program continuing from the nineteenth century, the purpose ostensibly to make the Indian a real man capable of standing on his own two feet as the peer of his civilized brothers—well, *almost* brothers; race distinctions were never for a minute forgotten.

President Herbert Hoover (1929–1933), a Quaker with humanitarian feelings, tried to alleviate the treatment by increasing funds for Indian welfare, but he held off reluctantly from letting them make their own decisions. The BIA agents remained almighty. During the twenties, however, change gestated in an organization called the American Indian Defense Association. Its president, John Collier, turned "reform" about in precisely the opposite direction from what it had been signifying until then. Collier personally was overwhelmed in a mystical way by the rituals of the Pueblo Indians functioning in worship of nature. Regardless of details, their general intent opposed the Christian ideal of acquiring mastery over nature and suppressing natural impulses seducing the person to sin. Aided by the general reduction of Christian sanctimony that occurred during the twenties, Collier's association aroused much public sentiment against the worst abuses of Congress and administrators of Indian affairs, and, with the election of Franklin D. Roosevelt in 1932, Collier got the chance to go from protest to creation. He seized it.

Roosevelt appointed Collier as Commissioner of Indian Affairs in which post his superior was Interior Secretary Harold Ickes who had been a charter member of Collier's Indian Defense Association. Under these auspices Collier planned a wholly new reform of government policy to reverse the pressures toward assimilation. Its most novel feature gave Indians some control over their own affairs and laid a foundation for a demand that Indians would raise in later years—the demand for tribal sovereignty.

Felix Cohen has summarized, "Although the eventual assimilation of Indians was a goal many in Indian affairs took for granted, Collier considered tribal governments and tribal ownership of land valid elements in the ultimate Indian adaptation to American society. The [Indian Reorganization Act] was intended to provide a mechanism for the tribe as a governmental unit to interact with and adapt to a modern society, rather than to force the assimilation of individual Indians."

Collier was not exempt from paternalism. He pushed his ideas hard and made enemies, some of them among Indians. His notion of a proper tribal government was one with a constitution and a system of elected officers (like the governments of civilized people). This conflicted with the traditions of many, perhaps most, tribes, in which government had been wholly or semi-hereditary. Some tribes therefore rejected the opportunity to set up governments under Collier's Act. Most tribes chose to cooperate, but had trouble adjusting traditional factional disputes to the new electoral systems.

The new government sponsored by Collier in the Navajo Nation nearly broke up at its beginning when he determined to reduce Navajo livestock herds. His logic was impeccable: reduction was necessary to preserve the range and to keep newly built Hoover Dam from silting up from erosion. But Navajo livestock owners did not subscribe to the same logic. Some of them complained, "We Indians don't think it is right for Collier to tell us we should govern ourselves, and then tell us how to do it." It was the dilemma eternally faced by reformers in a hurry; and it dogged Collier throughout his term in office.

Collier created a new Navajo government in 1938 to go along with his requirements, and his measures to control erosion were consummated by edict from Washington.

It has been desirable to take account of the conflict between ecological considerations and the wishes of tribal herd owners in order to show one facet of Collier's rather tempestuous career. This sort of conflict is not especially Indian in nature; it arises wherever property owners resist conservation regulations. Indeed, most of Collier's opposition came from the opposite end of the political spectrum, i.e., from politicians preserving the goal of forcing Indians to assimilate to the dominant culture, or hoping, at least, to unload all governmental responsibility for them.

Opponents of Collier's policies reacted strongly. For more than a century, Indians had sued for redress in United States courts, usually without success. In the twentieth century the tribes became more familiar with lawyers, or perhaps it would be more accurate to say that lawyers became more aware of what big fees might be gained "on a contingency basis"—i.e., on speculation—if they won a tribal claim case. With nothing to lose and much to gain, tribes clogged the courts with suits, and Congress decided to get rid of the nuisance and publicity by one sweeping gesture. In 1946, Congress enacted the Indian Claims Commission, and the commissioners held hearings of expert scholars as well as legal counsel. By 1978 when the Commission stopped work, it had adjudicated about 670 cases and awarded some $774,000,000 in damages to aggrieved tribes in order to quiet title to millions of acres of land. (It passed on about eighty more cases to the Court of Claims which awarded additional sums to bring the total over $1,261,000,000. But those big round numbers had some strings attached. Much money went into "trusts" not controlled by their tribes.)

A tribe that accepted a Commission judgment and its award thereby forfeited all right to sue again. To that extent the Commission fulfilled its purpose of getting the tribes out of the courts, but the process functioned also in ways not anticipated. The scholars drawn into hearings and who prepared evidential background studies became aware of their mutual interests and realized the importance of interdisciplinary research. They began to cross disciplinary lines, to share professional interests and information, and in 1953 they formed an association that evolved into the American Society for Ethnohistory. This society has now grown to more than 1200 members. It is international, meets annually, and publishes the quarterly journal *Ethnohistory*. It acts as an unofficial core group for several informal regional associations. Its members have published many books based on their researches which are generally favorable to the Indians concerned.

Besides the hearings of the Indian Claims Commission, governmental advocates of assimilation tried to reverse the Collier reforms by a new policy called "termination." Historian Harvey D. Rosenthal remarks, "In essence termination stood assimilation on its head; instead of the Indians removing from the reservation and allowing the government role to wither, the government would remove the Indians and allow them to wither."

Conforming to this purpose, Congress enacted laws in 1953 that named thirteen tribes for release from federal supervision and "termination" of rights and financial assistance formerly guaranteed by treaty. Congress also permitted state law to supersede federal law in five states. The tribes were not consulted. Indeed the new Commissioner of Indian Affairs, Dillon Myer, rejected their right to participate in their own disposition except to do as told. "We must proceed, even though Indian co-operation may be lacking in certain cases."

The kindest thing to say about the termination policy, from a congressional viewpoint, is that it was a serious mistake. For the Indians concerned, it was a disaster. Necessarily, termination involved the same deceitful techniques that the tribes were protesting against in their Claims Commission suits. The first tribe chosen for termination was the Menominee tribe of Wisconsin. In 1854 the Menominees had signed a treaty by which they were guaranteed federal jurisdiction and protection; in 1953 the treaty became a nontreaty. Louise S. Spindler tells concisely how the people were manipulated to give an appearance of legality to a violation of trust. The federal government had been withholding substantial per capita payments from tribal members. A question was put before them in two parts, for which they were to give a single yes-or-no answer for "release of their per capita payments *and* agreement to 'the principle of termination.' The vote was 169 for and 5 against the resolution. When it was understood what had happened, another meeting was held one month later where the nearly 200 members present voted unanimously against termination, even though they expected to lose the $1,500 payment; however, this later vote was not acknowledged in Washington."

Following this none-too-auspicious approach, the tribe's property was put into an involved financial structure controlled by outside interests with axes to grind, and its value deteriorated to the point where President Richard M. Nixon confessed that termination had "created rather than solved problems for Indian people." In 1973, termination for the Me nominees was rescinded and the federal reservation restored for "unencumbered Menominee property" which seems to have meant what was left by the locusts who had descended on it. It is notable in this situation that no one pretended that the Menominees had failed to adapt successfully to "civilization." Until terminated, they operated several business enterprises including a prosperous sawmill, but the success of these businesses did not survive the tender ministrations of the bank and businessmen into whose hands they were delivered. Anyone with elementary understanding of political patronage will be able to reconstruct the proceedings.

Without understanding that, the action of Congress regarding the natives of Alaska must be incomprehensible. In 1971, as the termination disaster for the Menominees was becoming plain, Congress enacted the Alaska Native Claims Settlement Act which was large-scale termination with a delayed fuse. This Act provided that *all* aboriginal title to land, including even hunting and fishing rights, "are hereby extinguished," along with all the rights "to sue the United States or any of its officers with respect to the claims extinguished by the operation of this Act."*

A prologue called this a "fair and just settlement" of claims because many millions of dollars were paid into a set of corporations that also acquired title to aboriginal lands, and the Indian, Eskimo, and Inuit natives were made shareholders in the corporations. Regardless of its honeyed preface, this Act was another seizure of aboriginal property. As had become too familiar in such affairs, there was a trick concealed in the machinery. To begin with, the native corporations created by the Act were bewilderingly complex to anyone without a specialized knowledge and expe-

*[Section 4(b); 2(f). Act is accessible as Appendix 1 of *A Guide to Alaska Native Corporation Publications*, ed. Phyllis Nottingham. Juneau: Alaska Dept. of Education, 1976.]

rience of finance, and certainly that was not possessed by seal hunters and muskrat trappers barely able to read, if at all. Out of all the confusion, however, two facts emerge clearly: (1) lands transferred to the corporations were patented "in fee simple," which meant that they could be sold without supervision or approval by government; and (2) corporation share ownership was restricted to natives for no more than twenty years.

As of 18 December 1991, the native shares were to be canceled and new shares issued in their stead, and the new shares will have no restrictions on ownership or alienation. It is allotment, and worse than allotment, all over again. At the time of writing this, one can sense the agents of corporate raiders burrowing about in Alaska to identify and get promises from the natives most in need of ready cash, and when enough of them have been found the rest will be outvoted in the corporations and will come under the sway of what are euphemistically called *arbitrageurs*. An earlier era called them Robber Barons. Their aim is to "milk" a corporation of its assets.

Those who cannot believe this analysis are requested to review what happened when regulations were removed from the Savings and Loan societies. In 1992, the Alaska gold rush is being repeated by prospectors in white shirts and three-piece suits.

This is not to imply that the reservation lands of the lower forty-eight States have ceased to interest financiers. Mineral deposits have been found on some of the larger reservations—coal and oil especially—and contracts made for extraction of the minerals with payment of royalties to the possessing tribes. The procedures for obtaining those contracts have rarely been above reproach. This is too large and complex a subject for description here beyond saying that the Indians involved generally protest that they have been entangled in legal webs that prevent them from getting anything near full value for their rights. It is a continuing struggle.

Though continuing conquest and exploitation present a sorry spectacle, the remarkable upturn in Indian population and morale is felt throughout "Indian country." As the young warriors of past centuries learned how to fight with European guns, the young warriors today are learning how to fight with law books; and what the law has taken away, the law can restore or compensate.

Public interest in Indian cultures and public sympathy for Indian aspirations have never been higher. Indian history is entering upon a new era about which the only safe prediction is that it will be different.

PART SEVEN

A Hazard of
New Fortunes

CHAPTER 45

Renewal

> At best the existence of a tribal society within the borders of a highly technical culture is tenuous. It is not that tribal society materially threatens the technological way of life, but that it presents a moral threat to settled myths . . .
>
> —HARVEY D. ROSENTHAL

Indian history in the twentieth century has been dominated strongly by population recovery. All other developments are subordinate to the renewal of social energy generated by renewal of numbers. That said, a caveat on the interpretation of census figures must be made immediately. Specific figures are open to question on several scores though the general trend is clear.

According to the U.S. Census, the country's Indians numbered about 228,000 in 1890. Growth was slow and erratic until 1950 when the census reached 357,000. At mid-century, however, a sudden spurt lifted the total to 524,000 in 1960, 793,000 in 1970, and 1,367,000 in 1980. Newest estimates raise the number to 2 million in 1990. As always in Indian history, there are complications in interpreting these figures.

On the one side, it is likely that census enumerators have been influenced by racial attitudes and have counted according to their preconceptions. This is very clear in the nineteenth century when enumerators simply classed Indians as Whites or Coloreds. Thus the 1870 census killed off all the Wampanoags of Gay Head (Martha's Vineyard, Massachusetts) where the Wampanoags have resided without a break since the discovery of the island by Europeans in the sixteenth century. At Mashpee on Cape Cod, the 1860 census showed 305 Whites and 17 Coloreds. By 1870, the same people had become 39 Whites and 307 Coloreds, "also 2 Indians." One has to suspect that the mid-twentieth-century spurt in Indian population may have been influenced to a degree by what C. Matthew Snipp calls "procedural changes."

From the other direction, improvement in racial attitudes among the general public has encouraged persons who formerly had feared discrimination and persecution to identify themselves as Indians.

A further very complex difficulty arises from intermarriage between Indians and others, and the tangle of attempted definitions. Just what *is* an Indian? In the late twentieth century, some very important people still use Dark Ages terminology about "blood quantums" denoting persons as having a half, a quarter, or a sixty-fourth Indian "blood," just as Nazi Nuremberg Laws defined Jews. Even scholars commonly refer to "full bloods" and "mixed bloods," and flatter themselves for not having said "half-breed." If genealogy is to be a determining factor, as it often is, we ought at least to realize that inheritance is transmitted by genes. Blood has nothing to do with it. Children of mixed marriages are *synethnics*, not "half-breeds" nor "mixed bloods."

Supposing the use of decent language, how much of Indianness is biological, how much cultural, and how much simply legal? I raise the question not in order to answer it in a phrase or two. No one else has given a definitive answer in even a long book. Among still other problems, C. Matthew Snipp remarks that "American Indians as a pure genotype probably disappeared at the beginning of the sixteenth century." The point of noticing such issues is to show the census-taker's dilemma and provide another reason for reading census figures with great care.

The upward *trend* of Indian numbers is clear, and there seems to be general agreement that one reason for population increase has been improved medical care. Despite much talk about Indians who prefer traditional medicine men to "western style doctors" (to which I, too, have contributed) smallpox raged unchecked until vaccination eliminated that scourge. As I write, the *Navajo Times* reports a measles epidemic which can be fatal to Indians even today.

It is noteworthy that after Indian health care was transferred from the Interior Department to the Department of Health, Education, and Welfare, appropriations for Indians tripled between 1955 and 1965. It is easy to correlate this fact to the reduction of infant deaths between 1955 and 1967, from 61 per 1,000 live births to 30 per 1,000—down 50 per cent. During the same period, Indian deaths from tuberculosis dropped 66 per cent. Romantic rhetoric about the wonders of folk medicine must take such figures into account. No shaman or powwow ever yet cured a case of smallpox. (The Navajos are hastily vaccinating against measles.)

This is not the place for detailed analysis of all the data for population recovery. That task has been performed in two excellent books by C. Matthew Snipp and Russell Thornton. (See the bibliography.) It is enough here to see the large fact of renewal and to realize the driving force of

Twentieth-Century Indian Reservations

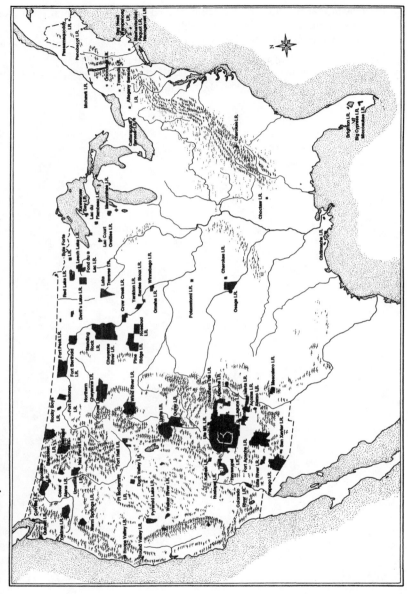

momentum on the culture. Amazingly, the recent rate of renewal implies that, if it is maintained, Indian population "will exceed four million by the end of the century" which would approximate what some demographers believe was the case before European invasion. Credibility is enhanced by something of the same sort having happened already in Mexico.

CHAPTER 46

Immigrants in Their
Own Country

When Indians surged in numbers in mid-century, they also became more urban. World War II seems to have given a push to this change, though other factors were also involved. In 1940, about 7 percent of Indians lived in urban centers, and the proportion nearly doubled to 13.4 percent in 1950. These were the years of the war, the "baby boom" that followed, and the many dislocations of all sorts of people brought about by the war. During that decade the increase of urbanism of Indians greatly outpaced their general increase. The overall great surge came in the following decade.

However that may be, urban Indians continued to increase in proportion to rural Indians until today at least half of all Indians live in urban areas. Not all such locations are big cities. Any town or village with a minimum of 2,500 inhabitants is urban for the census. Yet even the smaller places have a special significance for Indians because they are outside the reservations.

For better or worse, urban Indians are more intimately involved in the dominant culture than their reservation brethren, though even the latter have become more "urbanized"—more sophisticated—through travel, schools, movies, television, and their own production of news and entertainment media. Reservations with enough members publish their own newspapers—dozens of them—and operate their own radio stations. Some conduct their own schools and junior colleges (for instance Tsaile College of the Navajos), and they have created public libraries and tribal archives. Some, especially the Pueblos, have sent fellows to the Newberry Library and the Smithsonian Institution to search out materials on tribal histories. Some have mounted to the very apex of civilization by operating casinos and Bingo parlors. No universal rule of urbanism is valid for all the reservations; each must be studied individually.

Why did so many leave the reservation? Some young people may have gone to cities in the age-old quest for novelty and excitement, but most seem to have pulled up roots out of economic necessity. Judged by rates of unemployment, the reservations have been in a state of permanent economic depression. An unemployment rate of 80 per cent is not uncommon. Tribal leaders strive to cope by adopting a rule frequently seen in United States cities: i.e., they *create* jobs as patronage appointments. (We see the same thing in Chicago, for instance, when one man fixes a pothole while three others stand around with hands in pockets.) Federally recognized tribes can create quite a few jobs with funds derived from contractual annuities or federal subsidies, but this is still not enough to employ all the young people of that rising population, so the youth head off to where they think work may be available (whether or not it really is).

Indians who began to leave the reservation before 1950 found occupations that varied as widely as from "show business" in Wild West shows to "high steel" construction by Mohawks in New York, with more humdrum laboring tasks and domestic work in between. Fur traders hired some in the Far Northwest, and lumbermen took on more. If Mohawks were to be found high on the steel skeletons of New York City's towers, Senecas perched on redwoods in Oregon. Oklahoma Indians worked for oilmen, and some became oilmen themselves when their allotted properties gushed. In California, many Indian "alumni" of the missions stayed on to help build the cities that grew up around the missions. There is no set rule.

In 1950 the federal Bureau of Indian Affairs initiated a relocation program to assist Indian people to move to urban areas. The Bureau located or built housing, financed moving, and helped the migrants to adjust to customs and requirements in their new communities. This was a major project involving perhaps as many as 100,000 Indians in its first twenty years, which amounted roughly to an eighth of all Indians. Yet the statistics seem to say that the Bureau's project assisted less than half as many as those who migrated of their own accord.

Such developments within and without the reservations create great strain on tribal cultures and interpersonal relations. Some reservation traditionalists decry the migrants as having forsaken their people and thus having ceased to be genuine Indians. Young migrants who return to visit their reservation kin, as they all do, are likely to come up against deep suspicion from elders who see these kids with new ideas as threats to established culture—and to established leaders. Elders dub them "post-powwow Quarterbacks"—a curiously syncretic term. The youngsters become impatient with unifying rituals that have ceased to have meaning for them. (At Taos, I have seen young men with exquisite coiffures and expensively fashionable clothing being overtly resentful as their fathers lined them up and stood by them to enforce participation.)

Adjustment to urban life has not been easy for Indians who grew up in a wholly different environment. Added to normal homesickness, many migrants found that the towns had no more jobs *for them* than the reservations where traditional family support networks cushioned the pain of joblessness. The impersonality of big cities makes a terrible emotional strain, and it is all too easy for an isolated person to take refuge in the bottle.

The stress has been partly alleviated by social organizations in the big cities, typically multitribal, and the irony is that migrants from reservations are repeating many of the patterns of immigrants from Europe, but with this difference: the "old country" reservations are closer and easier to return to than Italy or Poland. A very high rate of return to the reservation prevails, but the statistics vary so much as to be meaningless. If half of all Indians now live in urban communities, a great many more must have experimented with that life before rejecting it.

Typically those who stay in the city are better educated (and therefore more employable), or have intermarried with non-Indians. "Generally," writes Russell Thornton, "it seems that the more Indian one is, the less likely one is to remain in the city."

Also in the pattern of immigrants from Europe, intermarriage dilutes ethnic self-identification, and economic success tends to reduce birth rates as the support and education of individual children becomes more expensive for upwardly mobile nuclear families shorn of the support of extended families on the reservation. In short, by surmounting the barrier of *caste*, such families have become subject to the restrictions and compulsions of social *class* under the rules by which class structure functions in the dominant American culture.

In that culture, individualism is the keynote. Insofar as group loyalties are demanded, national patriotism comes first. Religion is optional. Though tribalism is now respected, even encouraged, by a government that has turned off the fire under the melting pot, the tribes must now find ways to cope with the immense pressures of the mass media and individual mobility.

Perhaps, in the long run, the old adage will include Indians: "The more they change, the more they remain the same." Whether something of the same sort can also be said of their tribes is more problematical.

In May 1977, Congress's American Indian Policy Review Commission presented its final report. This commission differed from its predecessor official bodies by having five Indians among its members and six more on its executive staff besides sixty-odd in other capacities. This leaven baked a new loaf. As the report summarized: "It has been the fortune of this Commission to be the first in the long history of this Nation to listen attentively to the voice of the Indian rather than the Indian expert."

The commission made 206 specific recommendations to Congress. The "fundamental concepts" underlying them were stated concisely:

1. That the Indian tribes are sovereign political bodies, having the power to determine their own membership and power to enact laws and enforce them within the boundaries of their reservations, and
2. That the relationship which exists between the tribes and the United States is premised on a special trust that must govern the conduct of the stronger toward the weaker.

In 1978, the American Indian Religious Freedom Act declared the "inherent right" of all Native Americans "to believe, express, and exercise" their "traditional religions." Thus was rescinded the premise on which governments had sponsored and enforced missions since the beginning of European invasion.

In October 1990, President George Bush signed into law the Native American Languages Act to encourage perpetuation of languages sinking into oblivion. Completely reversing the policy of a ban on use of tribal speech that once had been enforced in BIA schools, the new law stipulates explicitly: "Sec. 105. The right of Native Americans to express themselves through the use of Native American languages shall not be restricted in any public proceeding including publicly supported educational programs."

In Canada also, new attention has been drawn to tribal relations with Canadian governments. An awakening was stimulated violently when an Indian member of a provincial parliament blocked confirmation of the "Meech Lake accord" between provinces and the federal government. After many meetings and compromises, the accord provided for a new constitution defining relations between the federal government and the provinces, but its authors had omitted a role for the tribes. Now that the Indian chief has prevented confirmation, the job must be started again from scratch, this time with a clear understanding that Indians may not be left out of its arrangements.

That this lesson has been taken to heart in some circles is evidenced by a new provincial agreement—the first ever—between Ontario and twelve Indian chiefs, recognizing the Indians' rights to self-government.

This new Statement of Political Relationship provides for negotiations between the Ontario government and the 200,000 Indians of the province (half of Canada's total) on a government-to-government basis.

As I write, the United States Congress is considering once more the relationship of tribes to the federal government. What may be more significant in the long run is that the Indians have learned some techniques indispensable in the American system of politics. Some, at least, now know how to voice their interests through the media of public opinion, and they have shown aptitude for lobbying agencies of government responsible for their affairs. In regions of the nation where Indian persons are concentrated, politicians begin to pay attention to them.

These things are new—unprecedentedly new. Where they will lead remains to be seen, but it seems unlikely to be a reprise of the bad old days in the same old ways.

Yet it would be very foolish to ignore signs of new ways to deal foully with America's Indian people. There was the hideous attack by federal troops in 1973 on the Pine Ridge Reservation, called by Lakota people "Wounded Knee II." This siege lasted seventy-one days and involved armored personnel carriers, automatic weapons, and elements of the 82nd Airborne Division, not to speak of U.S. marshals, the FBI, and BIA police. Though there was no outright massacre this time, writer Norma Clark Wilson claims that over sixty members of the American Indian Movement "died violently" on the Pine Ridge Reservation between 1973 and 1976, and that none of these deaths was ever solved.

On the legal front, in a book published in 1980, Russel Lawrence Barsh and James Youngblood Henderson foretell Supreme Court decisions hostile to Indian rights by the method of chipping away at them. The Court's 1978 decision in *Oliphant v. Suquamish*, they believe, showed that it "has moved definitively in the direction of tribal termination." As tribalism is the very core of Indian ethnic identity, tribal termination could lead inexorably to the extinction of Indianness.

I do not pretend to know which path the American government and people will take. In practice, the conclusion drawn by Barsh and Henderson seems sound:

"In the midst of this time of social and environmental reevaluation, in which Indian culture and Indian imagery have played so large a part, and in which a mixture of nostalgia and guilt over the passing of aboriginal America is so popular in the media, it is ironic that Indians are still not secure in the enjoyment of political liberty. . . . The white Americans of this decade consume an unprecedented number of books and films on Indian life and legends while they tolerate the legal dismemberment of tribal communities. It is not enough to mourn past misdeeds. It is necessary to challenge the power to repeat them."

CHAPTER 47

In Perspective

It has not been unknown for American practice to violate American principles.

—RUSSEL LAWRENCE BARSH and
JAMES YOUNGBLOOD HENDERSON

Among American intellectuals, a curious semantic cleavage has long existed. They expatiate grandly on the American empire, but shy away uncomfortably from saying *imperialism* to describe the process of acquiring that empire. American imperialism, for them, is something that happened only about the time of the Spanish-American War. It has a bad sound, like something that Old World Spain or Britain might do, not us. Frontier democrats conquered *wilderness* and *built* empires; they were not imperialists.

This is an aspect of the more inclusive myth of American exceptionalism, an invention to warrant just about anything our forefathers did, as long as it succeeded. Since Frontier democracy was Good and the Old World was Bad, whatever we did here was Different. This myth deflates as soon as Europe's history is given some factual attention. It was necessary, therefore, to maintain it by running Europe through a Hegelian sieve showing how the Spirit of History had risen from Asia to Europe (bypassing Africa) and leaped gloriously to America's pinnacle. In retrospect, it seems incredible that anyone would take this guff seriously, but much of it is still with us.

Indians know better. They have been overrun as the indigenous tribes of Europe were by conquering armies, and dispossessed by alien hordes. In matter-of-fact manner, Indians speak of the colonialism to which their peoples were reduced under the euphonious name of civilization. The colonies of Europe in America once formed tiny enclaves within surrounding populations of Indians. Now Indian reservations form enclaves within the all-conquering descendants of Europeans who include assimilated Africans and recently immigrated Asians.

Perhaps it may be pleaded that this situation came about less from outright combat than from treaty negotiations. Dorothy V. Jones illuminates those treaties in the very title of her fine book, *License for Empire: Colonialism by Treaty in Early America.* Treaties that had begun as a means of accommodation, she wrote, "gradually transformed into a system for transferring land ownership" and, we may add, under duress.

Treaties between Europeans and non-European peoples were far from unique to North America. The theory and practice of treaties had evolved in feudal Europe and were taken around the world in Europe's great age of imperialist conquest. "For example, in the brief period 1763–74," Dr. Jones notes, "North American Indians were signatories to thirty treaties, or 39 percent of the total" in the extended treaty system, "and Asian Indians to thirty-one treaties, or 40 percent of the total." North America and its European colonials were integral to the worldwide system, and the dominant European descendants continued the pattern after they gained independence for themselves.

Whatever the means, the effects are plain. Before Europeans invaded the American continents, Indians had mastered living in them. They had built cities in Mexico and Peru. They had established towns and villages, and had created well-used trails for commerce between them. They had, in short, conquered the wilderness for their purposes. Their power fell disastrously short in one crucial respect—defense against novel epidemic diseases. When the ravages of smallpox, influenza, measles, tuberculosis, and others enabled Europeans to conquer, a conception arose of "the vanishing Indian" who was fated to extinction because of inherent inability to survive in the presence of "civilization." Balm though it was for tender European consciences, this fallacy has now been exposed.

Even at nadir, the tragically diminished remainder of the original people clung to their special identity. Now that their numbers increase once more, it is certain that a degree of empowerment will recur, is indeed already doing so. The people who could master continents of wilderness may be expected to achieve a respected role for themselves amidst the culture that swept over them. Very clearly, American Indian cultures are taking their place among the others of a nation of plural cultures. To the extent that Indians assimilate, it will be on their own terms, by their own choices, and with the fierce preservation of their precious essence of identity.

Imperialism was not and is not just the conspiracy of a few villains. Worse, far worse. Though there was conspiracy enough, the program embodied an ideal enjoying full popular support. (Ideals are not always "idealistic.") Jacksonian democracy was popular, but not especially Jacksonian. His political enemy, Massachusetts' John Quincy Adams, was every bit as expansionist as Jackson, just a little less crude.

The popularity of expansionism among the American *Herrenvolk* derived from the same source as the same process in South Africa: to wit, general acceptance of racist conceptions that came to be known late in the nineteenth century as Social Darwinism. (When Rhodesia broke away from Britain, it proclaimed a parody of the American Declaration of Independence.) The conceptions were widespread long before the name of racism gave them dignity, and it is quite wrong to assume, as is often done, that they conflicted with religious teaching. They were part of the churches' assumptions as the "reformers" amply demonstrated. Religionists fully agreed that Indians should be conquered; they just wanted to do it *kindly*, for the Indians' own good. Clergy found plenty of biblical sanction for conquest and stratification of peoples, and for slavery too. Abolitionists were a disapproved, radical minority among churchmen.

Nineteenth-century scientists had no grounds to assume airs of holier-than-they. The very name Social Darwinism betrays what they were thinking, and Reginald Horsman has shown in precise, well-documented detail the connection between "scientific" racism and Manifest Destiny. Almost certainly, there must have been some voices raised in behalf of the common humanity of Indians and their conquerors, but such voices were very small indeed. The most cursory survey of the periodical literature of the late nineteenth century shows *race, race, race*, permeating every branch of thought.

Overt racism remained a constant in American life until the rise of Hitler's Nazis held up a mirror in which most of us—not all—beheld an appalling image. (Nazi race doctrines drew heavily from American pseudo-scientists.) The first American *scientist* of stature to repudiate and denounce racism was the German immigrant Franz Boas who transformed anthropology by substituting *culture* for *race* as its theoretical theme, and who insisted that the way to learn about a people was to go and study them as they were. Historians were harder to teach, and some still resist learning, but this is not the place for lists.

Now that Indians are under control and increasing again, they enjoy increased opportunities to participate in American society on something like equal terms if they accept the rules as given. Indeed there are special benefits for those who will accept them—scholarships, for example, all the way up through graduate school, but many reservation Indians cannot or will not reach out from the reservation nest.

As has long been true, all Indians are selective about what they accept and adopt from the dominant, surrounding culture. A Navajo cannot be parted from his beloved pickup truck which is certainly not part of traditional culture. The "constitutional" Indian nations have the forms of elected republics, but their parties still strongly resemble kin and clan structures. My experience has been that every Indian, even the most completely assimilated, cherishes something from ancestral culture, something of his "Indianness." Organized tribes sponsor projects and celebrations of renewal of the old ways. Such things seem quaint to tourists, but what they mean to participants needs further thought.

At a powwow in Oklahoma some years ago, I watched the "gentlemen's dance." The dancers were attired in ordinary street clothes with a few ornaments and pieces of jewelry. (Full regalia was reserved for the "fancy dancer" boys.) Leading the "gentlemen" was a tall, muscular man who never stopped until we dispersed after midnight. I learned later that he was an over-the-road truck driver who had to take his big rig out again at 4:00 A.M. What makes this account pertinent was the expression on his face. The movements of his body were the stimulants to transport his mind to a land far away and long ago. During the dance, this man *lived* with his people in their great days.

Indians cannot dance all the time, much as some would like to, but they find ways to preserve some of what they love against the most powerful pressures of the surround. When my party toured Acoma—the "sky city" of the Pueblos—I asked our guide how many tribal members belonged to the impressive Roman Catholic church from which we had just emerged. "All of us" was the response. "But why are there two separate graveyards?" I asked. "Oh, *that* one,"—she pointed to the plot at a small distance from the church—"is *our* religion."

In recent years anthropologists have become sensitive to this sort of melding of features from distinct cultures. *Syncretism* can be seen in politics and technology as well as religion. The dominant culture does this sort of thing too as, for instance, by adopting "Indian corn" and potatoes and tomatoes into agricultural production and Indian herbal extracts into medicines. When scholars outgrow the constraints of either-or thought and come to examine phenomena as they were and are, Indians may hope for genuine history. Happily, that process is now well under way.

Indians themselves begin to show interest and acquire the necessary historical skills though many traditionalists reject history as an alien way of thinking. Already a number of reservation communities are accumulating tribal archives and instituting programs of study. Highly educated Indians have followed a pattern familiar among immigrants by concentrating in fields for the immediate benefit of their people, such as medicine, law, and anthropology, but here and there a historian has emerged.

When the number of Indians in graduate school reaches a certain threshold, we may confidently anticipate transformation of Amerindian history.

In a sense, history is a luxury for people who have mastered the basic necessities of life and can afford time for contemplation. Seen another way, however, history empowers a people with knowledge of what they are and how they became so—knowledge essential to planning future progress. A people without understanding of their history is a people adrift.

We must not forget the tremendous changes in American society and culture that have taken place during the twentieth century. Computers, nuclear energy, labor-saving home appliances, automobiles, airplanes, movies, radio, television, sound tape and videotape players—all have changed the lives and minds of Indians as well as others. In an odd turn of events, this new technology, which is so much more advanced than that of earlier eras, makes adjustment and a degree of assimilation easier than it was. At just the historical moment when military and political repression are coming into bad repute among principled people, technology seduces Indians to want to join the dominant culture.

The reservation is no longer a place where Indians can be dumped and forgotten. It has become a base for action and publicity. Members move energetically back and forth for economic reasons and also simply for enjoyment of their heritage in the many powwow celebrations that have become as common as rodeos and more widespread.

Since the Collier revolution, the reservation has become a place for revival of tribal consciousness and autonomous management of the tribe's own affairs, and this occurs just as the people grow once more in numbers and morale. Land is important for reasons of sentiment, yes, but not only so. A land base is required for establishment of a reservation and tribal administration for tribal purposes. That is why some Indians will scrape together a tract far from where they were dispossessed. Without a land base, the people disintegrate. The fight for land, in a very real sense, is a struggle for survival as a people.

Our era is full of paradox. The reservations that were concentration camps have become bastions. The peoples were sent there to die away and vanish, but they have multiplied and gained strength, and they send out emigrants to the towns and cities of the conquerors. In a sense, these urbanites are missionaries in reverse. The technologies that mold Indians into the outward image of other people are also the instruments by which Indians unite and strive for their own goals more effectively than since the founding of the United States.

In saying this, and in writing this book, I do not wish to leave an impression either that all Indians are heroic—they are human—or that their conquerors have been more vicious than the same sort of people in the same sort of situation elsewhere. It was the process of intended conquest, and the proceedings that followed, that gave European colonizers their particular character. They, too, were human. That this was not only some mysterious product of racial identity is amply clarified by the Aztec example.

As Wilcomb E. Washburn has reminded us, some descendants of America's conquerors have shown more conscientious sense of responsibility, and have compensated the conquered people to a degree that is found in no other land where conquest occurred. A great reservoir of good will toward Indians has filled up from an abiding sense of guilt and a desire to use power fairly. To be sure, there are some whose spokesman was the southern Congressman protesting, "We stole the land fair and square," but not many people live comfortably with *stole*.

The mythology of conquest is embedded deeply in the national consciousness of Americans, most notably in the ideology of race. In exposing facts contradicting the myths I hope not only to recognize the achievements of the Indian pioneers who conquered the wilderness, but also to show how abhorrent conquest is, how it turns ordinary persons into monsters, how it poisons the integrity of statesmen, clergy, and scholars and creates the illusions of supermen and divinely chosen people which trouble the earth. Many Americans have tried to be decent; many others, unfortunately, have shown a mean streak in our national character. We cannot overlook how the United States has become massively militarist, nor the social implications of such a state. Predictions are not in order.

Part of the general wave of repression in recent years is the effort to keep Indians and other lowly persons out of sight in courses of study. Former Education Secretary William Bennett assailed Stanford University for its proposed new curriculum's inclusion of peoples and cultures other than WASPs. (Conservative Stanford!) As I write this (in June 1991) New York State is considering a curriculum with attention to "minority" peoples. Opponents denounce the proposition as "distorting history by suggesting that all interpretations are equally valid." This is a false issue. It is not equally valid to say that Columbus discovered America or that he arrived at an already settled land. One of these statements is false, the other true. The valid issue is whether our histories are to be mythical or to reflect reality.

Should we agree with the reported view of Columbia University Professor Kenneth T. Jackson that "history . . . has given Americans a culture that is mainly rooted in Britain but that has been greatly transformed by later tides of immigration"? The very statement discloses the massive ignorance about American Indians, not to mention other peoples, that makes necessary a new approach to education.

With the growth of Indian numbers has come the creation of new pan-Indian organizations entirely under Indian leadership and free from the foot-dragging hesitations of older leaders denounced as "uncle Tomahawks." Some of the new militants have engaged in such flamboyant actions as the seizure of Alcatraz, the trashing of the BIA office in Washington, and the armed seizure of a self-proclaimed "nation" in the Adirondack Mountains. Not all Indians approve such militant protest, but it seems to me that universal assent is given to the militants' main demand, which is for Indian *sovereignty*. This is worth serious attention on several counts. By the nature of Indian societies, the cry for sovereignty must be expressed in form as *tribal* sovereignty; there is no material at present for an Indian State. On the surface this appears like a mirror image of the termination idea—it is a demand to get the government off the tribes' backs, which the terminators would express as getting the tribes off the government's hands—but there is a substantial difference muddled by the rhetoric. What the tribes want is autonomy to manage their own affairs in their own ways. They do not want to absolve the federal and State governments of the contract responsibilities they undertook *in return for land cessions and seizures.* (Not as alms.) We must not be misled by empty gestures such as the Iroquois Grand Council's issuance of passports for international travel, which the federal government tolerates as a minor nuisance best not noticed. (There are demagogues and hot-air artists among all peoples.) The real issues are self-government *and* contractual obligations, and these have been the essence of formal relations between Indians and others since European invasion began.

Inevitably, opponents will cry as they have since 1776, "The Indians are not ready to govern themselves." Apart from the fact that they had managed well enough for thousands of years before Europe noticed, Felix S. Cohen has given a terse response: "Let us admit that self-government includes graft, corruption, and the making of decisions by inexpert minds. Certainly these are features of self-government in white cities and counties." He might have added the national empire of the United States or of any other independent nation-state. These are not self-governing because of virtue—that has long been too ludicrous to suggest. Rather, they govern themselves because they have power enough to fend off external governors. To consider that issue properly, however, would require another book.

Setting aside virtue, which is at least as prevalent among Indians as among others, the difficulty with tribal sovereignty is the nature of the tribe, especially in its relationships with the nation-state. Tribes are "kinship states," and modern American society scatters kin to the four corners of the country and the globe. In some ways, tribalism can teach lessons to nationalists about democracy and community welfare—if the nationalists will listen. In respect to power, however, it seems that the tribe must give way, regardless of rhetorical thunders and symbolic gestures. This puzzle also requires another book. It is time to end this one.

CHRONOLOGY

These dates are keyed to events mentioned in the book. Selective rather than comprehensive, they pull into one sequence the happenings treated in separate chapters and other studies in different fields of research. Sometimes their correspondences surprise.

68,000 years B.C.　L. S. Cressman's extreme guess for early migration to North America

30,000 years B.C.　Earliest estimates of hearth charcoal in Brazilian rockshelters

28,000 years B.C.　Earliest estimates of hearth charcoal on Santa Rosa Island (California)

25,000 years B.C.　Dean R. Snow's estimate of early migration to North America

40,000–23,000 years B.C.　Linda Newton's tolerance for early migration to North America

Ca. 20,000 years B.C.　Linda Newton's estimate of early migration to South America

16,000 years B.C.　An ice-free corridor existed between glaciers

12,000 years B.C.　Dating of Meadowcroft Rockshelter near Pittsburgh, Pa.

10,000 years B.C.　Beringia was submerged under glacier melt; all unglaciated regions of the Americas had been occupied by humans

7000–5000 B.C.　Mastodons, woolly mammoths, and other great mammals of North America became extinct

Ca. 8000 B.C.　Northeast region of U.S. occupied by humans

Ca. 7000 B.C.　Teosinte cultivated in Tehuacán, developed into maize

3500–1500 B.C.　Beginnings of horticulture in U.S. Southwest

Ca. 3000 B.C.　Villages appeared in Tehuacán Valley

Ca. 1400–900 B.C.　Olmec trade flourished

3000–1000 B.C.　Uto-Aztecan migration created Nahuatl-speaking urban culture in Mexico

Ca. 1000 B.C.　Poverty Point (La.) mounds built

Ca. 500 B.C.　Adena-Hopewell mounds in Ohio Valley

(*All dates from here on are Anno Domini*)

Ca. 1 Teotihuacán rose to prominence
500 Identifiable remains of Hohokam, Anasazi, and Mogollon peoples (in U.S. Southwest)
600 Beginnings of Cahokia (Ill.)
Ca. 750 Teotihuacán abandoned
Ca. 800 Mesoamericans in the Mississippi Valley; introduction to Mississippi Valley of improved variety of maize
900–1110 Toltecs flourished at Tula
1132 City of Texcoco founded according to Sahagún's informants
1200 Probable maximum population of North American Indians
1000–1300 Anasazi communities flourished
1300 Most recent migration of Delawares from west to east; Mississippians withdrew southward; Onondaga culture showed marked change; Apacheans began to separate into tribes
1358 Tlatelolco founded
1390 Traditional origin date of the League of the Haudenosaunee (Iroquois)
1400 Athapascans migrated to U.S. Southwest
1428 Alliance of Tenochtitlán, Tlatelolco, and Texcoco defeated Azcapotzalco
1430 Ruler Itzcoatl ordered destruction and substitution of Tenochtitlán's records
1473 Tenochtitlán triumphed over Tlatelolco
1486 Huitzilopochtli's new temple dedicated in Tenochtitlán
1490 Spain began to colonize the Canary Islands
1492 Columbus made landfall in the Caribbean Sea
1493 Pope Alexander VI granted Amerindian lands to the Spanish crown
1494 Columbus sent 500 enslaved Indians to the market in Seville; Rome was invaded by French King Charles VIII
1498 Census by Bartholomew Columbus listed 1,100,000 natives in half of Hispaniola
1500 Royal decree arrived in Hispaniola making Indians vassals of the crown, otherwise personally free; it was generally ignored
1502 Las Casas arrived in Hispaniola
1511 Montesinos preached against slavery on Hispaniola
1513 Balboa claimed for Spain the lands bordering the Pacific Ocean
1515 Las Casas converted to anti-slavery for Indians
1517 Martin Luther's attack on Papal Indulgences
1518 Population of Central Mexico estimated at 25,200,000 by Borah and Cook
1519 Cortés landed on coast of Mexico

1520 Smallpox carried from Cuba to Mexico

1521 Ponce de León failed to conquer Florida

1525 Probable time of Apacheans' arrival in U.S. Southwest; three of Cortés letters describing conquest published

1527 City of Rome plundered by army of Emperor Charles V

1534, 1535 Jacques Cartier voyaged and wintered among St. Lawrence Iroquoians

1536 Royal College of Santa Cruz founded in Mexico

1539 De Soto invaded Florida and the Gulf region

1540 Coronado invaded Acoma and other Pueblos

1551 Emperor Charles V founded the National University of Mexico

1559 Establishment of the Spanish Inquisition's Index of forbidden books

1564 Beginning of the annual fleet of trading galleons from Mexico to the Philippines

1565 Menéndez massacred the French colony at Fort Caroline; San Agustin founded in Florida

1570 Jesuit mission founded and destroyed by local Indians on Chesapeake Bay

1571 The Inquisition came to New Spain; it had little interest in Indians

1579 Francis Drake's *Golden Hind* harbored near San Francisco on its trip around the world

1580 By this year, 500 vessels per year took part in North American fisheries, making them one of Europe's biggest industries

1585 Ralegh's Roanoke colony founded

1588 The Netherlands and England defeated the Spanish "Invincible Armada"

1597 Guale Indians (of Georgia) rebelled against Spanish missions and were suppressed

1598 Juan de Oñate conquered the Rio Grande Pueblos; Philip II of Spain died

1607 Jamestown (Va.) founded

1608 Quebec founded

1609 Champlain aided Algonquins and Montagnais in war against Mohawks

1610 Santa Fé founded

1614 Dutch traders founded a year-round trading post on the upper Hudson River

1620 New Plymouth founded

1622 Powhatan rising against Virginia colony

1624   Dutch West India Company founded Manhattan and built Fort Orange (Albany, N.Y.)

1630   Massachusetts Bay founded

1632   Publication of Chronicles of Bernal Diaz del Castillo

1634   Maryland founded

1636   Massachusetts and Connecticut warred against Pequots; Harvard College founded

1638   New Sweden founded

1640   New Netherland's Willem Kieft warred against surrounding tribes, and had to hire English mercenaries to win.

1642   Montreal founded; Maryland defeated Susquehannocks

1643   Susquehannocks, with Swedish help, defeated Maryland; Mayhew mission began on Martha's Vineyard

1644   The second rising and suppression of the Powhatans

1646   Massachusetts founded John Eliot's mission with Col. Daniel Gookin as administrator

1648   Semen Dezhnev's voyage through the Bering Strait

1649–1655   Mohawks and Senecas broke up the Huron confederation and drove the people out of Ontario, after which they scattered the other Iroquoian tribes between lakes Erie and Ontario

1656   Jesuit mission founded near Ontario; Timucuans of Florida rebelled against missions and were suppressed

1658   Mohawks ruined the mission near Onondaga; Esopus Indians rose against New Netherland

1659   10,000 Florida Indians died of measles

1659–1660   Des Groseilliers and Radisson traded near Hudson Bay for the first time

1661   Louis XIV began personal rule

1664   Second Esopus rising; New Netherland conquered by Duke of York's fleet

1666   De Tracy burned Mohawk villages

1668   Des Groseilliers sailed from England to Hudson Bay wintered there at "Charles Fort"; Fathers Claude Dablon and Jacques Marquette founded Mission Saulte Ste. Marie

1669   Praying Indians of Massachusetts attacked Mohawks and were defeated

1670   Charles Town (S.C.) founded; English crown chartered Hudson's Bay Company

1671   Hudson's Bay Company set up its first "factory"; Father Marquette founded Mission Saint-Ignace at Michilimackinac; Daumont de Saint-Lusson officially claimed the entire Northwest for France; a French trading post was set up to compete with the Hudson's Bay Company

1673 Jolliet and Marquette found the Mississippi for the French, and canoed down it to Arkansas; Iroquois pleaded with Frontenac to save them from his rampaging allies

1674 Edmund Andros arrived as New York's governor

1675 Intersocietal wars in New England and the Chesapeake Bay region

1677 The Covenant Chain founded

1680 South Carolina, with Shawnee allies, destroyed the Westos; Pueblos, outraged by efforts to ruin their religion, revolted, captured Santa Fe, and drove out Spaniards

1681 French crown chartered Compagnie de la Baie d'Hudson; English crown chartered colony of Pennsylvania; proprietors of Carolina ordered trade in guns as means of creating tribal dependence

1682 La Salle cruised down the Mississippi River to its mouth; French took prisoner the crews of English ships in Hudson Bay; the Hudson's Bay Company expanded from one post to three

1684 Onondaga chief Garangula humiliated New France's Governor La Barre

1685 New York's Governor Dongan sent a successful trading party from Albany to Michilimackinac

1686 French intercepted a large trading party from Albany (intending to go to Michilimackinac) and confiscated its goods; French seized all but one Hudson Bay English posts

1691 Jacques Le Tort's expedition from Burlington (N.J.) via Susquehanna, Allegheny, Ohio, Mississippi, and Missouri rivers made contact with "over forty" native peoples

1692 Shawnee band, with Martin Chartier, arrived in Pennsylvania after leaving Tonty's Fort St. Louis; Spaniards reconquered Pueblo Indians and restored Santa Fé

1698 Dr. Daniel Coxe planned a giant English colony to be called Carolana which would conflict with territories pre-empted by the French; it never came to anything

1699 Le Moyne de Iberville built Fort Maurepas at Biloxi (Miss.); French mission founded at Cahokia

1700 Hopis massacred male villagers of Awatovi who had decided to receive Spanish priests

1701 Iroquois made peace with New France and its allies; French founded Detroit; Iroquois refused to attack Detroit, but gave New York a "deed" to it; William Penn treated with the Susquehannocks for trade and cession of their valley

1701–1713 Queen Anne's War

1703 French mission founded at junction of Kaskaskia River with Mississippi

1708 By this date, Carolina traders had seized 10,000 to 12,000 Spanish mission Indians and had sold them into West Indian slavery

1710 Treaty at Conestoga between Pennsylvania and the Iroquois League was kept secret from New York

1711 Mobile (Ala.) made capital of Louisiana

1712 Dubuisson and allies massacred Foxes fleeing from Detroit; Tuscaroras warred against Virginia; large-scale immigration began to Pennsylvania from Rhineland and Ulster; Louis XIV gave Louisiana to Antoine Crozat

1715 Yamasees warred against South Carolina

1716 Louvigny led a trading expedition in the guise of war against the Foxes

1717 Antoine Crozat surrendered his profitless charter for Louisiana

1718 New Orleans founded as new capital of Louisiana; John Law given Louisiana as the Company of the Indies which soon went bankrupt; Michel Bisaillon gave information to James Logan that stimulated the English Board of Trade to aggressive new policies; William Penn died in England

1724 Local French commander exterminated the Natchez nation to gain their lands; some survivors were given refuge and protection by the Chickasaws

1728 Vitus Bering's voyage through Bering Strait

1730 French and allies massacred Foxes trekking eastward in hope of sanctuary among Iroquois

1731 Company of the Indies surrendered its Louisiana charter

1733 English colony of Georgia founded

1734 French defeated by Foxes and allies in battle of Butte des Morts

1737 Beauharnois made peace with Foxes under pressure from his Indian allies; the "Walking Purchase" took place in Pennsylvania

1738 Gaultier de La Vérendrye made the first official visit to the Mandans; *coureurs de bois* had preceded him

1741 Bering's voyage to mainland Alaska

1742 Acceding to Pennsylvania's wishes, Onondaga Chief Canasatego ordered the Delawares off their land; he fabricated an Iroquois conquest supposedly making the Delawares into "women"; this became a support for the myth of a giant Iroquois "empire" over other Indians

1744 The Russian fur trade was extended to the Aleutian Islands

1744–1748 King George's War

1749 Céloron de Blainville toured Ohio tribes to demand expulsion of Pennsylvania traders and was rebuffed

1750 The Ohio Company of Virginia formed

1752 Virginia's treaty at Logstown (Ambridge, Pa.) with tribes resident in Ohio Country

1753 French expelled Pennsylvania's traders from Ohio Country; George Washington took Virginia's demand that French abandon their forts in the Ohio Country

1754 Washington capitulated to French at Fort Necessity; Albany Congress of English colonies with Iroquois

1754–1763 The Seven Years War (or "French and Indian War")

1755 Braddock routed at Fort Duquesne; Vaudreuil instigated Indian raids on English outpost colonials

1758 At a treaty at Easton (Pa.), Delawares agreed to leave the French in return for a promise of a boundary line between Indians and colonials; Forbes captured Fort Duquesne

1763 Treaty of Paris took France out of North America by cession of claimed lands to Britain and Spain; "Pontiac's Conspiracy" besieged British forts in the Old Northwest; Fort Pitt's garrison created a smallpox epidemic among the Delawares; British crown proclaimed a boundary line between colonials and Indians

1769 Captain Will's Shawnees captured Daniel Boone and freed him after confiscating his goods and gear; Spaniards founded Mission San Diego as the first in a series extending northward along the California coast

1773 Creeks ceded territory

1774 Lord Dunmore warred against the Shawnees; Iroquois refused to help them; Mingo James Logan's family massacred; the Quebec Act legislated a boundary between English colonies and crown lands reserved to the Indians

1776 United States declared Independence; Cherokee rising suppressed by South Carolina and Virginia

1776–1783 The War for American Independence

1777 The Battle of Oriskany set Iroquois against Iroquois; Iroquois grand council "covered the council fire"; Americans won the Battle of Saratoga

1778 Delawares proposed creation of an Indian state with themselves at its head; Congress ignored the proposal; Captain James Cook landed on Vancouver Island

1779 Sullivan's army destroyed Iroquois towns

1783 Treaty of Paris recognized U.S. independence and ceded British territorial claims; it made no mention of Indian rights

1784 Treaty of Fort Stanwix between Iroquois and U.S.

1786 New Mexico's Governor Bernardo de Galvez inaugurated policy of treaties and trade with Apacheans; Grigori Shelikhov began Russian conquest of Alaska

1787 Northwest Ordinance provided for organization of Old Northwest into States

1788 Kentucky lands claimed by Shawnees, ceded by Iroquois

1790 General Harmar's army defeated by western Indian confederation; the Trade and Intercourse Act enacted

1791 Vermont admitted as a State; General St. Clair's army routed by western Indian confederation

1792 Kentucky admitted as a State

1794 Russian missionaries arrived on Kodiak Island; General Wayne defeated the western confederation at Fallen Timbers

1795 The Treaty of Greenville re-established a boundary between Indian territories and the U.S.

1796 Tennessee admitted as a State

1799 Russian American Company granted monopoly of fur trade; most Russian missionaries died in a shipwreck; Onondaga Handsome Lake had a vision that began the Longhouse religion

1802 Tlingit Indians destroyed New Archangel (Sitka)

1803 William Henry Harrison's Treaty of Fort Wayne obtained cession of 1,152,000 acres under dubious circumstances; Napoleon Buonaparte sold the Louisiana Territory to the U.S.

1804–1806 Meriwether Lewis and William Clark explored the U.S. Northwest all the way to the Pacific Coast

1805 Tlingit Indians destroyed Yakutat

1807–1808 Black Hoof's Shawnee farm and mission ruined by official decision after hopeful start

1811 William Henry Harrison defeated Tenskwatawa's Shawnees and allies at Tippecanoe

1812–1815 "The War of 1812"

1813 William Henry Harrison defeated the British and Indian allies at the Battle of the Thames in which Tecumseh was killed

1814 Andrew Jackson defeated the Creeks at the Battle of Horseshoe Bend, after which he forced cession of 20,000,000 acres

1815   Jackson and Lafitte won the Battle of New Orleans
1818   Jackson seized Pensacola (Florida)
1820–1823   Mexico became independent and abolished the legal status of "Indian" by absorbing it into "citizen"
1821   Stephen Austin brought "Anglos" to Texas; Hudson's Bay Company acquired North West Company
1823   Oneidas settled at Green Bay
1825   Erie Canal opened
1830   President Jackson's administration enacted the Indian Removal Law to force Indians west of the Mississippi; ultimatum given to Choctaws at Treaty of Dancing Rabbit Creek
1831   De Tocqueville observed Choctaws on their "trail of tears"
1833   Japanese junk wrecked near Queen Charlotte's Island after drifting across the Pacific
1834–1836   California missions secularized by Mexico
1835   Cherokees, at Treaty of New Echota, accepted removal west of the Mississippi
1836   Cherokee "trail of tears"; Texas seceded from Mexico
1837   Seminole Chief Osceola was seized at treaty negotiations and imprisoned; he died in prison
1837–1838   Smallpox destroyed the Mandan Indians
1838   The "blatantly corrupt" purchase of Seneca land by the Ogden Land Company
1841   Migration began on the Oregon Trail
1842   Allegany and Cattaraugus reservations were confirmed to the Seneca Indians
1845   Texas admitted as a State
1846–1848   War between the United States and Mexico
1848   Mexico's provinces north of the Rio Grande were ceded to the U.S. by the Treaty of Guadalupe Hidalgo; most Senecas replaced their traditional hereditary government with elected officers; Tonawanda kept the traditional system
1849   The gold rush to California began
1854   Japan was opened to western trade by Admiral Matthew Perry
1857   Seminoles accepted a cash payment to move west; massacre at Mountain Meadows (Utah)
1861   Texas seceded from the United States to join the Confederate States
1861–1865   The Civil War in the United States
1867   Russia sold its North American colony to the U.S.
1869   Texas re-admitted to the United States
1870   Congress substituted "agreements" for "treaties"

1875 Comanches surrendered after war with the U.S.

1876 Massacre of Custer's cavalry troop at Little Big Horn

1880 Full publication of Fr. Diego Durán's manuscript about Mexican Indians

1887 The General Allotment Act (Dawes Act) passed

1890 U.S. Indian population at nadir; massacre of Chief Big Foot's Sioux at Wounded Knee; U.S. census proclaimed "the end of the frontier"

1893 Oklahoma Territory opened to homesteaders; Spanish-American War and cession to U.S. of Philippines and Puerto Rico

1900 Hawaii annexed as a U.S. territory

1900–1910 18,000,000 acres of tribal lands taken by U.S.

1924 American Indians made U.S. citizens

1934 John Collier's Indian Reorganization Act enacted

1946 The Philippines given independence by U.S. Congress; the Indian Claims Commission enacted

1950 BIA initiated a relocation program to move Indians from reservations to urban areas; by this date 13.4 percent of American Indians had become urban, mostly by personal action

1953 "Termination" begun with 13 tribes released from federal supervision; American Society for Ethnohistory founded

1959 Hawaii admitted as the 50th State

1971 Alaska Native Claims Settlement Act enacted

1973 "Wounded Knee II" on the Pine Ridge reservation; Menominee termination rescinded

1977 Final report of U.S. Congress American Indian Policy Review Commission

1978 American Indian Religious Freedom Act enacted; U.S. Supreme Court's decision in *Oliphant v. Suquamish* leaned toward tribal termination

1982 English translation of Sahagún's manuscript about the Aztecs completed and published

1990 At least half of U.S. Indians have become urban

18 December 1991 Alaska Native lands corporations to be opened to share ownership by non-Natives

NOTES

This book was written for the general public, who are usually averse to footnote citations. Upon its completion, however, it occurred to me that professionals might like some guideposts outside their specialties. The list, with the Bibliography, should be considered more as finding aids than the full-scale documentation usual in scholarly monographs. I apologize for gaps occurring because of the dispersal of my personal library when I moved from Massachusetts to Chicago.

Chapter 1. Except for Washington Irving, this chapter is based heavily on *Crossroads of Continents*, the prehistory articles in *Handbook of North American Indians*, and special articles in *Natural History*. **P. 29:** The shoreline route is mapped in *National Geographic* 174:4 (Oct. 1988), 436–37.
P. 32: Jenny Alowa entranced her listeners at the Newberry.
P. 32. Driver, v. **P. 33:** "became mighty hunters": *Atlas of Ancient America*, 33; "Others moved by land or water": Woodbury and Zubrow, 51, 52.

Chapter 2. P. 40: Hurt, 1–4, 17; Walker, 1–4. **Pp. 40–44:** based primarily on *Cambridge Encyclopedia of Latin American History*, vol. 1; **pp. 44–45:** "Platform mounds": Morgan, 48–49; **pp. 45–46:** Coe, 101, 124, 125–27; Sahagún, pt. 9, 166–70.

Chapter 3. Pp. 48–49: Woodbury and Zubrow, 46; Jesse D. Jennings, 114; Cressman, 104; Haury, 26; **Pp. 50–52:** Woodbury; Woodbury and Zubrow; Martin; Gumerman and Haury; all in *Handbook* 9.
p. 52: "Luxury items": Kelley, 93; Cordell, 258.
p. 54: Frazier, 108–9, 121, 126; Cordell, Ch. 8.

Chapter 4. P. 56–58: Morgan, 10; Brose, Brown, and Penney, 53, 51. Morgan's book has line drawings of "mounds" and "pyramids" that show very clearly their differences. The book also includes dimensions and dates. It is a fact hunter's delight.
P. 62: Smith, 30–35; **p. 64–67:** Brose, Brown, and Penney, 147, 150; **pp. 98–100:** ibid., 98–102, 198.

Chapter 5. Pp. 69–70: Brugge, Opler, Young, in *Handbook* 10; Hale and Harris in ibid., 9; Jacob E. Thomas, oral tradition recorded in F. Jennings, *Ambiguous*, 23–24; **pp. 70–72:** Heckewelder, 47–51; **p. 72:** Mooney, 17–23; Arthur C. Parker; **p. 72:** Chafe, personal letter; **pp. 72–74:** Mithun, "The Proto-Iroquoians" in *Extending the Rafters;* "evidence of predecessors": Bradley, 9; "*in situ*": Tuck; **p. 74:** Bradley, 21, 24; **pp. 74–75:** Heckewelder, 50–55; Colden, 3–6; *Traditional History*, 1; **pp. 68–69:** Trigger, *Children*, 1: 156–57; **p. 69:** ibid., 158–59, 174; Cartier: Quinn, *North America*. Throughout the early part of my book, I have relied very heavily on the works of David B. Quinn whom I (and many others) regard as the grand master of the "discoveries period" of North America.

Chapter 6. P. 78: Swagerty, "Indian Trade" in *Handbook* 4:351–53. William R. Swagerty seems to me to be our foremost authority on western trade between Indians and others, and he has made much progress on trade between Indians and Indians. He is my

Chapter 7. **P. 83:** *Jesuit Relations* 2:73. I have discussed the semantics of Turner and
Webb in F. Jennings, *Invasion,* ch. 5. **Pp. 83–84:** Vattel 3:38; **p. 84:** Gallatin, 152–53; **p.
85:** Kroeber, 150, 132, 134–35; Ubelaker, 247, 287; **p. 85:** Spinden, 470, 463; Kroeber,
177, 180, 181; Sauer, 65–69; **p. 86:** Borah and Cook, 180–81; **pp. 86–88:** Dobyns, "Estimating," 414; Thornton, 26.

Chapter 8. **P. 90:** "excavating ancient Troy": Ceram, 40; **p. 91:** Cressman, 200; "teeth":
Christy G. Turner II; **p. 94:** Tuck, *Onondaga;* **p. 96:** "Aztec ruler Itzcoatl": Leon-Portilla
in *Cambridge Encyclopedia,* 1:14.

Chapter 9. **P. 101:** Sauer, *Early Spanish Main* gives a complete description of the
culture of the islanders and what happened to it and them after the Spanish invasion. **P.
103:** "Canaries": Verlinden, *Beginnings.* Sauer believed that the funds came from the Santa
Hermandad. Recently it has been suggested that Genoese bankers residing in Spain might
have financed their countryman Columbus. I am skeptical. Bankers are not, and certainly
were then not, sentimentalists. There is no word in Columbus's contract of recompense to
any banker. The Spanish crown cooperated with Columbus and contracted with him. **P.
103:** Columbus's voyage: Morison, 191, 311, ch. 16; motivation: Morison, 486–87; Sauer,
35; "landing": Judge. In all the recent fuss about the proper characterization for Columbus,
I have seen nothing superior to Las Casas's carefully balanced description: Las Casas, *History, passim;* **pp. 101, 105:** Sauer, 88, 98–99; Las Casas, *History,* 69.

Chapter 10. **P. 108:** Durán, 325n2; **p. 109:** Davies, 9; **pp. 109–113:** editors' prefaces
and provenances are the bases for backgrounds of books in this chapter. See Cortés, Diaz,
and Sahagún.

Chapter 11. **P. 114:** Davies, 7–8; Sahagún, pt. 1:49, 69; **p. 116:** Sahagún, pt. 9:15;
Davies, 18–21; **p. 117:** Davies, 60–61; Durán, 49; **pp. 117–121:** Durán, ch. 15, 57–60;
p. 107; Davies, 79; Leon-Portilla in *Cambridge* 1:14.

Chapter 12. **Pp. 122–23:** Davies, 39, 128–31; **p. 125:** Davies, 42–43; Durán, 51, 70;
p. 127: Durán, 78–79. The economic background in this chapter is drawn from Ross
Hassig, *Trade, Tribute, and Transportation,* a very valuable book.

Chapter 13. **P. 130:** Diaz, 301, 311; **p. 131:** Sauer, 100–103; "rational souls": Hanke,
4; **p. 132,** Diaz, chs. 1–3. For Las Casas's life and work, see Manuel Gimenez Fernandez
in *Bartoleme de Las Casas in History,* 67–125.

Chapter 14. **P. 136:** Elliott, xv; Las Casas, *Tears,* 28; **Pp. 136–37:** Cortés, 73; Diaz,
258–59, 263; "uprising": Davies, 268; **pp. 137–38:** Diaz, 280, 301; "Cuitlahuac": Davies,
258, 268; Sahagún; Keen in Zorita, 7; Elliott and Leon-Portilla in *Cambridge* 1:183; 1:36;
pp. 138–42: "Pizarro": Parry, 92–93; "Acoma": Castañeda, xxiv; Minge, 1; **p. 127:** "Crusaders": their less than sanctified motives are very clear in Runciman, *History.* For recent
writing about Florida and de Soto, see Milanich in *Columbian Consequences* 2: *Archaeological
and Historical Perspectives.*

Chapter 15. **P. 145:** Gibson, *Spain in America,* 109; **p. 148:** ibid., 67; **pp. 148–49:**
Todorov, 205; "Virgin of Guadalupe": Davies, 302; "pagan gods": Seznec; "big churches":
Gibson, 78–80; **p. 150:** "Motolinía": quoted in *Bartolomé de Las Casas in History,* 324–25;
p. 151: De Roo 4:465.

Chapter 16. P. 152: Cronon, 165; **pp. 153–60:** Dobyns, "Who Killed the Gila?" 17, 26; **p. 161:** Cronon, 77. The chief investigator of phenomena in nature resulting from the macrocontact of Europe and the Americas is Alfred W. Crosby, whose deeply researched work is full of surprises.

Chapter 17. P. 165: Quinn, *North America,* 508–9; **pp. 166–67:** the Mississippians invaded by de Soto, and his effect on their societies, is in Milanich in *Columbian Consequences* 2, ch. 1; **p. 166:** Quinn, *North America,* 282–83; **p. 167:** ibid., 172–74, 186, 358–59, 514, 529; **pp. 167–68:** "escapee": Quinn, ibid., 260; "scurvy": Jennings, *Invasion,* 52; **p. 169:** Sources are in Quinn, *Roanoke Voyages.* **P. 169:** the effect of maize in Africa is in Tannahill, *Food in History,* 244–67.

Chapter 18. This chapter largely summarizes findings in Jennings, *Invasion of America, Ambiguous Iroquois Empire,* and *Empire of Fortune.* **P. 176:** "Quakers": See Proud, *History of Pennsylvania 1:224n;* **p. 177:** "torture in Jamestown": Canny, "Permissive Frontier" in *Westward Enterprise.*

Chapter 19. P. 182. George R. Hamell's remark is in his mss. "Trading in Metaphors," dated 12–13 June 1982, p. 4. **P. 185:** Van der Donck, 131. As noted above, I think William R. Swagerty is the foremost student of western frontier trade. For the east see Jennings, *Invasion of America,* ch. 6, *Ambiguous Iroquois Empire,* chs. 3–6, and "The Indian Trade of the Susquehanna Valley"; Trigger, *Natives and Newcomers.* See also *Old Trails and New Directions; "Le Castor Fait Tout."*

Chapter 20. P. 187: *Jesuit Relations* (1653), 39:141; **pp. 188–89:** Trigger, *Children* 2:840; **p. 189:** *Jesuit Relations* 44:155–61; "Mohawk heads"; pamphlet "Constitution" in *Parker on the Iroquois,* article 6; **p. 190:** "Buteux": *Jesuit Relations* 1:18; *Dict. Can. Biog.* 1:142–43; "intermarriage": Clark, *Acadia,* 361; **pp. 190–91:** "Rale,": *Dict. Can. Biog.* 2; **p. 191:** Washburn, "Philanthropy," 53–54; Jennings, *Invasion,* 53–56, ch. 14; Calloway, *Western Abenakis,* 48; **p. 192:** Eliot's reputed sins appeared in letters to the editor of the *Vineyard Gazette;* "Bourne": Brodeur, *Restitution,* 14; **p. 193:** The deal between Matthew Mayhew and Thomas Dongan is in an unpublished mss. by Jack Campisi. Some of it is in W. Simmons, *Spirit,* 16–28.

Chapter 21. Pp. 198–99. "Ojibwas": Moodie in *Old Trails,* 282; **p. 198:** J. R. Gibson, *Feeding the Russian Fur Trade;* "New Orleans": Usner in *Powhatan's Mantle,* 115; **pp. 201–02:** Milanich, "Franciscan Missions"; Hann, ch. 12; Bushnell, 145.

Chapter 22. Pp. 204–05: "Hudson Bay": G. L. Nute, "Chouart"; E. E. Rich, 69–70; Van Kirk, 4; **pp. 206–07:** Milanich, "Franciscan Missions" mss., 3, 9; Bushnell, 135, 142; Hann, 13.

Chapter 23. P. 209: Jennings, *Ambiguous,* 104–5; **p. 210:** "uprising": Jennings, *Invasion,* 78–79; "Florida": J. L. Wright, *Only Land,* Milanich, "Franciscan Missions"; **p. 211:** "S. Carolina": Crane, 17. Though more than sixty years old, Crane's book is still indispensable. **Pp. 212–214:** see Trigger's chs. on the Beaver Wars in *Children;* p. 194: Heckewelder, 78. For fuller documentation on events in this chapter see Jennings, *Invasion* and *Ambiguous.*

Chapter 24. The Covenant Chain is analyzed and documented in detail in Jennings, *Ambiguous.* See also *Beyond the Covenant Chain.*

Chapter 25. P. 223: Marc Simmons in *Handbook* 9:191; **pp. 226–27:** "Westos": J. L. Wright, 107; **p. 228:** J. L. Wright, 113.

Chapter 27. P. 238: "Pimas": Fontana in *Handbook* 10; **pp. 238–39:** "Apaches": Opler in *Handbook* 10; **pp. 245–46:** Spicer, *Cycles*, 191, 325; **p. 247:** ibid., 239–40.

Chapter 28. P. 247: "Galleons": Rolle, ch. 3; **p. 248:** Rolle, 22; "missions": *California's Missions*, quotation at 9: **pp. 249–51:** Castillo in *Handbook* 8, quotation at 101; **p. 251:** Guest, 78; Geiger, 73; Castillo, *Handbook* 8:102; **pp. 250–51:** Cook in *Handbook* 8:92; idem: *Population of California Indians*, 200.

Chapter 29. This chapter relies heavily on *Handbook* 7, *Northwest Coast*, and *Crossroads of Continents*. **Pp. 255–56:** "Labor shortage": Kan in *Handbook* 7, 506; "Aleutians": Black, "Story," in *Crossroads*, 72; **pp. 72, 75:** ibid., 75; **pp. 257–58:** "Tlingits": Frederica de Laguna in *Crossroads*, 60, 63; Richard A. Pierce in *Handbook* 4:122.

Chapter 30. This chapter was assembled from various sources. "Hudson's Bay Co.": E. E. Rich; "Iroquois 'conquest' ": Jennings, *Ambiguous* and *Empire of Fortune;* "mixing peoples": Van Kirk; Jennifer Brown; / *The New Peoples;* "trade journeying": Jennings, Swagerty; **pp. 263–64:** Jennings, "Bisaillon" in *Dict. Can. Biog.* 3; **p. 264:** "Cadillac": Zoltvany, 312; **p.** 266: "Mandan markups": Newman, 187; "French explorers"; *Dict. Can. Biog., passim.*

Chapter 31. See articles in *Dict. Can. Biog.* about both Frenchmen and Indian chiefs. Supplement with Louise Phelps Kellogg's book and article, and with Callender's "Foxes" in *Handbook* 15.

Chapter 32. The basic source for Natchez destruction is Le Page du Pratz. See also: **p. 274:** Giraud, 81; **pp. 275–76:** "Carolina proprietors": Merrell, 52. And background in Crane, 43, 45, 68–69, 71–73, ch. 7, 170.

Chapter 33. This chapter summarizes my own research in primary sources, heavily documented in my publications cited herein. **P. 284:** "treaty minutes, 31 July 1710": Penn Papers, Indian Affairs, mss., 1:34, Hist. Soc. of Pa.

Chapter 34. Summarized from Jennings, *Empire of Fortune*. **P. 293:** Quotation about Braddock: *Empire*, 125n46; "Braddock's remark": ibid., 159; **p. 294:** "French boast": ibid., 188–89; "Shirley": ibid., 199; **p. 295:** "Montcalm's aide Bougainville": ibid., 215.

Chapter 35. The bulk of this chapter is also from *Empire of Fortune*. **Pp. 301–02:** Graymont, 197, 199, 213, 262.

Chapter 36. P. 310: de Tocqueville, ch. 10.

Chapter 37. Horsman and Edmunds are basic for this chapter. **P. 313:** "population": D. D. Wallace, 146–47; Dinwiddie remark is from Richard L. Morton, *Colonial Virginia*, 2 vols. (Chapel Hill: University of North Carolina Press, 1960), 2:687–88; **p. 315:** "robbers": Bakeless, 48–52; **p. 316:** "Dunmore's remark": Downes, 164; **p. 317:** O'Donnell, 52.

Chapter 38. This chapter is based on Edmunds, Horsman, and Ronda. **P. 321:** Ronda, 252; **pp. 322–23:** Edmunds, 21; **p. 323:** idem, 64; Clark's remark is in *Reader's Encyclopedia*,

487; **pp. 324–27:** Horsman, 186–87; **pp. 324–27:** McKenney and Hall, 116, 118, Edmunds, 67–70; **p. 331:** Horsman, 186–87; Edmunds, 152.

Chapter 39. Pp. 330–31: Usner, "Frontier Exchange," 191; **p. 332:** idem, 168; *"Herrenvolk":* Christopher Saunders in *Frontier in History,* 169; **p. 332:** Perdue, *Slavery,* 62; **p. 333:** "Choctaws": De Rosier, 123; "Lumpkin": Perdue, 66–67; **p. 333:** "casualties of trail of tears": Washburn in *Reader's Encyc.;* **p. 334:** "survivors": Richard Sattler, personal communication.

Chapter 40. P. 338: A.F.C. Wallace, *Death and Rebirth,* 162, 183, 260; **p. 340:** Campisi, "Ethnic Identity," 101, 500–503; F. J. Turner, 1, 15.

Chapter 41. P. 347: "Mandan trade": Swagerty in *Handbook* 4: 351–74; **p. 352:** Swagerty, "Marriage and Settlement," **p. 356:** Peterson, "People in Between," 5; F. J. Turner, 23. See also Myers, *History of the Great American Fortunes:* for Astor, chs. 2–7. Myers treats also of the railroad fortunes derived from land grants from seized Indian territories.

Chapter 42. Pp. 363–64: Spicer, *Cycles,* 338; Spicer in *Handbook* 4:103, 109; Brugge in *Handbook* 10:495–96; **p. 365:** Castillo in *Handbook* 8:105; Adam Johnson in *Handbook* 8:107; **pp. 366–67:** "Truckee": *Reader's Encyclopedia,* 155; Unruh, 117, 121, 127–28; **p. 368:** "Young": in Unruh, 147; **p. 369:** Unruh, 157–58. We are most fortunate to have two such splendid books as Spicer's *Cycles of Conquest* and Unruh's *The Plains Across.* How they reveal the massive mythology that has passed for respectable history!

Chapter 43. Pp. 373–74: Washburn in *Reader's Encyc.,* 867; **pp. 373–74:** Cohen, 62–63, 127; "Whipple": Prucha, v, 64–65; **p. 375:** Cohen, 66; **p. 376:** "statistics": Kelly in *Handbook* 4:66–80; Cohen, 136; Williams, "American Imperialism," 238; "Lodge": ibid., 242; **p. 377:** Linda Parker, 122; Dee Brown, xi; **p. 377:** "Crook": *Reader's Encyc.,* 278; Dee Brown, 418; "Medals": *Report of U.S. Senate Comm. on Veterans Affairs, 14 Feb 1979;* **p. 380;** Hagan, 119; **p. 380:** Dee Brown, xi.

Chapter 44. P. 384: Kelly in *Handbook* 4:67; **pp. 385–88:** "Carlisle": see photos herein; **pp. 388–89:** Kelly, *Assault on Assimilation* is standard for John Collier; **p. 388:** Cohen, 147; **p. 390:** Shepardson in *Handbook* 10:626–30; **p. 390:** Rosenthal in *Irredeemable America,* 54; "Dillon Myer": Washburn, *Red Man's Land,* 85; Spindler in *Handbook* 15:722.

Chapter 45. P. 395: "national census": Snipp, 64; **pp. 396–98:** Snipp, 64, Snipp, 31; Snipp, 65–66.

Chapter 46. P. 399: "baby boom": Thornton, 227; **p. 400:** "BIA": Thornton, 228–29, 160; **p. 401:** ibid., 230; **pp. 401–03:** *American Indian Policy,* 3–4; "rescission of Premise": Prucha, *Documents,* 288–89; "Bush": *Congressional Record* S15-O24-15030, 11 Oct. 1990; **p. 352:** "statement of political relationship": *Chicago Tribune,* 7 Aug 1991, 16; "Wounded Knee": Wilson, 9; **p. 403:** Barsh and Henderson, 290.

Chapter 47. P. 405: Jones, 4, 16; **pp. 409–10:** "Jackson": *New York Times,* 21 June 1991, A1, B4; **p. 410:** Cohen, *Indian Self Government.*

BIBLIOGRAPHY

Tribute

EXEMPLARS

As pioneers in the reconceptualization of American Indian history, three men stand out: William N. Fenton, Alvin M. Josephy, Jr., and Wilcomb E. Washburn.

Already in 1950, in a conference and book, Fenton exhorted the Institute of Early American History and Culture to attend to the "needs and opportunities" of the field.

In 1957, Washburn overturned the traditional portrayal of Bacon's Rebellion by showing Indian roles in *The Governor and the Rebel*.

In 1961, Josephy edited *The American Heritage Book of Indians*, following it in 1968 with his own *Indian Heritage of America*. By insisting recently that I contribute a chapter to *America in 1492*, he forced me to lift my sights beyond my narrow specialty.

All three of these scholars have remained fruitfully productive to the present day, to the great good fortune of the historical profession (and mine).

We must not forget the giant in the background, who learned to fight racism and became its implacable foe. Franz Boas taught us to stop imagining Indian savages and to start studying Indian peoples.

PUBLICATIONS

Two large sets and a very special cooperative publication have contributed strongly to making the present study possible. They are the *Handbook of North American Indians* of the Smithsonian Institution, the *Dictionary of Canadian Biography*, which has included Indian leaders as respectfully as others, and *Crossroads of Continents*, the extremely valuable outcome of a joint undertaking by the Smithsonian and the Institute of Ethnography of the USSR Academy of Sciences. Every student should be acquainted with these treasures.

List

This is a select and personal list of works that have been consulted especially for the present study or have been especially influential in background. For recommended readings over a broader range see Bibliographical Series of the D'Arcy McNickle Center for the History of the American Indian at the Newberry Library, published sequentially by Indiana University Press and Oklahoma University Press.

Abler, Thomas S., and Elisabeth Tooker. "Seneca." In *Northeast*, ed. Trigger. *Handbook of North American Indians*, q.v. 15:505–17.

Adovasio, J. M., and Ronald C. Carlisle. "Pennsylvania Pioneers." *Natural History* 95:12 (Dec 1986), 20–27.

America in 1492. Eds. Alvin M. Josephy, Jr., and Frederick E. Hoxie. New York: Alfred A. Knopf, 1992.

American Indian Policy Review Commission. *Final Report, 17 May 1977*. 2 vols. Washington, D.C.: Government Printing Office, 1977.

Atlas of Ancient America. Eds. Michael Coe, Dean Snow, and Elizabeth Benson. New York: Facts on File Publications, 1986.

Axtell, James. *The European and the Indian: Essays in the Ethnohistory of Colonial North America*. New York: Oxford University Press, 1981.

Bakeless, John. *Master of the Wilderness: Daniel Boone*. New York: William Morrow and Co., 1939.

Barsh, Russel Lawrence, and James Youngblood Henderson. *The Road: Indian Tribes and Political Liberty*. Berkeley: University of California Press, 1980.

Bartolomé de Las Casas in History: Toward an Understanding of the Man and His Work. Eds. Juan Friede and Benjamin Keen. De Kalb: Northern Illinois University Press, 1971.

Best of Cahokian: 16 Articles Appearing in the Cahokian, *1974–1980*. Eds. William Iseminger, Dick Norrish, and John W. Strong. Collinsville, Ill.: Cahokia Mounds Museum Society, n.d.

Beyond the Covenant Chain; The Iroquois and Their Neighbors in Indian North America, 1600–1800. Eds. Daniel K. Richter and James H. Merrell. Syracuse, N.Y.: Syracuse University Press, 1987.

Black, Lydia T. "Peoples of the Amur and Maritime Regions." In *Crossroads of Continents*, q.v., 24–31.

———. "The Story of Russian America." In *Crossroads of Continents*, q.v., 70–82.

The Book of the Life of the Ancient Mexicans Containing an Account of Their Rites and Superstitions: An anonymous Hispano-Mexican Manuscript preserved at the Biblioteca Nazionale Centrale, Florence, Italy. Reproduced in facsimile. Tr. and ed. Zelia Nuttall. Berkeley: University of California Press, 1903.

Boone, Elizabeth Hill. *The Codex Magliabechiano and the Lost Prototype of the Magliabechiano Group.* Berkeley: University of California Press, 1983.

Borah, Woodrow, and Sherburne F. Cook. "Conquest and Population: A Demographic Approach to Mexican History." *Proceedings of the American Philosophical Society* 113:2 (April 1969), 177–83.

Bradley, James W. *Onondaga Iroquois Prehistory.* Syracuse: Syracuse University Press, 1971.

Brodeur, Paul. *Restitution: The Land Claims of the Mashpee, Passamaquoddy, and Penobscot Indians of New England.* Boston: Northeastern University Press, 1985.

Brose, David S., James A. Brown, and David W. Penney. *Ancient Art of the Woodland Indians.* New York: H. N. Abrams, 1985.

Brown, Jennifer S. H. *Strangers in Blood: Fur Trade Company Families in Indian Country.* Vancouver, B.C.: University of British Columbia Press, 1980.

Brugge, David M. "Navajo Prehistory and History to 1850." In *Handbook of North American Indians,* q.v., 10, ed. Ortiz. Pp. 489–501.

Bryce, George, *The Remarkable History of the Hudson's Bay Company.* Toronto: William Briggs, 1900.

Burch, Ernest S., Jr., "War and Trade." In *Crossroads of Continents,* q.v., 227–40.

Bushnell, Amy. "Ruling 'the Republic of Indians' in Seventeenth-Century Florida." In *Powhatan's Mantle, Indians in the Colonial Southeast.* Eds. Peter H. Wood, et al. Lincoln: University of Nebraska Press, 1989. Pp. 134–50.

California's Missions. Eds. Ralph B. Wright, John B. Anderson, and Benjamin M. Watson. Arroyo Grande, Calif.: Hubert A. Lowman, 1950.

Callender, Charles. "Fox." In *Handbook of North American Indians,* q.v., 15, ed. Trigger. Pp. 636–47.

Calloway, Colin G. *Crown and Calumet: British–Indian Relations, 1783–1815.* Norman: University of Oklahoma Press, 1987.

———. *The Western Abenakis of Vermont, 1600–1800: War, Migration, and the Survival of an Indian People.* Norman: University of Oklahoma Press, 1990.

Cambridge Encyclopedia of Latin America and the Caribbean. Gen. eds. Simon Collier, Harold Blakemore, and Thomas E. Skidmore. 2 vols. Cambridge: Cambridge University Press, 1985.

Campisi, Jack. "Ethnic Identity and Boundary Maintenance in Three Oneida Communities." Ph.D. diss., State University of New York, Albany, 1974.

———. *The Mashpee Indians: Tribe on Trial.* Syracuse: Syracuse University Press, 1991.

Castañeda, Pedro. *The Journey of Coronado* (mss. copied 1596). Tr. and ed. George Parker Winship. New York: Allerton Book Co., 1922. Reprinted New York: Readex Microprint, 1966.

Castillo, Edward D. "The Impact of Euro-American Exploration and Settlement." In *California,* ed. Heizer. *Handbook of North American Indians,* q.v. 8:99–127.

Ceram, C. W. *Gods, Graves, and Scholars: The Story of Archaeology.* Tr. E. B. Garside. New York: Alfred A. Knopf, 1952.

Champagne, Antoine. "Gaultier de La Vérendrye, Louis-Joseph." In *Dictionary of Canadian Biography*, q.v., 3:241–44.

Chaput, Donald. "Renaud Dubuisson, Jacques-Charles." In *Dictionary of Canadian Biography*, q.v., 2:563.

Clark, Andrew Hill. *Acadia; The Geography of Early Nova Scotia to 1760.* Madison: University of Wisconsin Press, 1968.

Codex Mendoza: Axtec Manuscript. Ed. Kurt Ross. Fribourg, Germany: Productions Liber, 1978 / 1984.

Coe, Michael D. *Mexico.* 3d ed., rev. and enl. New York: Thames and Hudson, 1984.

Cohen, Felix. *Handbook of Federal Indian Law.* Ed.-in-chief Rennard Strickland. Charlottesville, Va.: Michie Bobbs-Merrill, 1982.

———. "Indian Self-Government." In *Red Power: The American Indians' Fight for Freedom.* Ed. Alvin M. Josephy, Jr. Lincoln: University of Nebraska Press, 1971.

Colden, Cadwallader. *The History of the Five Indian Nations Depending on the Province of New York in America* (1727–1747). Reprinted Ithaca, N.Y.: Great Seal Books, 1958.

Columbian, Consequences 2: Archaeological and Historical Perspectives on the Spanish Borderlands East. Ed. David Hurst Thomas. Washington, D.C.: Smithsonian Institution Press, 1990.

Cook, Sherburne F. *The Population of the California Indians, 1769–1970.* Berkeley: University of California Press, 1976.

———. "The Significance of Disease in the Extinction of the New England Indians." *Human Biology* 45:3 (Sep 1973), 485–508.

Cook, Sherburne F. and Woodrow Borah. *The Population of the Mixteca Alta, 1520–1960. Ibero-Americana* 50. Berkeley, 1968.

Cook, Warren L. *Flood Tide of Empire: Spain and the Pacific Northwest, 1543–1819.* New Haven, Conn.: Yale University Press, 1973.

Cordell, Linda S. *Prehistory of the Southwest.* Orlando, Florida: Academic Press, 1984.

Cortés, Hernan. *Letters from Mexico* (1519–1526). Tr. and ed. Anthony Pagden. New Haven, Conn.: Yale University Press, 1986.

Crane, Verner W. *The Southern Frontier, 1670–1732.* Ann Arbor: University of Michigan Press, 1929.

Cressman, L. S. *Prehistory of the Far West: Homes of Vanquished Peoples.* Salt Lake City: University of Utah Press, 1977.

Cronon, William. *Changes in the Land: Indians, Colonists, and the Ecology of New England.* New York: Hill and Wang, 1983.

Crosby, Alfred W. *Ecological Imperialism: The Biological Expansion of Europe, 900–1900.* New York: Cambridge University Press, 1986.

Crossroads of Continents: Cultures of Siberia and Alaska. Eds. William W. Fitzhugh and Aron Crowell. Washington, D.C.: Smithsonian Institution Press, 1988.

Davies, Nigel. *The Aztecs: A History* (1973). Reprinted Norman: University of Oklahoma Press, 1986.

De Roo, Peter. *Material for a History of Pope Alexander VI, His Relatives and His Time.* 6 vols. New York: The Universal Knowledge Foundation, 1924.

DeRosier, Arthur H., Jr. *The Removal of the Choctaw Indians.* Knoxville: University of Tennessee Press, 1970.

De Ville, Winston, et al. "Louis Juchereau de Saint-Denis." In *Dictionary of Canadian Biography,* q.v., 3:317–18.

[Diaz del Castillo, Bernal], *The Bernal Diaz Chronicles: The True Story of the Conquest of Mexico* (1632). Tr. and ed. Albert Idell. Garden City, N.Y.: Doubleday and Co., 1956.

Dictionary of Canadian Biography. Eds. George W. Brown et al. Toronto: University of Toronto Press, 1966–

Dikov, Nikolai. "On the Road to America." *Natural History* 97:1 (Jan 1988), 10–14.

Dobyns, Henry F. "Estimating Aboriginal American Population: An Appraisal of Techniques with a New Hemispheric Estimate." *Current Anthropology* 7(1966), 395–416.

————. "Indians in the Colonial Spanish Borderlands." In *Indians in American History: An Introduction.* Ed. Frederick E. Hoxie, q.v., 67–93.

————. "Who Killed the Gila?" *The Journal of Arizona History"* (Spring 1978), 17–30.

Documents of United States Indian Policy. Ed. Francis Paul Prucha. 2d ed. Lincoln: University of Nebraska Press, 1990.

Downes, Randolph C. *Council Fires on the Upper Ohio: A Narrative of Indian Affairs in the Upper Ohio Valley until 1795.* Pittsburgh: University of Pittsburgh Press, 1940.

Driver, Harold E., and William C. Massey. *Comparative Studies of North American Indians. Transactions of the American Philosophical Society,* new series 47, pt. 2 (July 1957).

Durán, Fray Diego. *The Aztecs: The History of the Indies of New Spain* (1581). Tr. and ed. Doris Heyden and Fernando Horcasitas. New York: Orion Press, 1964.

Eccles, William J. "The Fur Trade in the Colonial Northeast." In *Handbook of North American Indians,* q.v., 4, ed. Washburn, 324–34.

————. "Marin de La Malgue." In *Dictionary of Canadian Biography,* q.v. 3:431–32.

Edmunds, R. David. *Tecumseh and the Quest for Indian Leadership.* Boston: Little, Brown and Co., 1984.

Eggan, Fred. "Pueblos: Introduction." In *Southwest*, ed. Ortiz. *Handbook of North American Indians*, q.v., 9:224–35.

Elliott, J. H. "Cortés, Velázquez and Charles V." In Hernan Cortés, *Letters from Mexico*, q.v., xi–xxxvii.

Extending the Rafters: Interdisciplinary Approaches to Iroquoian Studies. Eds. Michael K. Foster, Jack Campisi, and Marianne Mithun. Published for the Center for the History of the American Indian of the Newberry Library. Albany, N.Y.: State University of New York Press, 1984.

Fenton, William N. "Structure, Continuity, and Change in the Process of Iroquois Treaty Making." In *The History and Culture of Iroquois Diplomacy*. Eds. Francis Jennings et al. Syracuse, N.Y.: Syracuse University Press, 1985. Pp. 3–36.

Fisher, Raymond H. *The Voyage of Semen Dezhnev in 1648: Bering's Precursor.* Works Issued by the Hakluyt Society, 2d ser., no. 159. London, 1981.

Fitzhugh, William W. and Aron Crowell. "Crossroads of Continents: Beringian Oecumene." In *Crossroads of Continents,"* q.v., 9–16.

Fladmark, Knut R. "Getting One's Berings." *Natural History* 95:11 (Nov 1986), 8–19.

Fontana, Bernard L. "History of the Papagos." In *Southwest*, ed. Ortiz. *Handbook of North American Indians*, q.v., 10:137–48.

———. "Pima and Papago: Introduction." In *ibid*, 10:125–36.

Foster, Michael K. "On Who Spoke First at Iroquois–White Councils: An Exercise in the Method of Upstreaming." In *Extending the Rafters*, q.v. Pp. 193–207.

Frazier, Kendrick. *People of Chaco: A Canyon and Its Culture.* New York: W. W. Norton, 1986.

The Frontier in History: North America and Southern Africa Compared. Eds. Howard Lamar and Leonard Thompson. New Haven, Conn.: Yale University Press, 1981.

Funk, Robert E. "Post-Pleistocene Adaptations." In *Northeast*, ed. Trigger. *Handbook of North American Indians*, q.v., 14:16–27.

Gallatin, Albert. *A Synopsis of the Indian Tribes within the United States East of the Rocky Mountains and in the British and Russian Possessions in North America* (1836). Facsimile ed. New York: AMS Press, 1973.

Geiger, Maynard. *Mission Santa Barbara, 1782–1965.* Santa Barbara: Franciscan Fathers of California, 1965.

[A Gentleman of Elvas]. *True Relation of the Hardships Suffered by Governor Fernando de Soto and Certain Portuguese Gentlemen During the Discovery of the Province of Florida* (1557). Tr. and ed. James Alexander Robertson. 2 vols. De Land: Florida State Historical Society, 1932–1933.

Gibson, Charles. *Spain in America.* The New American Nation Series. New York: Harper and Row, 1966.

Gibson, James R. *Feeding the Russian Fur Trade: Provisionment of the Okhotsk Seaboard and the Kamchatka Peninsula, 1639–1856.* Madison: University of Wisconsin Press, 1969.

———. *Imperial Russia in Frontier America: The Changing Geography of Supply of Russian America, 1784–1867.* New York: Oxford University Press, 1976.

Giddings, J. L. "Seven Discoveries of Bering Strait." *Proceedings of the American Philosophical Society* 106 (1962), 89–93.

Giraud, Marcel. *A History of French Louisiana 1: The Reign of Louis XIV, 1698–1715* (1953). Tr. Joseph C. Lambert. Baton Rouge: Louisiana State University Press, 1974.

Graymont, Barbara. *The Iroquois in the American Revolution.* Syracuse, N.Y.: Syracuse University Press, 1972.

Griffen, William B. "Southern Periphery: East." In *Southwest*, ed. Ortiz, *Handbook of North American Indians*, q.v., 10:329–342.

Guest, Francis F. *Mission Indian Life: An Examination of the Thesis of S. F. Cook on the Forced Conversion of Indians in the California Missions.* Reprinted from *Southern California Quarterly* 61:1 (Spring 1979), 1–77.

A Guide to Alaska Native Corporation Publications. Ed. Phyllis Nottingham. Juneau: Alaska Department of Education, 1976.

Guidon, Niède. "Cliff Notes," *Natural History* 96:8 (August 1987), 6–12.

Gunnerson, James H. "Southern Athapaskan Archeology." In *Southwest*, ed. Ortiz. *Handbook of North American Indians*, q.v., 9:162–69.

Gurvich, I. S. "Ethnic Connections Across Bering Strait." In *Crossroads of Continents*, q.v., 17–21.

Hagan, William T. "How the West Was Lost." In *Indians in American History*. Ed. Hoxie, (q.v.), 179–202.

Hale, Kenneth, and David Harris. "Historical Linguistics and Archeology." In *Southwest*, ed. Ortiz, *Handbook of North American Indians* (q.v.), 9:170–177.

Handbook of North American Indians. Gen. ed. William C. Sturtevant. 20 vols. projected. Washington, D.C.: Smithsonian Institution, 1978– .

Hanke, Lewis. *All Mankind Is One: A Study of the Disputation between Bartolomé de Las Casas and Juan Ginés de Sepúlveda in 1550 on the Intellectual and Religious Capacity of the American Indians.* DeKalb, Ill.: Northern Illinois University Press, [1974].

Hann, John H. *Apalachee: The Land Between the Rivers.* Gainesville: University of Florida Press / Florida State Museum, 1988.

Hassig, Ross. *Trade, Tribute, and Transportation: The Sixteenth-Century Political Economy of the Valley of Mexico.* Norman: University of Oklahoma Press, 1985.

Haury, Emil W. "The Greater American Southwest." In *Emil W. Haury's Prehistory of the American Southwest.* Eds. J. Jefferson Reid and David E. Doyel. Tucson: University of Arizona Press, 1986.

———. *The Hohokam, Desert Farmers and Craftsmen: Excavations at Snaketown, 1964–1965.* Tucson: University of Arizona Press, 1976.

434 · *Bibliography*

Heckewelder, John. *An Account of the History, Manners, and Customs of the Indian Nations Who Once Inhabited Pennsylvania and the Neighbouring States* (1819). Rev. ed. edited by William C. Reichel. Memoirs of the Historical Society of Pennsylvania 12. Philadelphia, 1876.

Hess, Andrew C. *The Forgotten Frontier: A History of the Sixteenth-Century Ibero-African Frontier.* Chicago: University of Chicago Press, 1978.

Hinton, Thomas B. "Southern Periphery: West." In *Southwest,* ed. Ortiz *Handbook of North American Indians,* q.v., 10:315–28.

Hirst, Stephen. *Life in a Narrow Place.* New York: David McKay Company, 1976.

Honigmann, John J. *The World of Man.* New York: Harper and Brothers, 1959.

Horsman, Reginald. *The Frontier in the Formative Years, 1783–1815.* New York: Holt, Rinehart and Winston, 1970.

———. *Race and Manifest Destiny: The Origins of American Racial Anglo-Saxonism.* Cambridge, Mass.: Harvard University Press, 1981.

———. "Scientific Racism and the American Indian in the Mid-Nineteenth Century." *American Quarterly* 27:2 (May 1975), 152–68.

Hosley, Edward H. "Intercultural Relations and Cultural Change in the Alaska Plateau." In *Subarctic,* ed. Helm. *Handbook of North American Indians,* q.v., 6:546–55.

Hurt, R. Douglas. *Indian Agriculture in America: Prehistory to the Present.* Lawrence: University Press of Kansas, 1987.

Indians in American History: An Introduction. Ed. Frederick E. Hoxie. Arlington Heights, Ill.: Harlan Davidson, 1988.

Irredeemable America: The Indians' Estate and Land Claims. Ed. Imre Sutton et al. Albuquerque: University of New Mexico Press, 1985.

Irving, Washington. *The Adventures of Captain Bonneville* (1837). Eds. Robert A. Rees and Alan Sandy. Boston: Twayne Publishers, 1977.

Irwin-Williams, Cynthia. "Post-Pleistocene Archeology, 7000–2000 B.C." In *Southwest,* ed. Ortiz. *Handbook of North American Indians,* q.v., 9:31–42.

Jennings, Francis. *The Ambiguous Iroquois Empire: The Covenant Chain Confederation of Indian Tribes with English Colonies.* New York: Norton, 1984.

———. "Bisaillon (Bezellon, Bizaillon), Peter," in *Dictionary of Canadian Biography* 3. Ed. Francess G. Halpenny. Toronto: University of Toronto Press, 1974.

———. *Empire of Fortune: Crowns, Colonies, and Tribes in the Seven Years' War in America.* New York: Norton, 1988.

———. "The Indian Trade of the Susquehanna Valley," *Proceedings of the American Philosophical Society* 110:6 (1966), 406–24.

———. *The Invasion of America: Indians, Colonialism, and the Cant of Conquest.* Chapel Hill: University of North Carolina Press, 1975. (Paperback, Norton, 1976.)

Jennings, Jesse D. "Prehistory: Introduction." In *Great Basin*, ed. D'Azevedo. *Handbook of North American Indians*, q.v., 11:113–19.

The Jesuit Relations and Allied Documents. Ed. Reuben Gold Thwaites. 73 vols. reprinted facsimile in 36. New York: Pageant Book Co., 1959.

Jones, Dorothy V. *License for Empire: Colonialism by Treaty in Early America.* Chicago: University of Chicago Press, 1982.

Josephy, Alvin M., Jr. *The Indian Heritage of America.* New York: Alfred A. Knopf, 1968.

Judge, Joseph. "Where Columbus Found the New World." *National Geographic* 170:5 (Nov 1986), 566–605.

Kan, Sergei. "The Russian Orthodox Church in Alaska." In *History of Indian-White Relations*, ed. Washburn. *Handbook of North American Indians*, q.v., 4:506–21.

Keen, Benjamin. "Editor's Introduction" to Alonso de Zorita, *The Lords of New Spain*, q.v., 3–77.

Kelley, J. Charles. "The Mobile Merchants of Molino." In *Ripples in the Chichimec Sea*, q.v., 81–104.

Kellogg, Louise Phelps. "The Fox Indians During the French Regime." In *Proceedings of the State Historical Society of Wisconsin*. Pp. 142–203. Madison, 1907.

———. *The French Regime in Wisconsin and the Northwest. Publications of the State Historical Society of Wisconsin.* Madison, 1925.

Kelly, Lawrence C. *The Assault on Assimilation: John Collier and the Origins of Indian Policy Reform.* Albuquerque: University of New Mexico Press, 1983.

Kroeber, A. L. *Cultural and Natural Areas of Native North America.* University of California Publications in American Archaeology and Ethnology 38. Berkeley and Los Angeles, 1939.

Lange, Charles H. "Relations of the Southwest with the Plains and Great Plains." In *Southwest*, ed. Ortiz. *Handbook of North American Indians*, q.v. 9:201–5.

Langley, J. C. "Pre-Columbian Mesoamerica." In *Cambridge Encyclopedia of Latin America and the Caribbean*, q.v., 1:165–71.

Las Casas, Bartolomé de. *History of the Indies* (1560–61; first published in Spanish 1875–76). Tr. and ed. Andrée Collard. New York: Harper and Row, 1971.

———. *Tears of the Indians* (1552). English translation 1656. Reprinted, Williamstown, Mass.: J. Lilburne, [1970].

"Le Castor Fait Tout" Selected Papers of the Fifth North American Fur Trade Conference, 1985. Eds. Bruce G. Trigger, Toby Morantz, Louise Dechene. Montreal: Lake St. Louis Historical Society, 1987.

Le Page du Pratz, Antoine Simon, *The History of Louisiana* (1758), tr. from French (1774). Reprint ed. Joseph G. Tregle, Jr. Baton Rouge: Louisiana State University Press, 1975.

Linton, Ralph. *The Tree of Culture.* New York: Alfred A. Knopf, 1957.

Lomax, Derek W. *The Reconquest of Spain.* London: Longman, 1978.

Martin, Paul S. "Prehistory: Mogollon." In *Southwest*, ed. Ortiz. *Handbook of North American Indians*, q.v., 9:61–74.

Martinez, Manuel M. "Las Casas on the Conquest of America." In *Bartolomé de Las Casas in History*, q.v., 309–49.

McGhee, Robert. "Thule Prehistory of Canada." In *Arctic*, ed. Damas. *Handbook of North American Indians*, q.v. 5:369–76.

McKenney, Thomas L., and James Hall. *History of the Indian Tribes of North America*. 3 vols. Philadelphia, 1838–44.

Merrell, James H. *The Indians New World, Catawbas and Their Neighbors from European Contact through the Era of Removal*. Chapel Hill; University of North Carolina Press, 1989.

Milanich, Jerald T. "Franciscan Missions and Native Peoples in Spanish Florida." Unpub. mss.

Minge, Ward Alan. *Ácoma, Pueblo in the Sky*. Albuquerque: University of New Mexico Press, 1976.

Mithun, Marianne. "The Proto-Iroquoians: Cultural Reconstruction from Lexical Materials." In *Extending the Rafters*, q.v., 259–81.

Mooney, James. *Myths of the Cherokee*. 19th annual report, Bureau of American Ethnography, Washington, D.C., 1900.

Morgan, William N. *Prehistoric Architecture in the Eastern United States*. Cambridge, Mass.: MIT Press, 1980.

Morison, Samuel Eliot. *Admiral of the Ocean Sea: A Life of Christopher Columbus*. Boston: Little, Brown, 1942.

———. *Journals and Other Documents on the Life and Voyages of Christopher Columbus*. New York: Heritage Press, 1963.

Myers, Gustavus, *History of the Great American Fortunes* (1907), reprinted as a Modern Library Giant. New York: Random House, n.d.

Newman, Peter C., *Company of Adventurers*. 2 vols. New York: Viking, 1985.

The New Peoples: Being and Becoming Métis in North America. Eds. Jacqueline Peterson and Jennifer S. H. Brown. Winnipeg: University of Manitoba Press, 1985.

Newton, Linda. "Pre-Columbian settlement." In *Cambridge Encyclopedia of Latin America and the Caribbean*, q.v., 1:128–33.

Nute, Grace Lee. "Chouart Des Groseilliers, Médard." In *Dictionary of Canadian Biography* 1:223–28.

O'Donnell, James H., III. *Southern Indians in the American Revolution*. Knoxville: University of Tennessee Press, 1973.

Old Trails and New Directions: Papers of the Third North American Fur Trade Conference. Eds. Carol M. Judd and Arthur J. Ray. Toronto: University of Toronto Press, 1980.

O'Neill, C. E. "Le Moyne de Bienville, Jean-Baptiste." In *Dictionary of Canadian Biography* 3:379–84.

Opler, Morris. "The Apachean Culture Pattern and Its Origins." In *Southwest*, ed. Ortiz. *Handbook of North American Indians* 10:368–92.

Parker, Arthur C. "Origin of the Iroquois as suggested by their Archeology," *American Anthropologist* 18 (Oct 1916):479–507.

Parker, Linda S. *Native American Estate: The Struggle over Indian and Hawaiian Lands*. Honolulu: University of Hawaii Press, 1980.

Parker on the Iroquois, Ed. Wm. N. Fenton. Syracuse, N.Y.: Syracuse University Press, 1968.

Parry, J. H. *The Spanish Seaborne Empire*. New York: Knopf, 1966.

Perdue, Theda. *Slavery and the Evolution of Cherokee Society, 1540–1866*. Knoxville: University of Tennessee Press, 1979.

Peterson, Jacqueline Louise. "The People In Between . . ." Ph.D. diss. University of Illinois at Chicago Circle, 1981.

Pethick, Derek. *First Approaches to the Northwest Coast*. Vancouver: Douglas and McIntyre, 1976.

Pothier, Bernard. "Le Moyne d'Iberville et d'Ardillières, Pierre." In *Dictionary of Canadian Biography* 2:390–401.

Powhatan's Mantle. Eds. Peter H. Wood et al. Lincoln-University of Nebraska Press, 1989.

Proud, Robert, *The History of Pennsylvania* (1797–1798). 2 vols. Facsimile: Pennsylvania Heritage Series 2–3. Spartanburg, S.C.: The Reprint Co., 1967.

Prucha, Francis Paul. *American Indian Policy in Crisis: Christian Reformers and the Indian, 1865–1900*. Norman: University of Oklahoma Press, 1976.

Quinn, David B. *North America from Earliest Discovery to First Settlements: The Norse Voyages to 1612*. New York: Harper and Row, 1977.

The Reader's Encyclopedia of the American West. Ed. Howard R. Lamar. New York: Thomas Y. Crowell, 1977.

Rich, E. E. *The Fur Trade and the Northwest, to 1857*. Toronto: McClelland and Stewart, 1967.

Ripples in the Chichimec Sea: New Considerations of Southwestern-Mesoamerican Interactions. Eds. Frances Joan Mathien and Randall H. McGuire. Carbondale: Southern Illinois University Press, 1986.

The Roanoke Voyages, 1584–1590. Ed. David B. Quinn. 2 vols. Hakluyt Society Publications, 2d Ser., 104–105. London, 1955.

Rolle, Andrew F. *California: A History*. 3d ed. Arlington Heights, Ill.: AHM Publishing Corporation, 1978.

Ronda, James P. *Lewis and Clark among the Indians*. Lincoln: University of Nebraska Press, 1984.

Runciman, Steven. *A History of the Crusades* (1951). 3 vols. Cambridge: Cambridge University Press, 1987.

Sahagún, Bernardino de, *Florentine Codex: General History of the Things of New Spain*. Tr. and ed. Arthur J. O. Anderson and Charles E. Dibble. 13 parts. Salt Lake City and Santa Fé: School of American Research and University of Utah, 1950–1982.

Sauer, Carl Ortwin. *The Early Spanish Main*. Berkeley: University of California Press, 1966.

Schroeder, Albert H. "Pattern Diffusion from Mexico into the Southwest after A.D. 600." *American Antiquity* 31:5 (1966), 683–704.

Scullard, H. H. *Roman Britain: Outpost of the Empire*. London: Thames and Hudson, 1979.

Seznec, Jean. *The Survival of the Pagan Gods: The Mythological Tradition and Its Place in Renaissance Humanism and Art* (1940). Tr. Barbara F. Sessions. Bollingen Series 38. New York: Pantheon Books, 1953.

Shepardson, Mary. "Development of Navajo Tribal Government." In *Southwest*, ed. Ortiz, *Handbook of North American Indians* 10:625–35.

Shoemaker, Nancy. "Native American Families." Unpublished mss., 1989.

Simmons, William S. *Spirit of the New England Tribes: Indian History and Folklore, 1620–1984*. Hanover, N.H.: University Press of New England, 1986.

Smith, Bruce D. "Harvest of Prehistory." *The Sciences* (New York Academy of Sciences), May–June 1991, 30–35.

Snipp, C. Matthew. *American Indians: The First of this Land*. Published for the National Committee for Research on the 1980 Census. New York: Russell Sage Foundation, 1989.

Snow, Dean R. "Iroquois Prehistory." In *Extending the Rafters*, q.v., 237–40.

———. *Native American Prehistory: A Critical Bibliography*. Newberry Library Center for the History of the American Indian Bibliographical Series. Bloomington: University of Indiana Press, 1979.

South from the Spanish Main: South America Seen Through the Eyes of Its Discoverers. Ed. Earl Parker Hanson. New York: Delacorte Press, 1967.

Spicer, Edward H. *Cycles of Conquest: The Impact of Spain, Mexico, and the United States on the Indians of the Southwest, 1533–1960*. Tucson: University of Arizona Press, 1962.

———. "Mexican Indian Policies." In *History of Indian-White Relations*, ed. Washburn. *Handbook of North American Indians*, q.v., 4:103–9.

Spinden, H. J. *The Population of Ancient America*. In *Smithsonian Report for 1929*, 451–71. Washington, D.C.: Government Printing Office, 1930.

Spindler, Louise S. "Menominee." In *Northeast*, ed. Trigger, *Handbook of North American Indians*, q.v., 15:708–24.

Standen, S. Dale. "Beauharnois de La Boische, Charles de, Marquis de Beauharnois." In *Dictionary of Canadian Biography* 3:41–50.

Struggle and Survival in Colonial America. Eds. David G. Sweet and Gary B. Nash. Berkeley: University of California Press, 1981.

Swagerty, William R. "Indian Trade in the Trans-Mississippi West to 1870." In

History of Indian-White Relations, ed. Washburn, *Handbook of North American Indians*, q.v., 4:351–74.

———. "Marriage and Settlement Patterns of Rocky Mountain Trappers and Traders." *The Western Historical Quarterly* 11:2 (April 1980), 159–80.

Tannahill, Reay. *Food in History.* New York, 1973.

Thornton, Russell. *American Indian Holocaust and Survival: A Population History Since 1492.* Norman: University of Oklahoma Press, 1987.

Tiller, Veronica E. "Jicarilla Apache." In *Southwest*, ed. Ortiz. *Handbook of North American Indians*, q.v., 10:440–61.

de Tocqueville, Alexis. *Democracy in America* (1848). Tr. George Lawrence. Eds. J. P. Mayer and Max Lerner. New York: Harper and Row, 1966.

Todorov, Tzvetan. *The Conquest of America: The Question of the Other* (1982). Tr. Richard Howard. New York: Harper and Row, 1984.

Traditional History of the Confederacy of the Six Nations: The Constitution of the Five Nations Confederacy. Prepared by a Committee of the Chiefs. *Transactions of the Royal Society of Canada* (16 May 1911), 3d ser., 5:1911. Reprint ed., Wilsonville, Ont.: Iroquoian Institute, 1987.

Trigger, Bruce G. *The Children of Aataentsic* 2 vols. Montreal: McGill-Queen's University Press, 1976.

———. *Natives and Newcomers: Canada's "Heroic Age" Reconsidered.* Kingston and Montreal: McGill-Queen's University Press, 1985.

Tuck, James A. *Onondaga Iroquois Prehistory.* Syracuse: Syracuse University Press, 1971.

Turner, Christy G., II. "Ancient Peoples of the North Pacific Rim." In *Crossroads of Continents*, q.v., 111–16.

———. "Teeth and Prehistory in Asia," *Scientific American* 260:2 (Feb 1989), 88–96.

Turner, Frederick Jackson. "The Significance of the Frontier in American History" (1893). In *The Frontier in American History.* New York: Holt, Rinehart and Winston, 1920.

Ubelaker, Douglas H. "The Sources and Methodology for Mooney's Estimates of North American Populations." In *The Native Population of the Americas in 1492.* Ed. William M. Denevan. Madison: University of Wisconsin Press, 1976.

Unruh, John D., Jr. *The Plains Across: The Overland Emigrants and the Trans-Mississippi West, 1840–60.* Urbana: University of Illinois Press, 1979.

Usner, Daniel H., Jr. "Economic Relations in the Southeast Until 1783." In *History of Indian-White Relations*, ed. Washburn. *Handbook of North American Indians*, q.v. 4:391–95.

———. "The Frontier Exchange Economy of the Lower Mississippi Valley in the Eighteenth Century." *William and Mary Quarterly*, 3d ser., 44 (April 1987), 165–92.

———. *Indians, Settlers, & Slaves in a Frontier Exchange Economy: The Lower Mississippi Valley Before 1783*. Chapel Hill: University of North Carolina Press, 1992.

Van der Donck, Adriaen. *A Description of the New Netherlands* (ca. 1656). Tr. Jeremiah Johnson (1841). Ed. Thomas F. O'Donnell. Syracuse, N.Y.: Syracuse University Press, 1968. (A new translation by Charles Gehring is now available.)

Van Kirk, Sylvia. *Many Tender Ties: Women in Fur-Trade Society, 1670–1870*. Norman: University of Oklahoma Press, 1980.

VanStone, James W. "Exploration and Contact History of Western Alaska." In *Arctic*. ed. Damas, *Handbook of North American Indians*, q.v. 5:149–60.

Vattel, Emmerich de. *Le Droit des Gens, ou Principles de la Loi Naturelle . . .* (1758). Tr. Charles G. Fenwick. 3 vols.: facsimile and translation. Washington, D.C.: Carnegie Institution Classics of International Law, 1916.

Verlinden, Charles. *The Beginnings of Modern Colonization: Eleven Essays with an Introduction*. Tr. Yvonne Freccero. Ithaca, N.Y.: Cornell University Press, 1970.

Walker, Edwin F. "World Crops Derived from the Indians." *Southwest Museum Leaflets* 17 (1967). Los Angeles, Calif.: Southwest Museum, 1967.

Wallace, Anthony F. C. *The Death and Rebirth of the Seneca*. New York: Alfred A. Knopf, 1970.

Wallace, David Duncan. *South Carolina: A Short History 1520–1948*. Columbia: University of South Carolina Press, 1969.

Wallace, William J. "Post-Pleistocene Archeology, 9000 to 2000 B.C.": In *California*, ed. Heizer. *Handbook of North American Indians* 8:25–36.

Washburn, Wilcomb E., "Philanthropy and the American Indian: The Need for a Model." *Ethnohistory* 15 (1968).

———. *Red Man's Land/White Man's Law*. New York: Charles Scribner's Sons, 1971.

Webb, Stephen Saunders. *1676: The End of American Independence*. New York, Alfred A. Knopf, 1984.

Webb, Walter Prescott, *The Great Frontier* (1952). Reprinted Austin: University of Texas Press, 1979.

The Westward Enterprise: English Activities in Ireland, the Atlantic, and America, 1480–1650. Eds. K. R. Andrews, N. P. Canny, and P.E.H. Hair. Detroit: Wayne State University Press, 1979.

Williams, Walter L. "American Imperialism and the Indians." In *Indians in American History*, q.v., 231–50.

———. "United States Indian Policy and the Debate over Philippine Annexation: Implications for the Origins of American Imperialism." *Journal of American History* 66 (1980): 810–31.

Wilson, Norma Clark. "Wounded Knee in Literature." Institute of American Indian Studies *Bulletin*, Vermilion: University of South Dakota, Winter 1990.

Woodbury, Richard B. "Prehistory: Introduction." In *Southwest*, ed. Ortiz. *Handbook of North American Indians*, q.v., 9:22–30.

Woodbury, Richard B. and Ezra B. W. Zubrow. "Agricultural Beginnings, 2000 B.C.–A.D. 500." In *Southwest*, ed. Ortiz, *Handbook of North American Indians*, q.v. 9:43–60.

Wright, J. Leitch, Jr. *The Only Land They Knew: The Tragic Story of the American Indians in the Old South*. New York: Free Press, 1981.

Yinger, J. Milton, and George Eaton Simpson. "The Integration of Americans of Indian Descent." In *Annals of the American Academy of Political and Social Science* 436 (March 1978), 137–51.

Young, Robert W. "Apachean Languages." In *Southwest*, ed. Ortiz. *Handbook of North American Indians*, q.v., 10:393–400.

Young, Steven B. "Beringia: An Ice Age View." In *Crossroads of Continents*, q.v., 106–10.

Zoltvany, Yves F., "New France and the West, 1701–1713." *Canadian Historical Review* 46:4 (Dec 1965), 301–22.

Zorita, Alonso de. *The Lords of New Spain: The Brief and Summary Relation of the Lords of New Spain* (mss. ca. 1570; pub. 1891), tr. with intro. by Benjamin Keen. London: Phoenix House, 1963.

INDEX

Entries in this index refer to special mentions of their topics. It has not been feasible to note every appearance or to cross-reference comprehensively, but the book's wide range of names and themes can be found under related headings.